W9-BUF-837

Additional Praise for
STONE SOUP FOR THE WORLD

"Hopefully, this will inspire each of us to more fully appreciate and nurture children's and our own natural instincts for learning, caring, and growing fully human."

—John Vasconcellos, California State Senator

"A vivid gallery of can-do people who have done extraordinary things against extraordinary odds. By acting out their dreams, these heroes show how global dreams for a better world can actually come true."

—Harlan Cleveland, president of The World Academy of Arts and Sciences

"By telling stories of community service, Stone Soup plays an important role in reinforcing the values and inspiring the actions upon which a healthy civil society depends."

—Tom Chappell, president of Tom's of Maine

"Taps a universal longing to make a difference. These stories describe a way of seeing—and of being in the world—which could help us rekindle the human spirit in business."

—Joseph Jaworsky, author of *Synchronicity: The Inner Path of Leadership*

"Through these stories, I came to know people like Gandhi on an intimate level. While they lived through amazing hardships, they always found hope—by moving forward."

—Nancy Berg, American Red Cross

Stone Soup *for the* World

Life-Changing Stories of Kindness & Courageous Acts of Service

Collected by Marianne Larned

Foreword by Jack Canfield

MJF BOOKS
NEW YORK

Published by MJF Books
Fine Communications
Two Lincoln Square
60 West 66th Street
New York, NY 10023

Stone Soup for the World
Library of Congress Catalog Card Number 99-70070
ISBN 1-56731-321-3

This edition published by arrangement with Conari Press.

Cover illustration © 1997 Anthony D'Agostino, Santa Fe, NM
Cover design: Ame Beanland
Book design: Jennifer Brontsema

Manufactured in the United States of America on acid-free paper

MJF Books and the MJF colophon are trademarks of Fine Creative Media, Inc.

10 9 8 7 6 5 4 3 2 1

A Message from Colin Powell

During my travels around the country, visiting inner-city neighborhoods and talking to the young people I've met there, I have been struck again and again by the stark differences between their childhoods and my own. When I was growing up in the Bronx, I wasn't rich—at least, not in a material sense, but I had the matchless blessing of being reared by two devoted parents—backed up by a platoon of doting aunts and uncles—who gave me the love, discipline, and motivation I needed to succeed.

Too many of today's youth are not getting the same kind of nurturing environment that I—and most Americans—once took for granted. As many as 15 million youngsters are "at risk" in today's America. They are in danger of being lost for good unless the more fortunate among us step forward and lend a hand.

At the Presidents' Summit for America's Future in Philadelphia last April, several thousand of our nation's leaders endorsed five basic resources that our young people need to become successful adults: 1) a caring adult; 2) safe places and structured activities to learn and grow; 3) a healthy start; 4) a marketable skill through effective education; and 5) an opportunity to "give back" through community service. It is the mission of America's Promise, the organization I chair, to help provide every at-risk child in America with access to these resources.

It is this glorious cycle of giving, receiving, and giving back that we want to pass along to the next generation of Americans. We want them to believe in America, and we want them to know that America believes in them.

Sometimes the single best thing you can do for a child is to show him or her that there's a whole different world out there. An involved, caring mentor can plant a seed of hope in a child's heart that can flower into self-confidence, hard work, ambition, and ultimately, success. To do that is to know one of life's most exalting experiences.

Stone Soup for the World: Life-Changing Stories of Kindness & Courageous Acts of Service gives you 100 wonderful stories to share with the children in your life. These heartwarming, action-oriented stories will show them a different world—real heroes who had the courage to overcome obstacles in their lives and the determination to work hard and build a better world. Young and old alike will be inspired by the hundreds of ideas for how we can help our children, our schools, our communities and our country to be the best we can be.

Working together, we have the power to redeem our at-risk youth and to transform our nation in the process. Working together, we can reach across the racial, cultural, social, and economic gaps that divide us. We can recover our sense of community—our pride in being a nation of neighbors who care. We can revitalize the tradition of service to others that has been so much a part of our history and national character. We invite you to join us in this effort.

General Colin Powell
chairman of *America's Promise—The Alliance for Youth*

Table of Contents

Foreword

The world is hungry for positive, uplifting, and inspirational stories. I know this because, over the last five years, the *Chicken Soup for the Soul* books have struck a powerful chord with millions of people all across the country and around the world.

Everywhere Mark and I go, people now ask us, "What's next? I feel so much better about myself and my life; I want to give something back—but I'm not sure how." Once we feel better about ourselves, we naturally want to reach out to help others.

Stone Soup for the World: Life-Changing Stories of Kindness & Courageous Acts of Service is a beacon of light pointing the way to how to give back and contribute to our communities. It is, in a sense, a handbook for humanitarians, giving us hundreds of ideas for how we can make the world a better place.

In these one hundred stories, you will meet ordinary people doing extraordinary things, and extraordinary people doing ordinary things. Eleanor Roosevelt and Mother Teresa show us that greatness grows out of simple acts of giving, and stories about Martin Luther King Jr., Mahatma Gandhi, Cesar Chavez, and Nelson Mandela give us the courage to overcome the obstacles in our lives so that we can help others. Stories about the Peace Corps, Teach for America, and Christmas in April remind us that we can each make a difference and, when we work together, we can literally change the world.

The heartwarming stories in this book encourage us all to stretch—to go beyond ourselves and our own little worlds—and think about our fellow human beings and how we can work together to make the world a better place for all of us. They show us that with a little imagination, teamwork, and cooperation, we can outperform our new expectations and do things we never thought possible.

Based on the feedback we receive from the millions of teens who have read our books, we know that young people love these kinds of stories. They yearn to know that their lives matter and that the world is and can be a better place because of them and their efforts. As young children, they love to give and to help out, but somewhere along the way they often lose touch with the fact that they matter and that we need them to build a better world. Unfortunately, kids often have too few role models to show them the way.

Just think—if more teens knew people like David Levitt, an eleven-year-old boy who convinced the Tampa, Florida, school board to give leftover cafeteria food to homeless shelters, or, like fifteen-year-old Andy Lipkis, who got his fellow campers to plant a forest and help reduce the L.A. smog, just think what kids might be inspired to do with their friends, their schools, and their communities! It might just give us all hope for the future. Because of this, I encourage all of you who read this book to share these stories with kids. Read them stories, buy them copies of the book, and challenge them to find their own ways to contribute.

Over the twenty years that I have known Marianne Larned, we've become great friends, connected by our shared search for practical ways to build a better world and for positive stories that inspire people to take action to create that world. Marianne is one of those people who truly believes that somewhere on the planet there is a solution to each of the world's problems. She's always looking for ways to inspire others to join her in building a better world. This wonderful book is only the latest of the many ways that she has come up with.

Whenever we get together, Marianne shares inspiring stories about people she's worked with across America and from faraway countries, who are doing great things to make a better world. Up until now, many of those stories have not been widely known. Because of the media's lack of commitment to positive news, they have, in fact, been well-kept secrets. Thanks to *Stone Soup for the World,* millions of people will now know about and hopefully be inspired by these stories—inspired to take action to help build a world that works for everyone.

After you read these stories, I am sure you will have found lots of new ways to make a difference in your school, your community, and the world. So pick up the phone or a pen and get involved today. But wait—I'm getting ahead of myself . . . First you need to read the book that you are now holding in your hands. You are in for a wonderful treat, a wonderful meal of *Stone Soup for the World!*

Enjoy!

JACK CANFIELD
co-author of *Chicken Soup for the Soul*

Stone Soup, a Folktale

There was once a man who had been traveling for a long time. Having run out of food, he was weary and hungry from his journey. When he came upon a small village, he thought, "Maybe someone could share some food."

When the man knocked at the first house, he asked the woman who answered, "Could you spare a bit of food? I've traveled a long way and am very hungry." "I'm sorry, but I have nothing to give you," the woman replied.

So the traveler went to the next door and asked again. The answer was the same. He went from door to door and each time he was turned away.

But then one villager said, "All I have is some water." "Thank you," the traveler said smiling gratefully, "We can make some soup from that water. We can make stone soup."

He asked the man for a cooking pot and started building a small fire. As the water started to boil, a passing villager stopped and asked him what he was doing. "I'm making stone soup," the traveler replied. "Would you like to join me?" The curious villager agreed.

"First, we must add a special stone," said the traveler. "One with magic in it." He reached into his knapsack and carefully unwrapped a special stone he'd been carrying with him for many years. Then he put it in the simmering pot.

Soon people from the village heard about this strange man who was making soup from a stone. They started gathering around the fire, asking questions. "What does your stone soup taste like?" asked one of the villagers. "Well, it would be better with a few onions," the traveler admitted. "Oh, I have some onions," he replied.

Another villager said, "I could bring a few carrots." Someone else offered, "We still have some potatoes in our garden. I'll go get them."

One by one, each villager brought something to add to the pot. What had started as just some water and a magic stone, had now become a delicious soup, enough to feed the whole village. The traveler and the villagers sat down together to enjoy their feast, and the miracle they'd help to create.

Introduction

Each day millions of people commit acts of kindness and courageous acts of service.

Everyone of us has a favorite story about someone who touched our lives with their giving. One of mine is Mother Teresa: an ordinary person who became great by helping others. She welcomed everyone—the hungry, the homeless, the sick and the dying—with open arms, and inspired people all over the world to realize they too could help others. Her life was a shining example of the power of unconditional love, enduring faith, and ceaseless joy. Her simple acts of love were contagious. Presidents of countries and companies couldn't say no to her humble requests. Young and old traveled to India and other countries just to be with her and learn how to love.

When I met her in the Philippines, the radiance from Mother Teresa's eyes reflected her love for children and her commitment to do everything she could to make their lives better. When Princess Diana first met her, she asked Mother Teresa how to overcome depression. Mother Teresa encouraged her to reach out and help others, especially the poorest of the poor. From then on, Princess Diana's life was filled with more joy and meaning from her humanitarian efforts. "Nothing brings me more happiness than trying to help the most vulnerable people in society," said Princess Diana. "It is a goal and an essential part of my life."

Just as we were finishing this book, both Mother Teresa and Princess Diana died. At first people were stunned at the simultaneous loss of these two extraordinary women. Then something wonderful happened: people started asking themselves, "What can I do to help?"

From the youngest child to the oldest senior, each of us wants to help, to give back, to make a difference. We want to feed the hungry, care for the elderly, and teach the children. Sometimes we wonder what we can do, with too little time, money, and resources.

Stone Soup for the World reminds us of the wisdom in the children's folktale of a traveler and his stone soup. When we each give something, we can feed the hungry of the world and the hunger in our souls. My mother read me the 16th century folktale when I was a young girl. I remember being fascinated by the hungry traveler who made soup from just a stone. He inspired the villagers to each give something to "the pot" and together they created a feast, enough to feed the entire village. As the eldest of ten children, I learned the importance of working together at an early age. When we did, we could get more done and have more fun.

For the last 20 years, I've been a traveler, living and working in communities across the country and around the world. Everywhere I went, I heard people express a common longing: they wanted a better life for their families and a greater sense of community. Leaders realized they needed local people to help solve local problems. And most people, young and old, wanted to help, yet they didn't feel connected and they didn't know where to begin. Like the villagers in the Stone Soup folktale, they often didn't think they had anything to give; they thought they had too little time, energy, money or power to make a real difference.

Stone Soup for the World reminds us that with a little imagination, cooperation and goodwill, we can make the world a better place. These heartwarming stories feature ordinary people doing extraordinary things, and extraordinary people doing ordinary things. They show us that greatness grows out of simple acts of giving. A toolbox full of ideas and a resource guide, this book gives us hope and direction for how to build a better world, one day at a time. After reading these stories, we hope you catch the Stone Soup spirit. Like the traveler in the folktale, we each have a magic stone: the power to give and get others to join us in building a world that works for everyone.

These stories show what can happen when just one or two people decide to make a difference. Imagine what will happen when millions of people use their magic stone and become a "community hero," helping others and building a better world.

The final story, The 100th Monkey, shows what happened when an island of monkeys started doing things in a new way. The energy brought by the hundredth monkey created a spark, an idealogical breakthrough, that advanced the entire species. "The 100th Monkey phenomenon" will happen when enough of us realize our potential to change our world. You might be the 100th one, the person who tips the scale, and helps us all reach the dream.

As we near the millinenium, we wonder what the world will be like, especially for our children. We hope and pray they have a safe and healthy place to live. If we learn from what's working in the world, we can create a better life for everyone. If each one of us opens our heart and works together, we can create a more hopeful future for those we love.

This book is a wonderful collection of stories about what is working in the world. Their simple, transforming message can guide us into the new millennium. They are a beacon of light pointing the way, to the dawn of a new day.

Somewhere on this planet, someone has a solution to each of the world's problems.
It might be one of us.
The future is in our hands and the hands of our children.
With your help, we can build a more hopeful world.
What can you do today, tomorrow, next week, next year?
And if you sometimes think you haven't enough time, energy, or resources,
remember the Stone Soup folktale:
When we each give a little, we can feed the whole world.

What One Person Can Do

The heroes of all time have gone before us. We have only to follow the thread of the hero path. Where we had thought to travel outward, we will come to the center of our own existence. And where we had thought to be alone, we will be with all the world.

JOSEPH CAMPBELL

Have you ever wondered if just one person can really make a difference? Sometimes the problems around us can seem overwhelming. But think about it: it was one person who walked on the moon and and one person who discovered electricity. And if you've ever had the privilege of seeing a woman give birth to a child, you know what one person can do.

There are thousands of ways each one of us can make a difference. A helping hand to a neighbor or a stranger creates a more caring world. Reading to children enriches their life and changes their future. A generous gift to a church or a charity gives new energy to those helping others. One kind word or a thoughtful deed can change someone's day, or even make history. It's amazing what one person can do!

The stories in this chapter show how everyday heroes commit acts of human kindness and courageous acts of service each and every day. "A hero is someone who responds to a 'call to service' and gives his life to something bigger than himself," said Joseph Campbell after helping George Lucas with the movie *Star Wars.* Young Luke Skywalker becomes a hero after responding to a call, going on a quest, facing challenges, and coming back victorious with a gift for his people. In the climactic moment of the last fight, Ben Kenobi's voice comes back to Skywalker saying, "Turn off your computer, turn off your machine and do it yourself, follow your heart, trust your feelings." When he does, he succeeds, and the audience breaks into applause.

Like Luke Skywalker, the community heroes in this chapter responded to a "call" and began fascinating and life-changing journeys. People from all walks of life: mothers, fathers, students and seniors; nurses, doctors, firefighters, and ministers; artists, musicians, and presidents of countries and companies. Their journeys become paths of self-discovery, where they overcome obstacles and find the resources to fulfill their destinies. Good samaritans and great humanitarians, dedicated volunteers and corporate champions; they follow their hearts and trust their instincts to help others. In the end, they find the kind of joy and fulfillment others only dream of, and have an exciting adventure that lasts a lifetime.

"The ultimate aim of the quest must be the wisdom and the power to serve others," says Campbell. He describes "legendary heroes" as those who dedicate their entire lives to the quest and start a new way of life, a new age, a new religion, a new world order. Legendary heroes in this chapter: Mother Teresa, Robert Muller, Jimmy Carter, Nelson Mandela, and Eleanor Roosevelt, have left footsteps for others to follow.

Each and every one of us can become an everyday hero. As you read these stories, let your imagination take you on a hero's journey. What has been calling to you? Remember, it only takes one person to takes a stand and decide to do something. When one person makes a commitment and asks others to help, people give of themselves. As Martin Luther King Jr. said, "Everyone can be great because everyone can serve."

- If you had one day or even one hour to make a difference in someone's life, what would you do?
- What could you do to help your school or your neighborhood?
- When you take time to listen for your "call," you may be surprised.
- You may begin an adventure more exciting than any you could imagine!

May the force be with you.

Starfish

A young girl was walking along a beach where thousands of starfish had been washed up during a terrible storm. When she came to each starfish, she would pick it up, and throw it back into the ocean.

She had been doing this for some time when a man approached her and said, "Little girl, why are you doing this? Look at this beach! You can't save all these starfish. You can't begin to make a difference!"

The girl seemed surprised and deflated. But after a few moments, she bent down, picked up another starfish, and hurled it as far as she could into the ocean. Then she looked up at the man and replied, "Well, I made a difference to that one."

God Didn't Mean for Them to Be Hungry

STORYTELLER: DAVID MURCOTT

Sometimes, big things come in little packages. Take Isis Johnson for example. At the tender age of four, she took her first step towards making a gigantic impact in her community. "Grandma," she asked, "can we send the chicken we have left to the children in Ethiopia? God didn't mean for them to be hungry." Isis had just seen pictures of starving children on the TV news and she wanted to help.

"Isis," her grandmother said tenderly, "Ethiopia is too far away. The chicken would spoil before it got there." Not ready to give up so easily, Isis asked, "Well, are there any hungry girls and boys in New Orleans?" Her grandmother told her the sad truth. "Yes, I'm sure there are." That was all Isis needed to know. "Then let's send our chicken to them," she said.

That's how it all started. Isis began going door-to-door, asking her neighbors if they would donate food for hungry children. She and her grandmother drove around town, gathering even more. Isis put a sign in the window of their home asking people to feed the hungry. Soon, people started bringing food to them. Their home became a small warehouse of donated food and supplies.

Isis and her grandmother decided to give the food away on Saturday, just before Christmas. They told the Salvation Army, which, in turn, told needy families. That first year, four year-old Isis gave out over 1000 items to hundreds of people. Soon, there were stories in the media about her work. Even NBC Nightly News and Black Entertainment Television covered the story. People were surprised to hear how much one little girl could do.

Isis received calls of support from all over New Orleans. Everyone wanted to help. Some people gave money to buy goods, others continued to bring food to her house. The following year, Isis helped collect 1,300 items. The Salvation Army, which had agreed to distribute them, had to send seven men to load it all into a truck. The next year, it was 4,000, and each year it grows.

A few years ago, when Hurricane Andrew hit Louisiana, Isis was upset by the amount of suffering she saw. So, she branched out into clothing, collecting over 1,600 articles of clothing for the Red Cross to distribute. Whenever Isis hears stories that make her sad, she tries to find a way to help. One day she heard about a New Orleans child who had been accidentally shot and killed in a drive-by shooting. When Isis discovered that the parents couldn't afford the burial, she collected money for the funeral and gave it to the family so that they and their child could be more at peace.

So many people made contributions to Isis' projects that her grandmother and a lawyer helped create the Isis Johnson Foundation. Now, her donors can receive tax credit for giving money, food or clothes. Sometimes, it's still hard for Isis to believe she has a foundation named after her and a list of recognition awards, like being induced to the Mickey Mouse Hall of Fame, that are too numerous to name.

Sometimes other children act jealous of her. Isis simply tells them, "If I can do it, so can you. You can get involved in projects like mine or start a special one of your own. But, no matter how you do it, when you help people, you feel good about yourself."

Isis, who turned 13 this year, wants to continue helping people when she grows up—either as a doctor or teacher. "No matter who you are or where you come from, you can make a difference. You don't have to be old to make things better, you only have to care." For those who still don't know where to begin, Isis suggests listening to a child. For, as she has proven, the youngest will show us the way.

Good habits formed at youth make all the difference.

ARISTOTLE

Organize a food or clothing drive for those in need in your community. If you want to help Isis in her war on hunger, write to her grandmother, Claudette Jones, at the **Isis T. Johnson Foundation** at 333 Hodges Street, Memphis, TN 38111.

Working in the Schools

STORYTELLER: JONATHAN ALTER

Sometimes, hope is born of fear. In this case, it was the fear that volunteer tutors would be robbed as they walked to their cars.

The Byrd Academy is an inner-city public school, not unlike many others. It is overcrowded and understaffed. The school is located in Chicago's Cabrini-Green neighborhood, one of the most infamous housing projects in the United States. Only a mile away from the glittering lakefront, it is a place afflicted by poverty and violence. Children cannot walk across playgrounds without fear of crime, injury, or worse. Not long ago, a young boy was dropped to his death from a window by some older children.

The apartment buildings in Cabrini-Green are filled with young mothers, most on public assistance, many with drug problems, and others so young themselves that they have little idea how to raise children. Fathers, for the most part, are nowhere to be seen. They've abandoned the area, leaving it for gangs to rule.

Joanne Alter was well aware of the problems in Chicago's public schools. As a county office holder, she sometimes visited them. The first woman elected to countywide office, Joanne was ending an 18-year career in elective politics. In her mid-sixties, it was time to retire.

One day she talked with a third grade teacher at the Byrd Academy. The teacher was upset that her students were struggling to learn, battling fear and a need to be loved. On an impulse, Joanne offered to volunteer in the teacher's classroom, helping teach these kids how to read. The teacher enthusiastically agreed. Her children needed to know that someone besides her believed in them.

On Joanne's first day of class, as she was leaving home, she met her neighbor, Marian Stone, in the elevator of her apartment building. Joanne explained the school's need and invited Marian to join her. The two decided to go to the school together. They had a terrific time in the classroom. The young children, starved for attention, begged them to come back. That was the modest beginning of a program called Working in the Schools (WITS).

"We help the teachers with some of their most challenging students," Joanne says. "We find 200 ways to say to the child, 'You look wonderful today!' 'Your math is so much better!' 'Aren't you terrific?', and so on. The point is to let kids know, 'We're here for you — and we're coming back.'"

"When we first started, we thought we'd be doing something small to solve a problem in education," she says. "To our surprise, we found that the kids weren't the only ones who benefited. We learned of the tremendous pay-back to the volunteers."

But, as WITS began to grow, a problem emerged. Volunteers understandably feared driving to the school. No one felt comfortable walking to the parking lot after school. Unfortunately, most potential volunteers thought it was just too dangerous to help out in Cabrini-Green, even though that's where help was needed most.

Joanne looked for a solution and decided that if the children could take a bus to school, so could the tutors. So now, WITS buses pick up volunteers in middle-class neighborhoods and take them to inner-city schools, then bring them back again four hours later. Volunteers feel safe and secure. In WITS' five-year history, there have been no incidents.

The program rented a minibus for the first 11 volunteers, which included Joanne's husband, Jim Alter. Today, there are 300 WITS volunteers, so they need the biggest buses it can find. The buses are always full of chatter about this class, or that kid. Remarkable camaraderie develops, not to mention the occasional romance. (One widow met a widower on the bus and married him.)

What started as a tutoring program staffed by older, often semi-retired volunteers, now includes mid-career professionals. Companies in the community, like United Airlines and Smith Barney, grant their employees "release time," which allows them to tutor twice a month on company time. Jim Boris, CEO of Everen Securities, has made plans to expand the WITS "release time" concept to their offices in 10 cities nationwide. By the year 2,000, WITS plans to have 10,000 volunteers helping Chicago's children.

"Whether they go one morning a week, or more, once the volunteers get hooked, they almost never leave," Joanne says. "The kids really give you unconditional love. The volunteers are nourished by it, and they keep coming back." One little boy in particular still stands out in her mind. "Moncell was a good student," she recalls. "He tried hard, but he was in the third grade and had never learned to read." Joanne worked with him often but he just wasn't making the kind of progress he should have been. "One day I asked him if he was reading his books at home after class. He sheepishly said no. I reminded him that practice makes perfect and he smiled and said he would try harder." The next week, the class recited poems they had memorized for their visiting parents. Moncell's poem was short and not too difficult. He recited it brilliantly. His mother was deeply touched.

After the program, Joanne asked Moncell's mother if she read to him at night. "There was a group of people near us, so she mumbled something about not having enough time and quickly walked away." Later that morning Joanne felt a tug on her sleeve. It was Moncell's mother. "I'm sorry," she said, with tears in her eyes. "I don't know how to read." Now, it was Joanne who was touched. "I told her that was okay and suggested that she have Moncell read to her at night." Moncell's mother promised she would.

The next week Moncell came to class all excited. "Guess what, guess what," he said. "My mom read with me last night. Now I'm gonna read like a pro!" To everyone's delight, but no one's surprise, Moncell started to improve that very day.

This story of Moncell and his mother resonated with me because Joanne Alter, co-founder of WITS and an inspiration to me on the subject of service, happens to be my mother.

Give a few hours of your time to help a child learn to read and feel the rewards. To volunteer or to become a corporate partner at **Working in the Schools** call 312-751-9487 or write WITS, 150 E. Huron, Chicago, IL 60611.

Sidewalk Sam

STORYTELLER: ASHLEY MEDOWSKI

It's downtown Boston, rush hour. But no one is rushing. Instead, a large audience stands in awe, staring down at an 8x10 foot reproduction of the Mona Lisa beneath their feet. Crouched upon the sidewalk next to his dusty chalk masterpiece, "Sidewalk Sam" creates the perfect blush on the Madonna's cheeks; then smiles up at the crowd.

It's the same kind of crowd, with friendly faces and cautious feet, that he has brought together for the past thirty years. For this work of art will be washed away in a matter of minutes under the sprinkling rain. But this concrete artist does not frown. He just sits comfortably in his work jeans and blue denim shirt, feeling pure satisfaction in creating this community of admirers.

Robert Guilleman studied art in Paris, Chicago, and Boston, and his artwork has been in many galleries and museums. But something was still missing for him. "The pure white walls, the guards, and people whispering didn't seem real to me," he says. Art should be for everyone, he thought.

Guilleman realized that sidewalks were actually exhibition platforms where people played out much of their lives. "We treat sidewalks with such disdain, throwing cigarette butts, bubblegum, and trash on them," he thought. "What if we could show some respect in a place where people who live in a rough and tumble environment exchanged their daily hellos?"

And so, over thirty years ago, he crouched down upon a busy street corner — with a cigar box full of chalks — and began to draw. Spending 10-12 hours each day on a few square feet of sidewalk, he soon became known as "Sidewalk Sam." Instead of promoting his individual expression of art, he decided to unite a whole community in a lifetime art project. "I wanted to get people involved in art," he says. "Art is something that brings the extremes of society together. . . we've forgotten the part of our cities where everyone is entirely human together — the streets."

Sam didn't get to finish his first few creations. The Boston police threatened to arrest him for "defacing public property." Once the city realized that he was creating communal masterpieces, he's been allowed to draw just about anywhere he pleases. On Earth Day, 1990, for example, Sidewalk Sam turned one of the most congested highways in Boston back in time into the original lush green meadow it once was. With the full support of the City, Storrow Drive was shut down, and it became a giant one-mile long symbol of the Earth and the community supporting each other.

First, he filled the city's water trucks with environmentally-safe, grassy green paint and turned one mile of the highway into a rolling field beside the Charles River. Then he handed out 60,000 boxes of rainbow-colored chalk to the public, inviting them to become artists. They drew symbols of peace and growth- from butterflies to sunflowers. Corporate presidents traded pastel chalks with panhandlers and the city street became a meadow once again. "Everyone passing by was a co-creator of the art," Sam recalls. "Most Americans want to give of themselves. And this was art being made by all of us together."

As for Sidewalk Sam, he's become a symbol himself, using his artistic talent to get the public to realize the kindness in their own hearts. Reflecting upon his work, Sam explains, "I took my goodness and set it on the ground. I allow people to trample it, if they would. But instead, tens of thousands step around it everyday. "

Today Sidewalk Sam is no longer walking away from his masterpieces. He fell off a ladder in '94, and returned to his Boston streets in a wheelchair. His back fractured, he now leans from his chair to continue to chalk in his vision. He relies on others to help him finish his works now. "I have to fulfill my humanity. I have got to make my life worthwhile," he proclaims. "I have got to serve my fellow man."

His latest project involves the busiest highway in Boston, the Central Artery. The Federal Highway Department has decided to move the Artery underground in a 10-year, 10 billion dollar construction project. Sidewalk Sam was asked to beautify the area and entertain tourists during the massive construction. So most days, you will find him painting the tunnel's dull gray interior into a massive medieval cathedral! When he is finished, cherubs will shoot their love arrows from a blue sky. Bumper to bumper traffic will move slowly past gold-trimmed pillars and marble painted staircases.

The homeless, the children, and the community near the tunnel will join in by painting fluffy clouds above the rooftop of the cathedral. With Sidewalk Sam, it's all about painting the picture that will make people stop and look — whether it's at the clouds or the magnificent pillars. And like those cherubs, Sidewalk Sam's aim is true — striking the hearts of common pedestrians and everyday travelers.

We think too much. We feel too little.
More than machines, we need humanity.

CHARLIE CHAPLIN

Art can help bring your community to life in exciting, colorful new ways—and can help solve society's problems. To learn how, write to Sidewalk Sam at **Art Street, Inc.** 83 Church Street, Newton, MA 02158 or e-mail: artstreet@aol.com.

Hidden Treasures

STORYTELLER: JOHN MCKNIGHT

The most precious things in the world are not easily found. Gold, oil, diamonds—all take time and patience to find and cultivate. The same is true of people. More often than not, the most valuable thing a person has to offer is not in plain view. Unfortunately, most of us do not take the time or have the patience to search for the gems the eyes can't see. But, I met a remarkable woman who does just that.

She was responsible for assisting developmentally disabled people in southern Georgia. She and her colleagues had become concerned with their field's focus on people's disabilities instead of their possibilities. She realized that they rarely thought about the gifts, talents, and capabilities of those entrusted to their care. She became determined to begin spending more time with her "clients," to see if she could uncover the special gifts each of them had to offer. She went first to the home of a forty-two-year-old man named Joe. He was the product of a system that, despite its best intentions, had labeled and limited him. After years of special education, society had concluded there just wasn't a place in it for someone like Joe. So, he was sent home to his family's pig farm. Every day he did two things. He fed the pigs each morning and night, and he sat in the living room, where he listened to the radio. After four days at Joe's house, my friend was thoroughly dejected. She could not find Joe's gift. "Then, on the fifth day I realized what his gift was," she said. "Joe listens to the radio."

It might not sound like much, but to her it was a treasure. "After talking with those in the community, I found out there were three people in town who listened to the radio, and got paid for it," she said. "One was in the sheriff's office, one was in the police department, and the third was in the local civil defense and volunteer ambulance office." She went to each of these places to see if she could match Joe's gift with one of them.

The civil defense and ambulance office was located in a donated house that doubled as the neighborhood community center. It was a busy place, full of activities. Somebody was always there. People came in to talk and drink coffee in the dining room. Sometimes they showed movies. It was perfect. My friend noticed a young woman monitoring the radio for emergency calls, dispatching ambulances as needed. She told the dispatcher, "I know somebody who likes to listen to the radio as much as you do. I'd like to introduce him to you." Now, every day, Joe shares the office listening to the radio and helping the dispatcher. When Christmas came, the volunteers at the ambulance station gave Joe his own CB radio to listen to at home in the evening.

One day, he went to the local diner. "Hey, Joe, what's happening?", the owner casually asked. Joe looked at him and replied, "The Smith house over in Boonesville burned down this morning. And out on Route 90, at that turnoff where you can have picnics, there was a drug bust. And Mr. Schiller over in Athens had a heart attack." The diner fell silent, as all eyes turned to Joe. Everyone in the diner realized that if they wanted to know what was happening, Joe was the man to see. To the best of my knowledge, this is the only town in the United States that now has the benefit of a bonafide, old-fashioned town crier.

When I last spoke to my friend, she told me she had taken Joe to meet the editor of the newspaper. It occurred to her that although the town was small, he couldn't possibly know everything that was happening in the community. But, every day by noon, Joe knew. So now he is a stringer for the local newspaper.

Thanks to my friend's efforts, Joe, a man nearly written off by society, has become an inspiration—and a valuable resource to his community. But it would never have happened if one person hadn't dug a little deeper, searched a little longer, and tried a little harder, to find Joe's true potential. How many more Joes are out there, just waiting for someone to take the time to discover what they have to offer? If you look long enough, there's a treasure waiting to be found in each and everyone of us.

Learn how you can uncover the hidden treasures in your community by seeing people as assets instead of problems. Call the **Neighborhood Innovations Network** at 847-491-3395 to order a copy of John McKnight's book *Building Communities from the Inside Out,* or attend a training program to learn how to uncover and mobilize the gifts, capacities, and resources in your local neighborhood.

The Forgiveness Party

Storyteller: Jo Claire Hartsig
adapted from *Fellowship,* magazine of The Fellowship for Reconciliation

Nine-year-old Bess Lyn Sannino was hurt and confused. Some older neighborhood children had broken into her house stolen her favorite things, and vandalized her Virginia Beach home, pelting it with raw eggs and spraying graffiti on the garage door. Bess' shock quickly gave way to anger. Her first reaction was revenge: "I felt like going over to their houses and killing them." They had been in her room and gone through her personal things. It wasn't right. With great detail, she could list every item that was taken, including her $17 allowance money, her Valentine's Day candy, and her tape player.

Her mother, Grace, wrestled with the decision of whether or not to call the police, since the vandals were kids from the neighborhood and not hardened criminals. She called the father of one of the suspected teens, who identified the others involved. He encouraged her to work with the police to make this a lesson for the youngsters.

When Grace called the police, a compassionate and understanding officer responded. He spent a whole week tracking down the parents of all four burglars. One of the mothers worked two jobs and rarely got home until after 11 p.m. Another family was caught up trying to deal with their father who was hospitalized due to his own violent behavior.

The police officer, the parents, the teens, and Bess' family all agreed to try to avoid having the kids get criminal records. Curfews were set and other restrictions imposed. The teens had to "pay back" their neighbors as well. They returned the stolen property. They painted over the graffiti. They scrubbed the splattered egg off the garage door. They helped out with yard work and chores around the house. One of the boys even wrote an essay on integrity and read it to Bess.

Bess wasn't angry anymore, but she still felt unsettled. In her child's heart, she struggled with the grown-up truth that restitution is not the same as reconciliation. Though she and her neighbors had gotten to know each other better, she felt there would always be an awkwardness between them. From her confused feelings, a simple idea was formed. Bess decided to throw a party, not just any party, "A Forgiveness Party," she called it. She decided to host a party, for the people who only weeks before had pried open a window to her house and helped themselves to her special things.

The party was a huge success. Bess made a pināta and decorated the house and yard with balloons and lights. Not only did the teens from the break-in attend, they brought their families as well. It became a celebration. As people danced to music from the stolen then returned tape player, they moved from anger and shame through understanding and forgiveness to compassion and joy. That day enemies became friends.

How lovely to think that no one need wait a moment: we can start now, start slowly changing the world! How lovely that everyone, great and small, can make a contribution toward introducing justice straightaway!

Anne Frank

Teach your children conflict resolution skills. Learn how to create nonviolent solutions to conflict with the **Children's Creative Response to Conflict at the Fellowship of Reconciliation,** Box 271, Nyack, NY 10960, or http://www.nonviolence.org/nvweb/for.

Teaching Jazz, Creating Community

STORYTELLER: LESLIE R. CRUTCHFIELD

Most people know Wynton Marsalis as a musician. But for students in Washington D.C. schools the award-winning trumpet player is special kind of teacher. When he's not touring the country he spends much of his time teaching kids. But he doesn't just show them how to play jazz—he uses jazz to teach them about life.

For Roberto Peres, who had studied trumpet for eight years, Marsalis has been a role model. He thinks Wynton is the best. One day, Roberto's music teacher at Duke Ellington School of Arts in Washington D.C. surprised him by taking him to the local NPR station to meet his hero. The next day, Wynton gave Roberto a free two-hour trumpet lesson. Wynton's honest critique gave Roberto the encouragement he needed to do his best.

His next lesson would be five months later—this time over the phone. "We talked for three hours," Roberto says. But this time, it wasn't just about music: it was about life, and the importance of persistence, dedication, concentration, and consistent practice. Through this conversation, Roberto discovered that his favorite trumpet player was also a real person. "He's very giving, always making time for you," he says.

Over the past decade, Wynton has visited more than 1000 schools and has mentored several students like Roberto. "What a kid learns from jazz is how to express his individuality without stepping on somebody else's," he says. Wynton teaches them two main ideas. "The first thing I tell them is, 'Play anything you want, as long as it sounds like you. It's important to develop yourself and your own vision.' It's about finding one's purpose in life," he says, "Kids need to learn to walk their own path."

The second lesson is that individualism has a flip side: "While pursuing your individuality, recognize that other people are also pursuing theirs." So, he teaches them how to control their self-expression. "Don't just blurt something out. Adapt it to what the other guy is doing. Take your freedom and put it into the service of somebody else's," he tells the kids. "Being a good neighbor, that's what jazz is all about."

As a young child, Wynton learned some tough lessons about being a good neighbor. Born in New Orleans in 1961, the second of six sons, he remembers being called "nigger" and forced to integrate into hostile white schools. He was shocked to discover that the better a black student did, the more he was attacked. Despite hardship, Wynton became a straight-A student who won every musical competition he entered. At the age of seventeen, he was admitted to New York's elite Juilliard School—one of the youngest musicians ever to enter. But the school didn't fit his style, and Wynton left after his first year. He later joined a band, Art Blakey's Jazz Messengers, and eventually became the first artist to win Grammy awards in both classical and jazz categories.

Although Wynton's father, the great jazz pianist Ellis Marsalis, had the greatest influence on his musical life, it was his mother who taught him the most about life. He remembers her saying, "You better develop your mind, show some humility, and act like you had some home-training." Wynton says that, next to his parents, the writer Albert Murray had the most influence on him. "Murray said, 'To hell with whining,' Wynton explains. "Humanity doesn't move forward by complaining about the fact that life is hard. You can't discard the whole apple because one section is rotten." Optimistic to the core, Wynton adds, "You gotta cut that rotten section away and eat the rest."

Wynton says his greatest gift is the ability to listen to the soul of a musician. "When they play and I hear their sound, I can tell what kind of grades they make in school and what kind of habits they have. I can just hear it in their sound. I know what they're saying. Sometimes, what they're saying is 'Help'." Wynton reaches out to them with more than a helping hand. Through jazz, he gives them the gift of a richer, fuller life.

Roberto is now studying at Howard University and still playing his trumpet. Whenever Wynton comes to town, Roberto goes to see him perform. It's been two years since they first met and Wynton is still giving him direction and advice both about the jazz world and the world in general. "Wynton is the best teacher I've ever had," says Roberto. "He's taught me, 'If you love what you do, you'll always succeed.' By example, he's also shown Roberto how to work for that success. Roberto says, "If he wants something, he'll do whatever it takes to accomplish his goal."

If you want to bring music into the lives of children, call your local school principal. If you are a professional musician, look up the local public or performing arts school when you're on tour. When you're in Washington D.C., call the **Duke Ellington School of Arts** at 202-333-2555.

Thank You, Dr. Coué

Storyteller: Robert Muller
adapted from *Most of All, They Taught Me Happiness*

As Assistant Secretary General at the United Nations, when bad news dragged me down, I remembered a great lesson I had learned from Dr. Émile Coué when I was a student at the University of Heidelberg and a dying friend asked me to help him. It is a mystery to me. I do not understand it. But it has created miracles for me and it saved my life during the war.

"Could you please go to the library and borrow a book by Dr. Coué?," my friend in the hospital asked. "Bring it to me as soon as possible." I went the following morning and found *Self-Mastery Through Conscious Autosuggestion*. Looking through the book, I learned that this doctor, who was from my neighboring town in France, had gained worldwide fame for his healing methods which drew on the confidence and imagination of the patient.

The essence of his work lies in this simple practice: Every morning before rising, and every evening before getting into bed, you shut your eyes and repeat several times: "Every day, in every way, I am getting better and better." One can also add one's own words. I got accustomed to saying: "I feel wonderful, I feel happier than yesterday, I have never felt so good. It is marvelous to be alive and so healthy."

I thought at first that it was a little too easy—to seek happiness by just repeating to oneself that one felt happy! But after reflecting on it I could see that we have the choice of seeing everything in light or in dark. I now start the day with the conviction to feel good, healthy, and happy to be alive. My happiness, zest for life, attitude toward the world are affected by this "internal" decision, taken at the beginning of each day. Then when difficulties arise, I revert to an innermost part of myself, switch on optimism and confidence and return to peace of mind.

To the great surprise of the doctors, my friend recovered within a few weeks and was released from the hospital. I have never forgotten him and Dr. Coué's method. I have not always remembered to repeat the affirmation, but I have instinctively followed his philosophy of optimism and self-reliance all my life.

When I was 20, I worked as an informant for the French Resistance. Under the false identity of Louis Parizot, I had an administrative position in a French telecommunications center that enabled me to warn my friends of impending inspections by the Germans. One evening, I noticed that someone had gone through my possessions in my hotel room. I asked the hotelkeeper if anyone had entered my room. "Yes, two workers from the electrical company checked it." Had electrical workers really displaced some of my belongings, I wondered. Was it a routine inspection by the French police, or were the Germans on my trail?

The following morning I received a telephone call from the guard at the entrance of the office building. Three gentlemen wanted to see me on behalf of a friend named André Royer. My heart jumped violently when I heard his name. The news had just reached me that this good school-friend of mine had been arrested by the Germans during a raid. I suspected that the men who were on their way to my office were Germans. I told my secretary to receive them, to find out what they wanted, and to let me know by telephoning the secretary of a colleague in a nearby office, where I took refuge.

After a while the telephone rang and I could heard my secretary say over the phone: "I am looking for Mr. Parizot. Do you know where he is? Three gentlemen from the police want to see him." This message was clear enough. To gain time, I went to the hotel attic, and I asked the secretary who had harbored me to give a message to one of my Resistance colleagues. He soon joined me, and said: "You have little chance of escape, if any. There are five or six Gestapo in the building. They are systematically searching offices and appear quite relaxed, for they know that you are here. The entrance to the hotel is blocked and a prison van is stationed at the curb. To hide here in the attic or climb on the roof will not help. You know perfectly well that they will shoot you down like a pigeon."

Then he left me, promising to return if there were any new developments. I found myself alone to consider the trap I was in. "This is the moment of all moments," I thought to myself, "to keep cool and in full command of my mental and physical capabilities." Suddenly I remembered Dr. Coué. "I must feel relaxed and even elated about this situation." Following the good doctor's advice, I repeated to myself that it was indeed an extraordinary and thrilling adventure for a 20 year-old youth to be trapped in a hotel, pursued by the Nazis. Would it not be exciting if I could play a trick on them and slip through their fingers?

Having switched my perspective to a positive, confident frame of mind, I felt relaxed, even happy and cheerful, without any fear or thought of failure. I began to think calmly and decisively. "Nothing is hopeless in this world," I thought. "There must be at least once chance in a thousand to escape from this situation. I must find it. I must concentrate on the mentality of the Nazis. They know that I am in this building. They are convinced that they will get me and that it is only a matter of time and *Gründlichkeit* (thoroughness). There is no rational means of escape. I must think of something that is foreign to their psychology."

I examined various options. All but one led to certain arrest and possible death. Then a little flicker of hope arose. "There are many people in the hotel. My best chance of escape is to become part of the crowd. Why not walk downstairs and go straight to the group of people who must be gathered? The Nazis certainly do not expect me to do that. The worst that would happen is I would be arrested. But this is likely to happen anyway. If I have any chance at all, it is by doing the one thing the Germans do not expect me to do: to walk straight to them."

I put my plan into action. I changed my physical appearance as best I could, wetting my hair with water from a faucet, parting it on the side. I took off my glasses and lit a cigarette to gain a relaxed posture. I seized a file from a desk and put it under my arm. When I walked down the majestic staircase, a large gathering of people had assembled. I could not see very well without my glasses, but I distinguished a group dominated by shiny spots: These must be the bald heads of the Germans, I surmised. I walked straight up to them. A split second of silence set in when my French colleagues saw me appear on the staircase. But they immediately understood what I was doing, and chatted louder to create a diversion.

I walked up to the group of Germans and recognized my secretary, whom they were still interrogating. I asked her calmly: "What is all this turmoil about?" She answered very composedly: "These gentlemen are looking for Mr. Parizot." I expressed surprise: "Parizot? But I just saw him a few minutes ago on the fourth floor!" *"Schnell hinauf!"* (Quickly upstairs!) shouted one of the Germans and the whole group ran upstairs! I hung around casually for a few more minutes, in case I was being observed by one of the smarter Nazis. My French colleagues were careful not to pay any attention to me, returning to their desks.

Then I went to a compatriot's office and asked how I could get out of the building. "The main entrance is guarded, but there may be a way of getting to the garage through the cellars. The French superintendent downstairs should be able to help you." Under his guidance, I finally reached the garage, which was full of bicycles. I took a good, sturdy one and rode to the house of a member of the underground. I waited there for a few days until the search had abated and then proceeded to the hills.

Thirty five years later I flew to Paris to receive UNESCO's Peace Education Prize. At the ceremony I was astonished to see my former secretary, whom I hadn't seen since that memorable day. I embraced her warmly and listened as she told me the rest of the story. She said that the Germans had been so thorough and convinced of finding me that they had even unrolled old carpets stored in the attics!

She told me that when she had seen me walking down the staircase, she had recited to herself: *"Passera, passera pas, passera . . ."* (Will pass, will not pass, will pass . . .).

After several other instances in which Dr. Coué's method saved me from danger during the war, I have become a strong advocate for the power of optimism. Now I live on the positive and sunny side of life that God has given me. Optimism, hard work and faith are not only in our highest self-interest, they are also the affirmations of life itself. I was fortunate that one of my compatriots taught me this at an early age.

Thank you, Dr. Coué, thank you from the bottom of my heart.

We must make life a true miracle and our planet a paradise. Let us fill the last years of this century and millennium with our ideas and dreams for the future. You can send your ideas and dreams for a better world to Dr. Robert Muller at http://www.worldpeace2000.org/ideas. *Suggestions and Autosuggestions* by Dr. Emile Coué and C.H. Brooks is published by Samuel Weiser, New York, NY.

Father Joe

STORYTELLER: DENNIS MORGIGNO

The setting was San Diego's newest and most exclusive shopping center, home to Cartier, Ferragamo, Gucci, and Dunhill. On the third floor, around the walkway that circles the atrium, the clinking of fine crystal mixed with the easy laughter of the revelers at yet another grand opening. Among the guests that night was a large man dressed in black, though not quite like the others in their tuxedos and evening gowns.

The caterer was about to call the invited to his steaming pans of hors d'oeuvres and entrees when he noticed the man in black. He replaced the lid on one of the large warming pans and walked over to him. "Father Joe?" the caterer asked. "I once stood in your food line; now I want you to be the first to stand in mine."

It's the kind of story Father Joe Carroll never tires of telling. In the ten years since opening his revolutionary St. Vincent de Paul Village, he's seen thousands of people leave the streets, regain their dignity and return to productive lives. There's no better example than the caterer Jim Miller, a former construction worker whose alcohol and cocaine abuse led to his sleeping under cardboard by San Diego Bay. One day Miller stumbled onto the food line outside St. Vincent's. He took nourishment for his body while he sorted out his soul. "You have to be ready to kick," he says. "And when you are, you're really thankful for the programs and the support they offer here."

For Father Joe, a warm and friendly visionary of a man, his role at St. Vincent's is nothing short of divine irony. "From the time I was five until I was twelve, every Christmas present was from the St. Vincent de Paul thrift store in the Bronx. We were a poor family; and when we ran out of food, my mother would go to St. Vincent's. It's funny how God works. I was the one chosen to give back what my family had received all those years."

Not that young Father Joe didn't need a little push. "I never really wanted to do it," Carroll says. "But Leo [the late Bishop Leo Maher] called me in one day and said: "Tomorrow, you're the new head of St. Vincent's. You're the biggest New York hustler we have. We need you there."

Father Joe soon realized the old man simply had seen the real Joe Carroll, a young priest others would follow; someone who would not be afraid to use his peculiar powers of persuasion to build St. Vincent's into a force in the community. He would eventually become known far and wide as "The Hustler Priest," picking the pockets of average citizens and major philanthropists alike to turn his down-to-earth vision into reality.

The first test came at a local parish, where the pastor issued a challenge. He would support Father Joe's plan for St. Vincent's if Carroll could raise $5,000 from the second collection, always the hardest. Father Joe rose to the challenge. "Homelessness is a social disease," he preached. "It destroys communities like a cancer." The kid from the Bronx had their attention. "The cancer spreads. It gets neighbors fighting neighbors and, pretty soon, no one's working together."

Joe Carroll raised $20,000 that day—at one church. Others churches followed, joined by members of the community. Helen Copley, owner of San Diego's largest daily newspaper, was St. Vincent's first major benefactor. Her $250,000 donation gave the project credibility. McDonald's matriarch and former San Diego Padres owner Joan Kroc sealed the deal, giving Carroll three million dollars to finish the first phase of the Village.

Father Joe did more than just build a shelter; he changed the way a whole city dealt with homelessness. He insisted that communities must "break the cycle of homelessness," not just offer indigent people an occasional meal and a place to park their bedrolls at night. When he began his crusade in late 1982, San Diego was doing just that for the legions of homeless attracted by its warm weather.

The few shelters that existed were simply overnight havens from the storm drains and underpasses; the meal programs offered little more than meager breakfasts and dismal soup lines. Carroll changed all that, ignoring those who said his Village was "too nice" for homeless people. He believed that feeding and clothing the homeless is only half the battle. By restoring people's dignity, you can help them reclaim their lives.

Father Joe's Village is a community where dignity is being reborn every day; where there is hope for the future. He built apartments where homeless families could have their privacy as well as large, clean dormitories for single men and women. The Village now has a medical clinic to address the ills of life on the streets, job training, a school for the children and financial counseling for their parents. A huge central kitchen churns out three square meals a day for everyone who calls the Village home.

Nine years after the first residence opened its doors, St. Vincent's served its 10 millionth meal in September of 1996. The Village gets people back on their feet and into the world. The records show that after a year in Father Joe's program, more than 80% of all the families live in homes of their own and have a positive cash flow.

Father Joe has become a San Diego celebrity and an international symbol as a champion for the homeless. In January of 1988, the United Nations awarded him the International World Habitat Award. The City of Las Vegas has awarded Father Joe $10 million and asked him to do for them what he has done in San Diego.

But he never forgets his roots. "We have a policy here that, no matter what the size of the donation, if I'm here, you can give it to me personally. We used to have a little old lady who got five-pound blocks of cheese from the federal food program.

She would cut it in half every month and give half to us. My staff would call me out of a meeting and she'd hand it to me. Those people are just as important to what we do as the big donors," says Father Joe, and you can tell he really means it.

"St. Vincent's has become a catalyst for people who care," he says with more than a touch of awe and gratitude in his voice. "We're giving them an opportunity to give back, and people like Jim Miller an opportunity to live again."

★

The only solution is to love.

Dorothy Day

Help end the cycle of poverty for the homeless. Come visit **St. Vincent de Paul Village** and see how their "continuum of care" supports 855 residents and 1,200 non-residents with housing, meals, counseling, drug and alcohol programs, medical-dental care, children's services, job training—all at one site. Call 619-687-1066 for inspiration or for a tour.

Oakland's Fire-Fighting Peacemaker

STORYTELLER: PATRICIA WEST

On October 20, 1991, the Oakland/Berkeley Hills were a blaze of fire. Later, it would become known as the largest urban wildfire in U.S. history. One of the first people on the scene happened to be off-duty Fire Captain Ray Gatchalian.

Exhausted from fighting a five-alarm grass fire the day before, Ray was at home resting. Suddenly, his electricity went out. Fierce winds outside his window called to him. From his deck he could see smoke. It was about to engulf his entire neighborhood. The next thing Ray remembers is a helicopter warning his neighbors: "Evacuate the area! Evacuate the area now!"

Ray's first thoughts were of his wife, their daughter and their elderly neighbors. For a few moments, he was torn. His home was about to be in the middle of this raging fire: "Do I stay with them or do I go and fight the fire?" After securing their safety, Ray closed the door to his house, thinking it might be for the last time. Ray hopped in Oscar, his faithful 65 Chevy pickup truck, and headed to Fire Station 15. He and another off-duty firefighter, John Arnerich, loaded up the few remaining fire hoses and nozzles and made Oscar their honorary fire engine.

They sped to the edge of the fire—where it was threatening to jump into the next canyon. At once, Ray realized the danger lurking along this brush-choked hillside. In the intense heat of the first hour, homes were being consumed at the unbelievable rate of one every five seconds. By the end of that day, 25 people would lose their lives, 3,000 homes would be destroyed, and in its ashes the fire would leave an estimated $1.5 billion in damages.

In all his years, Ray had never seen a fire burn with such ferocity. He recalls, "I fought in Vietnam. I've witnessed the destruction of civil war in El Salvador and the earthquake in Mexico City. But I wasn't prepared to see the devastation of my own community. I was stunned, in total shock."

Ray called the Fire Department dispatch and urgently pleaded for immediate assistance. But there was nothing left to send. All 23 fire engines and 7 fire trucks were already on the fire lines. When he heard the dispatcher's last words, he realized they were on their own: "Ray, I will do the best I can to get someone up there, but I can't promise. God bless."

By now, the fire was threatening to engulf the entire neighborhood. If they were to have any chance whatsoever, somehow, they needed to slow the fire. Several curious onlookers stopped to help, and Ray quickly organized these willing folks into a makeshift fire brigade. Ray looked at his volunteers, a dozen young, untrained and unprepared people, but what they lacked in experience, they made up for with spirit.

With nothing but the spare supplies they'd loaded in Oscar, Ray led his makeshift fire crew in a courageous three-hour stand against the fire. The angry red monster roared, ready to turn on the firefighters without a moment's notice. In the end, they prevailed, saving many homes and preventing the fire from spreading to another canyon, where it would have gained even more strength. But their work was far from over.

When fire engines finally arrived to relieve them, one of Ray's volunteers, Rich Stover, heard that his own mother's home was on fire. His new friends were not about to let the fire destroy one of their own. Exhausted but determined, they worked tirelessly with limited resources to save his mother 's home and six of her neighbors'. In the heat of those critical hours, Rich, a 28-year-old general contractor, decided to become a firefighter. Rich explained, "Fighting the fire with Ray changed my life. It rekindled my desire to help others."

The TV cameras from around the world captured dramatic flaming footage showing the magnitude of the devastation, but they missed the selfless heroism of these volunteers and hundreds like them, who courageously battled the inferno. Without them, the loss of life and property would have been catastrophic. "Some might say they were stupid, while some would say it was valor," Ray says now. "But once you face such a monstrous thing, your life is transformed."

Rallying people to make a difference is nothing new to Ray. One might even say it's his "calling". A former Vietnam vet and Green Beret now dedicated to peace, he once organized doctors to donate their services to refugees, and then helped influence Congress with his award-winning documentary film *Unheard Voices* to stop military aid to El Salvador. He's even spent his vacation organizing a month-long, round-the-clock, torch-bearing vigil to rally his Oakland community to stop the violence and create peace.

For his courage and community service, Ray has won many prestigious awards. But he'll be the first to tell you that he's just a regular working guy. What makes him special is that he's always willing to give. His father once told him, "We're here to inspire one another, to bring out the best in each other." On that hot, dry and windy day of the fire, Ray did just that.

Those among you who will be truly happy are the ones who have sought and found how to serve.

Albert Schweitzer

Give thanks for the good works of 250,000 firefighters across the country. To support the **International Association of Fire Fighters Burn Foundation** and the national children's burn camp, write to them at 1750 New York Ave. Washington D.C. 20007.

The Power of an Idea

STORYTELLERS: JEB BUSH AND BRIAN YABLONSKI

One Sunday morning in the spring of 1993, eleven-year-old David Levitt read "The Power of an Idea" in *Parade* magazine. The story was about Stan Curtis, a Kentucky man who had founded a network of volunteers to transport donated food to hungry people. The program was called Harvest USA, with over eighty chapters across the nation. David was so intrigued, particularly by their motto "Feeding The Hungry Without Money," that he paid a visit to another food organization, the local Tampa Bay Harvest.

The president gave him all kinds of information about Stan Curtis' food donor program called "Operation Food for Thought" in Louisville, where donated leftovers from school cafeterias goes to the hungry. Why couldn't he create a similar program in his school so that leftover food could feed the homeless in local soup kitchens?

The sixth-grader first approached his school principal with his idea, but was told that there were probably government regulations that would prevent a program like this from getting off the ground. Even his new friends at Tampa Bay Harvest told him that several people had made similar proposals to the Pinellas County School Board only to be defeated. Nevertheless, David was not discouraged.

Over the next few weeks, David collected facts, figures, and success stories from Tampa Bay Harvest and Operation Food for Thought. He researched Florida's laws regarding food donations. He wrote a proposal, made eight copies of it, and personally delivered it to the superintendent and all seven members of the Pinellas County School Board.

While at the school board office, David asked to see the meeting room. Photographs of the board members were hanging on the walls, and as he looked at them he wondered how an eleven-year-old would be able to sway these powerful people when so many before him had failed. What if he called each of them individually to share his idea? He got the phone numbers of each of the board members, personally called each one, and asked their response to his idea. No one had ever taken the time to do this before and the school board members were really impressed with David's determination.

David's twelfth birthday was a big one. He found himself standing before the Pinellas County School Board in the very room he had been awed by only weeks before. His persistence and hard work had paid off. The school board unanimously approved his plan! David smiled in victory. "It just took a kid to help them see that this matters," he said.

Five months went by, however, and the program had still not been implemented. David was getting impatient. Food was being wasted and people were going hungry. David called the president of Tampa Bay Harvest to see what needed to be done. It turned out that they needed airtight containers to ship the food, and since the school system's budget had no money to purchase them, Tampa Bay Harvest was responsible for buying the containers. But they didn't even have a bank account, let alone the money.

David set out on a quest for containers. A visit to his local supermarket got him the addresses of companies that made containers. He then sent letters to every company he could find. Publix Super Market, Inc. was the first to help. They sent him a one-hundred-dollar gift certificate to buy containers. He was making progress, but it wasn't nearly enough. Next, David received a letter from an executive at First Brands Company, maker of Glad Lock bags. They were so impressed with David's project that they sent him eight cases of storage bags and later committed to providing an ongoing supply. David was delighted.

As he passed by the building on his way home, he couldn't even look at it. It took over a week to find out if his mother was dead or alive. Rescuers worked around the clock to clear rubble and recover victims. The news, when it came, confirmed their worst fear: Carroll Fields was one of the 168 people who lost their lives that horrible day of April 19, 1995.

People all over the country were shocked by this outrageous tragedy. Everyone wanted to help. They sent donations, along with their prayers. Car washes were held, lines at blood banks swelled, heartfelt letters were sent to inspire rescuers. In Lubbock, Texas a young child put a dollar in an envelope and addressed it to "Big Help" in Oklahoma City.

In Santa Clara, California, all Chris Gross could think about were the children. "I kept seeing the building and the images of the children who died in the day care center," he said. He kept thinking about them and the others, the ones who had lost their parents. "Imagine being one of them," Chris thought. "Put yourself in their shoes. They're going to be missing their parents for the rest of their lives." Twenty-seven-year-old Chris wanted to give these kids a little extra something.

Like Ronnie Fields, Chris had been close with his own parents. He had grown up knowing he was lucky and feeling grateful for his life. At an early age, his parents had instilled in him the Jewish tradition of *tsdaka,* giving to others. Chris remembers how his mother would always buy too many cookies from the Girl Scouts. "When young people are trying, give them an opportunity to succeed," she would say. "Never turn them away."

Chris' parents also fostered an appreciation for learning and worked hard to put Chris and his brother through college. "I always thought that if most parents had a dying wish for their children, they would say, 'Go to college, make something of yourselves,'" says Chris. He thought the Oklahoma parents would have wanted this for their children, too. He wondered how he could help make this wish come true.

He started by talking with his friends. "Wouldn't it be great if we created a scholarship fund and raised a million dollars to give these kids some hope for their future?" Chris asked them. "Right now, everyone is making them dinners and offering them clothes. But in five or ten years, will anyone really be there to help? If we start now, we could make a big difference in these kids' lives."

Chris searched for ways to jumpstart a scholarship fund. Having graduated only a few years earlier, he knew how expensive it was to go to college. As a financial analyst at Applied Materials, a semiconductor equipment company, his salary was $53,874. It was a good salary for a young man, but not enough to finance the education of so many children. Even if he gave it all, he would only have enough for one scholarship. But what if he could get others to match his salary? Chris decided to share his idea with Tom Hayes, Vice President of Corporate Affairs, and ask for his help. "What if we could get eighteen other Silicon Valley companies to match my salary?" Chris proposed. "We could raise a million dollars!"

"A couple years earlier, I wouldn't have had the money. In a couple of years, I'll be married with lots of responsibilities," Chris reflects. "I was at an optimal point in my life." He calculated his finances: he had $12,000 in the bank, no car payments or debt. He figured if he cut way back on his spending and planned things carefully, he could live on his savings for one year. So Chris learned to live with less: he slowed down his fast-paced life, gave up his cell phone and wore the same clothes, instead of buying new ones. He kept up his social life by going out with friends for dessert, instead of an entire meal.

When Chris' employer decided to match his salary, he was on his way towards meeting his goal. For the next several weeks, he spent many long days faxing and telephoning people in other Silicon Valley companies, inviting them to participate in the scholarship fund. When he felt tired, he gained strength knowing he would someday be able to help children in Oklahoma City.

His persistent efforts paid off: Chris succeeded beyond his wildest dreams. After about a year, he raised $400,000 from twelve of the eighteen corporations he had contacted. When the press ran a story, hundreds of people across the country wrote letters and sent checks, adding another $300,000 to the fund. Oklahoma Governor Keating was so impressed with Chris' scholarship fund that he added another $3 million to it from the general donation fund. "Giving people the chance to succeed stuck with me," Chris says. "I just wondered what one person could do."

Thanks to the Oklahoma City Scholarship Fund, 207 children now have hope for their future, knowing they will receive all the support they need when it's time to go to college. Ronnie Fields is one of the first to receive a scholarship. After the bombing, he didn't know if he would be able to continue his college education. Before his Mom was killed, his mother had paid his college tuition, and his father, his room and board.While Ronnie worked after school, he couldn't take on any more debts. At times, he even thought of dropping out of school. When he got a call from the Oklahoma City Community Foundation giving him the good news about the scholarship fund, he knew his prayers had been answered. He had prayed to God, hoping that some good could come out of the tragedy.

Ronnie thought long and hard about his future and how he could give his gifts to others. As a peer counselor, he had really enjoyed working with young people. An easygoing, fun-loving, and patient guy, he connected easily with them. He could also relate. "When I was a teen, sometimes I was a real jerk, thinking I was too cool to be with them," he remembers with regret, "and I have a video to prove it!"

Ronnie decided he could help young people create a strong foundation for their lives if he went to graduate school and became a youth minister. He is now in his second year at Brite Divinity School at Texas Christian University in Fort Worth. On the weekends, he volunteers at a crisis intervention hot-line, hoping to spare families from the pain of suicide. "Live life to the fullest, don't get stressed out about the little things and don't wait to enjoy your life," he counsels those who call in. "Do as much good as you can—and have some fun."

Ronnie thinks about his mother every day and often feels her loving spirit with him. "You never know when any of us are going to go," he tells young people. "So appreciate the time you have with your parents."

One day Ronnie hopes to meet Chris and thank him for helping to make all this possible. "I wouldn't be here if it weren't for him," Ronnie says gratefully. "It's done wonders for me. It's changed my whole life."

The next time you hear of a tragedy, think about the children who've lost their parents. If you want to give them encouragement and support, you could **start a scholarship fund**. To get started, just call your local community foundation or bank trust department.

She Kept Her Promises

STORYTELLER: TRUDE LASH

In her time, Eleanor Roosevelt became the most trusted woman in the world. Not because she was the President's wife, or because she was born into one of the leading families. Eleanor Roosevelt earned people's trust—by always keeping her promises.

When she was a young child, Eleanor Roosevelt's father promised her that when she was a little older the two of them would live together again. She lived for that day. After her mother died, she was very lonely, living with her grandmother who was very old, strict, and old-fashioned. When her father broke his promise, it broke her heart. At ten years old, she realized that she had to become strong in herself if she wanted to go on living. And she made a vow to herself that she would never break a promise. For the rest of her life, you could always count on Eleanor Roosevelt.

The soldiers in the hospitals in the Pacific Islands she visited during World War II believed her when she said she would telephone their families the moment she got home. Something in her manner made people know they could trust her.

The moment I met her, my life changed. I was married with three children, living a very comfortable life. I didn't think there was anything I could really contribute. "Well, that's very silly," she remarked. Since I had a good education, she expected me to not only be a good wife and mother, but to go out and work. She convinced me that I had work to do, so I concentrated on doing what I could do. I started by using my knowledge and my training, and then taking a leadership role and working hard. She always helped people to become stronger. She expected her friends to grow up and grow better, because they owed that to themselves.

In the early days of the United Nations, I was acting secretary to her Human Rights Commission. Later I became Executive Director of the Citizens' Committee for Children. I was 24 years younger than she was and worked with her wherever possible. In the beginning, I stood in awe of her, but eventually we worked together easily, though my admiration for her never changed.

She visited handicapped war veterans, who expected her to work miracles, to straighten out their cases with the Veterans Administration, provide a wheelchair or help in finding a special job. And she often did. I know of one man who was crippled during the war. She encouraged him when he had given up. She stayed in touch with him and he became a leader in the veteran organizations. And he is still alive and a man of some pride. Because she believed in him and helped him, both practically and financially, he was able to believe in himself.

"Mrs. Roosevelt, I have lost my job and can't find another," some would say. "If you help me think through what kind of job you would like," she would respond, "we could try and find one." The strange thing is that of all the things she was asked for, she quite often did the most impossible ones. She was a woman of much influence, and she was quite willing to use that influence to help others. She never hesitated to write to the Secretary of State or members of Congress if she thought they could do something and felt what she was asking for was important. She never tried to force people or throw her weight around. She just used her influence to get people what she really believed they deserved.

There was no stronger foe of racial discrimination than Eleanor Roosevelt. She would say "As long as we leave out some large number of people we are not yet one nation." When the Daughters of the American Revolution denied Marion Anderson the use of Constitution Hall for a concert, Mrs. Roosevelt got Harold Ickes, Secretary for the Interior, to arrange for her to sing at the Lincoln Memorial. And then she resigned from the DAR. During World War II, she fought for Negro rights in the Armed Forces. Once she arrived to speak at a meeting in the South and found that the white audience sat on one side of the aisle and the black on the other. She put her chair in the middle of the aisle and spoke from there. When a leading black educator, Mary McLoyd Bethune, needed help for her fledgling Bethune College for women, she invited her to the White House. She received an avalanche of hostile reactions for arranging for Marie to meet people who could help her, yet Eleanor Roosevelt carried on.

She also felt that womens' rights had been neglected, that women had fewer rights than men, and she worked for them tirelessly. When she first came to Washington she held press conferences just for women. The President was having press conferences, just for men. And at her press conferences she gave the women real news. The men began to complain bitterly. They would come and say "What did she say? What did she say?" After a while, there were no discriminations anymore against women in the press.

She was often called a "do-gooder," but she found companionship with other do-gooders like Gandhi, who also expected much of himself, and who moved through difficult situations so he could free people. Sometimes officials would say "Mrs. Roosevelt is a bother." Sometimes I'm sure she was, the way people who believe in doing things are bothers to others who don't really feel like it. It's necessary to be bothersome sometimes. She used to say that if you have power, you can contribute somehow. She felt it was always worth trying and she would do that very quietly without claiming recognition. People she dealt with often believed she could do miracles. They were not totally wrong: she always did what she could, and often that was a lot.

When her husband became President, the expectations for a First Lady were very limited. Through her significant contributions to her husband's administration, she changed all that and became a role model for the rest of this country, and for future Presidents' wives.

She did an invaluable service for the President, when he wasn't able to travel. She would scout things out for him, help people and give them comfort, and bring back the important information to him about what was happening in the country. She had started to serve as the President's "legs" when he was Governor of New York, where she inspected state institutions. The President trained her well. "I don't want any indirect reports," he would say to her. "You go and see for yourself." In the beginning he would ask her questions she couldn't answer after her visits. That didn't last. She learned quickly to observe carefully. To look behind the door to see where the dirty dishtowels were hidden and to look for the special staff menu. She was often the one who had to bring the President the bad news when others wanted only to please him.

Her heart went out to children all over the world to families who were refugees from Nazi terror. She visited refugee camps in Europe, Israel and Africa, and raised funds for services to their children. She led the fight for legislation which would have admitted thousands of children from beleaguered Great Britain to the U.S. The desperate political refugees often said that Mrs. Roosevelt was the one person who gave them the feeling that life was worth living. She believed in them, and she believed that the fight against Hitler was the absolute fight at that time. She arranged for an endless number of affidavits for people to come to this country.

She considered the United Nations her husband's greatest achievement. After his death, she became his surrogate, the most powerful advocate for the UN. As chairman of the Human Rights Commission, she labored ceaselessly to develop the Human Rights Declaration and to bring the underdeveloped and Western nations together. When she first became a member of the U.S. delegation, the men shrugged her off and gave her the unimportant assignments. But they came to respect her as the most thoughtful, hardest-working, most admired member of the delegation, the one most concerned about the inclusion of all, not only the powerful nations, in planning for the future.

Over time, she became a leader in her own right. She remained her own unassuming self, and her majesty combined with her modesty were irresistible to all who met her. She was a realist and knew how much struggle, how many battles between nations and factions lay in the path of progress, what hard efforts would be needed for even the smallest step ahead. Yet she remained a believer, her love for people was undiminished, her beliefs were passionate, her work was strong to the end of her days. Even grim disappointments did not discourage her. She simply tried harder the next time—her commitment and conviction that you had to fight for your beliefs were for life.

She never gave up. One thing she couldn't stand was someone saying, "But what can I do? I can't do anything." She would say, "We have gotten ourselves in a nice big hole and we have lost a lot of power, but that's because we weren't working hard enough for our country."

She often spoke of individual responsibility and thought we shouldn't blame everything on Washington or look for someone else to blame. "Let's look at ourselves," she would say. Maybe we did not live up to what we were supposed to do. Discuss it, talk about it, but do something about it. She would insist on bringing out the best in people. "You have something to contribute because much has been given to you. You must not forget that you are human and that you owe." That's what she always said.

She's been gone now for 35 years, yet she is still with us. Last year, a statue of Eleanor Roosevelt was unveiled in a beautiful spot in New York's Riverside Park. It is amazing that there hadn't been one before commemorating her, or any other

American woman. Thousands streamed into the surrounding streets and stood quietly through the dedication ceremonies. Even though they couldn't hear or see very much, they wanted to be there. They came to pay respect to a great woman who was important to them. And it's quite amazing to see the people who come and spend a while sitting on one of the benches, looking at the statue, honoring her work and her legacy.

To many of us it was her being there as an example of what one person could do that changed and enhanced our expectations of ourselves; to others it was the love and care she gave to those who she saw as the most needy and lonely. To all, it was her courage and untiring effort, her total dedication to service to others that were so inspiring. When she died, a columnist friend wrote, "While she was with us, no man had to feel entirely alone."

You must do the thing you think you cannot do.

ELEANOR ROOSEVELT

Next time you're in New York, take some time to visit the Eleanor Roosevelt statue at 72nd and Riverside Drive. **The Eleanor Roosevelt Center** continues her work. For more information, call 914-229-5302.

Peace for Their Grandchildren

STORYTELLER: JIMMY CARTER
adapted from *Talking Peace, a Vision for the Next Generation*

Shortly after my inauguration in 1977, President Anwar Sadat of Egypt came to visit me in Washington. He was interested in bringing peace to his own people and strengthening friendship between Egypt and the United States. However, he saw no chance to make real progress on resolving basic differences with Israel anytime soon. On several issues he responded, "Maybe in my lifetime."

I told him that I was prepared to use my full personal influence and that of my country in support of any effort he was willing to make. Later, during our private talks upstairs in the White House, he agreed to take major strides toward peace in the long-standing conflict between his country and Israel. This was very much in the interest of the United States.

My role as a mediator in the talks would be a challenge. To prepare, I studied thick books on the personalities of the two leaders, prepared for me by specialists. These books told me about each man's family relationships, religious beliefs, early life experiences, health, and most important friends. I also learned about how each had won office, how he responded to pressure, and what his hobbies and personal habits were. As I read, I took notes that later proved very useful in the actual meetings. I also prepared lists of points on which the Egyptians and the Israelis were in apparent agreement, points of difference between them, questions to be asked during the negotiations, and some compromises I thought both men might accept.

President Sadat was the first to arrive for the peace talks, and I was pleased to discover that he seemed quite flexible on most questions. When Israeli Prime Minister Begin arrived later, he and I also had a private discussion about the major issues. Yet I soon realized that he viewed our Camp David sessions as just the first in an ongoing series of negotiations. Sadat and I had hoped to settle all the major controversial issues between the two countries during the next few days, if we possibly could.

As we discussed various issues, I soon realized that Begin and Sadat were personally incompatible. The sometimes petty, sometimes heated arguments that arose between them when we were all in the same room convinced me it would be better if each of them spoke to me as the mediator instead of directly to each other. For the last ten days of the Camp David negotiations, the two men never spoke to or even saw each other except for one Sunday afternoon trip. Meanwhile, their teams of advisers continued to meet face-to-face.

Toward the end of the talks, Begin's foreign minister told Sadat that Israel would never compromise on certain major issues, and Sadat decided it was time to leave. The Egyptians began packing their bags and asked for a helicopter to take them to Washington so they could return home. When I heard about this, I said a silent prayer, quickly changed into more formal clothes, and went to confront Sadat in his cabin. After an intense argument in which I reminded him of his promises to me and stressed the global importance of his role as a man of peace, Sadat agreed to give the process another chance.

In the end, something unexpected miraculously helped to break the deadlock. We had made some photos of the three of us, and Begin had asked me to sign one for each of his eight grandchildren. Sadat had already signed them. My secretary suggested that I personalize them, and on each photograph I wrote in the name of one grandchild above my signature. Although Begin had become quite unfriendly toward me because of the pressure I was putting on him and Sadat, I decided to take the photographs over to his cabin myself.

As he looked at the pictures and read the names aloud, he became very emotional. He was thinking, I am sure, about his responsibility to his people and about what happens to children in war. Soon both of us had tears in our eyes. I was very grateful when he promised to review the language of my latest revisions.

Shortly thereafter, Begin called me and said he would accept my compromise proposal. This was, indeed, a framework for peace: a laying of the foundation for a future treaty between Israel and Egypt.

That afternoon, Begin, Sadat, and I left Camp David in my helicopter and flew to the White House for the signing ceremony. Six months later, a formal treaty was signed between the two countries—the first treaty ever between Israel and an Arab nation.

Cooperation is a state of mind. There is little hope of real progress until we make this discovery and act upon this knowledge.

THOMAS JEFFERSON

Find a cause that is close to your heart and support it. To learn more about and support **The Carter Center,** call 404-420-5119.

A Long Road to Freedom

STORYTELLER: NELSON MANDELA
adapted from *Long Walk to Freedom*

I awoke on the day of my release after only a few hours sleep at 4:30 a.m. February 11 was a cloudless, end-of-summer Cape Town day. I did a shortened version of my usual exercise regimen, washed, and ate breakfast. I then telephoned a number of people to come to the cottage to prepare for my release and work on my speech. As so often happens in life, the momentousness of an occasion is lost in the welter of a thousand details. My actual release time was set for 3 p.m.

By 3:30 p.m., I began to get restless. I told the members of the reception committee that my people had been waiting for me for twenty-seven years, and I did not want to keep them waiting any longer. Shortly before 4 p.m., we left in a small motorcade. About a quarter of a mile in front of the gate, the car slowed to a stop, I got out and began to walk toward the prison gate.

At first, I could not really make out what was going on in front of us, but when I was within 150 feet or so, I saw a tremendous commotion and a great crowd of people: hundreds of photographers and television cameras and newspeople as well as several thousand well-wishers. I was astounded and a little bit alarmed. I had truly not expected such a scene. At most, I had imagined that there would be several dozen people, mainly the wardens and their families. But this proved to be only the beginning. I realized we had not thoroughly prepared for all that was about to happen.

Within twenty feet or so of the gate, the cameras started clicking, a noise that sounded like some great herd of metallic beasts. Reporters started shouting questions.

Television crews began crowding in. ANC (African National Congress) supporters were yelling and cheering. It was happy, if slightly disorienting, chaos. When a television crew thrust a long, dark, furry object at me, I recoiled slightly, wondering if it were some newfangled weapon developed while I was in prison. Winnie informed me that it was a microphone.

When I was among the crowd I raised my right fist and there was a roar. I had not been able to do that for twenty-seven years, and it gave me a surge of strength and joy. I felt—even at the age of seventy-one—that my life was beginning anew. My ten thousand days of imprisonment were over.

At my first speech at a rally during the Grand Parade festivities in Cape Town, I spoke from the heart. I wanted first of all to tell the people that I was not a messiah, but an ordinary man who had become a leader because of extraordinary circumstances.

Friends, comrades, and fellow South Africans. I greet you all in the name of peace, democracy and freedom for all! I stand here before you not as a prophet but as a humble servant of you, the people. Your tireless and heroic sacrifices have made it possible for me to be here today. I therefore place the remaining years of my life in your hands.

It was my desire for the freedom of my people to live their lives with dignity and self-respect that animated my life. It transformed a frightened young man into a bold one that drove a law-abiding attorney to become a criminal, that turned a family-loving husband into a man without a home, and that forced a life-loving man to live like a monk.

It is from my comrades in the struggle that I learned the meaning of courage. Time and again, I have seen men and women risk and give their lives for an idea. I have seen men stand up to attacks and torture without breaking, showing a strength and resiliency that defies the imagination. I learned that courage was not the absence of fear, but the triumph over it. I felt fear myself more times than I can remember, but I hid it behind a mask of boldness. The brave man is not he who does not feel afraid, but he who conquers that fear.

To survive in prison, I developed ways to find satisfaction in my daily life. One can feel fulfilled by washing one's clothes so they are really clean, by sweeping a hallway so that it is empty of dust, or by organizing one's cell to conserve as much space as possible. The same pride one takes in consequential tasks outside of prison, one can find doing small things.

While I have always enjoyed gardening, it was not until I was behind bars that I was able to tend my own garden. A garden was one of the few things in prison that one could control. To plant a seed, watch it grow, tend to it, and then harvest it offered a simple but enduring satisfaction. The sense of being the custodian for this small patch of earth offered a small taste of freedom.

In some ways I saw the garden as a metaphor for certain aspects of my life. A leader must also tend his garden. He, too, plants seeds and then watches, cultivates, and harvests the result. Like a gardener, he must take responsibility for what he cultivates; he must mind his work, try to repel enemies, preserve what can be preserved, and eliminate what cannot succeed.

The authorities supplied me with seeds. I initially planted tomatoes, chilies, and onions—hardy plants that did not require rich earth or constant care. The early harvests are poor, but they soon improved. I coaxed a tender seedling into a robust plant that produced deep red fruit. Once the garden began to flourish, I often provided the wardens with some of my best tomatoes and onions.

I always knew that deep down in every human heart, there is mercy and generosity. No one is born hating another person because of the color of his skin, his background, or his religion. People must learn to hate, and if they can learn to hate, they can be taught to love, for love comes more naturally to the human heart than its opposite. Even in the grimmest times in prison, when my comrades and I were pushed to our limits, I would see a glimmer of humanity in one of the guards, perhaps just for a second, but it was enough to reassure me and keep me going. Man's goodness is a flame that can be hidden but never extinguished.

I have walked that long road to freedom. I have tried not to falter; I have made missteps along the way. But I have discovered the secret that after climbing a great hill, one only finds that there are many more hills to climb. I have taken a moment here to rest, to steal a view of the glorious vista that surrounds me, and to look back on the distance I have come. But I can rest only for a moment, for with freedom comes responsibilities, and I dare not linger, for my long walk is not yet ended.

Our deepest fear is not that we are inadequate. Our deepest fear is that we are powerful beyond measure. It is our light, not our darkness that most frightens us.

Your playing small doesn't save the world. There's nothing enlightened about shrinking so that other people won't feel insecure around you.

And as we let our own light shine, we unconsciously give other people permission to do the same. As we are liberated from our own fear, our presence automatically liberates others.

MARIANNE WILLIAMSON

Help build a strong, free South Africa. Invest in South Africa's democratic and equitable development: call **Shared Interest** at 212-229-2709. Work with **The Africa Fund** to support **South Africa's Trauma Centre for Victims of Violence and Torture:** call 212-962-1210 or send e-mail to africafund@igc.apc.org.

Mother Teresa

STORYTELLER: NAVIN CHAWLA,
adapted from *Mother Teresa: The Authorized Biography*

It was 1981. Mother Teresa had just returned from a mission to Ethiopia. A terrible drought in the northern part of that country threatened hundreds of thousands of lives.

She had carried a few hundred kilos of medicine and food from Calcutta, but that was a tiny drop in the vast ocean of need. Although there were many international relief agencies helping the beleaguered Ethiopian government, there appeared to be more confusion and less coordination. The poor state of the roads also made it difficult to get supplies to the scores of villages in the interior where they were most desperately needed.

Even after she returned to Calcutta, her concern did not lessen. Together with her Sisters, she prayed (and even fasted) that further tragedy be averted. Finally, as an inspiration, she wrote a letter to the president of the United States.

It was about a week later that she received a telephone call from the White House. President Reagan himself came on the line. He thanked her for her letter and assured her on behalf of the American people and himself that he would do everything possible to see that help arrived quickly where it was most urgently needed.

He was as good as his word. Not only did the U.S. government rush in food and medicine, but cooperation with other relief agencies improved significantly. After that, the supplies started to flow, and helicopters brought food to the villages.

It was then that I had remarked for the first time, half-teasingly but with an undercurrent of seriousness, that she was the most powerful woman in the world. In an unaffected way, she had replied with a smile, "I wish I was. Then I would bring peace to the whole world."

Join Mother Teresa's revolution of the heart by caring for the poor in your community. To directly support Mother Teresa's work around the world, please write to the **Missionaries of Charity,** 54-A, AJC Bose Road, Calcutta, 7000016 India.

Everybody in America is Helping

STORYTELLER: RAM DASS AND PAUL GORMAN
adapted from *How Can I Help?*

I am talking to a woman who is working for the Gallup poll. She's actually doing a poll on how much time people spend helping. She's trying to explain the criteria. I finally start to crack up, seeing something of the absurdity of it all.

"You all are crazy! 'How much time are people helping?' What kind of question is that? Tell Gallup he's nuts!"

She started to laugh as well. "I know. That's what I said too. What can I tell you? It's a job." She was sort of whispering, which made me laugh more. We got into this conspiratorial, infectious laughter at it all. When we stopped laughing, I asked, "Was that helping?" She said, "I guess so, sort of. Why was it?"

I said, "That's your job. You tell me why." And then I threw in, "We were trying to make the best of a nutty situation. In fact, that's what I'm trying to do all the time. That's it—I want you to put me down in the Gallup poll as someone who helps all the time."

More laughter. She said, "We don't have a category for 'All the Time.'"

"Oh ye of little faith."

"But we do have a line here that says, 'All of the Above.'" (At this point I didn't know if she was kidding, but I went for it.) "Perfect. Put me down under 'All of the Above.' I am very All-of-the-Above. In fact, you have to put everybody down under 'All of the Above.' Everybody's trying to make the best of a nutty situation. Gallup can release a poll saying, 'Everybody in America is Helping.'"

"God," she said, "I wish I had the nerve. Maybe I'll do it with an alternative answer. 'One Out of Every Two People in America Is Helping.' The other half is being helped."

By this point we were just in love with the idea of throwing the topic back into blessed confusion, which is where it really is anyhow. Finally, we said goodbye.

"It's been great," I said. "Very helpful," she agreed.

Months later, there's a story in the newspaper: Gallup Poll Reveals Half of All Americans Help Out as Volunteers. Right there in the paper. She did it! She pulled it off!

I rush into the kitchen reading the headline to my wife. "That's me!" I exclaim. "Which half?" says my very formidable and wonderful wife.

"All of the Above!" I answer triumphantly. "Just wash the dishes," she replies.

One Person's Voice

adapted from *The Weight of Nothing*

"Tell me the weight of a snowflake," a coal mouse asked a wild dove.
"Nothing more than nothing," was the answer.

"In that case I must tell you a marvelous story," the coal mouse said.
"I sat on the branch of a fir, close to its trunk, when it began to snow.
Since I didn't have anything better to do, I counted the snowflakes settling
on the twigs and needles of my branch. Their number was exactly 3,741,952.

"When the next snowflake dropped onto the branch
—nothing more than nothing, as you say—the branch broke off."

The dove, since Noah's time an authority on the matter,
thought about the story for a while and finally said to herself:

"Perhaps there is only one person's voice lacking
for peace to come about in the world."

Cultural Healing

News Flash

How many people *didn't* shoot each other today?

Just think what could happen if the nightly news featured as many stories about people who are committing acts of goodness as those committing acts of violence. What message would we give to our children? Who are these cultural heroes and what can we learn from them?

The history of America is one of the most amazing Stone Soup stories of all. In just 300 years, people from all corners of the world have gathered together and formed the most culturally diverse country on the planet. We come together with our struggles and challenges as well as our hopes and dreams. We each bring a wealth of resources as well as our nationality, race, religion, color, and culture. When we combine our gifts and talents, we form a rich multicultural community that gives our nation an unique advantage in the world.

The cultural heroes in this chapter show us when we teach tolerance, learn forgiveness, and practice compassion we can heal our collective wounds and move forward. When we bring people from different heritages together, we can find common ground and solve our common problems. When we accept and even appreciate our differences, we can rise above the distinctions which divide us. They renew our faith in our capacity to bring about cultural healing among all Americans.

These stories honor people from every culture, giving young people real heroes to identify with and footsteps to follow. Compelling stories of African-Americans, Native Americans, Hispanic Americans, and Euro-Americans who overcame obstacles, endured personal sacrifices, and courageously persevered to better the lives of their people. Through their noble efforts, they dispel negative stereotypes, work for justice and restore cultural pride. They also give us powerful lessons for how we can bring cultural healing to our country. While not everyone can be a Cesar Chavez or a Martin Luther King Jr., a Gandhi or an Aung San Suu Kyi, we can all learn from them and can help carry out their legacy.

Each one of these cultures has a long history and rich tradition of helping others. In the Native American culture, children are taught to think about how their actions will affect the next seven generations. The African proverb, *It takes a whole village to raise a child* has become a popular metaphor, reminding adults that we are *all* responsible for raising *all* of our nation's children. In Puerto Rico, people believe by working together they can move forward: *Nos estamos moviendo nos para adelante.* The Jewish tradition of *tikkun olam* encourages people to carry out their responsibility of mending the world.

Included in this chapter are a few of the hundreds of courageous acts of service from the civil rights movement. These stories remind us of what it takes to stand up for what we believe in, especially in spite of injustice. We learn about the power of committing to a noble goal: once we decide to work for justice, somehow we find the strength to make tough choices and the hard sacrifices. We also discover how to become cultural heroes by transforming obstacles, despair and hatred, oppression and resentment, into hope and new opportunities for ourselves and the world.

To reclaim our human dignity, cultural healing sometimes requires humility and honesty. Stories in this chapter remind us that terrible mistakes have been made, often by well-intentioned people. Everyone likes to be right and no one wants to admit they were wrong. Alabama Governor George Wallace's ability to admit his mistakes, apologize for his hateful words and deeds during the civil rights movement and try to make amends took great courage. It also took courage for others to forgive him, and allow him to join the 30th anniversary commemorating the march from Selma to Montgomery.

These stories show how one person can turn the tide against racism and make a difference in someone's life. For some, it was a parent's commitment to build a better life for their children. One Christian mother began the cultural healing process in her community by rallying her neighbors to stand together and stop the hate crimes against their Jewish neighbors. An African American minister teaches tolerance, to be willing and able to accept others and their differences so "... all different colors of hands, reach down to help each other."

Some cultural heroes broke free from the vicious cycle of poverty and then reached back to help others. Through these stories, we come to understand their struggles and celebrate their victories. For many cultural heroes, it took tremendous courage, yet they knew change had to start somewhere. George Sarabia asked himself in the story about Edward James Olmos' work with young gang members in Los Angeles, "If I'm not able to forgive, when will it ever stop?"

Each one of us must decide to create cultural healing in our communities. When we nurture our shared legacy for helping one another, we bring out the best in ourselves and each other. Together, we can rebuild our inner cities, strengthen our democracy, and create a safer, healthier world for everyone. Together we can keep our promise of being "one nation, indivisible, with liberty and justice for all."

You could be the one to reach out, to teach tolerance, learn forgiveness, and practice compassion. You could help break the cycle of poverty by teaching a child to read, giving someone a job, standing by them as they struggle to turn over a new leaf.

- When you hear of stories about people from different cultures who are committing acts of goodness, spread the good news.
- Share these stories with your friends, your newspaper editor, your TV reporter.
- Challenge your friends and family to think and act differently.
- Take small steps towards healing our country.

Young Acts of Courage

Storyteller: Melba Pattillo Beals
adapted from *Warriors Don't Cry*

My Grandmother India always said God had pointed a finger at our family, asking of us just a bit more discipline, more praying, and more hard work because He had blessed us with good health and good brains. My mother was one of the first blacks to integrate the University of Arkansas, graduating in 1954. Three years later, I was one of nine black teenagers who integrated Central High School in Little Rock, Arkansas.

It was not yet eight o'clock in the morning when Mama and I parked at the curb just outside Mrs. Bates' home. Everybody spoke in whispers. I was ushered through the crowd and into the living room, where radio and news reports about the integration held everyone's attention.

As we filed silently out of the house, I waved good-bye to my mother. I wanted to hug her, but I didn't want everyone to think I was a baby. Other parents milled about, looking as if we were being carted off to be hanged. As we started to walk to the cars, they clutched at us as though they weren't completely certain we'd be coming back.

When we arrived at the school, the driver urged us to get out quickly. The white hand of a uniformed officer reached out toward the car, opened the door, and pulled me toward him as his urgent voice ordered me to hurry. The roar coming from the front of the building made me glance to my right. Only a half-block away, I saw hundreds of white people, their bodies in motion and their mouths wide open as they shouted their anger. "The niggers! Keep the niggers out!" The shouts came closer. The roar swelled, as though their frenzy had been fired up by something. It took a moment to digest the fact that it was the sight of us that had upset them.

"The principal's office is this way," whispered a petite woman with dark hair and glasses. "Hurry, now, hurry." We were shoved into an office where a row of white people, mostly women, stood staring at us as though we were the world's eighth wonder. "Here are your class schedules and homeroom assignments. Wait for your guides," Vice Principal Mrs. Huckaby said. Each of us was assigned to a different homeroom. "Why can't any of us be in the same homeroom or take classes together?" I asked. From behind the long desk, a man spoke in an unkind booming voice, "You wanted integration . . . you got integration."

I turned to see the hallway swallow up my friends. None of us had an opportunity to say a real good-bye or make plans to meet. I was alone, in a daze, following a white woman up the stairs. Frightened does not describe my state of mind at the time: I had moved on to being terrified. I had fantasized about how wonderful it would be to get inside the huge, beautiful castle I knew as Central High School. But the reality was so much bigger, darker, and more treacherous than I had imagined.

Suddenly, I felt the sting of a hand slapping the side of my cheek, and then warm, slimy saliva on my face, dropping to the collar of my blouse. It was the first time I had ever been spat upon. I felt hurt, embarrassed. I wondered if I'd catch her germs. Before I could wipe it off, my guide's harsh command summoned me to move. "Get going. Now. Do you hear me? Move! Now!" I brushed the saliva off my face with my hand and stumbled after her.

As I entered a classroom, a hush fell over the students. The guide pointed me to an empty seat, and I walked toward it. Students sitting nearby quickly moved away. I sat down surrounded by empty seats, feeling unbearably self-conscious. One of the boys kept shouting ugly words at me throughout the class. I waited for the teacher to speak up, but she said nothing. My heart was weeping, but I squeezed back the tears. I squared my shoulders and tried to remember what Grandma had said: "God loves you, child. No matter what, He sees you as His precious idea."

Walking the gauntlet to my next class was even more harrowing. "You'd better watch yourself," the guide warned as we moved at high speed through the hostile students. The next class was gym. Out on the playing field, groups of girls were tossing a volleyball. It took me a moment to realize it was whizzing awfully close to my head. I ducked, but they hit me real hard, shouting and cheering as they found their target. And even as I was struggling to escape their cruelty, I was at the same time more terrified by the sound of the angry crowd approaching in the distance. Suddenly things got out of control. "Get inside, Melba. Now!" The face of the gym teacher showed both compassion and alarm as she quietly pointed to a group of women jumping over the rear fence as they shouted obscenities at me.

I was in tears, ready to give up, paralyzed by my fear. Suddenly Grandma's voice came into my head: "God never loses one of his flock." Shepherd, show me how to go, I said. I stood still and repeated those words over and over again until I gained some composure.

"I've been looking for you." My stocky guide's voice was angry, but I was so glad to see her I almost forgot myself and reached to hug her. "Let's go to the shorthand class." She didn't know it, but she was the answer to my prayer. I looked over my shoulder to see the group of mothers standing still, obviously unwilling to come after me with a school official at my side. I choked back tears and speeded my steps.

As I headed for the last row of empty seats by the window, my shorthand teacher called out to me, "Melba, stay away from the window." Her voice was sympathetic, as though she really cared what happened to me. The ocean of people outside stretched farther than I could see—waves of people ebbing and flowing, shoving the sawhorses and the policemen who were trying to keep them in place. From my seat I could hear the crowd shouting,"Get the niggers" and "Two, four, six, eight, we ain't gonna integrate."

I looked up from my notes to see my guide entering the classroom. "Come with me now, to the principal's office," she called out nervously. I heard her frantic tone of voice and heard someone else say the mob was out of control and that they would have to call for help. "There must be a thousand people out there, armed and coming this way," "Some of these patrolmen are throwing down their badges," another breathless voice said. "We gotta get these children out of here."

I heard footsteps coming closer. A tall, dark-haired man came toward us. "I'm Gene Smith, from the Little Rock Police Department. It's time for you to leave for today. Come with me now." Right away, I had a good feeling about him. He urged us to move faster, and acted as though it mattered to him whether or not we got out. I decided to forever remember this man in my prayers.

Outside, two cars were sitting with engines running, lights on, hoods pointing toward the door. "Hurry, now . . . get in," Smith said as he held open one of the doors. Their expressions told me we were in the kind of trouble I hadn't even imagined before. "Hold on and keep your heads down," the driver shouted. The deafening noise of the mob engulfed us. That's when the car really began moving fast, faster than I'd ever ridden before. Finally, there were fewer hands and faces on the car windows and the noises subsided. I took a deep breath. I wanted to tell the driver, "Thanks for risking your life to save mine." It was an awkward moment with a stranger, a decent white man. He took me home, dropping me off right at my door. "Get in the house now—go," he said, pausing for an instant, then gunning his engine and pulling away. He was the second white man I would pray for God to protect.

That night in my diary I wrote, "There seems to be no space for me at Central High. I don't want integration to be like the merry-go-round. Please, God, make space for me."

Speaking from the White House that night on national television, President Eisenhower said he sent troops because "Mob rule in Little Rock menaces the very safety of the United States and the free world." That night a man handed my mother an envelope from the President and said to her "Let your daughter go back to school, and she will be protected." The next morning, I saw them, about fifty uniformed soldiers of the 101st, with well-shined boots and rifles at their sides. There were tears in my mother's eyes as she whispered good-bye. "Make this day the best you can," she said.

For the next several months, I got up every morning, polished my saddle shoes, and went off to war. I entered Central High School, a building I remember only as a hellish torture chamber, a place that was meant to nourish us and prepare us for adulthood; instead, it was like being a soldier on a battlefield.

I had always imagined that my last day of the term at Central High School would be marked by a grand ceremony, with a massive choir singing hallelujah or perhaps some wonderful award from my community—a parade maybe. But it was the same as any other day. "It's over," my brother Conrad said. "You don't have to integrate anymore."

The next September, we waited in vain to return to Central High. But Governor Faubus closed all of Little Rock's high schools. Segregationists were squeezing the life out of the NAACP, the Bateses' newspaper, and the State Press. In an effort to get us to voluntarily withdraw from Central High, our people continued to lose their jobs, their businesses, and their homes. In despair, NAACP officials sent an announcement to chapters across the country, asking for families that would volunteer to give us safe harbor and support us in finishing our education. I was fortunate enough to go to the Santa Rosa, California, to the home of Dr. George and Ruth McCabe and their four children. They were a family of politically conscious Quakers committed to racial equality. More than their guidance, it was their unconditional love that taught me the true meaning of equality. Their love helped to heal my wounds and inspired me to launch a new life for myself.

Inspired by the journalists I had met during the integration, I followed my dream and became a news reporter. I always remembered that it was the truth told by those reporters who came to Little Rock that kept me alive. Later, as an NBC television reporter, I would take special care to look into those unexposed corners where otherwise invisible people are forced to hide as their truth is ignored.

Forty years later, Little Rock's Central High School is peacefully integrated. I look back on my Little Rock integration experience as a positive force that ultimately shaped the course of my life. Because we dared to challenge the southern tradition of segregation, this school became a furnace that consumed our youth and forged us into reluctant warriors for civil rights. As Grandma India had promised, it taught me to have courage and patience.

I for one am grateful for the courage of youth.

ELEANOR ROOSEVELT

Smile at a neighbor. Help a stranger. Be grateful for your blessings and share them with others. Every child deserves a loving home. Join with Melba Beals and **Adopt a Special Kid** who have placed 11,000 special children in 20 years. Call 510-451-1748.

Miracle in Montgomery

STORYTELLER: REVEREND JOSEPH LOWERY

adapted from *Fellowship,* magazine of The Fellowship for Reconciliation

In March of 1995, many of us from the civil rights movement who had walked the historic path to freedom so long ago, retraced our steps from Selma to Montgomery, Alabama. This sacred trail, forever stained with the blood of martyrs, is hallowed by the hopes and dreams of those for whom we walked. We marched again to remind ourselves of the bitter price we paid thirty years ago for the right for all Americans, Black and White, to vote and of the painful price we pay today for failing to exercise that precious right.

With this march, we hoped to encourage a heightened level of voter activism and revived movement energy. We sought to gain support from politicians and dignitaries, from business people and journalists. We accomplished all of those things and much more, for on this day, we were witnesses to a miracle.

In 1965, Martin Luther King Jr. appointed me to chair a committee of marchers, assigned to present our demands to Alabama's Governor George Wallace. This was the man whose troops had brutalized us. He was the man who stood in front of the schoolhouse door to stop Blacks from attending the University of Alabama.

As a Methodist preacher speaking to a Methodist layman, I told him that God would hold him accountable for his hateful words that others had transformed into hateful deeds. Those deeds took a heavy toll on people like Viola Liuzzo, Jimmie Lee Jackson, and many others who lost their lives in the struggle. At the time, his response was, at best, indifferent. Yet thirty years later, in 1995, he was the man who wanted to welcome us back to Montgomery!

While some were opposed to granting Governor Wallace's request to greet us at the close of the march, I did not dare stand in the way of an act of repentance. Since he had nothing to gain politically, I accepted his offer of reconciliation. That he wanted to join us and affirm our purpose was like the flash of light that shines across a way filled with shadows of malice.

By car, it's less than three hours from the University of Tuscaloosa, where Wallace had blocked the door, to St. Jude High School in Montgomery, the end of our march. But, by way of the heart, it has taken more than thirty years. That's the tortured distance traveled by Governor Wallace that day. At the end of that journey, here he was paying honor to those he had stood against.

In 1972, Governor Wallace was shot and paralyzed by an enraged citizen. Later he said, "In a way that was impossible before the shooting, I think I can understand something of the pain that black people have come to endure. I know I contributed to that pain, and I can only ask forgiveness." In his last term as governor, in the late 1980s, he appointed more than 160 blacks to state governing boards and doubled the number of black voter registrations in Alabama's counties.

Remembering the angry days of the 1960s and the hate, violence, intolerance, and stubbornness of this man, I am amazed at the governor's transformation. None of us could ever have dreamed that a man like Wallace would come to embrace our cause, hold our hands, and sing our songs.

Well, almost none. Martin Luther King Jr., that dreamer whose life was cut short, had a vision:

I have a dream that one day, down in Alabama, with its vicious racists, with its governor having his lips dripping with interposition and nullification, that one day, right there in Alabama, little Black boys and little Black girls will be able to join hands with little White boys and girls as brothers and sister. I have a dream today!

DR. MARTIN LUTHER KING JR.

Encourage racial harmony in your school and community, and in your world. Learn how from the **Racial Dialogue and Reconciliation Program** at the **Fellowship of Reconciliation**, Box 271, Nyack, NY 10960 or reach us at http://www.nonviolence.org/~nvweb/for.

Letter from a Birmingham Jail

STORYTELLER: ANDREW YOUNG
adapted from *An Easy Burden*

After some initial setbacks in the struggle for civil rights, some said we were beaten, but in fact we were more ready than ever to wage our nonviolent campaign. So we set our sights on the toughest town in the south: Birmingham, Alabama.

The Birmingham campaign was a turning point for the national civil rights movement. It was also a turning point for Martin Luther King Jr. Until then, he had always been cautious, even reluctant, about being a leader. It had been thrust upon him, and occasionally he would try to retreat from it all. But in Birmingham, I believe, he finally accepted that he could never walk away from the awesome responsibility that had fallen upon his shoulders.

Shortly after our campaign began, the city of Birmingham got a state court injunction against demonstrations. We knew that marches would result in certain imprisonment.

One morning about a dozen of us were squeezed into the sitting room of Martin's hotel room. We were facing a difficult decision and our unity began to fray. "Martin, you've done all you can do here," one said. "Forget Birmingham for a while." Another explained, "You can't put more people in jail now. We can't bail out the ones already in there. Sending more people to jail is just out of the question."

In this atmosphere of utter depression, Martin said very little. He just listened. Suddenly, he rose and retired into the bedroom. When he had been gone for a while, the discussion finally slowed to a halt. Almost on cue, Martin and Ralph Abernathy came out dressed in denim jackets and jeans: our work uniform in Birmingham, worn to dramatize our solidarity with working people. "The only thing for me to do is go to jail and join those people already there," Martin said, "and stay there until people see what we're dealing with. Those who are going with me: get ready."

We didn't know it yet, but Martin's decision to go to jail on Good Friday, 1963, made it possible for us to sustain both the Birmingham campaign and the movement throughout the south. The march did not last long. Martin, Ralph, and some fifty others strode past Kelly Ingram Park. A huge crowd of Black citizens gathered around the march. Martin led the marchers along the sidewalk and stopped for red lights, but still the marchers were arrested for parading without a permit. We were stunned by the aggressiveness of the police, who began to push and shove the marchers, including Martin, into the paddy wagon.

One of the intimidating tactics used by the city of Birmingham was to set the bond at one thousand dollars or more for each marcher. This was incredibly high for what was essentially jaywalking. Martin was placed in an isolation cell, and no one was allowed to see him for a day or so. He couldn't even make a call to his wife, Coretta, who had just given birth to their fourth child.

Martin did not like being in jail: it was a cross he had agreed to bear, but it made him very moody. So he put tremendous pressure on us to maximize the impact and significance of his time in jail. "You must resume demonstrations immediately," he said. "Don't let the local support committee stop you. We have got to keep the pressure on Birmingham."

Despite Martin's impatience, the situation was already changing for the better. The news and the images of the Good Friday arrests were sinking in. Photographs of Martin and Ralph being hustled off to jail were shown on television and published all over the world. The reaction was tremendous. For the first time, the Birmingham campaign was being taken seriously. That same weekend, singer Harry Belafonte, a committed supporter of our cause and a close friend, was hard at work in New York securing new funds to replenish the critically short bail money. By Monday, Harry reported that he had raised fifty thousand dollars and that more would be forthcoming. To us this sounded like a miracle.

From his cell, the week after Easter, Martin began what would become his famous "Letter from a Birmingham Jail." He wrote in the margins of newspapers and on the back of legal papers and slipped us the text bit by bit. In this letter, he provided us with comprehensive, far-ranging answers to all the objections to our campaign. He also articulated the religious basis for the nonviolent protest movement in Christian theology. Martin's letter answered the charges of "ill-timing" by reminding our critics that blacks had waited more than three hundred years for justice in America; we could afford to wait no longer.

Within a few weeks, thousands of copies of Martin's letter were distributed around the country and published in national and European journals; it was being quoted from as the rationale behind the Civil Rights Movement. This letter helped establish the strong moral and intellectual basis not only for our struggle in Birmingham, but for all subsequent campaigns in the south. It has since become a classic in American literature.

The intense media attention, combined with an effective economic boycott, began to put a lot of pressure on the power structure in Birmingham. For nearly two months, black citizens purchased very little but food and medicine. In Birmingham, blacks spent a lot of money downtown, but businessmen didn't seem to appreciate just how much until their patronage was withdrawn. The lack of retail sales during the Easter season was visibly hurting the targeted stores, just as we had hoped.

Part of what made Martin's leadership so powerful was his ability to put our movement and trials in Birmingham into its proper context as a world movement. He was able to make us feel as if we were more than our daily selves, more than we had been—a part of a beautiful and glorious vision that was enabling us to transcend ourselves—to lift the people to another place so that they could almost feel themselves moving. Each night of the campaign, after Martin concluded his speeches to tumultuous applause, we would all rise, join hands, and sing "We Shall Overcome."

As usual, Martin was right. The work we did in Birmingham did help launch a worldwide movement. The model we developed for nonviolent social change in this small southern town has since been used to help campaigns for human rights and freedom in Poland, South Africa, and other countries. Trusting in Martin's wisdom helped us persist in the struggle. Now, looking back, it's very rewarding to know that the suffering we lived through was not in vain. It was all an integral part of God's plan for a better tomorrow.

In the spirit of his commitment to service, the **Martin Luther King Jr. Holiday** in January is now a national day of service, interracial cooperation and youth anti-violence initiatives. People and organizations are keeping the "Dream" alive by opening their hearts and offering their hands to bring diverse peoples together. For more information, call the **Office of Public Liaison at the Corporation for National Service** at 202-606-5000.

Fulfilling Martin's Dream

Storyteller: Rosalind Barnes

On the morning of August 18, 1963, Frank Carr got up at 2 a.m. to join a bus bound for our nation's capital. This white businessman from Chicago wasn't quite sure why he was going. He'd read about Reverend Martin Luther King Jr. and the March on Washington. He'd heard about their call to action for equal rights for all Americans. He just knew he had to go. Later standing among a quarter of a million other people, he listened to Dr. King's awe-inspiring speech, "I Have A Dream!" It became the turning point in his life.

". . . Now is the time to open the doors of opportunity to all God's children. Now is the time to lift our nation from the quicksands of racial injustice to the solid rock of brotherhood . . . When we let freedom ring, when we let it ring from every village and every hamlet, from every state and every city, we will be able to speed up that day when all of God's children, black men and white men, Jews and Gentiles, Protestants and Catholics, will be able to join hands and sing in the words of the old Negro spiritual, 'Free at last! Free at last! Thank God Almighty, we are free at last!'"

After hearing these words, Frank knew in his heart that he must do something to help make Martin's dream come true. When he arrived back home, he talked with his friends, people in business, people with influence. He spoke with a new confidence, "There are students in the ghettos and barrios with real talent," he said. "They can play important roles in our corporations and our communities, if we give them a chance." Frank's friends knew he was right. They had all seen young people with enormous potential denied opportunities because of corporate prejudice.

The key to their own success had been mentors, people who had taken time to listen to their hopes and dreams, show them the ropes and introduce them to the network. So, they each made a commitment to mentor one student, and to get their companies to place them in summer internships. In 1970, they opened the first INROADS office in Chicago, with 17 corporate sponsors and 25 eager students. "We had no track record, just a dream, and enough people willing to take some risks," says Carr.

Juan was one of the first 25 students. Originally from a small village in Mexico, when he was in the 6th grade, he joined his father, who was working hard to improve his family's life in Chicago. At first, he was thrilled, thinking that in this new world he could accomplish just about anything. Soon the unfriendly streets of Chicago, gave him a quick lesson in reality. In his Mexican village, he had been revered as a leader. In Chicago, he was an outsider, just another poor Hispanic kid, with broken English and an accent. But, following his father's example, Juan worked hard to get by.

Within three years, he graduated with honors from his high school. He was proud to be the first in his family to enter college. Juan did his best, but his first year was rough. He struggled without extra help to understand a new language and culture. Some days, he even thought of quitting. Unexpectedly, Juan's life took a dramatic turn. "This white man picked me out of the many students passing through a hallway, and said, 'Would you like to intern with a major corporation this summer?'" Juan couldn't believe his ears. "I thought: summer job? . . . major corporation? Sure. What do I have to do?"

The man in the hall was Frank Carr. He took Juan under his wing and introduced him to INROADS. That summer, Juan got a great job and for the first time in his life, he had opportunities to work with business leaders. "These people became my mentors, showed me the ropes, guided me throughout the summer," he recalls. "They really wanted me to make it in the business world." That summer's work experience with the Wm. Wrigley, Jr. Company convinced Juan that he really could, too. "For the first time since I was a boy in Mexico," he says, "I knew I could be somebody!"

Twenty-five years later, Juan is still with the company where he interned that summer. He's now a manager and a member of the INROADS/Chicago board of directors. Knowing what a difference a mentor made in his life, he's working with 6th and 7th graders of Mexican descent. He's helping others to be somebody. Juan will never forget Frank Carr. "He is as right today as he was all those years ago," Juan says. "There is so much talent in our youth. We all need to take the time to harvest it and help them realize their dreams."

Today, INROADS is a thriving career development organization. Over 6,000 African-American, Hispanic, and Native American young people have been interns in one of the 900 sponsoring companies in 49 U.S. Cities, Toronto, Canada, and even one in Mexico City, Mexico. And it all started with one man's response to another man's dream.

If you are in high school and want to apply to become an INROADS student, or a corporate executive who wants to learn more about sponsoring INROADS students, call **INROADS** at 800-642-9865 or reach them at http://www.Inroadsinc.org.

Shine On in Montana

STORYTELLER: JO CLARE HARTSIG
adapted from *Fellowship,* magazine of The Fellowship for Reconciliation

Early in December, Tammie Schnitzer helped her son, Isaac, stencil a menorah on his bedroom window in Billings, Montana. Like any five-year-old, he was proud of his holiday decorations. The family was celebrating Hanukkah, the Jewish festival of lights. Many non-Jews don't know the meaning of the holiday or of the menorah, the candleholder with eight candles. If you ask Tammy and Isaac, they'd be proud to tell you about it.

The story begins over two thousand years ago, when Judea was invaded by the Syrian Greeks. A small, yet determined band of Jewish freedom fighters waged an incredible and victorious guerrilla war against the Syrian army. During the bitter conflict, the Greeks tried to destroy the Jewish culture and religion. They ransacked the holy temple and extinguished the altar's eternal flame.

The Jewish people worked day and night to clean and restore their place of worship. Then they consecrated the temple once again. All that remained was to light the eternal flame. But they had only enough of the precious oil used in the lamp for one day. Nevertheless they were committed. If they could burn the lamp for only one day, so be it. Miraculously, the light didn't die on that day, nor the next. For eight days, the lamp burned, as brightly as it had on the very first day, shining on the altar. Ever since, Jewish families have celebrated Hanukkah with the menorah. They remember the miracle of the wondrous little lamp that kept the altar lit for eight amazing nights.

Shortly after Tammie and Isaac had finished stenciling their menorah, a brick flew through the decorated window, shattering it. The image of Issac's menorah lay in bits and pieces on the bed. The next day, the *Billings Gazette* described the incident. Tammie was reported to be troubled by the advice of the investigating officer. "You'd better remove the symbol from your house," he had told her. But how could a mother explain this to her son? He was so young, too young to be introduced to hatred like that.

As Margaret MacDonald, another Billings mother, read the paper that day, she was deeply touched by Tammie's question. She imagined having to explain to her own children that they couldn't have a Christmas tree in the window because it wasn't safe. That was no way for a little boy to remember the holidays. She wanted Isaac to be able to look back on this as a season of love, not hate and fear.

She remembered a story she'd heard about the King of Denmark during the Nazi occupation of World War II. Hitler had ordered the Christian king to force all Danish Jews to wear the Star of David on their chests, and he had refused. In an act of courageous defiance, the King placed the yellow star over his own heart, declaring he and all his people were one. If Hitler wanted to persecute the Jews, he would have to take the King as well. The King was not to stand alone. His example inspired his countrymen, people of all religions, to wear the stars in solidarity with the Jews. Because of their courage, the Nazis were ultimately unable to find their "enemies." In Denmark, there were no Jews, no Gentiles: only Danes.

Margaret wanted to make a similarly powerful statement against hate for Tammy and Isaac and for all the children of Billings. She phoned her pastor, asking him to tell the Danish story during his Sunday sermon and to pass out paper menorahs so that families could hang them in their windows. The pastor immediately agreed and spread the word to other churches. That Sunday, members of the congregation could be seen all over town hanging menorahs in their windows. By the following weekend, other churches, businesses, and human rights and community groups had followed suit. Soon, hundreds of menorahs appeared in the windows of non-Jewish homes. When Tammy drove Isaac to school, they could see them shining in the windows. They felt a special connection with their community.

Some concerned citizens called the police department, asking about the danger of this action. They were told, in no uncertain terms, by Chief Wayne Inman, "There's greater risk in not doing it." Hate crimes in Billings had been on the rise. A small contingent of skinheads, Klan members, and other white supremacists had targeted Jews, non-whites, gays, and lesbians for harassment, vandalism, and personal injury. If there was a time to stand together, it was now. The townspeople of Billings rallied around Tammy and Isaac.

Soon it spread from homes into the entire community. A sporting goods store proclaimed on its large billboard: "Not in Our Town! No hate. No violence. Peace on Earth." A local high school posted a sign reading, "Happy Hanukkah to our Jewish Friends." A vigil was held outside the synagogue during Hanukkah services to protect those who worshipped inside.

But the battle of light against darkness was not easily won. Bullets riddled the high school windows. Two United Methodist Churches, adorned with menorahs, had their windows broken. Six non-Jewish families had car windows smashed; a note left behind simply said, "Jew lover." The violence continued.

The *Billings Gazette* published a full-page drawing of a menorah and invited its readers to cut out the picture and place it in their windows. In this town, with fewer than a hundred Jewish families, the menorah was proudly displayed in thousands of homes. Now the hate groups couldn't find their enemies. In Billings, there were no Jews, no Gentiles: only friends.

As the holidays wore on, incidents of violence slowed. New friendships formed and greater understanding developed. Ironically, the violence intended to rip the community apart only served to make it stronger. Now, the people of Billings have new reasons to celebrate. If you ask them about their menorahs and what Hanukkah means to them, they'll be proud to tell you. It's about standing together in the face of hatred, overcoming violence with love, and the miracle of the light shining through the darkness.

Darkness cannot drive out darkness; only light can do that.
Hate cannot drive out hate; only love can do that.
DR. MARTIN LUTHER KING JR.

Want to help your church foster better relations in your community and undermine the appeal of hate groups? The **Interfaith Department** at the **Fellowship of Reconciliation** will show you how. Write to Box 271, Nyack, NY 10960 or visit http://www.nonviolence.org/~nvweb/for.

We Walk Our Talk

STORYTELLER: CECIL WILLIAMS,
adapted from *No Hiding Place* with Rebecca Laird

In the heart of San Francisco is the Glide Memorial Church. Glide is much more than a church, it's a community: a place of unconditional love and support. For thousands—rich and poor, young and old—Glide is a place of healing and of starting over. My African ancestors, who endured slavery, carried with them across the Atlantic a tradition that remains solidly rooted in African-American culture today. At Glide, we speak our truth by storytelling, engaging one another through dialogue, and immersing ourselves in the Spirit.

We estimate that 80 percent of the people who come to us are in recovery. One of the first things we learned about fighting the war on addiction is that traditional drug treatment programs don't work for most African-Americans. Twelve-step programs focus on individual recovery, as if independently getting clean and sober were the ultimate goal. But African-Americans are a communal people: we fight for our freedom together.

I grew up in San Angelo, Texas, which was a segregated town prior to the civil rights movement. The buses, the drinking fountains, the railroad tracks, the rest rooms, everything in San Angelo constantly reminded me that I was colored, black, a nigger. When I grew up and became a minister, I wanted to change that—to make life better for my people. Over 65 percent of blacks in San Francisco live in crime-ridden, boarded-up, graffiti-plastered housing projects. Many folks are on drugs. And even if they manage to stay drug free during the day, they eventually have to go home to projects that have become havens for every imaginable habit. The temptations are great. Since our people were living in the projects, Glide had to go there, too.

One of the things I preach at Glide is: "walk the talk that you talk." So, we walked our talk and decided to march on the most troubled housing projects in San Francisco: Valencia Gardens. On February 17, 1990, we decided to march and call out the good news of recovery to our brothers and sisters. We spent dozens of hours gathering people together from the community, the public housing tenants association, the mayor's office, and people from Glide. We also decided not to be stupid with our faith. We took the police with us, too.

We created a human force to influence the people in the projects. Our goal was not to run the pushers, pimps, and drug users out of public housing; we were coming to embrace them with unconditional love and declare that there was another way to live. So, we boarded buses, drove up Market Street, and turned on to Valencia Street, singing songs of freedom. When we arrived, we got off the buses and marched around the projects. Those in the front carried a street-wide banner that declared our nonviolent battle cry: "It's Recovery Time." Others carried placards reading: "The User Needs Recovery" and "Welcome Home to Recovery."

We marched as a posse of lovers, heralding freedom from drugs, addiction, and despair. As Jesus has said to each of us, "I'm with you," Glide marched to say to our hurting extended family, "We are with you." Each heart bore a commitment to accepting those we met. No one marched empty-handed either. Some carried paintbrushes and gallons of paint. Others bore heaping plates of fried chicken and potato salad. It does no good to go in shouting and screaming for change with your empty hand shaking in the air. You've got to have something to offer.

When the hundreds of marchers had converged in the center of the housing complex, I took a bullhorn and began to shout to those peeking out of the top-floor apartments. "C'mon down. Join us. It's recovery time! We know who you are. You're our sons and daughters. It's time for you to take control of your lives!"

Slowly, people started coming down, some from apartments currently serving as crack houses. We put them right up on stage and gave them the microphone. They talked about their lives. Then, late in the day, one of my staff members came up to me and said a group of pushers wanted to play a tape over our public address system. I said okay, seeing it as an opening to talk with the young men. I walked up to the door where these young pushers were holed up. Someone from the crowd yelled to me, "You ought not do that, Cecil." But I did it anyway, and that's how I met Alex.

Earlier in the week Alex had begun to reflect on his life. He later told us, "I had been taught by my father that if I was going to live, then I should be the best at whatever I was doin'. I took the bad road, being crooked, a criminal, and I was good at it. I had no mercy or concern for another's physical well-being. I did some time in jail. I was growing tired of life.

"I was thinking, 'I can get a job, and if I don't make it, I can always turn back to what I was doin': selling drugs.' But the one who is always by my side, my baby's mother, said, 'You can make an honest living.' So, I started thinking about it. That Saturday was the day Cecil and all the people came in marching.

"I listened to Cecil. What he was talking about was what I wanted to be about. After the walls at Valencia Gardens got painted, I realized that the march wasn't about covering up the dirty walls; it was about the people. There was a total change in the people who lived in the projects. People in the projects who never talked to each other were now talking. There had been so much bad around V.G. [Valencia Gardens]; I wanted to help make some good."

Soon after, Alex started coming to Glide. Many months later, he spoke about the march on Valencia Gardens to some visitors who were interested in our recovery program. Alex said, "I remember my father telling me so many times that by being born in 1968 I missed out on everything: Malcolm X, the Reverend Martin Luther King Jr., Vietnam, the hippie movement, and the Black Panthers. After I came to Glide, I began to see that I hadn't missed everything. I've lived to see Glide and to know the Reverend Cecil Williams, who is not a killer but a saver. Glide saved me and my family from the madness. One of the coolest things about finding myself is: I never had to go find Glide, Glide came to my home and found me."

Alex now has a job; he's good at it. He's a new man. "Coming to Glide was like facing a mountain where there weren't any stairs or a clear-cut path. Instead there were hands, all different colors of hands, reaching down to help me. All I had to do was hang on and keep climbing until I got to the top. When I reached the top, then I looked back and saw how far I'd come. It was, and is, a beautiful view. This is recovery."

Lift up your eyes upon this day breaking for you.
Give birth to the dream.

MAYA ANGELOU

Join the Sunday celebrations at **Glide Memorial Church** with Reverend Cecil Williams and inspirational gospel music from the Glide Ensemble. To support Glide's thirty-seven comprehensive programs that serve thousands of homeless, drug addicted, downtrodden, hopeless, or outcast people, including the Daily Free Meals Program that serves three free meals a day, 356 days a year, for over a million meals annually, call 415-771-6300.

The Banker with Heart

STORYTELLER: ALEX COUNTS

adapted from *Give Us Credit: How Muhammad Yunus' Micro-Lending Revolution is Empowering Women from Bangladesh to Chicago*

Giving America's poor a handup rather than a handout is an approach that has its roots in an unlikely place: Bangladesh. It began as one man's desperate attempt to make sense of his life in a country devastated by famine.

In his early twenties, Muhammad Yunus was an impatient young man brimming with self-confidence, optimism, and ambition. Before planning his trip to America, he had never heard of Vanderbilt University in Tennessee, where he had received a Fulbright scholarship. Looking at a globe, he realized it was almost exactly halfway around the world from Bangladesh. After he graduated, he wanted to apply some of the lessons he had learned studying economics and launch one of the many ideas he had toyed with during his student days.

Soon after his return, the famine of 1974 devastated his country. At the time, Henry Kissinger called Bangladesh "the world's basket case." But for Yunus, it was home. He got a job teaching economics at the university. On his way to class, he had to walk past hundreds of his countrymen, dying from starvation. Yunus realized he had to do something, even if it was only a small gesture. He had no grand illusions about what one man could do, working alone.

He began by talking with poor people on the street and in the villages. He immersed himself in their world and came to believe that the lack of investment capital was one of the root causes of the poverty. Yunus found villagers who earned as little as two cents a day making bamboo stools and paid exorbitant interest rates (as much as 10 percent a week) on the money they borrowed to buy materials for their stools. Yunus was appalled. "I felt ashamed to be part of a society which could not make twenty-seven dollars available to forty-two hardworking, skilled human beings so they could make a decent living," he said.

So, he started lending tiny amounts of money—as little as ten dollars—to destitute people from his own pocket. They invested their money in building small businesses like poultry farming, ricksha pulling, stool manufacturing, and other cottage industries. He created the Grameen Bank, which means "village," to give these people a strong foundation they could count on. Twenty years later, more than two million people, mostly women, have received loans from the Grameen Bank. On an average working day, Grameen disburses more than sixty million Bangladeshi taka, or roughly 1.5 million dollars. The return on Yunus' first investment has been astounding. An unprecedented 98 percent have paid their loans back in full.

The bank's secret is that they get poor people to help themselves while helping each other. People without credit are organized into borrowing support groups. They meet every week to troubleshoot their challenges and celebrate their successes. Each borrower also has a real financial stake in all the others in the group; if anyone defaults on a loan, the other group members must repay it. With the help of the Grameen Bank, millions of Bangladeshis are now working together to escape poverty and build a life of promise for themselves and their families.

Yunus is spreading this simple story—and its success—to people around the world. In 1986, then-Governor Bill Clinton invited him to rural Arkansas to see if it was possible to start a similar program in the U.S. At first, poor people couldn't believe that anyone would lend to them.

Yunus asked the welfare recipients and unemployed people he met to imagine what they would do with the money if a bank agreed to give them a loan. Almost everybody said that a bank would not give them money, so there was no point in talking about it. So he asked them again, but he just got more blank stares. Then he decided to take a more direct approach. "Look," he said, "I run a bank in Bangladesh that lends money to poor people. I am thinking of starting a bank right here. But if there is no business, why should I come?" He explained that they didn't need any collateral or anything else usually required for bank loans. All they needed was a good idea.

One woman who had been listening very carefully said, "I would like to borrow some money from your bank!" When Yunus asked her how much, she said $375. Surprised at the precise figure, he asked her what she would do with it. She said that she was a beautician and that her business was limited because she did not have the right supplies. If she could get a box of supplies costing $375, she was sure she could pay him back with the extra income. She also said she did not want a penny more than what the box cost.

Another woman, unemployed after the textile factory she had worked at closed and moved to Taiwan, needed a few hundred dollars for a sewing machine. Another woman wanted six hundred dollars to buy a pushcart to sell hot tamales.

For years Yunus had been saying that his program would thrive anywhere poverty existed, but many experts had told him that America was different. "Poor Americans are lazy Americans," they told him. After his trip to Arkansas, Yunus thought otherwise. Convinced that his program would work in America, he charged a handful of mavericks working for nonprofit organizations with making it happen. Within months, the Good Faith Fund was established in Pine Bluff, Arkansas. At about the same time, the Women's Self-Employment Project started making loans to women in Englewood, Chicago.

Since then, nearly forty American nonprofit organizations have started peer-lending programs based on the model of Yunus' Grameen Bank. They serve African Americans and Mexicans in South-Central Los Angeles, Native Americans in South Dakota, poor

Whites in Arkansas, North Carolina, and New England, and refugees from Southeast Asia—the entire spectrum of the disadvantaged in the United States. The Grameen strategy gives the poor the opportunity to create their own jobs rather than waiting around for someone else to do it for them. Today, in addition to Grameen's two million borrowers in Bangladesh, another six million poor people in fifty countries around the world—in the Philippines and South Africa and in cities like Brooklyn and Paris—are part of a powerful group of peers who are changing the entire banking industry. The goal for the year 2005 is to have one hundred million of the world's poorest families join them with access to credit and the opportunity to create their own livelihood.

In 1988, I arrived in Bangladesh, having been invited by Yunus to come and work at Grameen for a year. Within a few days of arriving, he took me to a huge celebration that his borrowers had organized in one village to commemorate the founding of their local branch office. I was surprised by how festive and even outrageous the event was. Near the end, Yunus whispered to me, "These events are times when the poor can show off, be heard, be loud, make a stir. The slogans, the fanfare, it's all part of a process of overcoming the shame and isolation of poverty. Society has always told the poor, 'Stay in your crummy houses; you are neither to be seen nor heard.' Grameen invites them to come together, hold their heads up high. Be seen! Be heard."

★

Never doubt that a small group of thoughtful committed citizens
can change the world. Indeed it's the only thing that ever has.

MARGARET MEAD

Help end poverty in the world, one person at a time. Join the campaign to give one hundred million poor families access to microloans by 2005. Call the **Grameen Foundation** at 202-543-2636 to learn how you can develop partnerships with the Grameen Bank.

A Man with a Past Gives Back

STORYTELLER: DIANE SAUNDERS

It's ironic, Will agrees, that a man with his past now works with the police, some of whom have become his best friends. And it's sad, he tells young people, that it took his brother's death for him to find life. He often looks back to that turning point. Though he wishes it had come sooner, he's grateful it came at all.

William Morales was in solitary confinement, called "the hole," where all he could do was think. There wasn't much else to do. Screaming, bragging, blaming, tripping on the past, plotting revenge, he'd done all that, and it had gotten him nowhere. And now his young brother Hector was dead, shot during a gun battle with the police.

Will could never change that fact. As he sat alone in the hole, thinking over his life and Hector's death, he finally realized things would never change for him unless he changed himself. With a determination he had never felt before, he decided to let go of his past and start working on his future.

Up to that point, his life had consisted of one bad choice after another. When he was sixteen, he founded a gang, the X-Men, on the lucrative profits of cocaine trafficking in Boston. Known for their targeted attacks on police officers, other gangs knew better than to mess with the X-Men. Will went from infamy to incarceration within a year. By the age of seventeen, he was a prisoner of his own bad choices.

His long road to self-rehabilitation began with Perez, a lifer who'd gotten his master of education degree inside the walls. Perez agreed to teach Will to read. Starting with Little Bo Peep coloring books, Will started learning words, then sentences, then paragraphs, and then chapters. He absorbed everything Perez taught him, nourishing himself with each word.

Will joined a speaking program that gave him the chance to talk to troubled teens, in real street terms, about his brother's death and how it had changed him. The kids listened. Will began to understand that if it came at the right time and from the right person, intervention could keep a teenager out of trouble.

Four years after Hector's death and six years after he was locked up, Will was released. He got a job at a pizza company. One day he met up with his friend Luis who had also been paroled. Together they formed a group called X-HOODS and began making presentations to high school kids about staying out of trouble.

Will and Luis knew they would always be associated with their former violent gang, the infamous X-Men, so they decided to use that association to reach kids. They told Boston students that the *X* was a symbol for crossing out drugs, gangs, violence, and all the other bad elements in their community. *HOODS,* they said, stood for Helping Out Our Dysfunctional Society. They added the caution that if not used wisely, the X could be the mark of poison, ruining a young life. But, the same X could also mark the spot where you'll find the buried treasure within yourself.

Gradually, Will's dream of bringing the community together to help kids began to take shape. He met the Reverend Wesley Williams, a Methodist minister who directed an urban youth service program. The Reverend had already developed the idea of bringing the kids, the police, and the church together. Through applying tough love, solid values, and by using open communication to solve problems, the Youth and Police Partnership was born. "Even though the police and the church both wanted to keep kids out of gangs, they weren't working with each other to do it," says Will. The Youth and Police Partnership was the first sign of real cooperation and was the first outreach program in Boston's history run by teenagers. Today, they organize and run a crime watch and lead workshops for adults, teaching them how to start crime watch groups. Between talks at high schools with the D.A.R.E. (Drug Abuse Resistance Education) program and meetings with city officials to plan a neighborhood crime watch, Will's days are pretty full. He recently got the Massachusetts School of Law in Andover to create a special curriculum for his kids. The school teaches them to think and act like lawyers. "Now when the kids see a problem, they can analyze it in their minds, then verbally say, 'This is why that's wrong'. They can state their arguments clearly and defend themselves with words, not fists, knives, and guns."

On some nights, Will visits gang members. Only now he talks with them about jobs and other opportunities. Occasionally, he meets with the police to mediate and resolve problems. Officer Juan Torres, who coordinates the Youth and Police Partnership program, says, "There is definitely a new trust between us and the kids. They get to know us, in and out of uniform, as real people. We're constantly reminded that these are good kids who want to make a difference. They just need to know someone cares." Torres continues, "When they see a guy like Will let old wounds heal and move ahead, then they can also trust us and work with us to make the community a safe place where they'll have opportunities for personal growth."

At the end of his speeches, Will always reminds everyone it's a tough world out there. "Hey, I still carry a gun, but it's not a physical gun, it's a mental gun. And what I'm shooting for is the sky: the hope, peace, and freedom in the sky."

There are two ways of exerting one's strength: one is pushing down, the other is pulling up.

BOOKER T. WASHINGTON

Learn how you can bring the youth and police in your community together to build healthy relationships and teach children how to prevent violence through problem-solving forums and recreational activities. Call Will Morales at the **Urban Edge's Youth Police Partnership** at 617-989-0217.

A Healing Heart

STORYTELLER: SUSAN BUMAGIN

As far as Juan was concerned, there was really no choice. As a surgeon in his homeland of deeply troubled El Salvador, he felt it was his sacred duty to heal the sick. For many long days and nights he worked in the countryside, giving free medical aid to the peasants who desperately needed his services. For this, he was imprisoned by the government.

The peasants, Dr. Juan's captors said, supported the communist guerrillas. This made them enemies of the government. And, in their eyes, giving these poverty-stricken people the gift of life made Dr. Juan a dangerous man. Government agents slit his wrists and severed the tendons in his hands that had allowed him to perform the delicate maneuvers of surgery. Then they shot him and left him to die.

Barely alive, Juan was smuggled out of prison and out of the country. After two surgeries and two years in Mexico, he made his way to the United States, receiving political asylum in 1988. Although capable of giving basic medical treatment, his damaged hands would never again master the fine details of surgery. Still, Dr. Juan was determined to help heal his people from the pains of war.

He came to live in Washington, D.C., in the Mount Pleasant community, home to thousands who had escaped El Salvador's bloody war. Many had been victims of torture; others had been forced to watch as loved ones were killed. The collective trauma in this ghetto was almost beyond imagination. Dr. Juan saw that the physical wounds, bad as they were, paled by comparison with the spiritual and psychological damage these people had suffered.

As executive director of La Clinica del Pueblo, he began to train displaced, uneducated people to provide basic health care services to each other. When he began, the clinic was only open on Tuesday nights. Today, more than one hundred volunteer health care workers serve 7,000 residents a year on a full-time basis, providing free health care to 60–70 percent of the Washington D.C., Latino community. In addition to health care, people are given access to counseling services so they can begin to heal their minds and souls as well as their bodies.

One of Juan's greatest challenges happened one day as he walked his rounds in Washington D.C. A drunk man who seemed to recognize him staggered to his side. It was the very same man who had slit his wrists, crippling his agile surgeon's hands forever! It was Arturo from the torture squad, the one who had shot him and left him to die.

Juan stood in stunned silence for a moment. But all he saw in this broken man was one more member of his devastated community, greatly in need of healing. He looked Arturo directly in the eye, and said, "I'm still doing the same work I did before the torture cell. As a physician, I offer to help you, too."

Arturo experienced a deep healing that day, and it was a tremendous moment for Juan, as well. "I am grateful for my ability to help my torturers," says Juan, simply. "I can forgive them and offer my services. In spite of having suffered, we can pardon our torturers, so they can heal themselves." He adds, "People like Arturo need a special love, they need more compassion, and they need a democratic system like the one in the U.S. to relearn how to be human again." As for Arturo, he had never known it would be possible to respect another human being so deeply. When he sees Juan in the streets, he always says, "How are you, Doctor?" and his admiration is clear.

At La Clinica del Pueblo, there are many echoes of the old community in the new. Once, a new patient entered the doctor's office for treatment. She suddenly gasped, asking, "Juan is it you? This must be a dream. I thought you were dead." Dr. Juan's eyes filled with tears. "Maria Manjivar, I can't believe you are alive," he said.

Years ago, Juan had met Maria in El Salvador's war-torn countryside. He had trained her to be his surgical nurse, to take bullets out of the bodies of relatives and friends. Now, so many miles away, they would once again work together at the clinic, healing wounds of the spirit. And those who had survived the unthinkable would find a source of renewal they never dreamed possible.

When the power of love overcomes the love of power, then there will be true peace.

SRI CHIM MOI

Volunteer at your local free clinic and give the gift of health. Medical professionals and bilingual translators who want to help Dr. Juan provide free medical care, health education, mental health, and social services to immigrant Latinos at the **La Clinica del Pueblo** can call Renee Wallis at 202-332-1134 or write to 1470 Irving Street, N.W., Washington, D.C. 20010.

Viva! Barrios Unidos

STORYTELLER: PEGGY R. TOWNSEND

His grandmother called him "Nane," meaning "walks in peace." It's an unusual name for one who spends his days in the toughest neighborhoods of the country. Then again, Nane is a rather unusual man. His real name is Daniel Alejandrez. In barrios throughout the nation, he fights the violence and addictions killing America's youth.

The barrio where Nane started his work lies in the shadow of the Giant Dipper roller coaster in Santa Cruz, California. It's a tiny neighborhood filled with rundown homes and broken dreams. Drug dealers man the corners, gang graffiti litters the walls, and the thousands of tourists who pass by on their way to the nearby amusement park don't even know it exists.

It is here that Nane began Barrios Unidos. He combines messages of hope and understanding with practical programs like job training, computer courses, and even art classes. "Kids aren't born gang members or racists," he says. "They become that way." But they don't have to: a lesson Nane knows from personal experience.

He was born in Merigold, Mississippi; the child of migrant workers who followed the crops through America's heartland. By the age of five, he was picking cotton, asparagus, and beets alongside his family. Living in noisy labor camps, mostly in dusty tents, but once even under a tree, was a natural way of life. "I just accepted it," says Nane. He'd never known anything different.

The day his grandfather died, Nane's life which had been simply hard, turned bad. The patriarch, Don Pancho, returned home from a long day of chopping beets with a short-handled hoe. Soon after, he collapsed. Twelve-year-old Nane held his seventy-two-year-old grandfather in his arms, begging him not to die, but it was too late.

After Don Pancho's death, Nane's family fell apart. His father began to drink, and jobs became more scarce. Nane felt his father's pain as he bowed his head before the patrons and searched for work. He wanted nothing more than to escape, but there was nowhere to go. He decided if he couldn't run from his pain, he'd numb it. At twelve years of age, he started sniffing glue. By thirteen, he'd smoked his first joint. When he was seventeen, he tried LSD. He returned from Vietnam a heroin addict.

During a short jail sentence for drug use, he took a hard look at himself. He knew if he didn't change his path, he'd wind up like the gangsters and drug dealers around him: in prison for a very long time or dead.

When he got out of jail, Nane used the GI Bill to attend Fresno City College and the University of California, Santa Cruz. As he studied, he understood that the same despair that had nearly destroyed him runs rampant in the barrios. Without help and with few choices, many young boys were destined to repeat the mistakes he had made.

Nane decided he had to do something, so he went out into the streets and started talking to kids. It was that simple. He hung out with them, counseled them, and talked to them about a better way of living, one that would keep them out of prison or a graveyard. To better reach the kids, he decided to walk his talk: he conquered his own drug addictions.

But the way out of addiction and despair was not a smooth road. He had lost twelve relatives and friends in twelve years: his two brothers, his childhood hero, Uncle Pancho, and his grandmother. Finally, all he could feel was pain. "I didn't know how to let go of the tragedies in my life," he said. Seeking to numb the pain, Nane overdosed and almost died.

As he was rushed to the hospital's emergency room, Nane had a vision. He could see his brother Leo at the end of a tunnel of flashing light, "Go back, go back," Leo said, "It's not your time." Then he saw his other brother, Tavo, who said the same thing. "When I woke up, I realized the Creator had given me the opportunity to see my brothers and to know they were OK," Nane remembers. "After that I could let go of the pain."

The next day, he went to the cemetery and quietly prayed with his brothers. "I realized that I needed to deal with my own life—to move forward," he said. From then on, Nane found strength from being spiritually connected through traditional Native American ceremonies and sweat lodges. He sought guidance from tribal elders and also spoke with people of different faiths. "I began to focus on my own mission in life," Nane says, "to better our communities and to stop the violence among our young people."

At first, working from the trunk of his car, Nane founded Barrios Unidos, a group focused on providing new role models for America's troubled youth. It was 1977 and he was twnety-seven years old. While his wife sold tacos to make ends meet, he and his small band of volunteers went to schools, walked the barrios, and worked late into the night in pursuit of their vision of a world free from violence, drugs, and alcohol abuse. From the car trunk they moved to a small office. A small grant was used to buy a computer so they could write applications for more grants. Soon their message spread, as did their impact.

Today, Barrios Unidos has a staff of thirty-four people in twenty-seven chapters across the country. Their programs are extensive and they have a room full of computers. Free food and free counseling are given to those in need. Three summer Kids' Klub programs reach out to the youngest residents of the barrios.

To foster an entrepreneurial spirit, Barrios Unidos started a silk-screening business run by teens. The proceeds of the business help fund their initiatives. One of their most exciting projects is the Cesar Chavez School for Social Change in Santa Cruz near where Cesar organized in the fields of Pajaro Valley. Here, future community leaders like fifteen-year-old Miriam Garcia are raised up in the tradition of Cesar Chavez, Martin Luther King, and Mahatma Gandhi. "I am grateful for this opportunity," says Miriam, "and I'm looking forward to becoming a creator of positive change in my community."

Of course, there is still much to do. Sometimes it may even seem that Barrios Unidos is fighting a losing battle. Youth crime in our country is projected to more than double over the next decade, fueled in large part by gang activity. The FBI reports nearly one-half-million youth are now involved in gangs. For Nane and Barrios Unidos, that simply means more lives to turn around, more young people who need more choices for the future. Nane finds hope in young people like Alejandro Bilchez who is now the director of Barrios Unidos in San Mateo. "My father taught me to be a man," says Alejandro. "Nane taught me to be a warrior for change."

At forty-seven, Nane is still the guiding spirit of his organization. He still works in the office, travels across the country giving speeches calling for crime prevention funds, and meets children of the barrios. And he always takes time to pray, honoring the Creator. He now awaits the arrival of someone younger to take his place. In the kitchen of his modest home, Nane snuggles his three-year-old grandson close and talks of his hopes for peace. "Not for me," he says, "maybe not for my children. But if we all keep working towards it, maybe for my grandson."

We challenge people from all walks of life to help us save our children. To get involved with **Barrios Unidos** call 408-457-8208.

By Giving Our Lives, We Find Life

STORYTELLER: MARC GROSSMAN

For the migrant farmworker, each day was endless; each night he was exhausted and often hungry. His life stood in stunning contrast to the comfortable lives of the families who savored the fruits of his labor. In a land that promised plenty, migrant farmworkers in the 1960s had no voice, no rights, and no protections. Cesar Chavez knew their troubles firsthand. Once a migrant farmworker, he was small, soft-spoken, and low key; a guy you could easily lose in a crowd. But this gentle giant woke up the drowsy conscience of the most powerful country in the world.

For years, Americans had brought home sweet, plump clusters of table grapes without a second thought. By the late 1960s, Cesar Chavez had turned the decision of whether or not to buy grapes into a powerful political act. This quiet man with dark Indian features had changed the ordinary act of buying groceries into an opportunity to help others by exercising the power of socially responsible buying habits.

Farmworkers had been trying to organize a union for more than one hundred years. In 1965 they began a bitter five-year strike against grape growers around Delano, California. Two and one-half years later, in the hungry winter of 1968 with no resolution in sight, they were tired and frustrated.

Cesar had already decided to ask for help. He believed that if people in communities throughout the nation knew about the needless suffering of farmworkers, they would rise to the occasion and do what they could to help. Taking a bold leap of faith, Cesar invited consumers to join in solidarity with his United Farm Workers

(UFW). He asked them to send a message to the grape growers by boycotting California table grapes. The boycott began slowly, but built steadily over the next couple of years. First California, then the rest of the nation, and even Canada joined in support of the strikers.

In the meantime, some of the strikers had become impatient. Among some of them, particularly some of the young men, there began the murmurs of violence; some wanted to strike back at those who had abused them and their families. By fighting back, they thought they could prove their machismo, their manliness. But Cesar rejected that part of our culture "that tells our young men that you're not a man if you don't fight back." The boycott had followed the tradition of Cesar's hero, Mahatma Gandhi, whose practice of militant nonviolence he embraced. And now, like Gandhi, Cesar announced that he would undertake a fast as an act of penitence and as a way of taking responsibility as a leader for his people.

The fast divided the UFW staff. Many didn't understand why Cesar was doing it. Others worried about his health. But the farmworkers understood. A mass was said nightly near where Cesar was fasting at the Forty Acres, the UFW's headquarters in Delano. Hundreds, then thousands, came. People pitched tents nearby. They brought religious offerings: pictures and small statues. Farmworkers waited in line for hours to speak with Cesar in his tiny room, while he refused interviews with reporters.

After twenty-five days, Cesar was carried to a nearby park where the fast ended during a mass with thousands of farmworkers. He had lost thirty-five pounds, but there was no more talk of violence among the farmworkers. Cesar's message had gotten through. Senator Robert Kennedy came to the mass, he said, "out of respect for one of the heroic figures of our time."

Cesar was too weak to speak, so his statement was read by others in both English and Spanish. "It is my deepest belief that only by giving our lives do we find life," they read. "The truest act of courage, the strongest act of manliness, is to sacrifice ourselves for others in a totally nonviolent struggle for justice. To be a man is to suffer for others. God help us to be men."

Cesar's efforts connected middle-class families in northeastern cities and midwestern suburbs with poor families in the hot California vineyards. Motivated by compassion, millions of people across North America stopped eating the grapes they had loved so much. At dinner tables across the country, parents gave their children a simple, powerful lesson in social justice by reaching out to those less fortunate than themselves. By 1970, the grape boycott was an unqualified success. Bowing to pressure from the boycott, grape growers at long last signed union contracts, granting workers human dignity and a more livable wage.

In the years that followed, Cesar continued to use strikes, boycotts, marches and fasts to help farmworkers stand up for their rights and to gather support from ordinary Americans to aid them in their efforts. In 1988, at the age of sixty-one, Cesar undertook his last public fast, this time for thirty-six days, to draw attention to the pesticide poisoning of farm workers and their children.

By the values many used to measure success in the 1990s, Cesar Chavez was not very successful. He had been forced to quit school after the eighth grade to help his family. He never owned a house. He never earned more than six thousand dollars a year. When he died in 1993, at age sixty-six, he left no money for his family. Yet more than forty thousand people marched behind the plain pine casket at his funeral, honoring the more than forty years he spent struggling to improve the lives of farmworkers.

An all-night vigil was held under a giant tent before Cesar's funeral at Forty Acres, where his body lay in an open casket. Thousands and thousands of people filed by until the morning. Parents carried newborn babies and sleeping toddlers in their arms. One farmworker explained, "I wanted to tell my children how they had once been in the presence of this great man."

What was the secret behind such a remarkable display? A reporter once asked Cesar, "What accounts for all the affection and respect so many farm workers show you in public?" Cesar just looked down and smiled his easy smile. "The feeling is mutual," was his simple reply.

Support the **United Farm Workers of America** and their nonviolent work to carry on Cesar Chavez's dream of dignity for farmworkers across America by calling (805) 822-5571, ext. 3255.

Our Touchstone

STORYTELLER: JOSEPH RODRIGUEZ

Every Saturday night when I was growing up, the Rodriguez household in Paterson, New Jersey, joined millions of other Latino families from Alaska to Argentina to learn, laugh, and feed our souls! I remember how we'd sit around after dinner eating my mothers best Cuban desserts, watching *Sabado Gigante Internacional* and waiting to see what extraordinary feat Don Francisco would pull off each week.

For thirty-five years and to this day, Don Francisco hosts a unique four-hour TV show that unites one hundred million Spanish-speaking viewers in twenty-eight countries. At a time when so many TV shows prosper by exploiting human frailties, Don Francisco teaches his viewers the values of giving and helping others: the joy of compassion and human dignity.

I remember when I first saw Jose Reyes on the *Sabado Gigante Internacional* show. Jose was like a member of our family; he re-upholstered our old furniture and made it look like new. When we'd go to his shop, he always treated us special. His work was always flawless, full of pride and craftsmanship. Suddenly, there Jose was on TV: the same man who upholstered our furniture! When he was fifteen years old, Jose had been wounded, losing his right arm and leg during the civil unrest in his native El Salvador. Despite these physical limitations, he had mastered a craft requiring great physical skill. Now he was being celebrated and honored by Don Francisco. At the time, I was a young teenager, "too cool" to reveal my sense of awe in front of my parents, but Jose made a lasting impression on me.

One week Don Francisco might host Jose or others like him, who had overcome hardship and adversity. Another time, it might be a story of a man who was reunited with three sons he had not seen in twnety years. Don Francisco's stories have a common thread: to remind the Latino community that one of our greatest gifts is helping others. Every Saturday night, we reconnect with our most precious touchstone: the unity and importance of our family.

Perhaps the most amazing thing about Don Francisco (besides being listed in the *Guiness Book of World Records* as having the longest-lasting TV show) is his endless selflessness in spite of personal hardships; a lesson all too important for the Latino community. Born in 1940 to German-Jews who emigrated to Chile to escape the tragedy of the Holocaust, he overcame language and cultural barriers and rose to become one of the most successful businessmen in the Latino community. Today, despite his hectic schedule, he serves as a major figure in UNICEF (United Nations Children's Fund) and heads the Institute for Paraplegic Children in Chile, which he founded over eighteen years ago.

Today, I no longer sit around the TV with my mother and father waiting for Don Francisco. Despite the fact that I am thousands of miles away from them, Don Francisco's hand still touches our family. Each week, his show somehow manages to be a thread that still connects me with my parents. I think about Don Francisco and Jose from time to time when I'm confronted with a seemingly insoluble problem. I think to myself that if he could overcome obstacles despite his limitations, then I should be able to overcome mine too.

Recently, I asked my parents if they had heard anything about Jose. They told me that he had successfully expanded his business, and was in the process of starting an upholstery school to teach Paterson kids his trade. Some of his current employees were once the students he taught for free: former street kids who were lost and without direction. Today, his biggest challenge is recruiting enough volunteer craftsmen and funds to keep his dream alive. Given his track record, I'm sure he will reach this goal. The road behind him is littered with the obstacles he has overcome, and that is one of the most important lessons he teaches his students.

I remarked to my parents that Jose's perseverance was the root of his success. To my surprise, my father replied, "Not exactly. The love and support he received from his family and friends was as much a factor as his personal determination." That started me thinking about the first time I saw Jose on the show.

As a teenager, I had only seen the obvious: a man with one leg and one arm skillfully working his trade. I had completely missed the more important message. I now remember that Jose talked about how those around him had loved him so much that they hadn't allowed him to get lost in his limitations. They had nurtured him and helped him discover that his true potential didn't depend upon having two arms and two legs, but in the freedom that lies in being able to relearn how to live with what he had. "A man's greatest victory is not in never falling, but in rising every time he does," Jose had said. His words, lost on me at the time, now come back to me with real force.

Don Francisco and the everyday heroes he presented to us week after week are the touchstones I now use to measure my life. I know that no matter what seemingly insurmountable limitations confront my family, I can take comfort in the fact that we are all there supporting each other's steps into a better future. I also know that for four hours every Saturday night, Don Francisco helps us discover the strength that flows from our families and the value of unity and perseverance. And I, too, can count on people who love me enough to help me stand when I fall down and to help me celebrate when I succeed.

Watch Don Francisco on **Unavision's Sabado Gigante Internacional** every Saturday from 7-10 p.m. Call other talk-show hosts and encourage them to invite Stone Soup "community heroes" to share their ideas about what we can do to build a better world.

We Are Moving Forward

STORYTELLER: MATT BROWN

Marilyn Concepcion fondly remembers her simple childhood in Puerto Rico. Each morning she awakened to her grandmother's voice calling the chickens to feed. She remembers wearing a *mochilias* [sack] around her waist, and picking the red coffee beans from the trees in her yard. Her grandmother taught her how to dry, roast and grind some of the best coffee in the world. All this changed when Marilyn was 10 years old.

Like many young Puerto Rican women, Marilyn's mother left school when she was only in the sixth grade so she could help her family She wanted to give her four daughters a better future. With hope in their hearts, they left their beautiful paradise and moved to Providence, Rhode Island.

In this new country, Marilyn started a new life. The sounds of the city replaced her grandmother's morning calls to the chickens. The fast-paced urban lifestyle and social pressures confused her. For several years she struggled, trying to adjust, drifting aimlessly until she finally dropped out of school when she was 16 years old.

She threw herself into a series of jobs, factory work, delis and any work she could find. Between jobs, she stayed home and watched soap operas. "I worked very hard," she remembers. "But I knew that without an education my opportunities would always be limited."

Marilyn wanted to make something of her life, but how and what could she do? Then one day, a school counselor gave her a flyer about City Year. Marilyn was curious to know what was meant by "a new urban Peace Corps, the experience of a lifetime." The next day, she attended a meeting at her local library about this new youth organization that was starting in Providence.

Before she knew it, Marilyn was interviewed and officially welcomed into City Year's first-year corps. She loved their two-day retreat. Latinos, African-Americans, Asians, Native Americans, and white kids from Providence, all speaking different languages becoming a team. Working together, they learned how to turn vacant lots into gardens, build new playgrounds, and renovate community centers.

Because Marilyn could read and write both Spanish and English she worked with first and second graders in the English as a Second Language program. "One seven-year-old boy, Miguel, had problems pronouncing the letter "F," remembers Marilyn, "so I made a puppet of a frog for Miguel. Every now and them I would ask him what letter 'frog' began with. 'F,' he'd say with a huge smile. I felt so great that day! Here I was a high-school drop-out and I taught a child something."

As a City Year corps member, Marilyn was required to work on her GED. She studied so hard she passed in just one month, becoming the first person in her family to receive a high school diploma. On that memorable day she was called out of a corps meeting to receive the good news. She bolted back to the meeting and received a standing ovation from her entire team. "I couldn't believe it," she said. "I knew from that point on that if I put my mind on something, I could accomplish anything."

City Year was so impressed by Marilyn's enthusiasm, commitment and budding leadership, she was picked to help start another program in San Jose, California. At age 19, it wasn't easy living alone for the first time. But she worked hard, learned a lot, and helped even more. And when she gave of her heart, it caught on like wildfire.

Marilyn was invited to be a City Year spokesperson for the National Governor's Association conference. She so impressed Puerto Rican Governor Rossello that he invited her to come to Puerto Rico as a guest of honor to speak at the Summit

Against Crime. Marilyn was ecstatic—and a bit nervous. This would be the first time she would see her country since she left nine years ago. She wasn't sure what to expect, but she knew she had to go.

For three days, 300 university students shared how the high crime on the Island was limiting their future, they exchanged ideas and discussed new solutions for ways to prevent crime on the Island. Marilyn talked about her new life in America and the challenges she had faced. She talked about City Year and her experiences with helping herself by helping others. The young Puerto Ricans were impressed to see that someone their age, who came from simple beginnings like theirs, could transform her life by helping others.

Marilyn listened to these young Puerto Ricans debating the important issues facing their island, everything from the environment to domestic violence. It gave her hope that the Puerto Rican community was really moving forward. "Marilyn's integrity and dedication to serve others makes her an exceptional human being," says Governor Rossello. "It is a great pride for our Island to have a youth like her work with our young citizens. I am proud to see that a new generation is taking care of the young ones."

Marilyn returned to the United States with a new commitment to help her people. Now a pre-med student at Brown University, she wants to be a doctor so she can set up a free childhood immunization program. "If you aren't immunized you can't go to school, and getting an education is the key for our people," she says.

After attending the Presidents' Summit for America's Future, Marilyn decided to bring City Year to Puerto Rico so other young people could have the opportunities she's had. The response from the Puerto Rican community has been amazingly positive. The Mayor of Isabela has offered his community as the start-up site. From there, Marilyn hopes it will spread across the entire island.

When Marilyn spoke at the 1996 Democratic National Convention, she told her story to millions of people on national television. Reflecting back on her experience, Marilyn remembers the many Latina women who came up to talk to her after her speech. One of those who thanked her with tear-filled eyes was her high school Spanish teacher who said, "Thank you. You don't know what this means to all of us."

Marilyn says she realized in that moment that "It wasn't just me up there telling my story. It was much more than that." She pauses with tears in her own eyes, "I feel like we are all moving forward. As we say in my country, *Nos estamos moviendo nos para adelante*."

If you know of a child who needs immunizations but can't afford them or if you want to join with Marilyn and others who are committed to helping children become immunized, call the **National Immunization Hotline** at 800-232-2522. If you want to learn more about **City Year Puerto Rico** call Juan Rodriguez, Human Resource Manager for Timberland-Puerto Rico at 787-872-2140 (ext. 2313).

Hope for "Los Chavalitos"

STORYTELLER: DICK RUSSELL

Inside a classroom on New York City's upper east side, mostly affluent young teenagers listen in awe to their Spanish teacher, Alejandro Obando. Watching an inspiring slide-show, they see the grateful faces of three hundred Nicaraguan families who now have running water thanks to a sister-city project organized by their teacher with their New York neighbors. Modeled after the teachings of Dr. Martin Luther King Jr., the Manhattan Country School offers its students opportunities to make a difference in the world.

One student, Daniel Eddy, listened attentively as Alejandro shared his dream. After teaching Spanish in New York for seven years, his teacher had gone home. His heart had ached thinking about *los chavalitos*, the homeless children who live on the streets of Nicaragua, hustling trinkets and stolen goods. They sit together in alleyways, sniffing glue. Sometimes, they even sell their own bodies just to live.

This is what twelve long years of war will do to a country's children. More than 6,000 Nicaraguan children are orphaned and homeless. Thousands more, lucky enough not to have lost their parents, work long hours at menial jobs to help support their families. Eighty-five percent of Nicaragua's children under the age of fifteen live in poverty.

Alejandro, too, grew up destitute in central Nicaragua. He, too, had sold fake watches and shined shoes to survive. His parents divorced when he was a baby and placed him in the care of his grandmother, Celia, in the town of Camoapa. She scraped out a meager living, selling fried bananas. But she had real dreams of something better for her grandson and insisted that he read books instead of hanging out at the pool hall.

Under the Somoza dictatorship, Alejandro and other children in little towns like Camoapa were denied education after grade school. So the boy and his grandmother made their way to Managua, looking for jobs and an education. The little money he made selling lottery tickets was enough to pay for night school. One day, a doctor from his hometown found him on the streets; if Alejandro would sweep the school, he said, he could be among its first nineteen high school students. Alejandro happily accepted the offer.

After he graduated, Alejandro was fortunate enough to receive a baseball scholarship to Managua University. Working part time, he made enough money to travel to New York with his baseball teammates. There, Alejandro's dream of becoming a teacher took root. He decided to leave his homeland to study at Columbia University.

Now forty-eight, Alejandro is an American citizen with big dreams, and the Manhattan Country School is helping to make his dreams come true. Alejandro asked his students if they would help him create a farm-school for abandoned children. He wanted to bring some hope to these poor children and give them the second chance he was once given. "This was a ray of light in a war-torn land," Daniel recalls. "There was no way to hear him speak without wanting to help him."

School administrators arranged donations of clothing and school supplies. Friends of the school and cultural organizations raised funds. Several alumni traveled to Nicaragua during the summer to help build dormitories and classrooms. One of Alejandro's first Spanish students spent an entire year as a volunteer, helping set up the curriculum. A baseball field built by Alejandro and a group of American volunteers awaits the debut of its first team. The school, built in the town where Alejandro was born, is becoming a reality.

"Over the next five years, I want to create a wonderful life for fifty homeless children," he says. "Together, we will live on a three-hundred-acre countryside farm with a clear-running stream and wildlife-like monkeys and deer. Here children will learn to read and write, how to grow their own food, and how to be leaders. The older children will teach the younger ones."

The students back in New York City write Alejandro letters. "What you are doing is hard. We miss you, but we're proud of you." "I want to come help you during my summer vacation," one wrote.

"I cried when I received their letters offering to organize raffles and bake sales to buy the children pencils and supplies," says Alejandro. "The human heart knows no geographical boundaries."

At the school's opening ceremony, some twenty children stood together in a large circle. Their eyes brimming with hope, each one planted a small tree. "I want to teach the children to preserve the beauty of this land," Alejandro says. But before celebrating the fruits of his dream, he first made a pilgrimage to his grandmother's grave. "I hope to accomplish what she always told me," he says. "Be a good citizen, get your education, and help other people."

Education makes people easy to lead, but difficult to drive,
easy to govern, but impossible to enslave.

HENRY BROGHAM

Bring hope to the **"Los Chavalitos" school** in Nicaragua by volunteering. Call Ginny Scheer at the Manhattan Country School Farm at 607-326-7049. Send donations to: **Madre/Los Chavalitos,** 121 West Twenty-Seventh Street, Room 301, New York, NY 10001.

Democracy in Action

Storyteller: Marion Silverbear

Ada Deer grew up living with her parents and four siblings in a log cabin on the Menominee Reservation in Wisconsin. They had no electricity, running water, or telephones. They were poor, but so was everyone else she knew. Her tribe nurtured in her a healthy respect for the land, and the belief that members of the tribe should work together for the good of everyone.

Connie, Ada's mother, had come to the Menominee Reservation as a public health nurse. She met and married Joe Deer, a nearly full-blooded Menominee Indian, who kept alive many of the old tribal ways. As one of the tribal elders, "Mom" Deer taught her daughter to be a spirited student of tribal life and to commit herself to public service and social justice. "Ada Deer, you were not put on this planet to indulge yourself," her mother would say. "You are here to help people." After she had completed high school, Ada's tribe awarded her a scholarship to attend college. In gratitude for having been given this opportunity, she committed her life to helping the tribe.

Ada's path to leadership was shaped by many experiences. One of the most important and lasting influences was the Encampment for Citizenship, a six-week summer camp she attended when she was nineteen, along with more than one hundred other young people. "It was two years after the Supreme Court decision, *Brown v. Board of Education,*" she recalls. "I didn't know anything about race relations or this important piece of U.S. history."

"I participated in a workshop on segregation, led by a southern, African-American school teacher. She gave me a much greater understanding of racism's impact on individuals and the power of the federal government to affect positive change." As part of that summer's encampment, Ada's group visited for several hours with Eleanor Roosevelt at her Hyde Park home.

"I was impressed that the former first lady would spend so much time in discussion with us. She told us about how she had helped to create the United Nations Commission on Human Rights and the charter supporting peace and the brotherhood of man. I challenged her," Ada recalls. "I asked her, 'What about South Africa oppressing Black people? Why doesn't the U.N. do something?'

"Mrs. Roosevelt replied, 'We have to understand that it takes time. We need to educate people that violence is not the answer. We have to have faith in humans. Eventually, justice will prevail.' Of course, she was right. Forty years later, apartheid is over and Nelson Mandela is the president of South Africa.

"On another occasion, Dr. Kenneth Clark, the African-American psychologist, spoke to us about his work with school desegregation. I thought to myself: 'I want to make the kind of difference in the lives of my people that he has made for his.' Little did I realize where that desire would lead me."

Back in the early 1950s, Congress had "terminated" the Menominee Tribe, along with many others. Through an act of Congress, the government broke its treaty relationships in an attempt to force Indian tribes to assimilate into the mainstream culture, to live like non-Indian people. By the 1970s, Ada's tribe had sunk to even lower levels of poverty, and they had nearly lost their tribal identity and culture. Their beautiful hunting and fishing grounds had been sold to pay taxes, the local hospital was closed, and there were very few jobs. One senator described the reservation as "teetering on the brink of collapse."

For years, tribal elders had been fighting to overturn the termination of their tribe. While she had no formal training in politics, Ada could not just stand by while Congress wiped out her tribe's history. She joined with her mother and the other women elders and founded DRUMS (Determination of Rights & Unity for Menominee Shareholders).

No one thought they could succeed. Earlier attempts to reverse the law had failed. But Ada was determined to work with her people to correct this injustice. She had learned that a key to success was mobilizing a group effort. She and the volunteers drove from home to home across the beaten roads of the reservation. They spoke with each tribal member to explain what termination meant to the tribe and what needed to be done to change it.

Then she headed to Washington, D.C. with a busload of volunteers and set up a makeshift office. They continued to engage everyone they could from congressional committee chairs and members, aides, secretaries, doormen, and parking attendants. They worked day and night to convince members of Congress to reverse what had been law for nearly twenty years.

Meanwhile, back in Wisconsin, members of DRUMS marched 150 miles from the Menominee Reservation to Madison, the capital city. The march drew widespread media attention to the plight of the tribe.

On October 16, 1973, the moment of truth arrived. Ada and her associates had gotten Congress to vote on whether or not to restore the Menominee tribal status. It was an historic occasion. If the tribe was to be given back its rights, it would be the first time that the government's Indian policy had been reversed by Indian people. If they succeeded, many other tribes would be able to use this victory as a precedent to regain their rights too. On the day of the vote, Ada, the volunteers, and other members of DRUMS attended the congressional session. They watched the vote with excitement.

One by one, the "ayes" and "nays" lit up. By the vote's conclusion, the Menominee tribe had been reinstated by a landslide 404 to 3! Her brother Bob, who had worked alongside Ada in the struggle, remarked that the Memomiee treaty chiefs, Grizzly Bear, Great Cloud, and Oshkosh, would be proud. Ada was ecstatic. "This is democracy in action!" she cried. "This is how we, the citizens, can make a change. We can do it! We *have* done it!"

From 1994 to 1997, Ada Deer was the assistant secretary for Indian Affairs in the U.S. Department of the Interior. By working to restore the rights of Native American tribes, she helped to preserve the richness of their culture and of our country's history. She had the opportunity to participate in the dedication of a new tribal health clinic on the Menominee Reservation. "In the last two generations, I've seen my tribe come back from near collapse to restored physical and cultural well-being," she says. "Our tribe has a saying that 'the hard work and determination of our people will benefit the next seven generations to come.'"

Teenagers who want to learn how to create democracy in action in their school, organization, or community by attending our six-week national training program, can call the **Encampment for Citizenship** at 888-EFC-5097.

Freedom from the Madness

STORYTELLER: ARUN GANDHI

Souren Bannerji had always thought of himself as a peaceful man. But when his wife, son, and daughter were raped and murdered by a hate-filled crowd of Muslims in Calcutta, he was led to an unthinkable response. Souren found himself joining violent Hindu mobs, seeking revenge. Before he had time to realize what he was doing, he was involved in the massacre of a Muslim family. Having killed a child, Souren knew he'd be haunted forever.

Souren only knew of one man who could return him to a path of peace. His name was Mohandas Karamchand Gandhi, but people called him "Mahatma," which means "great soul." Gandhi's remarkably ambitious mission at the time was to teach total nonviolence to the people of India. He had successfully used active nonviolence to free India from British imperialism in 1946; many desperately needed to believe that the Mahatma had at least one more miracle.

Gandhi knew all too well that anger, unchecked and uncontrolled, turned people towards mindless violence. He described anger as an energy as potent as electricity itself. He felt that if anger was abused, it could destroy and kill. But used intelligently, that same energy could enlighten human lives.

Gandhi had had to face his own anger when, as a young lawyer, he was rudely awakened to the reality of racial prejudice in South Africa. One fateful day, a white man refused to share a railroad compartment with a "Blackie." The railroad officials physically threw Gandhi off the train. His humiliation sparked an intense emotional response, but Gandhi chose not to act impulsively.

Instead, he took deep, meditative breaths, chanted the name of Rama, and found peace descending upon him. As he calmed himself, he concluded that justice is not revenge but enlightenment. And enlightenment cannot be beaten into people, it can only be revealed through active nonviolence. Throughout his life, Gandhi came to see nonviolence as more than just a means toward conflict resolution. He saw it as the building of a spiritual relationship—a relationship of Oneness.

"I don't know what I would have done if I had not met Gandhi," Souren Bannerji says. "My life, like a railway train, had been completely derailed by this hateful violence. Gandhi put the carriages back on track, and now I am moving forward again."

Gandhi himself had reached a moment of profound personal discouragement in 1946. When the British left and the country was divided—India for Hindus and Pakistan for Muslims—hundreds of thousands were uprooted from the homes and land they had occupied for generations. Murder, mayhem, and rape were widespread. Gandhi's efforts to teach people to live as one family, to put religious and personal prejudices behind them, were forgotten.

"If inhumanity is what my countrymen want, I have no desire to live," the anguished leader said. He embarked on a fast. "I tried to teach people humanity, but they prefer bestiality," he lamented. "It is better that I die than live to see this carnage." Although he was a Hindu, the Mahatma chose to fast in a little hut in the poorest Muslim ghetto of Calcutta.

If the people did not stop fighting, Gandhi would most certainly die. At seventy-eight, he no longer had the strength nor the stamina to sustain complete starvation for a prolonged period of time. Hindus and Muslims alike also realized that if Gandhi should die, they would carry a burden of guilt. The paternal relationship that Gandhi had cultivated through the years made each Hindu and Muslim feel as though their own father were about to die for the wrongs they had done.

Souren Bannerji, for one, knew he could not let the Mahatma lose his life. In his heart, he knew his own worst act of violence had been committed just the day before Gandhi announced his fast. Now this news about his hero was exactly the motivation he needed to detach himself from the mob. After about a week of internal searching, he summoned up the courage to approach Gandhi face to face.

His face streaked with tears, Souren hiked to the hut where Gandhi barely hung on to life. Quietly and reverentially, he entered the room where a medical doctor, an old friend, was patiently rubbing the Mahatma's forehead. Souren placed his head on Gandhi's feet and sobbed uncontrollably, asking forgiveness. *"Bapu* [father], forgive me. I am a sinner and deserve to die, but you must live," Souren pleaded. "We are all sinners, my son," Gandhi answered, his voice barely audible. "Come close and tell me about your sin."

Souren let the words tumble in a torrent. "I have committed a heinous crime. I murdered a Muslim family after my family was killed. My life has become a living hell. I can't accept the additional burden of your death on my conscience, Bapu. Please give up your fast."

"If you want to save my life, go and work for peace and harmony. And if you want to atone for your sin, I have a suggestion," Gandhi said. "Tell me, Bapu," Souren said. "I will do anything you say. I want peace, and I want you to give up your fast."

"First, for yourself, go and find an orphan Muslim baby and nurture the baby as your own. You must allow the baby to grow up in its own faith." Gandhi was finding speech exhausting. He lapsed into silence, then added, "We are one human race. Religion must unify us, not divide us." With these words, Souren went on his way, thinking about the great man's counsel.

Word of Gandhi's fast and his appeal for unity and harmony was broadcast widely and repeatedly. Whether the people stopped fighting because they understood his message of Oneness or simply because they wished to save his life, it is difficult to say. In any case, peace came quickly.

Souren did not forget the words Gandhi had spoken to him. In his search for an orphaned Muslim child, he found a young Muslim mother with an infant baby who had miraculously escaped death. Her husband and family had been killed, she had been repeatedly raped, and now she was an outcast. One moment of madness had changed her life forever, just as it had changed Souren's life.

As they told each other of their suffering, Souren and Miriam found they had much in common. Slowly a relationship developed. One day Souren shared with Miriam the last words he had heard from Gandhi: "We are one human race. Don't let religion divide us." Souren and Miriam were married. In the spirit of Gandhi, they decided they would study both of their religions and absorb the good each had to offer.

I met Souren in Bombay several years later. He and Miriam had two children; Miriam's son, whom Souren had adopted, and a daughter. They never forgot my grandfather's role in bringing them together: in making love and new life triumph over a past scarred by hatred and violence. Before we had parted that day, they told me how they had learned an important lesson from Mahatma. Looking at each other and at their two precious children, they confided, "We understand what Gandhi meant when he said, 'Change can come only one life at a time.'"

Experience the power of nonviolence as a proactive tool to build and maintain human relationships and avoid conflict. Call the **M. K. Gandhi Institute for Nonviolence** at 901-452-2824.

Walking Shield

Storyteller: Jane Harvey

His Lakota name is "Walking Shield." Outside the Sioux nation, he's known as Phil Stevens. For those on the Pine Ridge Reservation, he is the right man in the right place at the right time. Phil has brought together his Native American heritage, his engineering expertise, and his federal and military contacts to bring hope to his people. He is forging a renewed spirit of community where there has long been none, and he is rebuilding his nation's homeland while also rebuilding his people's trust in the United States Government.

Phil grew up in a tough East Los Angeles neighborhood with only the stories told by his dad to connect him to his Sioux roots. As the great-grandson of a Lakota chief who fought in the Battle of Little Big Horn, leadership was in his blood. He worked hard in school, went to college, and earned two engineering degrees. Eventually, he became TRW's technical director, managing a major national defense project. He then built his own multimillion-dollar engineering business.

Phil didn't think about his heritage much until a group of Native Americans took over Alcatraz in 1969, protesting generations of injustice. As he read about the dramatic events, he wondered if there was anything he could do to help. In those moments, a sense of responsibility toward his people was born in him. Later, he would recall, "I wanted to help them—but from within the existing system of government."

For the next twenty years, Phil volunteered his time with various Indian tribes throughout the country. He worked with American Indians struggling to survive in the business world. He helped negotiate various land disputes between tribes and the federal government. In 1986, he was invited by tribal leaders to visit his homeland, the Pine Ridge Indian Reservation in South Dakota. What he saw changed the course of his life.

In weather that was forty degrees below zero, people were living in one-room, unheated shacks. They slept stacked like a cord of wood. Entire families were living in old cars. Some people lived in caves. For many, there were no toilets, and water was a quarter of a mile away. It was heartbreaking, particularly the predicament of the children who had to endure poorly outfitted schools and grossly inadequate health care. The shockingly high rates of alcoholism and domestic abuse suggested a people in despair. An oppressive sense of hopelessness hovered, as it had for generations, like clouds over the reservation.

When Phil got home, he told his family, "Our people are refugees in their own land." That day he made the decision to do whatever he could to make the Sioux a strong, self-sustaining community once more. He sold his business and poured all his energy and expertise into helping his people rebuild their hopes, their dreams, and their dignity.

Phil wanted the Sioux to be the strong, proud people they had once been. He wanted them to enjoy the same benefits enjoyed by everyone else in America, but it wasn't going to be easy. "In order to succeed, people must first believe that they can," he said. "But self-esteem was scarce on the reservation. And without hope, all is lost."

"What happened a hundred years ago is current in the minds of our children," he says. "But despite the injustices done to my people, this is a great land, truly a land of opportunity." Without glossing over the tragic history of the Sioux, Phil wants to help them get over the past and get on with building their future. "I grew up with very little material wealth, but I learned that if you work very hard and you have certain abilities, you can be blessed in our society," he says. "I want to give other Native Americans a chance."

Phil worked with tribal leaders, asking them what the people wanted and needed and how they might work together to achieve those goals. They came up with a long list of needs: food, clothing, building supplies, and better health care and education. The Sioux people were willing to work hard to rebuild their lives and their reservation if Phil could help supply the resources.

From his work with government agencies, Phil knew that military bases often discarded their outdated or unused materials and supplies. He developed a strategy to get these supplies donated to the reservations and founded the Walking Shield American Indian Society to coordinate the logistics. The society started by gathering food and clothing for reservation families. Then collected books and computers for reservation schools. "We focus heavily on education so the children can have a choice for their future," Phil says. "I tell the young people they need to learn how to live in both cultures—with a moccasin on one foot and a tennis shoe on the other."

To help people on the reservation rebuild their homes so they could be warm for the winter, they took on their most ambitious undertaking and called it Operation Walking Shield. Phil learned that because of post–Cold War military cutbacks, 463 newly refurbished houses at the Grand Forks Air Force Base in North Dakota were scheduled for demolition. He called the base and a few senators from North and South Dakota. "These homes are just going to be bulldozed," he told them. "We need them for the reservations." After negotiating with the Department of Defense, he arranged for the houses to be taken to seven Sioux reservations. He even got military personnel to install the foundations for the three-bedroom, two-bathroom homes as part of their military training exercises.

Phil then turned to the Internet to locate extra construction supplies. When he found them at various military bases, he asked the Air Force if they could deliver them free of charge to the reservation. Now, instead of flying in circles above their bases to log in training flight-time, military pilots are moving supplies from bases throughout the nation to Indian reservations in South Dakota.

Since 1995, Operation Walking Shield has been able to gather more than a half-million pounds of building materials so that the Indian people can repair and rebuild their own homes. They are also talking with other military bases that are being closed to obtain additional homes, and for the U.S. Navy's Seabee construction brigades to grade and repair over 200 miles of road on two Sioux reservations in South Dakota. They have secured medical supplies and equipment from the U.S. military hospitals being shut down in Turkey, Germany, Korea, and England, resulting in treatment for 5,300 patients on the Pine Ridge Reservation.

The Society's five hundred volunteers have helped thirty of the nation's 557 tribes, about 350,000 of the one million Native Americans who live on our nation's Indian reservations. Honoring the differences between the military and Indian cultures hasn't been easy. And relationships are not always smooth. Some of the military personnel were concerned about how they would be received on the reservation. On the other hand, some tribal members were wary of trusting the government to deliver on its promises. But as the digging of the first foundations began, their fears and concerns began to fade.

Homer Whirlwind Soldier, descendant of a Sioux chief, has watched cooperation build as Phil has created magic. "There are four types of people in the world," he says. "The first two, poor-rich and poor-poor have a miserly view of life and people," he explains. "Then there are the rich-poor and the rich-rich. They are full of spirit. They do things for others. Phil is one of those."

For his work with the tribe, Phil was the first person named Special Chief of the

Great Sioux Nation. It is an extraordinary honor that many equate to the honor accorded Sitting Bull, who helped unite the Sioux people more than a century ago. But for Phil, the reward isn't in the honor, or even in the improved standard of living on the reservations. "It's not the clothing, the medical equipment, or the houses that are really significant," he says. "The most important thing that we are doing is providing hope for our people."

Let us put our minds together
and see what life we can make for our children.

SITTING BULL

Help the **Walking Shield American Indian Society** provide food, shelter, medical assistance, and education for Native Americans. To volunteer, call 714-573-1434 or visit their website: http://www.netgate.net/~ddc/walkingshield/.

A Messenger of Hope

STORYTELLER: NANCY BERG

People thought he had lost his mind when he chose to film *American Me* on East L.A.'s most dangerous streets. But growing up in East L.A.'s barrio of Boyle Heights, Edward James Olmos never did follow the rules: he was more likely to create them. Early on, the Latino actor and activist used his head, heart, and talent to find a way to succeed so others could follow. He carefully chose his acting roles to set an example. As Don Johnson's firm but fair Lieutenant Martin Castillo in *Miami Vice,* he earned great respect. When he played the tough math teacher, Jaime Escalante, in *Stand and Deliver,* he taught the lost youth of East L.A. how to earn respect.

When he was ready to direct his first film, he wanted to deliver a strong anti-drug and anti-gang message to kids in the barrios, so he went right back to East L.A. Using gang members as extras and crew, Eddie showed the painfully harsh reality of their brief, violent lives. For many of these kids, their only ambition was to one day go to San Quentin or Folsom Prison. "They go from being streetwise gang members into prison. They don't see alternatives to the gang life," Eddie says. "Without skills and with jobs hard to come by, kids start dealing to make a buck, and gangs control that world," he adds.

Eddie wanted to give them real jobs with a real future and an opportunity to break out of the gangbanger world. He also wanted to show the little ones—the ones who see everything—that people who look just like them can succeed and make their dreams come true in a healthy, positive way. "Kids in East L.A., like any kids, need hope. You get hope by having the opportunity to see a future. Right now, it looks pretty dark," Eddie says. "I think that role models could be the most important thing in these kids' lives now."

Eddie has been blessed by role models who showed him that helping others can be a way of life; he carries this on within his own family. His mother, Eleanor, worked for fifteen years in the L.A. County General Hospital AIDS ward, and his father, Pedro, helped coordinate Little League baseball in East L.A. His actress wife, Lorraine Bracco, volunteers for a group that provides housing for disabled adults, and their six children helped paint murals in L.A. inner-city schools. "It's all a labor of love," Eddie says.

Known for his big heart, Eddie encourages others to give of themselves. After the 1992 L.A. riots, he galvanized people from across the city to unite in cleaning up the horrific rubble. With the simple but powerful gesture of holding up a broom and a dustpan on TV, he invited all who were watching to join him, to take to the streets, day after day, to clear away the debris. At the 1994 Democratic National Convention, he challenged the nation to join in: "It is the task of all caring adults to be messengers of hope to these disenfranchised youth."

By filming scenes from *American Me* right in East L.A.'s streets and at Folsom Prison, Eddie helped demystify the glamour of the gang world. While he got his message across to the young actors, he soon realized it wasn't enough. Even before *American Me* was released, two of the young men from the film crew had been killed by rival gangs. When the L.A. riots nearly destroyed South Central, Eddie decided he had to do something more. "These young people just want to make a mark on the world," Eddie says. "They're in search of identity, a sense of belonging. We each have the need to belong. It's an instinctual part of being human."

Eddie thought that if other young people could see what they had learned from gang members in *American Me*, it might help to change their lives. After convincing the U.S. Department of Justice to fund an educational documentary, Eddie and his team filmed the real-life drama behind the making of the movie. Named after the Hazard Grande barrio and the Big Hazard gang, they called it *Lives in Hazard* and depicted the social power and the strange and tragic choices these young people are forced to make. They also created a study guide and national resource guide to give teachers, counselors, and ministers the practical tools they need to help at-risk youth. The team now travels across the country sharing the film with teenagers and giving them the chance to talk about their struggles and concerns.

Whether speaking at schools, churches, jails, or juvenile halls, Eddie's message is the same: "My hope is that after watching *Lives in Hazard*, each of you will be inspired to move beyond what you think is possible by helping each other take ownership of your lives, your futures, and your communities."

For thousands of Latino teens like George Sarabia, Eddie has become a messenger of hope. Before he met Eddie, George had only one goal in life: to come back from prison a hero, having earned his "stripes." By age twenty-one, he'd been in a gang for seven years, been shot, and lost his brother, Javier, to gang violence. When he was offered a small part in *American Me*, he refused, afraid of betraying his brother's memory. But then he thought of his four younger brothers, all living in jail. "If I'm not able to forgive, when will it ever stop?" he asked himself. His decision to work with Eddie and his team was the turning point in his young life.

"Eddie helped turn our community upside down," George says. "He treated me like a human being and gave me an opportunity to help and the responsibility for cleaning up the graffiti." Working with Eddie's team on *Lives of Hazard* inspired George to begin a new career producing educational videos. "It was as if he took me by the hand and showed me a different life," he says.

Gil Espinozo is another young man who now has a more hopeful future, thanks to his experience with *Lives of Hazard*. After working as a production assistant on the film, he got a job working for a casting director for a film company. His experience gave him more than just on-the-job training, it provided him with a healthy place to belong, instead of in a gang. " I spend a lot of time at the theater," he says. "They are like a family to me, they accept me for what I am, and I like that."

When Eddie is praised for his work, he always gives credit to the "real heroes" like Father Gregory Boyle, a Jesuit priest who works with young people in East L.A.'s Dolores Mission Church. "I've had to bury and say good-bye to thirty-one young men and women, all killed in this madness called gangbanging," Father Boyle says. "These were kids I knew well, who were warm, unique, and full of potential. They should not have died so young."

Young people like George and Gil are now using their life experiences to create better futures for themselves as well as others. At twenty-seven, George runs a non-profit organization, Inner City Focus, that creates violence-prevention programming that is shown in five of L.A.'s housing developments through a local cable company. Taking a moment out of his busy life, he pauses to think about his mother and those who never gave up on him. "Before she died of cancer last year, she got to see that I have a good life, that I'm married and have a family," he says. "She was happy to know her son had chosen to walk the other way."

Knowing that young people often listen better to someone their own age, Eddie sometimes invites George and Gil to share their story and their message with other young people. "We all have choices," Gil tells them. "You can do whatever you want to do. You don't have to prove anything to anyone, just to yourself." Then he pauses for a moment and says, with quiet intensity, "Think about it. What you could do. What you could be."

Whatever you can do to uplift the life of a child
is a step in the right direction toward creating true civil rights for children.
If you don't have children, find someone else's!
Take them to the library, the theater, a picnic in the park.
Use your own life to help point a young life in the right direction.

OPRAH WINFREY

Be a messenger of hope to young people in your neighborhood. Give them an opportunity for a better life. To bring *Lives in Hazard* to your school, church, or community center, call 310-557-7010.

Community Cooperation

Imagine, if you can, a society formed of all the nations of the world.
People having different languages, beliefs, opinions;
in a word, a society without roots, without memories, without prejudices,
without routines, without common ideas, without a national character,
yet a hundred times happier than our own.

ALEXIS DE TOCQUEVILLE, Democracy in America, 1835

When you get together with your family and friends, do you often find yourselves talking about what's not working: in your school, your job, your neighborhood? Do you throw up your hands in frustration thinking the problem is just too confusing, too complex or too big? Do you sometimes think you're too busy, too tired or too unimportant to make a difference?

Many of the people you meet in this chapter faced challenges similar to yours. They rallied others to overcome obstacles and found ways to make things better. Through their stories, we learn that when we work together, we can tackle some of the toughest challenges facing our communities. "Never doubt that a small group of thoughtful committed citizens can change the world; indeed, it's the only thing that ever has," said Margaret Mead.

Our communities are increasingly being asked to do more with less: to feed the hungry, care for the elderly and teach the children. At times like these, we need more community heroes: men, women and children, young and old working together, side by side for the greater common good.

Alexis de Tocqueville had great faith in the power of the American people. In 1831, when he was just 21 years old, he came from Paris to study what makes the United States such a great country. As he traveled across the country, he was impressed with the helpful, inventive and energetic people he met, gathering in small groups to solve local problems. "In France, decisions are made by professors, elected officials, professionals and managers," he said. "In the United States, it's the common people who are making these decisions." In his book, *Democracy in America,* he told how these small groups, or associations as he called them, were the building blocks for a strong society. A century and a half later, his book is a blueprint for how we can renew our country's great legacy: people working together, shaping our own future and healing our communities.

Today, there is an exciting renaissance of people in communities across the country who are rebuilding America. This chapter features just a few of the hundreds involved in this renaissance. From Boston's Dudley Street Neighborhood Initiative to Chicago's Bethel New Life Church, from the New York Restoration Project to Los Angeles' TreePeople, these stories give us tremendous hope, especially for how we can renew our inner cities. As someone once said, "Sometimes it's not enough to give someone a fish or even to teach them to fish. We have to ask who owns the pond."

These community heroes give us lots of new ideas and offer valuable life lessons. They remind us how lucky we are to be American citizens, to have the power to change things, with our votes or our voices; our time or our money. They show us that when we work together, we can have far greater impact than any one could have alone. They help us see that people power is our greatest hope for the future. Like those in these stories, we can realize our dreams and make miracles happen.

These community heroes work with others to plant a million trees, build a community playground or clean-up an entire city park. They build partnerships with schools and churches, hospitals and civic organizations and transform toxic waste dumps into vibrant neighborhoods and a struggling economy into an economic miracle. With a little imagination and ingenuity, they connect people with a common goal, rekindle the old-fashioned barnraising spirit and reweave the fabric of their community.

These community heroes each have a different story about how they started and how their lives have been transformed by getting their communities to cooperate. Just as there is no one right way for a community to solve its problems, there's never just one community hero. Each person gives what they can and enjoys creating the spirit of togetherness. Together they discover, while each one of us can make a difference, when we work together, we can make history.

- The next time you get together with your family and friends, try talking about what you could do to improve things in your world.
- Where would you begin?
- Who would you ask to join you?
- And most importantly, how would you celebrate when you get the job done?

Just think, if we all work together, we can make things better for everyone!

Ashley's Big Plans

STORYTELLER: DAWN M. HUTCHISON

Seven-year-old Ashley looked out from her bedroom window. A tall white man, wearing a baseball cap, was measuring the vacant lot in front of her apartment, and she thought she'd better have a talk with him. He probably didn't know it, but she had big plans for this space. Ashley pulled on her red and blue jumper and scampered down the stairs, braids bobbing. She darted past her mother and little brother, and ran outside.

People in the neighborhood had been watching Darell Hammond all morning from their apartment windows. Some had even walked by for a closer look at what he was doing. But Ashley was the first to speak to him. "Have you come to build the playground?" she asked. "A playground, what a great idea!" said Darell, with a smile. How could she know that? he thought to himself.

"I'm Ashley," she said. "I've been praying for a playground and I have big plans for it!" "What exactly are your plans?" Darell asked. Ashley dashed back into her apartment, returning with a handful of drawings. By then, other kids had started to gather. Darell looked at Ashley's drawings and listened to the neighborhood kids. It seemed they all had big plans. "A dinosaur you can climb on," said one. "A big ship," said another.

Darell looked around at the dry, dusty, grassless area. He could just imagine what the area was used for at nights. And he was right. The Southeast Washington D.C. housing complex was poorly maintained. The neighborhood was known mostly for its poverty and crime. The lot had become a breeding ground after dark for illegal activity: drugs, gangs, and violence.

Darell immediately liked Ashley. She reminded him of himself, when he was her age. He had lived in a children's home with his eight brothers and sisters. He was a dreamer too, always coming up with ways to build a better world for children like him. Now 24-year-old Darell had an idea to turn this place around.

A week later, he returned. This time Ashley's mother and neighbors, Ms. Marshal and Ms. Law, came out to talk with him. He told the women about Ashley's dream and how he wanted to help make it come true. "But it's going to take a lot more than imagination," he told them. That was an understatement. What it would take was one hundred volunteers and about $40,000, Darell added, as Ashley's mother stared in disbelief.

There weren't many more than one hundred adults living in the entire complex, and many of them were single mothers who had little spare time. As for the $40,000, well, that was simply going to take a miracle. Darell understood Ashley's mother's concerns, having heard them from other parents in other housing projects. But he knew they could do it. He told stories of how other neighborhoods had come together and accomplished the impossible.

The mothers weren't sure how they were going to make it happen, but for the children, they wanted to try. Even the kids wanted to do their part. "I'll help out, Darell!" Ashley yelled, as she disappeared down the sidewalk with a trail of children following her, in search of one hundred adults.

And her work paid off. A week later, the community meeting was so packed, the kids had to gather outside. With paper and crayons the youngsters drew more of their playground ideas. Inside, the adults talked excitedly. Before long, churches, grocery stores, and even the local gas stations had posters advertising the community playground project. Ashley and the other kids led a penny drive to raise money.

But as the time to build the playground neared, they were desperately short of the funds. Many people were convinced the project would never happen. "Not in that neighborhood," they said. "You'll never raise that kind of money or get enough volunteers." After a while, even Darell became disheartened.

One day when he was almost ready to give up, Ashley ran up to him, out of breath. "Darell, we raised $9.97 in pennies this week! Isn't that great?" she asked. "That can buy something, right? A sliding board maybe?" In that moment, Darell knew Ashley would never give up. "Yes, Ashley," he said, "that will buy something wonderful," as he put his baseball cap onto her little head. If this little dreamer wouldn't quit, neither would he.

That's when fate stepped in to lend a hand. Later that day, Darell got a call from the local lumber yard. They wanted to donate a semi-trailer full of wood and five truckloads of wood mulch to spread around the playground! The next day, someone else called, donating some old tires. A woman from the paint store contributed paint and brushes. The church offered to make breakfast for volunteers and send their youth group to help. The miracle Ashley's mother had asked for began to materialize.

Before long, the empty lot was filled with piles of donated supplies and swarms of people! These volunteers worked tirelessly for four straight days. On the second day it rained, but they just kept building.

The whole apartment complex was filled with the echoes of hammers and saws, and clouds of sawdust. It was a beautiful sight to see. On the last day of construction, there were nearly five hundred volunteers! Even the children helped. They filled wheelbarrows and buckets with mulch, spreading it across the enormous playground. They screwed the last bolts into the dinosaur made of tires and hung the tire swings.

When the work was done, Ashley's mom and the other neighbors stood back, amazed. Their community playground was finally finished. And they did it for the children. Ms. Marshall just shook her head, saying softly, "I never would have imagined . . ." But Ashley wasn't surprised. "Darell and I . . . we always knew," she said with confidence, as she stared at the 24-foot sliding board. "We had big plans."

Adults need children in their lives
to keep their imagination fresh
and their hearts young
and to make the future a reality
for which they are willing to work.

MARGARET MEAD

This was the first playground built out of a partnership between Darell Hammond and Dawn Hutchison, who went on to co-found **KaBOOM!,** a national nonprofit organization. KaBOOM! inspires individuals, organizations and businesses to join together to create much needed, safe, and accessible places for children to play. Through this team effort KaBOOM! helps communities create a model of partnerships that achieve positive and sustainable changes in neighborhoods nationwide. For more information, call 888-789-PLAY.

TreePeople

STORYTELLER: SKYE TRIMBLE

Camp was great fun that summer of 1970. The roasting of marshmallows and the woodsy smell of the fire made fifteen-year-old Andy Lipkis fall in love with the great outdoors. But as he looked out over the forested mountains above the city of Los Angeles, his heart sank. He knew that bark beetles were killing the pollution-weakened trees at a rapid rate.

Andy couldn't just stand by and watch them die. So he rallied his fellow campers in an amazing tree-saving adventure! They started by planting smog-tolerant trees in an old parking lot at the camp. As they swung picks and sowed seedlings, they brought life back into that piece of earth. When camp was over, one fellow camper put his hand on Andy's shoulder and said, "Let's visit the trees when we're old." Andy smiled back, knowing they would someday.

For Andy, that summer inspired an idea. "We need to spread this work to more land and more people," he thought. Then he suddenly felt afraid: not of failure, but of success. He knew that if he got people to join him, he would be responsible for something very important. It might mean he would be planting trees for the rest of his life.! But he decided to follow his heart, wherever it might lead him.

A few years later, Andy heard that the California Department of Forestry was about to destroy twenty thousand surplus seedlings. Andy asked if he could have them for another tree planting project. "That would be considered a 'gift of public funds,'" the department told him. "We're prohibited by law from giving them to you."

But Andy did not give up that easily. He called newspapers, senators, and anyone else who could pull some strings. He told them what was about to happen and begged them to do something. His calls paid off. When the *Los Angeles Times* called the governor's office to confirm the story they were planning to run, the governor's office responded by ordering the bulldozers stopped—it was just as the seedlings were being plowed under.

Andy was allowed to adopt the remaining seedlings and brought together the kids and counselors from twenty summer camps for a major replanting project. Newspaper coverage led to more donations, more volunteers, and a new law requiring the government to give surplus trees to nonprofit groups who wanted them. People from all backgrounds joined Andy and his growing pack of citizen foresters. The group's nickname, "TreePeople," took root.

In 1980, Los Angeles Mayor Tom Bradley heard about TreePeople's success. He'd read that massive city tree-planting could reduce pollution and wondered if planting a million trees in L.A. could breathe life back into his city. The Mayor was told that it would take twenty years and two hundred million dollars to accomplish such a project. But the city couldn't wait twenty years; it had to be done now. So Mayor Bradley asked TreePeople to take up the challenge. "L.A. had just been selected as host of the 1984 Olympics," says Andy. "I saw this as a perfect opportunity to demonstrate the power of cooperative action to a global audience. I told the mayor I was sure the people of L.A. could do it, at virtually no cost to the government."

Response to the Million-Tree Campaign was enthusiastic from the beginning. One nursery offered to donate one hundred thousand surplus trees to get it started if TreePeople could find a way to transport them. Through the help of Air Force Officer Andy Drysdale, TreePeople had gotten air force transport before, and once again the air force came through. Early one morning in November 1981, eight massive trucks arrived in a convoy that stretched a quarter-mile on the freeway to move the seedlings across the L.A. Basin. The Million Tree Campaign was underway. Three hundred volunteers and soldiers worked side by side all day long to move the seedlings.

As the soldiers prepared to leave at day's end, they were stopped by a beautiful sight. Standing before them, a group of volunteers holding hands had formed a circle, the sunset's glow bathing them in a warm light. The soldiers were so moved that they stopped and joined the circle, making it twice as big. Hand in hand, they celebrated not just the day, but their power to contribute to life. That day, the troops used the tools of war to create peace and unity.

With this auspicious beginning, TreePeople inspired hundreds of volunteers with an ambitious goal: they would plant the millionth tree by the 1984 Summer Olympics. For the next three years, this goal united people from all over Los Angeles to work together to create an urban forest. Billboards proclaimed, "Turn Over a New Leaf, Los Angeles." Bumper stickers read, "Rooting for the Future." People were connected by the hope that the trees they had planted could help heal their home and the planet too.

Four days before the Olympic flame was lit, the millionth tree was finally planted. The people of Los Angeles were amazed that they could do something so profound with their own hands. To celebrate, volunteers gathered in the mountains overlooking the city. Old and young, men and women, leaders from corporations, gangs, and government agencies shared smiles and danced on the mountain together.

Since the Million Tree Campaign, TreePeople has been training young people to become "managers of the environment." They teach kids that the city is a living ecosystem that can be healed and nurtured only by the informed actions of caring citizens. They deliver fruit trees to low-income families across the city so they can grow their own fresh fruit. On Martin Luther King Jr. Day, they got thousands of Angelenos to plant the largest living memorial to Dr. King ever created. Five hundred trees now line the entire seven miles of King Boulevard. TreePeople's Citizen Foresters are now organizing neighborhoods to plant and care for trees throughout Los Angeles.

Andy's summer camp dream has become the gift of a lifetime. Andy now tells city kids across the country, "Believe in your dreams. That's what made mine grow."

We have a responsibility to the largest population of all,
the hundreds of billions of people who have not yet been born,
who have a right to be, who deserve a world at least as beautiful as ours.

David R. Brower

Plant a tree and take care of it. Learn how you can help rebuild the forests in your community by calling your **state forester** or **National Association of Service and Conservation Corps** at 202-737-6272 If you live in Los Angeles and want to help Andy rebuild the forests, clean the air and strengthen the economy, call Leslie Mylius at **TreePeople** at 818-753-4600.

The Great Martha's Vineyard Barn Raising

STORYTELLERS: RICK GLASSBERG AND SUSAN SPENCE

When people heard that the Agricultural Society was selling the beloved old Ag Hall, they were sick at heart. The charming building with its gingerbread eaves had been a center of community gatherings since it was built 139 years ago. More than just a building, it was an icon, representing a cherished, old-fashioned way of life. For as long as anyone could remember, it had been home to the society's annual Livestock Show and Fair and for the past 20 years, weekly farmers' markets. Losing it would be like saying goodbye to an old friend.

Unfortunately, the society's leaders felt the hall had become too small for its needs and the growing Island community. But when drawings for a new steel-framed building were unveiled, there were lots of rumblings. This break with tradition was a bitter pill for many in the community to swallow. One young society member, Andrew "Woody" Woodruff, echoed their sentiments when he quietly said that the new plan was "a very low moment for the Agricultural Society." Like every Island kid, he had regarded the fair at the old Ag Hall as the biggest event of the year. He just couldn't let it all be lost and let go of a lifetime of wonderful memories.

Community spirit on this little patch of land just off Cape Cod is legendary. Having weathered many storms together, Islanders have developed an unwritten code that when something important needed doing, neighbors helped out. And although Woody didn't know it, he was about to embark upon a year-long struggle that would arouse the community to fight for its cherished traditions and values.

Andrew knew he had to act quickly. He turned to Rick Anderson, a respected contractor, lover of traditional buildings and restorer of old barns. Rick's building expertise and relaxed, patient manner were a perfect complement to "Hurricane Andrew's" intense energy. Rick soon located a three-story, ninety-year-old dairy barn for sale in New Hampshire and knew immediately it would be a perfect replacement for the old hall. When Woody saw it, he agreed. The barn had that special feeling.

The Ag Society leadership, however, was not convinced. They were concerned that moving, reconstructing, and adapting the New Hampshire barn would be too costly. Woody and Rick remained determined. They lobbied sympathetic society trustees and reached out to builder friends for pledges of labor, materials, and equipment.

The local newspapers closely followed the struggle and soon eloquent letters of support began appearing in every issue. "This may be the last barn erected on the Vineyard in the old style and I want my grandchildren to see it," declared one. But a good number of society leaders held fast. So Woody decided to bring his cause to the people. The petition he circulated generated 700 signatures in the first week alone. The steadily rising support of the community and outpouring of volunteered goods and services began to change opinions. A key member of the society building committee visited the snow-covered New Hampshire hilltop to inspect the barn. When he came back a believer, the tide had turned.

Woody and Rick quickly organized what came to be called the Vineyard "Barn Busters"—55 volunteers of all ages who traveled to New Hampshire to take down the barn. For five bone-chilling days, the "Busters", under Rick's direction, disassembled the huge building, tagged every piece, and packed it into trucks loaned by Island businesses. John Keene, who donated heavy earth-moving equipment, will never forget heading back to the Island in the dead of night. "We had the road to ourselves and shared a sense of history. We were bringing home this barn where we'll be looking at it for the rest of our lives."

The weather gods blessed the early November barn raising with cloudless skies and 60-degree temperatures. The "Barn Busters" were joined by scores of craftspeople and unskilled workers who volunteered to do whatever was needed. A large crowd gathered to experience the historic event. Picnic tables groaned under the weight of an endless supply of hearty food, coffee, and cold drinks. Lee Waterman, the barn's former owner, came down to the Vineyard for the event, beamed and said her late husband Asa "would have loved to be in the thick of it."

By mid-afternoon, under Rick's precise orchestration, the 150' x 45' barn frame was raised exactly as thousands had been before it—by many strong hands and open hearts. Fittingly, Woody and Rick rode up on the final piece of massive framework as it was hoisted to its resting place. Throughout the night, visitors and photographers came to pay homage to the magnificent, flood-lit skeleton glowing in the midst of a 22-acre field. A farmer descended from one of the Island's first families, commented, "It was a once in a 100-year thing—kind of religious experience."

The next morning, hundreds of volunteers returned to sheathe the roof and sides, set the windows, and begin the massive shingling. "I counted 110 people shingling—two of them five-year-old boys with their little hammers," says Andrew. "It was the greatest."

The magic continued as artisans and volunteer laborers worked to finish the building and donations of every kind poured in. In August, the society's 134th Livestock Show and Fair, appropriately called "Dawn of a New Era," was held at the new Ag Hall and received universal praise. And two ex-Vineyard summer kids, James Taylor and Carly Simon, reunited for a spectacular "barn-raising thank you" concert. It was the first time the two had shared a stage since the "No Nukes Concert" in New York City so many years before. Ten thousand people shared in the glow of that special evening and funds contributed from the concert covered a sizable portion of the project's cost.

Today the new Ag Hall, built with the love of a special community, is in great demand for meetings, weddings, special parties, concerts, pot lucks, and the premier event, the annual fair—the highlight of the Island summer.

Woody and Rick succeeded beyond their wildest expectations. The society has a magnificent new home, Vineyarders have a new community resource, and the Island has a new legend. But most importantly, the community learned once again, that while individuals can really make a difference, when they work together, they can make history.

Visit the Vineyard in mid-August and you'll be truly inspired by the community spirit radiating from the **Agricultural Society's** magnificent barn and its renowned **Annual Livestock Show and Fair**. Call the Martha's Vineyard Chamber of Commerce at 508-693-7157.

Food from the 'Hood

Storyteller: Jeffrey Madison

In 1992, when the Los Angeles riots broke out, fifteen-year-old Karla Becerra was on the bus heading home from school. She could smell the smoke and see the fires. She saw people running down the street, wheeling strollers packed with things stolen from vandalized stores. But it wasn't until a week later, when she finally got the courage to leave her house, that Karla saw the true extent of the damage.

Everywhere she looked, buildings were burned to the ground. The National Guard was patrolling the streets. To Karla, it no longer looked like the Los Angeles she knew, but like her native El Salvador. The city and its people were lost. "Everyone at our high school was talking about what needed to be done," she remembers, "but we all felt there was nothing we could do. We were afraid to even go outside."

Karla's biology teacher, Tammy Bird, was deeply upset about how her Crenshaw High School students had suffered during the riots. She wanted to help Karla and the others regain a sense of control over their lives, and that sprouted an idea. Directly behind their classroom was a cluttered, weed-infested lot. Tammy invited her students to clear this little quarter-acre plot of land and create a community garden. One by one, the students began to pull weeds, making room for the new life to come. They planted herbs and tomatoes. Next came cabbage, lettuce, and carrots. "When we first started, I knew nothing about gardens or plants," says Karla. But she quickly learned enough to be put in charge of the crop watering, weeding, and harvesting operations.

The once vacant lot was soon blossoming with colorful and tasty vegetables. The student gardeners had transformed a wasteland into a wonderland. Everyone loved it!

Their once damaged community was coming back to life. Ms. Bird and her urban farmers then formed a company, using a vacant classroom as an office. The students would own and operate their business, naming it "Food From the 'Hood." Ms. Bird invited another adult volunteer, Melinda McMullen, to teach the students how to create a successful company through public relations.

The students were all very proud when they shared 25 percent of their first harvest with the homeless at Crenshaw's Community Outreach Centers. "We all fell in love with the garden because we were growing happiness there," recalls Karla. "Knowing that people in our community were fed by our food and that Thanksgiving or Christmas dinners would be extra special for our neighbors made me grateful to be a part of this."

The rest of the crop was sold at local farmers' markets. The student-owners were happy to be able to provide fresh vegetables to the community and make money in the process! As the business thrived, they took it a step further, investing the profits in their own future. They decided to use the money earned from produce sales as college scholarships for seniors graduating from their school. Now they were starting to really reap the fruits of their labor. But the proceeds supported only a few scholarships.

The students wanted to create something that might help all of them pay for college. Looking at the wide variety of vegetables they were growing, they saw the ingredients for a wonderful salad. The only thing missing was the dressing! So, the students created their own; they called it, "Straight Out of the Garden: Creamy Italian Salad Dressing."

The student-owners had to learn a lot about accounting, as well as making, marketing, and distributing a new product. They had to learn to understand the distinct language of business in order to meet with grocery executives to talk about their salad dressing. "In the beginning, I was very shy, a little girl stuck in the corner with nothing to say," Karla says. "The first time I had to give a presentation, I cried. I didn't want to face those business people," she now says, laughing. But over time, with the support of her fellow students, Karla found the confidence to speak with ease and from the heart.

In November 1994, His Royal Highness, Prince Charles of England, accepted an invitation to visit the Food From the 'Hood garden. The students voted to select one student to give the prince the tour of the garden. They chose Karla. The girl who was once too shy to speak out in the classroom braved a crowd of more than two hundred reporters armed with cameras and microphones.

"Karla was never one of those kids in danger of being involved with crime. What she was in danger of was never realizing her potential," says Tammy. "Food From the 'Hood changed all that. Just as our garden blossomed, so did she; into a confident, supportive, and outgoing person." Karla adds, "We had a goal of doing something that would help everyone, all races, come together. And we did it. We showed the world that with hard work and a dream, anything is possible."

Today, Food From the 'Hood's salad dressings are sold in more than two thousand grocery and whole food stores nationwide. The students' business has grown just as their vegetables did. Thanks to the scholarship fund, graduating seniors go straight out of high school into college. And it all began by planting a few seeds in a vacant lot and from a teacher's desire to bring out the best in her students.

Buy our **Food From the 'Hood** Straight Out of the Garden: Creamy Italian Salad Dressing and Straight Out of the Garden: Honey Mustard Salad Dressing and help our graduating seniors go straight out of high school into college. If you don't find it, ask your grocery store to join the more than 2,000 grocery and whole-food stores nationwide who carry it.

It Will Take a Miracle

Storyteller: Patricia Broughton

"It's like a war zone." That's not a nice way to describe the neighborhood you call home, but for Porter Billingsley of Chicago's West Garfield Park, that's simply the way it is. He has lived here for twelve years and can hardly recall a day gone by that somebody hasn't been shot, stabbed, beaten, or killed. "On every corner, we've got kids selling drugs," he says. "As a black man, I see our race going down the drain. Somebody has to do something."

And so he has; he and hundreds like him. They've joined with the African-American congregation of Bethel Lutheran Church and its community outreach program, Bethel New Life. Their mission, Take Back the Streets, seeks to reclaim their neighborhood from drug dealers and gangbangers. Intensive street action is combined with other community policing strategies to combat the highest murder rate of Chicago's seventy-seven districts. The battle is being waged against the core cause of the murders: a thriving open-air drug trade that makes a mockery of law and order.

Recently, one hundred men from Bethel took to the streets. Their enemies carry automatic weapons and a chilling disregard for human life. But these peaceful warriors were armed only with flashlights and black T-shirts calling for a "Cease Fire." Porter marched that Saturday night, as he has on countless other nights. He says of the marches, "Maybe they don't do much, but they're something. They show the gangs there are people out here who are not going to take it any more. As men, we must set the tone for the young ones." He adds, "We're supposed to be examples."

Reflecting on Saturday's march, Mary Nelson, president of Bethel New Life, quotes one of her favorite scriptures from Luke 1:8, the story of the persistent widow: "'Won't God protect His chosen ones who pray to Him day and night? Won't He be concerned for them? He will surely hurry and help them.'" "We must continue to be faithful," Mary exhorts her staff. "God will make a way out of no way." She has staked her life on this promise. Together with a strong and committed staff and board, she has brought new life to this struggling community on Chicago's west side.

Mary came here in 1965 to help her brother David move from his comfortable pastorate in Country Club Hills, Illinois, to a new congregation in West Garfield Park. She was planning to return home, but when she saw the magnitude of the work to be done, she had a change of heart. "I couldn't leave my brother here by himself. I had to stay," she says. Three days after arriving, they were pelted with rocks and stones, caught in the first of five riots that nearly destroyed Chicago's west side. "In the beginning, we moved quickly. There wasn't a lot of time for committee meetings and long-range planning," Mary recalls. "If the church was going to do anything, we had to be out in the streets. That's where the hurt and agony is. So, that is where we've been for over thirty years."

Over the years, she helped David turn a dying church into a robust spiritual community of more than six hundred active members. They started taking risks early. Their community outreach program began in 1979 with the purchase of a crumbling three-flat apartment building. Using borrowed money from personal credit cards, they raised the funds for renovations.

A deep and abiding faith sustains David, Mary, and the members of Bethel. It is this faith that allows the church to offer its property as collateral, time and time again, when banks refuse to make a loan. It is this faith that allows Bethel's community-based board of directors to take on massive projects like the Beth-Anne Life Center.

In 1988, St. Anne's Hospital closed its doors to the community. Shirley McDonald lived across the street from the hospital. She noted, "When the hospital closed down, the crime rate went up." A headline in *Crain's* business newspaper declared, "It will take a miracle" to resurrect the facility.

But they hadn't counted on the people of Bethel. Together, they bought the 9.2 acre site, adapted it for community use, and named it the Beth-Anne Center. It now boasts a state-of-the-art child development center and a small business center for local entrepreneurs. It is also home to the area's only bank and drug store. Senior housing and a cultural center are also currently under development.

Residents like Shirley are delighted. She was especially glad to see construction of the day care center. At the time, she was pregnant with her sixth child. Her daughter, Richelle, now three, has just started attending the center. "I love it," Shirley says. "It's really a beautiful godsend for all of us."

The Beth-Anne Center is only one example of the miraculous work of this congregation. In 1993, when the Chicago Transit Authority (CTA) seemed determined to close down the west side elevated transit line, Bethel helped rally community and suburban leaders. The coalition convinced the CTA not only to *not* close the line, but to invest $350 million to completely renovate it and to construct a three-story commercial "Superstation" at a key stop in West Garfield Park.

The Bethel success stories go on and on. Garbage-strewn vacant lots and unemployed residents became the building blocks for creating a recycling buyback center, which put more than $1 million into the hands of local residents. A Senior Services program employs more than two hundred formerly out-of-work residents and keeps some 750 seniors out of nursing homes by providing in-home care.

Bethel has also gotten twenty-five women off welfare by helping them start day care programs in their homes. "There truly has been a miracle worked in my life," said Nora Bryant, who lived in a roach and rat-infested basement apartment not so long ago. She put some 750 hours of hard labor into building her home, enough "sweat equity" to earn the down payment.

Today, Bethel New Life serves as a model for and gives hope to the entire nation. Through his efforts, twenty thousand people are participating in rebuilding the political, economic, and spiritual fabric of their community. They are living proof of what a group of inspired people can do for a community they love. Reflecting on the many miracles brought to West Garfield Park through this church, Pastor Nelson says, "Even though we didn't know what was ahead, God did. He brought together committed people who have labored hard to produce far more than we ever imagined. We thank God for his Spirit moving in these people."

If you can see problems as possibilities, can hang in for the long haul, and want to partner with a community rebuilding itself from the inside out, call **Bethel New Life** at 773-826-5540. Come help us weave a healthier sustainable community on Chicago's west side.

Rebuilding L.A. in a Day

Storyteller: Tom Dellner

"Today," said organizer Marianne Tyler with confidence, "we will change our city forever." It was the first L.A. Works Day, and several busloads of nervous, yet excited, volunteers were heading for projects all over Los Angeles. Hundreds of citizens were joining together, taking the first step on the road to rebuilding their struggling community.

Known worldwide for its bright sun, beautiful scenery, and Hollywood stars, L.A. has also gained a reputation for violence, poverty, and racial tension. The L.A. riots of 1991 was the latest black eye on the face of this high-profile city.

Richard Dreyfuss was profoundly upset by what he saw happening and he knew that the answers to many of the city's problems were in the hands and hearts of its people. "I sensed an enormous untapped resource in our community," he said. "People wanted to help, but didn't know what needed to be done or how to get involved." One day, he joined with a group of young professionals, mostly from the entertainment community, who wanted to mobilize their energies for the community. Richard wrote a check to get it started and L.A. Works was born.

On the first L.A. Works Day in 1993, a thousand volunteers traveled to work sites from South Central to the San Fernando Valley. They took shovels, paint, brushes, trees, and flowers. The army of volunteers painted murals, restored playgrounds, removed graffiti, beautified schools, and planted trees. And each year since, people from all over Los Angeles join together one day a year to renew this tradition and repair their city. A lot of work gets done in one day, but perhaps even more important is the boost in morale it brings to L.A.

Volunteers working with local neighbors share stories about their lives and families and talk about the city's problems. "When you're working together side by side, splattered in paint, barriers that might otherwise exist tend to go away," says Dreyfuss. "It's very simple," he explains, "A school needs a sandbox. So people help build one: the teachers and students from the school as well as people from the neighborhood."

"Maybe it sounds superficial, cleaning up school grounds when there are so many deeper and more complicated social problems in Los Angeles," says site coordinator Bill Schwaab, "but you've got to start somewhere." And when you do, the magic spreads. He continues, "Caring becomes contagious. The attitudes of entire neighborhoods change. People take more pride in their community. Now when they see graffiti being painted, they call the police. This didn't happen before. It can all be traced to one day's work." Even some gang members show respect by not repainting the graffiti.

Marianne and thousands like her have discovered that L.A. Works Day makes it easy to volunteer. "You make a minimal time commitment in an absolutely safe environment," she says. "You're with thousands of other people on a Sunday afternoon. You need no special skills and they provide all the supplies."

During the rest of the year, L.A. Works guides many people toward giving more of their time to other organizations. Volunteers renovate lower-income housing with Habitat for Humanity, care for those living with AIDS, and go hiking with runaway teens from the Angel's Flight Shelter. And L.A. Works' seventy-five hundred volunteers are as diverse as the projects they undertake.

"Los Angeles is celebrated for its wealth of talented people in different fields, but these groups never interact. The downtown business society, the aerospace engineers, the west-side money, the east-side academics, the artists, the Hollywood people, and the Black, Hispanic, Asian, White, and Jewish communities," Dreyfuss says. "The irony is that our strength as a city and a country is not in our commonalities, but in our differences. We are not linked together by ancestry, religion, or experience, but by a set of ideals that are uniquely American." And, as Dreyfuss puts it, "L.A. Works manifests those ideals."

When L.A.'s diverse people come together, synergy happens. "There is excitement in the air," says Dreyfuss. "To see thousands and thousands of people, who don't have to be there, turn out to paint, plant, and help rebuild the city, it's enormously moving."

As a result of his experience with L.A. Works, Dreyfuss believes that everyone should give a year of service to their country before graduating from high school. "The military, hospitals, agriculture, or community service, it's their choice," he says. "It would help our young people feel connected to their country and to the world. People see the problems in our society and say they can't be solved," he says. "This isn't really true. At L.A. Works we solve small problems each day. This means more to people than all the good work that is done. It means that together we can solve the larger problems, too."

Florencia Lopez agrees. As the president of the Resident Advisory Council for the Ramona Garden Development, she saw what happened when L.A. Works Day came to her neighborhood last year. "It was a very special day," she says. "Everyone was really motivated with a spirit of harmony and cooperation to do something positive for our community. Thank you L.A. Works for this opportunity. It was especially good for our young people. Working together we can accomplish more than we ever could alone."

Join the seventy-five hundred volunteers who contribute more than seventy-five thousand hours each year to help more than 650 southern California communities. Call **L.A. Works** at 213-936-1340 and help rebuild our great city.

The Healing on the Mountain

STORYTELLER: SUKI MUNSELL, PH.D.

Mount Tamalpais, a home of northern California's magnificent giant redwood trees, is a magical place. From just about anywhere in the San Francisco Bay area you can see the mountain's crest form the reclining profile of the sleeping Indian princess, Tamalpais, her face lifted upward to the sky. Legend tells that this Miwok Indian maiden was cast under the spell of her shaman mother, who feared the girl's betrothal to a warrior brave of a neighboring tribe. The princess will awaken, the story goes, when peace reigns among all people.

For those living nearby, the beautiful mountain offers a reprieve from overcrowded and overbusy lives. We walk through the fragrant forests, camp in the lush green valleys, and celebrate marriages on the sunny slopes overlooking the vast panorama of the Pacific Ocean. But in a heartbeat, the mountain was violated; the cherished serenity it offered was stolen.

In 1980, a killer stalked the trails. One by one, he murdered four women who were climbing in the quiet hills. The mountain, once a safe haven and source of refuge for city dwellers, quickly became a symbol of fear: a place to be avoided. Campers sought other grounds. Hikers chose other paths. In the months that followed, frustration and rage tormented the people of the surrounding communities. Our beloved Mount Tamalpais was held hostage, and we felt powerless to set her free. Until the day Anna invited us to help heal the mountain.

Anna Halprin is a dance teacher with a special passion for helping people heal themselves. A refugee from the traditional world of modern dance, Anna has pioneered ways of helping communities to heal through expressive dance. "Cultures everywhere in the world have channeled the power of dance to help bring rain, hunt, raise crops, and initiate the young," she said. "Dance can renew, inspire, create, and heal the life of a community."

In the ghetto of Watts, Anna inspired people to heal racial tensions in the community. She's helped San Francisco's gay community face the AIDS crisis and heal their torn lives. And in hospitals, she's encouraged patients to challenge their illnesses as she herself had done to free her own body from cancer.

That Easter, she and her husband, Lawrence, gathered members of our community together to help us discover our power to heal the mountain. We explored our feelings for the mountain and recalled why it was special to each of us. We remembered why it was worth reclaiming. Anna and Lawrence encouraged us to face our fears and express our rage artistically through dance. Under her guidance, we became a thundering tribe who danced our mountain alive. Through our performance, we evoked the spirit of Princess Tamalpais and enacted the capture of the killer. In the audience, the mothers of the four slain women openly wept.

At sunrise the next morning, we gathered to pray on the mountain. Spiritual leaders from many faiths helped us strengthen our community's soul. Our "tribe" reconnected with the healing spirit of Mother Nature. Dancing and chanting as we made our way down the mountain, we stopped to pray at the trail-side murder sites. Several days later the killer was captured and peace returned to the mountain.

Since 1980, Anna and community returned to dance every year on Easter Sunday to continue to purify the mountain. For years, one hundred dancers trained for a full week, performed on Friday and Saturday night, and returned to the mountain on Easter Sunday morning. The dance developed into a dance for peace, and by 1985, this celebration had gained worldwide exposure. It was performed at the United

Nations Plaza in New York City, on Hitler's grave in Potsdam, Germany, and traveled across the Pacific to Australia and Asia. Eventually, Anna created a score which could be done by people of all ages all around the world. It is called the "Planetary Dance," and has been danced all around the globe. Each year on Easter Sunday, the dance is performed in as many as thirty-six countries on six continents as the first worldwide dance for peace. But to us, it will always be a dance for our mountain.

Each Easter morning as the sun rises, our community gathers in prayerful celebration. Families come, bringing their youngsters who join the Children's Dance. By sunset many of us journey down to the beach where the mountain is kissed by the Pacific Ocean. We dance exuberantly with gratitude. The flames from the bonfire caress the shadow of Mount Tamalpais. In the fire, I think I can see her spirit dancing with us.

The hikers and campers have returned to the mountain. Laughter and song once again echo throughout its valleys. The mountain has been healed, and so have we.

Hope is the thing with feathers
that perches in the soul.
And sings the tune without the words
and never stops at all.

EMILY DICKINSON

Organize a dance, theater, or other arts group with your local church, synagogue, or community center. Come to the Anna's Planetary Dance next Easter Sunday or invite her to bring transformational healing through dance to your community. Call the **Tamalpa Institute** at 415-457-8555.

From an Acorn to an Oak

STORYTELLER: FRANCES MOORE LAPPÉ

Phil Donahue enthusiastically introduced his next guest. "And now please welcome Elena Hanggi, just an ordinary American!" The huge crowd roared its approval. Elena sat between a Democratic congressman from Massachusetts and a Republican congressman from Texas who was also a government banking official.

It was the late 1980s, and Donahue was diving into the savings and loan crisis. In her disarmingly soft southern-accent, tinged with a slight lisp, Elena proceeded to straighten out the viewers and her distinguished copanelists. "Every single one of us will pay at least one thousand dollars in taxes to clean up this mess created by a few high rollers," she told us. Her indignation was palpable.

Elena was a guest on one of TV's most-watched shows because she is an authority on the banking industry—the intricacies of which baffle most of us. But that was only one reason why she had been invited. Elena was also speaking from a moral ground and from her deepfelt sense of what was fair.

In her late 40s, Elena had already become a national leader of one of the largest citizen groups in the country—ACORN: The Association of Community Organizations for Reform Now—which was built from the ground up by low-income people.

Soon after Elena's appearance on Donahue, ACORN succeeded in getting the desires of ordinary Americans into the law governing the fallout from the savings and loan collapse. This crisis threw a lot of foreclosed property onto the market. The question was, who would get it? Thanks to a law conceived largely by ACORN, tens of thousands of low-income Americans had a chance to buy some of that property, including families for whom home ownership had seemed an impossible dream. Perhaps even more important, the law specifies that ordinary citizens like Elena will now have an official seat on the board governing the thrift industry, through citizens' representatives who are there to make sure that savings and loans serve the needs of all Americans.

Ever since I met Elena, I had pondered that elusive question, "Why her?" And therefore, "Why any one of us?" What makes it possible for anyone of us growing up within narrowly prescribed boundaries to transcend them and to break new moral ground for our society?

Elena's early upbringing gave little indication that she would have a future as a national leader. Growing up in Little Rock, Arkansas, in the 1950s, her home was typically blue-collar: her mom was a hairdresser and her dad was an army man. They didn't teach her to take a public stand for her beliefs, although she does say, laughing, that her mom sent a few signals that set her family apart. "We were the only kids on the block allowed to buy music by black artists. So all my friends came to my house to listen to Chuck Berry!"

But there was one particular moment, Elena remembers, when what she had been told to believe all her life suddenly collided head-on with what she could see for herself. It was 1957 and Little Rock's Central High, Elena's school, was being forcibly integrated. One day, as she and her classmates rose to pledge allegiance to the flag, she looked out the school's big open windows.

"Standing there, hand on my heart, I could hear the roar of a crowd getting louder and louder," she told me. "I looked to my left down Park Street in front of the school, and I saw a mob of white people chasing an elderly black man. I thought, 'Oh my God, if they catch him, they'll kill him!' Suddenly, everything seemed unreal. It felt like I was in a science fiction movie or something. How could I be standing here mouthing these beautiful words about liberty and justice while that was happening right outside?" In that moment, Elena questioned everything her friends accepted.

It was a moment she never forgot. But for the most part, in the years that followed, she went along quietly. She got married, had two daughters, and lived an everyday kind of life. Then one day in the summer of 1974, there was a knock on Elena's door. A neighbor asked Elena whether she would attend a meeting to help fight a proposed freeway threatening to cut through their neighborhood. Her neighbor was a member of ACORN, which had formed just a few years earlier. "Sure, I'll be there," she told them, "I'll fill up a chair at your meeting but don't even think of asking me to speak in public."

"Even though I told them I would not speak, they didn't listen," Elena says now. "They wanted me to lay out reasons ACORN was opposed to the freeway. When my turn came to speak, I was so frightened, they almost had to push me to the mike. I was terrified . . . but at the same time I was grateful," she remembers. "Someone saw something in me I didn't see in myself."

Having experienced the power of being pushed, Elena now heads the official "pushing-people" arm of ACORN: The Institute for Social Justice. This traveling training institute prepares the housekeepers, clerks, shopkeepers, secretaries, cooks, waitresses, and truck drivers of ACORN's one hundred thousand members. She's seen people so afraid of speaking out in her training class that they break down in tears when asked to introduce themselves to the group. And she's seen those same people emerge five days later as moving public presenters and confident activists.

"Looking out my window now," Elena said, "I can see city workers cutting the curbs to put in ramps for wheelchairs. Another example of what we've accomplished."

The benefits to society are clear, but for Elena there are personal rewards too. "My four daughters are not afraid, like I was, to speak out," Elena says with obvious satisfaction. One daughter is even hoping to buy a house soon because of the affordable, subsidized interest rate made possible by the law ACORN helped create and pass.

"You know, I never thought that acting on what I believe is right would have led me into learning all about banking," Elena says, surprised herself about the path her life has taken. "It all seemed so far out of reach, but I found out a big secret along the way . . . that all that stuff they want you to believe is out of reach for average, working people is really understandable by any of us."

★

If you think you are too small to be effective
you have never been in bed with a mosquito.

BETTE REESE

Want to uncover your potential for working with neighbors to bring change to your neighborhood, city, state, and nation? Call **ACORN** at 202-547-2500.

Making Lemonade from Lemons

STORYTELLER: JENNY MIDTGAARD

Joe Tysdal was the kind of volunteer everyone would love to have. Dedicated to the success of each year's Gilroy Garlic Festival, he carried out his volunteer duties enthusiastically. Even when he was battling leukemia, being kept alive with an oxygen tank strapped to his side, he would arrive on Monday with a crew of guys to construct the Festival's "Gourmet Alley" by Friday. Then, he'd put in three long, hot, and tiring days over his famous pasta pots, cooking *pasta con pesto* for the thousands of annual visitors.

Joe's superhuman commitment and his perseverance were not unusual, however. The Gilroy Garlic Festival inspires extraordinary dedication, it brings people together, and it has bolstered a community in need of pride and a sense of identity.

Rudy Melone remembers coming to Gilroy in the late 1970s and being shocked. He had heard the snide remarks and the backhanded jokes. He'd seen the self-deprecating attitude of the residents. When people visited this California town of thirty-two thousand, residents would apologize for the odor. If asked about Gilroy, few townsfolk would mention the beautiful garlic fields, which stretched for many miles, or the huge garlic processing plants. They figured it was better to just ignore the garlic. Lots of people hated the smell and the taste, anyway.

"There was a general embarrassment about the garlic," says Melone, who had been hired as president of the local community college. "But as I saw it, it was something to be proud of." An Italian American who had been raised on garlic, he set out to remedy the problem of the town's low self-esteem, using his own version of making lemonade from lemons.

Enter the Gilroy Garlic Festival. Melone had heard of a small town in France, Arleux, which hosted eighty thousand people at its annual garlic festival. In fact, they were claiming to be the garlic capital of the world. Melone knew Gilroy's garlic production and processing far surpassed that of any other area. He needed a way to convince Gilroyans that they should have a garlic festival of their own.

Volunteerism had always been strong and vital to the town's character. Community groups were big in Gilroy, as were bake sales, car washes, door-to-door magazine peddling, and lots of little sales to raise money for good causes. Appointed as the Rotary's fund-raising chairman, Melone was charged with raising money for their projects and for the Chamber of Commerce. If he could package a garlic festival as a fund-raising effort, he might just get the town's support, he thought.

His first step was to sell the idea to his Rotary Club. He copied reams of documents, all about the healthful effects of garlic, the abundance of garlic recipes, and the love of garlic in Arleux and pasted them around the room at the next meeting. Interesting stuff, said the members, but so what? Undeterred, Melone drove down to the local cafe and had coffee with the garlic growers who gathered there every morning.

"Couldn't we get all the growers together, put on a nice lunch, and really show the Rotary people the value of garlic?" he asked them. Don Christopher, now one of the world's largest garlic shippers, agreed to cohost, with Melone, a lunch prepared by chef Val Filice.

They invited both local and national media to the garlic meal, which they called "incredible." The Gilroy community leaders stood around chatting with the visiting journalists. Betsy Bosley of the *Los Angeles Times* took Christopher aside and urged him to run with the idea of a garlic festival. "This is going so well, we should do it every year," Melone said casually to Harvey Steinem of the *San Francisco Chronicle*. The next week, Steinem wrote about the luncheon and the festival idea in his column and the bulb was rolling.

Of course, there were skeptics. In fact, several of the town's big shots laughed out loud when Melone suggested the First Annual Gilroy Garlic Festival. But he kept asking, and when planning started, they were all there to help. Seven months later, the first Gilroy Garlic Festival was held, funded on borrowed money and planned by a small committee with big hopes and more than a few doubts.

Melone remembers the quiet on the first morning of the festival: the stillness, light traffic, and slight fog. "We wondered if anyone would come to our party," he says. But after awhile the sun popped through, bringing with it hordes of garlic lovers. The crowd was overwhelming. The fifteen thousand tickets printed for the event ran out, so volunteers were forced to collect them at the entry and run back to the ticket booth to recycle them!

Meanwhile, local women were frantically cooking pasta in a house on Bloomfield Road. In his booming voice, Filice, head chef of Gourmet Alley, ordered several men to drive to Monterey for more prawns and squid. Halfway through the first day, the beer committee chairman called Budweiser: "Heck, forget the kegs. Start sending us the trucks!"

That first festival netted nineteen thousand dollars. In the eighteen years since, the festival has brought more than four million dollars to the community. More than four thousand volunteers from all parts of Gilroy have worked hundreds of jobs, earning an hourly wage which they then get to donate to the charity of their choice. Collectively, they make big contributions to the community they care so much about.

In 1995, the local Elks Lodge raised more than ten thousand dollars to buy eyeglasses for poor children, aid a family who had lost their home in a fire, and build a flag-lined walk to honor veterans. Hope Rehabilitation, which teaches disabled people to work, earned more than three thousand dollars. Melone's idea of getting the town to celebrate garlic rather than being ashamed of it has clearly been more than successful. But there were other benefits as well.

"What I'm most proud of is how the festival has brought the people of Gilroy together," says Melone, now seventy-one. Gilroy's multicultural community—Hispanic, Caucasian, Asian, as well as the original Italian families—all pitch in. Festival volunteers often find themselves working elbow to elbow with someone they might never have met. School parents work with Gilroy Hispanic Chamber of Commerce members. Boy Scouts sell programs alongside 4-H members. High school football players dish up pasta next to choir members.

Melone asks, "How often can you raise dollars for your favorite cause, but also have fun yourself?" Enjoyable as it is, the festival is only half of the event for the volunteers. Each year they're rewarded for their hard work at the volunteers' barbecue, hosted by the festival on Labor Day weekend. At the barbecue, volunteers share stories and greet the people they now know so well after working together.

Sadly, Joe Tysdale didn't make it to the 1996 volunteers' barbecue. He'd been too ill to come to the festival as well. But he did send his son, daughter-in-law, and even several relatives from out of state, to work his shifts.

As the exhausted crew began to close down Gourmet Alley Sunday night, they received word that Joe was dying. Steve Morrow, his friend and fellow Elks member, says, "We were closing down shop at roughly the same time Joe was dying. As exhausted as we were, we felt as though Joe was there, watching over the last detail, holding on just long enough to be sure we had done a good job."

Joe died that night. But his spirit lives on in the hearts of all the dedicated volunteers who make Gilroy a pretty special place to visit and a very proud community in which to live. "It's an incredible success story," says Rudy Melone, "for all of us."

Volunteering is good for the soul.

STEVE ALLEN

Work with your local **Rotary Club** to turn your community's problems into win-win situations. Come to the 20th annual **Gilroy Garlic Festival** July 24–26, 1998, and see how we have made lemonade out of lemons. Call 408-842-1625 or visit our website at http://www.garlicfest.com.

Streets of Hope

Storyteller: Holly Sklar

Ché Madyun remembers the stench of smoke and garbage. She remembers the piercing wail of sirens, day and night. She remembers lying awake, heart pounding, afraid her home would be the next to burn.

In 1976, Boston's Dudley neighborhood looked like an earthquake had hit it. There were blocks and blocks of vacant land where homes and stores used to be. As the neighborhood became more racially diverse, it was abandoned by government, banks, businesses, and landlords. Some landlords burned down apartment buildings to collect insurance money.

By the time the smoke cleared, one-third of the Dudley neighborhood was a wasteland. People and businesses from outside the neighborhood used the vacant land as illegal dumping ground for all kinds of garbage, from old refrigerators to toxic chemicals. Kids vomited from the stench.

Ché and her neighbors were not about to let their children's future be thrown away. That's how the Don't Dump on Us campaign was born. Organized by a group called the Dudley Street Neighborhood Initiative (DSNI), hundreds of neighborhood residents held meetings and marches and actually convinced the new mayor to help clean up the dumps and enforce the laws against illegal dumping. After that, Dudley people felt a new kind of fire: they believed if they could clean up the dumps, they could do anything.

Working together in DSNI, Ché and her neighbors became powerful visionaries. They turned the usual top-down urban planning process upside down, they made it into bottom-up urban planning, so the people who actually lived there would have the greatest say in what happened to their own neighborhood. With support from the local Riley Foundation, hundreds of residents participated in planning their urban village. They dreamed of a livable place with affordable housing, community centers and gardens, playgrounds, small businesses, and a town common. Together, in 1987, they moved the city of Boston to endorse the plan and become a partner in rebuilding the neighborhood.

Dudley residents then made history by becoming the nation's first community group to win eminent domain authority. That gave the community the right to buy and develop thirty acres of vacant land in the most burned-out part of the neighborhood. A decade later, the area that once looked like an earthquake had hit it is alive with families living in new homes.

Yet Dudley would need a lot more than new housing to really transform the neighborhood. "You can build all the doggone houses you want," says Ché, who served as DSNI's president from 1986 until 1995, "but if you're not trying to touch people's lives, you're just putting up bricks and mortar." So DSNI restored a local park and started a summer camp. It continues to sponsor annual festivals and neighborhood cleanups. The group organizes tenants, works with employment programs, and much more. It encourages local nonprofit service agencies to be responsive to resident needs and priorities. In 1992, when Los Angeles exploded with the fury of urban America's crushed dreams, Dudley was surging with the power of dreams unfolding. As Ché says, "Hope is the great ally of organizing."

An African proverb teaches: "Together, we find the way." DSNI's Declaration of Community Rights reads:

> We, the youth, adults, and seniors of African, Latin American, Caribbean, Native American, Asian, and European ancestry, are the Dudley community. [Once] we were Boston's

dumping ground and forgotten neighborhood. Today, we are on the rise! We are reclaiming our dignity, rebuilding housing. and reknitting the fabric of our communities. Tomorrow, we realize our vision of a vibrant, culturally diverse neighborhood where everyone is valued for their talents and contributions to the larger community.

Today, a beautiful town common provides a welcoming gateway to Dudley. People come from different states and even other countries to exchange ideas about community building with Dudley residents.

In 1996, DSNI launched a new series of community visioning meetings, where residents dream aloud and plan how to make those dreams come true over the next ten to twenty years. "Our village is a culturally vibrant, active, people-centered, mutually supportive community with a sense of can-do optimism," they wrote. Their vision of the future includes lifelong learning in schools and community centers, thriving businesses, organic farming, and a safe and healthy environment.

Of course, Ché Madyun is far from the only community hero in this story. "People worked like a family," she says. DSNI, in fact, is an extended family, with over twenty-five hundred neighborhood members and thousands of outside supporters. Hundreds of residents have actively served on DSNI's board and committees over the years. Young people are encouraged to serve on the DSNI board and its varied committees, as well as their own youth committee. To illustrate their theme of "unity through diversity," the youth committee created a beautiful mural featuring neighborhood children, teenagers, and elders. Ché is dancing in it.

Now Dudley's youth help run summer programs. They grow food on neighborhood land and are mentors for younger children. They even planned a future community center during Dudley's Young Architects and Planners Project. The success of the project in Ché's words, is "based on the dreams and creativity of youngsters too often written off by others as worthless." Youth Leader Carline Dorcena remembers the words of former DSNI Director Gus Newport, "'The seed you plant on the first day of spring—it's going to grow and keep on growing.'"

The attitude of its youth is a measure of this once devastated community's extraordinary progress. Carline Dorcena, a child of Haitian immigrants and who knows prejudice firsthand, is always trying to build bridges where other people put walls. Now in college, Carline hasn't decided yet what career she will choose. But whatever it is, she plans to use her education to improve life in Dudley. "Whatever I am, be it a lawyer, an educator, a philosopher, a corporate psychologist, or an international businesswoman, I want to come back to our community," she says. She's definitely proud of her neighborhood. "People can look at you and say, 'I respect you because you're from Dudley and I know you're trying to do something.'"

The vision of a new Boston must extend
into the heart of Roxbury and into the mind of every child.

MARTIN LUTHER KING JR.

Reclaim a vacant lot in your neighborhood, and put it to communmity use. To learn from **Dudley Street Neighborhood Initiative** and their dynamic community work in progress, visit them at www.cpn.org/DSNI or call 800-533-8478 to order the book **Streets of Hope** and 201-652-6590 to order their film **Holding Ground.**

Papa to His People

STORYTELLER: DON CORATHERS

In the end, they took Ernie back to Kentucky and laid him to rest on top of a hill in Knox County. He had been away for almost forty years.

He had left his Eastern Kentucky home as part of the greatest internal migration in this country's history. Beginning as a trickle out of the hills and hollers of Kentucky, Tennessee, and West Virginia in the early part of this century, and becoming a torrent during and after World War II, hundreds of thousands of families moved from hard-scrabble farms and played-out coalfields in Appalachia to find a better life in the city.

The Appalachian migration is not as well known as the Dust Bowl exodus of the thirties because it didn't have a John Steinbeck to write about it, but it did have a Tom Joad. His name was Ernie Mynatt, and this is his story.

It was 1959 when Ernie, then in his mid-thirties, moved from Harlan County, Kentucky to Cincinnati, one of the primary destinations for Appalachian migrants. He had been to war, had earned a college degree, and had taught for ten years in the public schools of Harlan County. And he had met Purley Ayer, a charismatic Appalachian preacher, educator, and social activist, who persuaded Ernie that there was important work to be done on the streets of Cincinnati.

By that time, the formerly German Over the Rhine neighborhood on the edge of downtown Cincinnati had been transformed into a medium-sized Kentucky town in the middle of an Ohio city. "It was a common practice," said Marlin Wightman, a Tennesseean who lived in Over the Rhine in the fifties, "when you met someone, you'd ask them, 'Where you from, Kentucky or Tennessee?'"

For many Appalachian migrants, the city was a hard place. They came to Cincinnati for jobs, and found them, but often the wages and working conditions were exploitive. Raised in a culture that valued home and family and connection to place, they found themselves living in cramped walk-ups rented by the week, cut off from their extended families, in a place where there was nothing, really, for them to connect to. Their pain is expressed in bluegrass music, the soundtrack of the migration, sad songs about separation, loss, and regret.

It was hardest on the children. Scorned by their classmates and misunderstood by teachers who considered a Kentucky mountain inflection to be a sign of ignorance, many of the children of Appalachian migrants dropped out of school in junior high or earlier. They very quickly learned how many ways a hillbilly kid could get into trouble in the streets of the city.

It was in that environment that Ernie Mynatt set up shop in an Over the Rhine storefront in 1961. With the support of the Appalachian Fund, endowed by Herbert Faber, president of the Cincinnati-based Formica Company, Ernie began at age thirty-eight what would become his life's work: helping his friends and neighbors, and especially their children, learn how to cope with life in the city.

Early on the work was retail, one kid at a time. He began by hanging out on the streets, earning the trust of the kids, who at first suspected he must be a cop, a truant officer, or even a pederast. He went to juvenile court every morning, and through sheer persistence persuaded the judges to assign youthful offenders to his care instead of sending them to jail or reform school.

Eventually he had responsibility for more than six hundred teenagers. They could shoot pool on the table in his Main Street storefront, watch TV there, use the telephone to call about jobs. Most important, they could talk to Ernie, a country boy who had figured this city out.

Ernie was more or less officially "Papa to His People" in Cincinnati. That's what it says on the plaque he was given a few years ago, and it's a home truth in the hearts of hundreds of now middle-aged, middle class Cincinnati residents who still refer to themselves as "Ernie's kids."

Larry Reddin, now a senior staff member at Cincinnati's Urban Appalachian Council, is a member of that fraternity. He was an Over the Rhine street kid, essentially homeless, at the age of eleven. Ernie welcomed him into the fold, helping him out, at first, with what might be called small matters of great importance, like lunch money. Eventually Ernie arranged a placement for Larry in a residential program for teenage boys.

"The way we were growing up, there was no vision of the future," Reddin said. "There was no light at the end of the tunnel, because you're only thinking about that day, about where that next meal is going to come from. What Ernie did was give us a way to see what might be.

"When you needed Ernie, he would be there. You'd be thinking, 'Where's Ernie?' and a few minutes later he'd come walking down the street. It was sort of magical.

"And it was totally unconditional. With Ernie it wasn't just a second chance. For a lot of us there was a third chance, a fourth chance."

"Ernie shepherded an entire generation to adulthood in Over the Rhine," said Michael Maloney, who began working with Ernie while he was a student in the sixties. "And he mentored a generation of social workers, many of whom are still working in the inner city."

When he wasn't working in the streets, Ernie was agitating at City Hall on behalf the people who lived in Cincinnati's hardest neighborhoods. Over time, his community organizing began to take hold and expand in ever-widening circles. The organizations he started ultimately became the Urban Appalachian Council, an umbrella agency that today oversees a broad range of social service and cultural programs for the Cincinnati area's 250,000 citizens of Appalachian descent.

I met Ernie in the last year of his life, while I was working on a series of interviews with Appalachian migrants and their children. Even then it was easy to see the man who, without much more than the force of his intellect and personality, salvaged a generation of hillbilly kids thirty years ago: a big, powerful man with a broad, open face that never met a stranger. He had a smile that said, "Come in. Sit down. Let's talk."

Ernie's step had been slowed some by a broken hip he suffered a couple years earlier, and his vision wasn't as good as it used to be. But his mind, his fierce commitment to social justice, and his love of telling stories were undiminished.

Especially that storytelling part. It's a mountain thing: Ernie's response to any question was to tell a story. It takes longer, but in the end there's more truth in it than if he just gave you the facts. If you'd ask him straight out, as I did, what inspired him to devote his life to community organizing, he would start to tell you a story about World War II. He was a twenty-one year old Navy rigger on a PT boat in 1944, part of the secret campaign to soften up German coastal defenses before the Normandy invasion. On D-Day, he was on Utah Beach.

"You know," he said, "the little old town I grew up in had about six hundred people in it. And do you know that most of the guys that I ran around with in that town are dead, were killed. They were called up, and it was because we were a bunch of ignorant hillbillies who didn't know how to do anything but shoot a rifle.

"From the beach, you know where the water slushes up on the beach, from the water slushing up, the white, it's not white, it's red. For maybe ten yards, twenty yards. I had that blood all over my clothes, you know, it soaked in my britches and everything, and it was stiff as a board. And it was my buddies, it was their blood, it wasn't mine."

Even after fifty years, the memory brought him to the verge of tears. "If I get through this one, I said to myself, I'll never get into another one. I said if I lived, and got back to the United States, it was going to be different."

He got back, and he kept his promise. And now, finally, he's home.

I shall pass through this world but once.
Any good that I can do or any kindness that I can show to any human being,
let me do it now. Let me not defer or neglect it,
for I shall not pass this way again.

MAHATMA GANDHI

Empower individuals within local Appalachian communities to strengthen families, develop community resources, and reform the systems that impact their lives. Call **The Urban Appalachian Council** at 513-251-0202.

Giving Kids a Fighting Chance

STORYTELLER: ROBERT MARRA

Judith Kurland wasn't easily shaken, but this time she actually felt sick to her stomach. It was her first walk through the nurseries of Boston City Hospital, and she was enraged by what she found there: not by the outrageous conditions—after all she had been hired to figure out a way to build a new public hospital to replace the ancient building, she expected the deteriorating facility, the gloomy atmosphere. She was enraged at seeing the rows of tiny, tiny babies, born too soon and too little to thrive or even survive.

When Judith saw the faces of those children, saw the tubes running into their thin bodies and the respirators doing their breathing for them, she thought about the lavish buildings and fancy lobbies being built by the world-class hospitals that served Boston's wealthier neighborhoods. Boston: the world's center of high tech medicine, the mecca of medical teaching hospitals, had already spent far more on hospitals than any other city in the country. Yet these babies she looked at were born to women who had little or no prenatal care, poor nutrition, were homeless or with no access to information to help themselves. There were sixteen teaching hospitals, three medical schools and two schools of public health, but in the shadow of those glittering buildings was what amounted to infant death zones. Babies in Boston were dying at higher rates than in many Third World countries. The more she thought about it, the more enraged she became.

It was 1988, and the mayor of Boston had just appointed Judith as the head of Boston City Hospital and Commissioner of the Public Health Department. For many, it was a surprising choice. Not only was she the first woman ever appointed, she was an outsider, unconnected to those who ran this very political city. A small Jewish fireball from Brooklyn by way of New Jersey in a city that identified birth by neighborhood; an activist and progressive set loose smack in the middle of a conservative medical community.

Her first day on the job and Judith had seen enough to know what her mission would be. It was inexcusable that this could happen here. "This is a rich city," she said, "there are enough resources to make sure that every child in Boston be given a fighting chance to live a happy, healthy, and productive life."

Every day for the next five years, Judith used her savvy, chutzpah, and clout in every way she could: she pushed, she prodded, she pressured, and she pleaded. She shared her vision with legislators, philanthropists, policy makers, and foundations, She shared her information; health statistics, budget numbers and profit statements, with community groups, policy makers and the media. She believed the saying "Knowledge is power" and wanted power to be shared. And she made history by building a new $180 million hospital for Boston's most needy citizens: a yardstick of excellence against which to measure other hospitals' services to the poor.

But she wouldn't just raise funds or "throw money at the problem." She got people involved with the desperate of Boston, professional women mentoring teenage mothers, grandmothers knitting sweaters and booties for the new born babies, volunteers reading to children and tutoring their parents, college students providing skills to high school students, and hospital workers becoming involved with the communities outside their walls.

Judith also believed that many of the solutions to a community's problems were within the untapped resources of the community, that the problems of infant mortality, violence, and substance abuse required not only the resources of large institutions, but the ideas and understanding of the city's neighborhoods. She had learned while visiting community health centers and public hospitals in Africa that when the poor were expected to help provide health education and health care for themselves and their families, they do so with remarkable creativity and enthusiasm, healing themselves in body and spirit as they help others. So, she dramatically expanded public health programs that empowered families and their communities.

Judith wanted to tap community resources to find long-term solutions to the complex problems with a unique mix of public and private support. She gathered 250 health and community development leaders from Boston and around the world. Their conclusion was straightforward: If you want to improve the health of children, then you must raise the educational level of the mother.

That led to the creation of Healthy Boston. With great care, Judith brought together people from all parts of the community to create good health through jobs, schools, housing, and medical care. Through Healthy Boston, people from Boston's richest and poorest neighborhoods began working together, some for the first time in their lives. Both groups were amazed to discover such gifts in people they'd been trained to distrust for as long as they could remember.

She was also determined to engage Boston's wealthy hospitals in her cause. After three years of politely urging hospital leaders to share more of their great wealth with the community, she decided they needed a push. So she commissioned a report that the *Boston Globe* ran as a three-day front-page series. It contrasted the high infant mortality rate with the wealth of Boston's hospitals. Finally, the most recalcitrant hospital administrators loosened their grip on their wallets.

Challenging powerful institutions and driving major changes creates powerful opposition. Judith's strongest supporter, partner and anchor was her husband, Benny, the father of their three children. Whenever she was attacked he would remind her of why she had taken on this work: in Gandhi's words, to "make injustice visible," and in the admonition of the Talmud, "to repair the world."

Tragically, without any warning, Benny had a fatal heart attack at age forty-six. Her greatest friend was gone and her children needed her. Judith's term as commissioner was coming to an end, and she had rooted changes so that there was no way the hard-won progress she had made would reverse itself. Judith's labor of love resulted in dramatic improvements for Boston's children. During her tenure, Black infant mortality and teenage pregnancy rates decreased significantly; where immunization rates were the highest in the country, and neighborhoods were now working together to solve problems.

Those of us who have worked with Judith say she reminds us of the Glinda in *The Wizard of Oz.* With tornado-like force and Glinda-like magic, she turned Boston upside down and shook it mightily until rich and poor alike rediscovered the good within themselves. Now they are using that good—their brains, courage, and heart—to build a real Emerald City on the hill.

Get your hospital and community organizations to work together to build a healthier community. To learn about this growing community movement across the nation, call **The Coalition for Healthier Cities and Communities** at 312-422-2635 or visit their website at http://www.healthycommunities.org.

Polishing the Big Apple

STORYTELLER: NANCY BERG

Annette Williams had been on welfare for ten years when Joseph Pupello offered her a job with the New York Restoration Project (NYRP). After volunteering for the past five years as a reading tutor in the New York City public schools and as a garden helper, she'd become known as a dependable, hard worker who was exceptionally good with people. For seven summers, she worked with Joseph at Success Gardens, a nonprofit organization that turned vacant lots into little community Edens.

Annette remembers her first NYRP meeting with Joseph; it was in an abandoned park. "It looked more like a jungle," she says. Seeing the overgrown area and temporary homeless shelter behind the playground, she wondered if this sad patch of land could ever be turned into a park again. But just one month later, she witnessed what seemed like a miracle. "People started coming back," Annette said. "The kids came first, asking questions about what we were doing. 'We are giving you back your park,' was all we said."

As a mother raising six children in an economically troubled area, Annette knows the importance of having safe places for children to play. "Kids nowadays don't have places to play," she says. "Our cities are full of concrete and our parks with drug addicts, homeless people, and unleashed dogs. The kids say, 'We have nothing to do.' No wonder they get in trouble." Thanks to Annette and her team, they now have a safe place to go.

After a year at the NYRP, Annette was promoted to field director, managing a team of four employees, twenty Americorps volunteers, and supervising thirty-four members of the Work Experience Program (WEP). Together, they are responsible for restoring six of New York City's parks to their natural beauty. "The Americorps volunteers are like my kids," she says. "I become their mother, sister, brother, and friend. We're like a family." Through working with Annette, the WEP members learn job skills and build self-esteem. By getting up each morning and doing something positive for themselves and others, they gain confidence that they can get a real job. "I know what it's like to be on welfare," Annette says. "It's easy to get stuck in the cycle." She encourages people to start moving away from welfare by volunteering "so people can see you as more than a mother on welfare." After two years, she has seen five of her Welfare to Work people get good jobs. "One just got married and drives a Lexus!" she says happily.

Most people would be surprised to find that Annette Williams has a good friend and partner named Bette Midler who founded the New York Restoration Project. They have more in common than first meets the eye: both women had to learn, firsthand, how to work their way out of poverty, but while Annette spent her childhood in the concrete maze of New York, Bette grew up surrounded by the beauty of Hawaii.

Growing up in the Halawa, one of the poorest neighborhoods on Hawaii, Bette Midler and her family were the only non-Hawaiians for miles around. Treated like something of an outcast as a young child, she found solace in the awe-inspiring natural beauty around her. In the crystal-clear aquamarine sea, the little girl swam alongside bright magenta *kuma* and dazzling indigo parrot fish. Words like smog and pollution held no meaning for her. She thought the whole world was as beautiful as Hawaii. When she grew up, she made her first journey to the mainland. It was as if she had just stepped off a time machine from some pre-industrial age. She was shocked by the careless way people treated the earth.

For years Bette lived in southern California, developing her career. Later, she and her husband Martin moved to New York to raise their daughter Sophie. In a sense, the entertainer found a spiritual home there. "I love New Yorkers, and I'm like them," she says. "I'm noisy. I have my opinions." Bette exudes an energy and drive that has led most Americans to assume she was a New Yorker all along.

But the extent of careless waste and filth in New York took her by surprise: people were throwing their garbage out the windows. The city's once majestic parks were marred by refuse, old furniture, and even abandoned toilet bowls. "We love this city. The degradation was heartbreaking and unacceptable," says Midler. "I realized I had to do something. Even if it meant I had to go out and pick up all that stuff up with my own two hands."

It was obvious to anyone who had walked in New York City's parks that a volunteer effort was needed. The city once had 80,000 Parks Department workers to care for the more than thirty thousand acres of playground, woodlands, recreation centers, trails, gardens, and miles of protected waterfront. Cuts in public funding eliminated a staggering 77,600 of those jobs. With only 2,400 workers, there's just too much litter, illegal dumping, and vandalism to keep up with.

Bette decided to call her friend Scott Mathes at the California Environmental Project, an organization that had removed more than 3.5 million pounds of debris from Los Angeles since 1989. Bette enlisted Mathes' help to set up a similar project in New York. The NYRP was born and funded by a special benefit premiere of her film *The First Wives Club* and $250,000 out of Bette's own pocket.

Joseph remembers his first day as NYRP's director. it was at the Little Red Lighthouse under the George Washington Bridge. Midler was joined by Mayor Rudolph Giuliani, volunteers, and sixty schoolchildren from upper Manhattan to begin to clear away dump sites, plant trees, and remove rusted cars in a massive effort to reclaim the Fort Tryon and Fort Washington parks and restore beauty to seven miles of the Hudson River waterfront. Since then, with help from the Americorps volunteers and the Army Corps of Engineers, they've carted away more than fifty thousand pounds of refuse from the city's parks. "The Divine Miss M. brings style to the project, and she really gets her hands dirty," Joseph says. "She shows New Yorkers that they can be involved."

When people ask Annette about her job, she proudly says, "I pick up garbage." She finds working with Bette a real joy. "Bette is part of our extended family," she says. "She's very down to earth and just does her job. In her overalls and sneakers, she picks up trash, showing others there's a cleaner way to live. People walk by and say 'Hi' to her, not knowing who she is. She just goes on about her business."

Bette's willing to use her celebrity status if it get results, particularly with kids. "As long as I can remember, there have been antilittering campaigns, but nobody pays attention to them," Midler says to a group of children, making them laugh as she slips into her famous flamboyant persona. "They drop their lunches on the grounds and that's the end of it. And I have to come along and sweep it up and I mean, kids, I'm pooped, I'm exhausted. There's more trash out there than I can handle and if we keep this up there won't be any place left to walk; we'll be picking our way over mounds of cans and bottles, acres of egg cartons, and oceans of shrink wrap. So please, please, let's stop treating the earth like it was an ashtray. Tell your friends, tell your moms, tell your kids, we just have to stop! I really feel that if everybody did their part it would be a beautiful world."

Organize a cleanup day in your community. If you want to help beautify New York City's parks and rivers, call the **New York Restoration Project** at 212-258-2333.

Growing Nationally

Like the traveler in the Stone Soup folktale, Johnny Appleseed sparked a spirit of community when he planted apple seeds across America. This legendary American hero was born John Chapman in 1774, and grew up in Boston. Like Alexis de Tocqueville, he was just a young man in his twenties when he set out to travel across the country. Before leaving, he collected hundreds of apple seeds and spread them wherever he went. He wanted families who were moving West to see the apple trees growing everywhere and feel at home. For the next 40 years, Johnny Appleseed visited his apple orchards, pruning and caring for them and teaching hundreds of settlers how to grow their own. Twenty-five years later, when de Tocqueville traveled across the country in 1831, he probably enjoyed these fully grown trees, blossoming fragrant flowers and bearing delicious fruit, as much as he appreciated our country's rich community spirit.

Like Johnny Appleseed, the national heroes featured in this chapter have been planting seeds of hope and teaching others how to care for their communities for many years. Some "community heroes" in this book have been helping others for 20, 30, even 40 years.

Today, there are over 600,000 non-profit organizations with 14 million employees and over 100 million volunteers who serve America's people. No other country in the world has such a richly developed public sector. Each and every day, we benefit from the fruits of their labor. Their gifts to our country are invaluable, providing a strong backbone for our precious democracy.

The stories in this chapter honor just a few of the many Americans who have dedicated their lives to service. Many strive to create a safety net for those who are less fortunate, yet struggling to realize the American dream. These stories recognize these national heroes, acknowledge their great gifts and describe the amazing impact they've had on our country.

Their stories show that the path of service is never predictable. While some community heroes started with a dramatic turn in the road, for many it was a gradual evolving commitment, one step leading to another, and then another. Marian Wright Edelman's son Jonah tells us about the inspiration behind his mother's life-long commitment to making the world a better place for all children. Harris Wofford shares the experience of working side-by-side with John F. Kennedy in the founding of the Peace Corps.

Some stories show how national heroes, like Billy Shore at Share Our Strength and Patty Johnson at Christmas in April, are building public-private partnerships with companies to more effectively realize their organizations' noble goals. Other national heroes, like Dorothy Stoneman, have built a coalition among hundreds of youth organizations and partnerships with government agencies to use federal funds more effectively to meet community needs.

Some of these stories show how young people have carried out the legacy of their heroes. For Alan Khazei and Michael Brown, it was President Kennedy, who inspired them to found City Year. Gandhi's ability to mobilize millions of people with the simple act of fasting, led Nathan Gray to found Oxfam-America's Fast for World Harvest.

Sometimes as their work grows from one small office to a large national organization, these national leaders get tired. After years of writing grants, working with bureaucracies and dealing with politics, they sometimes even lose hope. We hope these stories will energize you, and reconnect you with the power and the promise in the spirit of service.

We are living in a time where there are many great, yet mostly unknown leaders in the world. This chapter tells some of their stories. They are among the finest teachers the world has ever known. Their hands-on experience and wealth of knowledge are among our country's greatest resources. Just as Alexis de Tocqueville reaped the harvest that Johnny Appleseed had sown 25 years earlier, we can reap the benefits of these community heroes and their years of service. Not everyone dedicates their lives to service, yet we can all learn from those who have and discover how we can help them with this important work.

Every one of these people and their organizations could use your help: your special gifts, skills and resources.

Give them a call and learn how you could change your life and the world, one day at a time.

Stand for Children

Storyteller: Jonah Edelman

In 1967, Mississippi was a dangerous place to be if you were black. Cora Bell Shade knew that all too well. Still, life had given her Efrem Douglas, her five-year-old son, and his birth had renewed her hope for a better future.

Cora Bell gave Efrem just about everything in her power, and he was generally about as happy as you could expect a little boy to be. Then one day they went into town in their beat-up green pickup truck. As they reached the main intersection, she pointed out a group of black children playing on the elementary school grounds nearby and said, "When you go to school next year, Efrem, you'll be playing over there."

Efrem looked at the playground she was pointing at, and then he looked across the road. "But I don't want to go to school there, Mama," he replied. "I want to go over here." Cora Bell's heart sank. Efrem's finger was pointing at the all-white elementary school right across the street from the black one.

"Oh, you can't go there, Sugar," Cora Bell was forced to tell her son. "That school is for white children." Efrem's small face crumpled. The sight of her son's tears tore Cora Bell up inside. She thought about how she had always told Efrem he could be whatever he wanted to be in life if he had an education, even if he was black and poor.

In that moment, something in Cora Bell changed, and her resolve strengthened. She couldn't let her son compromise his dreams. Before she knew what she was doing, she found herself pointing to the White school and saying, "When it's time for you to go to school, you'll go there."

She heard those words come out of her own mouth as if someone else were saying them. Then she just shook her head and sighed. Cora Bell Shade had absolutely no idea how she would make her promise come true.

Then a friend told her about my mother, Marian Wright Edelman, who was working as an NAACP Legal Defense Fund lawyer. When Cora told my mother her story, it spurred her to intense action. First, she checked into the legal and political ramifications of enrolling a black child in the white school. Then she arranged special tutoring for Efrem so he would be prepared to attend the white school, if and when they won their case. They did win, and because Efrem had gone to Head Start, he had a strong foundation. That fall, he went to the formerly segregated school and forward into his life.

When my mother moved from Mississippi to Washington D.C., she left a rich legacy. Because of her work with the NAACP, hundreds of children like Efrem were able to attend formerly segregated schools. By bringing Head Start to Mississippi, she gave thousands of poor children the chance to learn. Because of national nutritional programs she helped to expand, tens of thousands of children and families no longer went hungry. And hundreds of children whom she had personally touched came to believe in themselves. Where did she get the courage to serve so well for so long? Part of the answer is in a story my mother often told me when I was growing up.

On the night my grandfather, Arthur Jerome Wright, died of a heart attack in 1954, he asked my mother to ride with him to the hospital in the ambulance. My granddaddy knew he had precious little time left, and he didn't want to lose his last chance to counsel his youngest child.

My mother climbed in next to where her Daddy lay on a stretcher. By this time his feet were itching terribly from poor circulation, and he asked her to scratch them for him. As she began to untie his shoes, she was dumbstruck by what she saw. Her father was a minister and one of the most respected Negro leaders in the segregated town of Bennettsville, South Carolina. He had built a new church, a parsonage, a Sunday School building, and a home for the aged. He had put three of his children through college and had taken in his deceased sister's children and other orphans. And this man who had done so much for so many had holes in the bottoms of his shoes!

Those beat-up soles left a lifelong impression on my mother. Her father and my Grandma Maggie had told her time and again that material things were not the measure of our success. The true measure of our success, they said, was our service to others. "If you see a need, don't sit by and think someone else will do something about it," Daddy Wright always said. "Stand up and address the need yourself and don't worry about getting money or credit for it." The sight of my grandfather's beat-up shoes drove that advice home in a lasting way.

As the ambulance wove its way through Bennettsville's sleepy streets toward the black hospital ward, Grandpa Wright grabbed my mother's hand and shared with her a final lesson. "People will tell you that because you are black and a woman, you can't do what you want to do in life," he said, looking intently into her eyes. "But don't you ever believe that. If you get an education, you can accomplish anything you want to." My mother, tears rolling down her face, drank up her father's words. A few hours later he was gone.

My mother never had holes in her shoes, but she followed directly in her father's footsteps and has spent her life standing up for people who need help. Her father's words gave her the strength and courage to carry on, even when the odds were against her.

As her father did before her, my mother walks her talk. When I was growing up, she was extremely busy with her work. Yet even though she traveled a lot, my brothers and I always knew that we came first. Most mornings my Mom somehow managed to make what I thought was the best French toast in the world. She attended all of our parent-teacher nights, and cheered us on at important athletic contests. And, as her parents had done for her, she was always bringing us along with her on trips, taking us to hear speakers and introducing us to interesting people. She wanted to be sure we were never lost in her shadow. "Have you met my son?" were always her first words when we went to a new place. It means everything, having your parents always put you first like that. It gives you the feeling that you can do anything.

So when she asked me to help her jump-start a powerful movement for children in this country, I gladly stood by her side. She felt it was time to inspire hundreds of thousands of adults to recommit themselves to improving the quality of young people's lives in their communities by calling for a day to Stand For Children.

Although many said we had too little time and too little money, my mother took a lesson from Daddy Wright and paid the can't-do critics no mind. She booked the Lincoln Memorial in Washington D.C., for June 1 and secured office space for our headquarters. In January, we hoped forty or fifty organizations would join the Children's Defense Fund's call to action. By May more than thirty-seven hundred organizations had endorsed Stand for Children Day.

Soon thousands of people from every walk of life were spreading the word about the rally. Henry Bird, a grandfather in Maine who had never considered himself an activist, organized a busload of marchers. The Jacobsens, a family whose members were scattered around the midwest, made Stand For Children into a family reunion, picking up three generations of family members along the route from Wisconsin to Washington D.C. Cory Fischer-Hoffman, a twelve-year-old Philadelphia girl, organized a bus from her synagogue for her Bat Mitzvah project.

In all, well over a quarter of a million people answered my mother's call for Americans to recommit themselves to our children. They came from every state in the U.S. to the Lincoln Memorial on June 1, 1996, to Stand For Children. Those who attended heard the same simple message that Grandpa Wright passed on to my mother, that Cora Bell Shade passed on to her son, Efrem, and that my mother has passed on to my brothers and me: that caring, concerned people standing for children enable them to eventually stand for themselves.

"Every one of us can do more to ensure that our children grow up safe, healthy, and educated in nurturing families and in caring communities," my mother said. "Together we can give our children back their childhoods, safety, hope. We can improve millions of young lives right now." She added, "Return home and keep standing together for children every day until all America stands with us."

In our struggles, if we are to bring about the kind of changes
that will cause the world to stand up and take notice, we must be committed.
There is so much work that needs to be done.
It is a big job, but there is no one better to do it than those who live here.
We could show the world how it should be done and how to do it with dignity.

DR. MARTIN LUTHER KING JR.

To build a better life for children in your community join **Stand For Children**, a network of local children's activists who are developing direct service and advocacy initiatives. Call 800-663-4032 or e-mail cats@stand.org to form or join a local Children's Action Team.

Share Your Strength

STORYTELLER: BILLY SHORE

Battles are won or lost and the future is decided, all from inside one room. In a presidential campaign, it's called the War Room. In the White House, it's called the Situation Room. At Boston City Hospital's Growth and Nutrition Clinic, the doctors call it what it is: a coat room. It's the only place they could find. But, don't let the name fool you. The work done here is often a matter of life or death.

This is where Dr. Deborah Frank and her team—a doctor, a social worker, a nutritionist, a community worker, and a psychologist—meet every Wednesday. They ask themselves what can be done for Boston's malnourished babies, born into the poorest of families. Every day, Dr. Frank and this dedicated team face medical problems that medicine can't cure. They look for symptoms, not with a stethoscope, but by examining a family's lifestyle, parent-child dynamics, and household budgets.

From this coat room, Dr. Frank has helped nourish "at risk" babies for nearly two decades. She and her team sit on lopsided swivel chairs, crowded around a small table, reviewing cases and choosing strategies. All around them are supplies to meet the needs of their patients—coats, shoes, faded second-hand clothing, and a makeshift food pantry.

Today, the team is working on a case that has everyone stumped. Rosie Smith, 26 months old, has not gained an ounce in four months. The doctors classify her as "failing to thrive." With her height and weight far below normal for her age, the tiny girl faces the likelihood of life-long health problems and learning difficulties. Rosie's worried parents insist that they always give her enough food, even though their income is below the federal poverty line. Dr. Frank hunts for clues as to why the markers on Rosie's growth chart won't budge.

This five-foot-tall dynamo doctor is passionate about kids. She will be the first to tell you it takes more than food to fight hunger. She knows that in America, childhood hunger masquerades as a sleepy kindergartner, a toddler with an earache that won't go away, or a seemingly healthy two-year-old who is really an undernourished four-year-old.

She reaches beyond the limits of traditional medicine, investigating the homes of families in need. Low test scores, less active learning behavior, and under-developed bodies and brains are some of the clues she looks for. For some, she prescribes enrollment in federal nutrition programs; for others, it is adequate housing. She even stocks peanut butter and raisins right next to the cotton swabs and bandages in her tiny office.

She also coaches thousands of parents through the daily dilemmas of raising children under less than ideal conditions. Many parents must choose between heating their homes and eating; between giving an infant all the milk or watering it down so the other kids get some; and between filling growling tummies with water until the next meal or distracting them until the hunger passes.

Dr. Frank must be doing something right. Eighty-five percent of the children from her clinic have reversed their malnutrition and are growing normally.

Back in the coat room, Dr. Frank has a winning idea. She shouts out, "A high chair! Do Rosie's parents have a high chair?" That was it! Evidently, Rosie was eating while rambling around the house in her walker, and never stopped long enough to digest her food so she could grow. The clinic team will get a high chair for

Rosie, and Dr. Frank will make certain that the family receives extra support, as well as a follow-up home visit.

"Hungry children need more than a high calorie, high protein diet," Dr. Frank says. "They need medical care to address the serious complications of malnutrition. They need teachers who have the time to give individualized attention to their learning style. They need their parents' workplace to offer health insurance, and of course, they need love."

Dr. Frank is one of the thousands of extraordinary people involved with Share Our Strength, the anti-hunger organization that provides opportunities for people to connect with something special within themselves, and contribute to something larger than their own lives, like Dr. Frank's clinic. Since 1984, Share Our Strength has mobilized over 10,000 people nationwide—chefs, writers, business leaders, and artists—to lend their skills and talents, granting out more than $43 million in the fight against hunger.

Through a unique partnership with American Express and other corporate partners, Share Our Strength is able to help people like Dr. Frank and her team bring kids like Rosie back to health. For example, the creative "Charge Against Hunger" fundraising program generated more than $22 million from 1993 to 1996 to fight hunger.

Funds raised by SOS are used to invest in local leaders who are reaching out to families in need. Share Our Strength grants funds to distribute food, create community kitchens, plant gardens, educate families about nutrition and support clinics like Dr. Frank's.

Share Our Strength measures its success not by the number of meals they've served, but by the families they've helped: families like Rosie's, who no longer rely on going to a food pantry at the end of the month. With a healthy start in life, Rosie faces a brighter future. Her strength will help her learn better in school, live a better life, and build a better tomorrow. For Rosie, the help offered by Share Our Strength will make all the difference in the world.

There's a country at the end of the world
where no child is born, but to outlive the moon.

William Butler Yeats

Spend at least one holiday each year volunteering in a free food program, call: 800-532-3663. If you want to contribute your talents or mobilize your industry to fight hunger while investing in long-term solutions to hunger and poverty, call **Share Our Strength** at 800-969-4767.

Something Greater Than Themselves

STORYTELLER: ROSABETH MOSS KANTER

As a young boy growing up in Boston, Herman lived in a broken and abusive home with little little love or support. His backyard was a vacant lot where he played with his friends amidst broken bottles and trash. One afternoon when Herman was playing outside with his friends, a dozen young people wearing bright red jackets with the words "City Year" written across the backs suddenly appeared. To his surprise, they began to clean up the vacant lot. They were still hard at work that evening when he went home.

When Herman returned the next day, he was amazed. He had never seen anything so wonderful happen in his neighborhood before. Not only was the lot completely clean, but the young people were starting to build a playground! It was Herman's introduction to City Year, and it was a magical day.

Several years later, on his first day of middle school, Herman was nervous, wondering whether or not he'd fit in. As he turned the corner to enter his classroom, he saw one of those familiar red jackets. Khary, a City Year corps member, had been assigned to assist Herman's teacher. When Khary smiled at him, Herman knew things would be just fine. And, for a while they were. Khary was funny and warm and gave Herman lots of one-on-one attention. When Herman entered the Boston Public Schools oratorical competition, an entire City Year team encouraged and coached him. They were as proud as he was when he actually won!

However, through the years, the encouragement Herman received from City Year volunteers wasn't enough to combat all the things working against him. He fell behind in school, failed the 11th grade and eventually dropped out. He was near despair when a guidance counselor suggested that he join the Boston youth corps. City Year, he was told, took committed young people of all backgrounds, even high-school dropouts, as long as they agreed to try to get their GED's. He was thrilled when he was accepted to the program, and it was the beginning of a big turnaround in his life.

City Year was started by two young people who dreamed of making a difference in the lives of inner city kids. In 1978, two Harvard freshmen, Michael Brown and Alan Khazei, found that they shared more than a dorm room; they shared a passion for wanting to make the world a better place. Each night they would stay up late, talking about ways to solve the problems their country faced. They had heard how President Roosevelt's Civilian Conservation Corps helped rebuild America during the depression of the 1930s. And they studied the civil rights movement and the Peace Corps, which had brought people together in the 1960s.

Michael and Alan knew they wanted to make a difference, like their heroes—Gandhi, Martin Luther King, Jr. and President Kennedy. These men had led people, especially young ones, into service, creating something greater than themselves. Michael and Alan wanted to do the same. So, in the summer of 1988, their formal education complete, they started City Year with 30 young people, and a long list of community projects.

Today, clad in uniforms of khaki pants, white shirts, and those bright red jackets, over 700 City Year graduates from all walks of life continue to live City Year's motto: "Putting idealism to work," serving inner-city neighborhoods and brightening the lives of many kids like Herman. Since it's inception, City Year has helped inspire a renewal of citizenship across the country. In 1993, President Clinton used City Year as a model for his national service program, Americorps. And every year, tens of thousands of adults join these dedicated young people in Serve-a-Thons, giving a day of their own time to work on special community projects.

Herman now serves with his City Year team working with handicapped children at an elementary school in Boston. He has become another of the growing links in the chain of national service; from Franklin Roosevelt, John F. Kennedy and Martin Luther King Jr., to Michael, Khary and now Herman. He has learned that what might seem like small steps to others are leaps and bounds for "his" kids. Helping them learn to read, paint, and accomplish other new things makes him happy. Belonging to City Year has also given Herman a chance to transform his own life. He has earned his GED and will receive financial aid to go to college, where he plans to become a sign language interpreter to work with the deaf. Like the ripple effect when a pebble is tossed into a pool of water, this work goes far beyond good deeds done today. City Year workers help the Hermans of this world, so that they too can leave behind something greater than themselves.

Each time a man stands up for an ideal, or acts to improve the life of others,
or strikes out against injustice, he sends a tiny ripple of hope,
and those ripples, crossing each other from a million different centers of energy,
build a current which can sweep down the mightiest walls of oppression and resistance.

ROBERT F. KENNEDY

If you're 17-24 years old and want to give a year of your life to help public schools and urban neighborhoods or if your company is looking for ways to change communities by producing leaders to engage in service projects, call **City Year** at 617-927-2500.

Read Baby Read

STORYTELLER: JENNIFER POOLEY

At 11:00 am on a Saturday morning, cheers are erupting, as in the final seconds of a Houston Rockets game. "What room is this?" Mike Feinberg asks. "This is the room . . . that has the kids . . . who want to learn. . . . to read books . . . to build a better tomorrow," his fifth-graders chant, drumming their hands on their desks. Their enthusiastic voices form a deafening roar as they sing the continents, harmonize fractions and hip-hop long division.

Teachers Dave Levin and Mike Feinberg clap encouragement, chant with the students, and constantly invent new challenges. These fifth-graders can't take their eyes off them as they fire off questions and explain problems. With fourth-quarter do-or-die urgency, they seize every minute to learn. Hands wave. Volunteers read. Every student contributes. Motivation flows around the room, student to student. They all pull for each other. They succeed as a team. Learning is a celebration.

Outside Mike and Dave's classroom in Houston, the obstacles have been fierce. Poverty, deficient school systems, and street violence have shadowed these students' young lives. In most inner city schools apathy reigns, gangs organize, and academic performance falls. Mike and Dave's alternative middle school, and their Knowledge Is Power Program (KIPP), offer students a choice, and the students choose to learn. Mike and Dave take these kids and keep them off the losing teams of drug users, gangs and drop-outs. They replace these dead ends with a future for these youngsters.

Students at the KIPP Academy attend school 9 1/2 hours a day Monday through Friday, and four hours on Saturdays. Even though they attend school year-round, they rarely miss a day or take a vacation. They boast an enviable 99% attendance rate. "We are a team and a family," they explain. "We're climbing the mountain together."

For Mike and Dave, KIPP is a 24-hour effort. To stay connected they have an 800 number, a work number, and a cell phone. They even buy alarm clocks for the students so that they can take charge of their prompt arrival at school. Anxious students can call from local pay phones when they need to talk about their homework, or just talk. Every day Mike and Dave invigorate students by sitting with them at lunch tables, showing them new dance steps or shooting baskets with them. They are ready to do whatever it takes to get these kids to college: university banners hang alongside the posters with positive slogans, colorful decorations and math problems on the blackboards.

"There are no short cuts. There is no margin for error," says Mike. "We must play a perfect game." In KIPP classrooms, students must learn to take responsibility for themselves and their education. Self-sufficiency and self-esteem are cultivated daily. These virtues are as important as practicing spelling. The kids know the odds are against them. But they also know that they can win.

As a senior at Princeton, Wendy Kopp started Teach For America (TFA), the national teacher corps that has mobilized some of the nation's outstanding college seniors to improve our schools. Each TFA teacher gets real life experience by committing to work for two years in some of America's most under-resourced urban and rural public schools.

When Dave and Mike joined TFA they were both rookies with nothing more to give than their promise and natural talent. A few years later they opened their own school, the KIPP Academy, in Houston. Their energy, innovation, and impressive results caught the attention of school administrators in New York. Dave is now in the South Bronx, operating the second KIPP Academy, for grades 5 through 8.

After completing his two years in TFA, before moving to the Big Apple, Dave joined Mike and the Houston students on a trip to celebrate the end of the 1995 school year. They raised enough money to travel all the way to Washington D. C. When they arrived, they used the city as an open classroom. In the nation's capitol, U. S. History took center stage, generating fascinating discussions. Questions and answers were electric.

During a tour of the Supreme Court, the students even got to meet Justice Bryer. Mike introduced the fifth-graders to the Justice as the hardest working kids in the country. "Are you enjoying your trip?" the Justice asked the kids. One small hand started waving frantically. "Excuse me sir," asked Ruben Garcia. "But were you here when *Miranda v. Arizona* was decided?" "No, that was before my time," replied the astonished Justice. "Well then, how would you have decided?" pressed the confident eleven-year-old. "You GO Ruben!" his classmates cheered. The Justice thoughtfully replied, "I would have agreed," and added, "The Constitution was designed to safeguard the rights of all our citizens." Ruben listened carefully: It's not often that a fifth-grader's question of law is answered by a Supreme Court Justice! For this young American citizen with Hispanic origins, the Judge's response was especially meaningful.

On their last night in Washington D.C., excitement and wonder filled these eleven-year-olds. Dave and Mike had arranged for a trip to the White House the next day. Who knows what secret ambitions and dreams danced through the minds of these youngsters? How could they forget their big wish to see the President? As they stood on the front lawn, they chanted "WE WANT BILL!" and followed this chant with their own original *School House Rock*, "This is KIPP in the house! Give me a beat! You gotta read, baby, read!"

A large crowd gathered around the students and listened to them as they serenaded the President. They sang the Preamble to the Constitution, and belted out the Declaration of Independence. From the rooftops the Secret Service agents spontaneously began waving their arms, conducting the students.

Then, out came President Clinton and excitement overcame the kids. They hugged each other, cheering, crushing their teachers in their enthusiasm. In a moment reminiscent of the day the young Bill Clinton shook President Kennedy's hand at the White House, their radiant faces exuded the joy of their big day, and all the hope for bright futures.

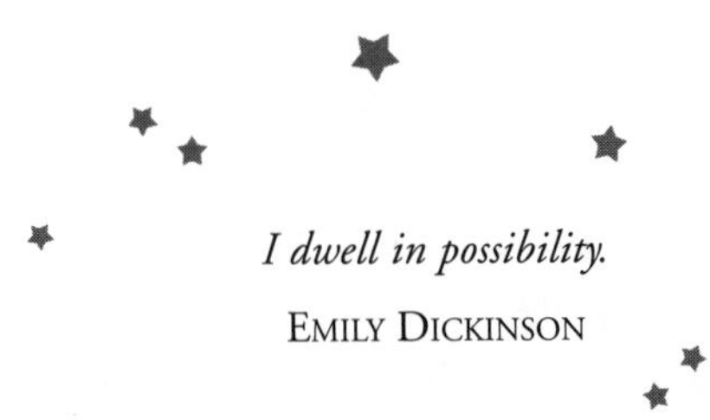

I dwell in possibility.

EMILY DICKINSON

Like Mike and Dave, you can open up a world of opportunities for some of America's most under-serviced students. Join **Teach For America** and other outstanding recent college graduates who commit two years to teach in America's under-resourced urban and rural public schools. Call 800-832-1230 or visit www.teachforamerica.org.

YouthBuild

STORYTELLER: JOHN BELL

Chantay Henderson Jones was just 14 years old when Dorothy Stoneman asked her and her teenaged East Harlem friends a question that would change their lives. "What would you do to improve your neighborhood if you knew I would do everything in my power to help you succeed?" she asked them. "If I helped you think through the project, got other adults to support you, and helped you raise money? What would you really like to do?"

It was as if Chantay and her friends had been just waiting for someone to ask them. "I would fix up the broken down buildings so homeless people could live in them," said one student enthusiastically. "I would fix the elevators in the projects so old people wouldn't have to walk up the stairs," another added thoughtfully. One teenager spoke up, "I would make a place for us to go, so we wouldn't have to hang out on street corners." "I'd eliminate crime!" another excitedly said. Still another quietly added, "I'd make beautiful parks for little children to play in." When Chantay shared her idea, the others nodded approvingly. "What about hiring unemployed young people like us to rebuild the abandoned buildings and make housing for the homeless?"

They all agreed that if given a chance, they would make permanent improvements such as fixing buildings, instead of cleaning the streets and parks, since those would just get dirty again the next day. "We would do something we could show to our grandchildren," they said.

It was 1978, and Dorothy had been teaching and working in the community for

14 years. She'd taught Chantay and many of these students when they were in the first grade. She was deeply troubled that some of her favorite students had died as teenagers in the tough city streets. She thought that the waste of their brilliance and goodness was a national shame that could and should be reversed. She also thought these youngsters might know how to help her do just that.

So Dorothy listened carefully as Chantay and her friends shared their ideas with her. She was impressed with their ability to see what was needed in their community—and their energy and caring to do something about it. They reaffirmed Dorothy's belief that young people could be a vital force for improving their communities. And they confirmed her desire to build a national movement of young people as leaders for positive social change. Dorothy asked Chantay and her friends to join her in taking the first steps towards this big vision.

At the time, there were tens of thousands of unemployed young people in New York City. Dorothy had also discovered that there were 10,000 abandoned city-owned buildings and 50,000 homeless people living on New York's streets and in its subway tunnels. If these kids were given real jobs, Dorothy knew they could contribute to their families' incomes as well as their community's well-being. She thought this was a perfect opportunity to put Chantay's great idea into action.

So Dorothy invited me, her long-time work partner—and husband—as well as other teachers and parents, and Chantay and her friends, to begin with an abandoned building on 107th Street between Lexington and Third Avenues. When we started fixing it up, all we had were garbage bags, a couple of shovels, and gritty determination. During the days, we'd all work together. The neighbors pitched in, bringing us refreshments and organizing bake sales to buy tools and supplies.

But at night the building belonged to the winos who drank and slept there. So we bought cinder blocks and cement and boarded up the windows. One night by the light of the streetlights, we spent five hours laying 14 bricks. We used the water from the fire hydrant two blocks away to mix the cement in a little bucket. But the night-time "tenants" just knocked in the bricks and took over again. While we were forced to abandon that building, we carried on—chalking it up as a "learning experience."

For the next six months, Dorothy went about rallying support from different community leaders, and organized various volunteer projects. We got the East Harlem Block Schools, a parent controlled school where we'd been working for many years, to agree to house us and our Youth Action Program (YAP). We put our ideas into a proposal and received a start-up grant from the federal government. Our first official project was to rehabilitate a six-story tenement building on 2nd Avenue and 119th Street.

It was a big job—and it took us five years to finish. We had to tear out the old before we could build the new. Day after day, young people volunteered their time and energy. It was hard work, but fulfilling. At the end of each day, these teens felt proud of the contribution they'd made to the neighborhood. And in the process of rebuilding the building, many of them rebuilt their own lives. For the homeless youths who worked on the project, the building became their new home. For others, it was an opportunity to make a difference. As one young man put it: "The building was like me, messed up on the inside. But we cleaned it out, fixed it up, and now it's new, just like me!"

Over the years, Chantay and her friends also worked to make their other dreams a reality. In addition to rehabilitating the building, they built a park, organized a crime prevention patrol, created a "Home Away From Home" for homeless teenagers, and a child care center for children of working single mothers. They also started a leadership school and organized the East Harlem Youth Congress.

It wasn't long before the YAP became famous for giving youth the opportunity to become leaders in their neighborhoods. There, teenagers learned how to turn their ideas into action plans, and to develop good sense about how to make them happen—with guidance from experienced adults. They helped make all the decisions—hiring the staff, managing the program and even helping Dorothy make policy decisions. In the process, they showed what a powerful force teens could be for social change—if given the chance.

Then they started thinking really big. If they could make things better in East Harlem, why not all over New York City? Their East Harlem Youth Congress began a network of community organizations, called the Coalition for $10 million, to persuade the New York City Council to fund programs like YAP throughout the city. Hundreds of young people testified in City Hall, calling for the resources to rebuild their crumbling neighborhoods. Council members were impressed with their track record, as well as with their sincerity and their heartfelt call for real jobs to rebuild their communities.

By 1988, calls were coming from people all over the country who wanted to put young people to work fixing up housing for homeless people. So we launched our model nationally, and named it YouthBuild. We worked with local community organizers in other cities who wanted to rebuild their communities like the East Harlem youth had done. There now are 108 YouthBuild programs in 38 states, putting 4,600 youth to work each year. And our network has grown to 650 organizations in 49 states—advocating for federal funds. Over the years, the YouthBuild Coalition has raised $158 million in federal funds to employ and train tens of thousands of young people in housing rehabilitation projects. One student in that first East Harlem project predicted our future when he said, "There's a lot of love in the Youth Action Program, and some day we're going to spread it around the world."

Chantay is now the program coordinator for a drug rehabilitation program in

Brooklyn. She uses many of the leadership skills she learned during her years in the Youth Action Program: writing, negotiation, challenging people to think, and mobilizing communities. Standing on 119th St. and Second Ave., looking at that first building she helped to rebuild almost 20 years ago, she says "There's an old African proverb: it takes a village to raise a child. Well, it also takes a child to raise a village," she says. "Everyone, no matter how young or how old has a responsibility to help their community. Young people can take the lead."

When I dare to be powerful—
to use my strength in the service of my vision,
Then it becomes less and less important whether I am afraid.

AUDRE LORDE

Want to join the **YouthBuild** movement of young adults who are rebuilding housing for low-income and homeless people, achieving higher academic skills, and taking leadership to improve their lives and their communities? Call **YouthBuild USA** at 617-623-9900.

Christmas in April

STORYTELLER: SKYE TRIMBLE

It was 3:30 in the morning, and Frances Vaughn had just finished her shift at the *Washington Post.* Her hands were ink-stained from hours of sorting papers. By moonlight, she hurried to make the last bus of the night. Holding tightly to the driver's hand, Frances climbed aboard. She sat in the first empty seat and closed her tired eyes. To pass the time, she began to quietly hum a tune. Soon, the engine's roar shifted. The weary woman knew her stop was next. After the driver helped her down, Frances thanked him with her genuine, dark eyes.

She followed the streetlights to her house and stared up at her stairs. Those *darn* steps. With two artificial knees, it was a real struggle for Francis. She'd done it before and she would do it again. But at 72 years old, it wasn't easy.

Frances went to bed that night, thinking about her future. She lay on her old mattress, looking around the dilapidated room. Over the years, her house had fallen apart around her. She wished she could take care of it as she used to, before she got sick. She hated to think of moving to a nursing home or even living on the streets. Tonight, as she did every night, Frances prayed with a hopeful heart.

Little did she know that in the morning, her prayers would be answered. She awakened to a surprising phone call from Patty Johnson, the co-founder of Christmas in April USA. For the last 10 years, the now more than 205 chapters across the country have been organizing volunteers, rekindling the tradition of neighbors helping neighbors. Their 'helping specialty' happened to be repairing low-income homes.

Frances stood awestruck, wrapped in her flannel nightgown, she listened to

Patty's enthusiasm pour out over the phone: "One Saturday in April each year, we send our crew to homes all over the country," she explained. "By dinner time, neighbors like you have a little comfort and security back in their lives. This year, we'd like to come to visit your house!"

Frances was quiet for a moment. She searched her memory for a time. She realized that, in all her years, nobody had ever helped her with her home. Patty Johnson's news was music to her ears. "This is an extra-ordinary day!" Frances exclaimed to Patty. She hung up the phone in amazement. Her heart raced as her excitement built, just thinking about fixing the long awaited repairs.

Then, on the last Saturday in April, 30 eager volunteers arrived at Frances' door. They carried supplies donated from corporate sponsors like Home Depot. Under Patty Johnson's guidance, they carried the old-fashioned barn raising spirit to new heights! As Frances puts it, "They tore my house up and put it back together again, like it was brand new!" With Frances beaming by their side, a team of volunteers joined together to fix the most important part of the house—the stairs. They built the strongest banister possible, so Frances could get up and down the steps more easily. If that was all Christmas in April did, she would have been happy. But, these kind folks had more in store for Frances!

While some patched her leaky roof, others laid down tile and carpet. Others brought safety to her home with a new lock, stove and smoke detector. Volunteers planted a lawn and shady tree.

Every corner of the homestead was filled with smiles and stories sung by Christmas in April voices. Anyone passing by the 'neighborhood family' would see all segments of the community pitching in. Street kids worked side by side with volunteers like the Junior League. These well connected ladies join the cause each year in communities across the country. "They turn their white gloves to white paint," as Patty puts it. They add their skills of organization while others add their muscle. "It all comes from caring people," Patty describes, "There are no suits, no white or blue collars, just people. That's the way it should be." Even President Reagan sent his staff to chip away the old paint and put on a fresh coat of white.

One teenage boy sat outside with Frances, breathing the sweet smell of new grass. He told her how Patty Johnson came from a poor home and grew up determined to help people feel secure in theirs. A grin came to his face as he described her work as "building miracles, one house at a time". Frances was impressed when he explained that their energetic leader had worked overtime in her unheated cellar, just to get the program going nationally, nearly 10 years ago. Frances felt a deep sense of gratitude—and a real sisterhood with Patty's spunky spirit.

That evening, everyone gathered outside Frances' beautiful new house. As she proudly walked up the stairs, holding on to the new banister, her new friends cheered, "Fran-ces! Fran-ces!" She couldn't believe what Christmas in April had created in just one day. She felt grateful that her number one dream, to stay in her own house as she grew old, had become a reality. She would never forget them; they made it the happiest day of her life.

The world needs friendly folks like you.
In this troubled world, it's refreshing to find someone who still has the time to be kind.
Someone who still has the faith to believe that the more you give, the more you receive.
Someone who's ready by thought, word or deed to reach out a hand, in the hour of need.

HELEN STEINER RICE

Spend the last Saturday in April with thousands of **Christmas in April** volunteers rehabilitating homes and renewing lives of the elderly. Call 202-483-9083 to join one of the 580 communities nationwide.

Opening Hearts

Storyteller: Elaina Verveer

While most seventy-nine-year-olds have settled into retirement, Louise Jackson is much too busy to even think of slowing down. The mother of four, grandmother of eleven, and great and great-great grandmother of seventy-seven, is taking time to care for the neglected children of our nation's capital. Don't look for her to stop anytime soon. She thinks her work has just begun.

Actually, it started when she was about eight years old. Louise accompanied her great-grandmother, a midwife, to the bedsides of poor women. Often given the responsibility of cradling the newborns, she learned to care for little ones at a very young age. Over the years, she instinctively allowed this caring to become an important part of her life.

Now, as a volunteer with the District of Columbia's Foster Grandparent Program, Louise works with families affected by child abuse. She teaches adults parenting skills and helps them find employment. But Louise's greatest gift is her love for the children. "Every child deserves to be loved," says Louise. "If I find children whose tears are caused by neglect, I'll help open their hearts so they can love again."

In 1985, Louise did precisely that for baby twins, Phyllis and Phillip, and their single mother. During their first meeting, Louise noticed the mother's bloodshot eyes and blackened veins. She saw the children's bandaged limbs and tear-stained faces. Sensing the magnitude of her challenge, Louise dedicated the next few months to helping this troubled family.

She gave the mother cooking lessons and job-training advice. But the young woman, overwhelmed by her difficult life, continued to put her need for drugs over her children's needs. Louise was upset to find the babies alone and unfed several nights each week. She knew their unchanged diapers and empty stomachs were signs of a much larger problem. When their mother was incarcerated for drug possession and child abuse, the baby twins were left with no one to care for them.

Every time Louise saw children thrown randomly into foster homes, she suffered. "Haven't these two little ones been through enough?" she thought. Rather than standing idly by, she took a leap of faith. Louise knew that what the baby twins needed more than anything else was a mother. Though at the time she was 70 years old, she accepted the judge's suggestion to officially adopt them. "I felt, within my soul, they were meant for me," she says. "From the start, I loved them as if they were my own."

It was her special love for these children that helped Louise get through the difficult and lengthy adoption process— her love and the memory of how she had first discovered the twins, crammed into one crib, faces red from hours of crying. Thanks to Louise's courageous caring, the symptoms of neglect now are gone and the children are thriving.

Today, Phyllis and Phillip are happily and healthily engaged in the rites and rituals of a normal childhood. When they are not studying for spelling bees or earning A's in arithmetic, they can be found kicking soccer balls in their front yard, singing out songs in their church choir, and dreaming of their futures as a dancer and a police officer. They show that they care for each other too, with hugs, handshakes, and high-fives.

Louise is committed to giving Phyllis and Phillip a solid foundation and a more hopeful future. Actively involved in her children's education, she hovers over fourth-grade textbooks and readers. "She helps the kids with their homework, and advises them on their future," says Constance Todd, director of the Foster Grandparent Program. "She picks them up from school, and does everything else a mother does for her children." But Louise is more than a mother. Despite her many years of parenting, she still knows what it's like to be a kid. That makes her a friend.

What does Louise expect in return for all that she has done? "To see my little angels walk across the stage and receive their diplomas," she says. "That would mean that I did my job. After all, what more could a mother want?" Imagine what would have happened to the twins if Louise had believed she was too old to make a difference. Instead, for as long as she lives, she'll be giving the greatest gift anyone can—the gift of love.

It may not make the evening news
when a Foster Grandparent takes the hand of a child
who has never had anyone raise a hand to her, except in violence.
It may not be what people write about,
when seniors understand that they too have something to continue to give,
but countless Americans benefit from their actions every single day.

FIRST LADY HILLARY RODHAM CLINTON

If you are over 60 years old and love children, call the **Foster Grandparent Program** at 800-424-8867 for the local office nearest you. Join the 24,000 older Americans who are helping 80,000 children in schools, hospitals, institutions, Head Start, and day care centers through the Senior Corps.

Helping Others to See

STORYTELLER: RAM DASS

If you are at a point in your life where you are ready to grow, to push yourself a little, to open your heart to a deeper compassion, drop in at the Aravind Eye Hospital in Madurai, India. Offer yourself up as a volunteer—for as long you are comfortable. Even a week would work, as it did for me. Then watch with awe as Dr. V, or Thulasi, his second-in-command, finds a place just for you.

In your "free" time, don't miss 6 a.m. in the waiting room of the hospital when Dr. V walks about in the river of humanity. Hundreds of village folk stand in lines, waiting patiently for inexpensive, often free, outpatient eye care. In an adjoining wing, long lines of the blind and the near-blind, guided by friends and relatives, await the 10-minute miracle of surgery that will give them back their sight.

Or join Dr. V's sister, a brilliant eye surgeon in her own right, as she, after six hours of surgery, leads a class of nurses in meditation and song.

After you have wandered around enough to begin to understand what this hospital is really about, ask Dr. V if you could visit one of his Sunday morning family sessions with his brothers, sisters, nieces, nephews, in-laws and all the children. Each week a different child presents something: it could be one of the holy stories of India through which the Hindi people contemplate their values and incorporate them into their lives. Or a political issue, a world public health issue, an environmental issue, a family issue. After the presentation, all three generations hang out together and discuss the way they can put into practice the values brought forth in the presentation.

Dr. V is a hero for these people for alleviating preventable and curable blindness in the world. He is a winner of the highest honors, and "chief" of this huge, world-class eye hospital complex. A strangely arresting man—with his gnarled arthritic hands and feet, his gray rumpled suit, his seventy-odd years and a perfect "poster man" at the same time—a brilliant mirror of compassion to all. His work is not only a response to the great need he sees every day. It is motivated by his belief that "intelligence and capability are not enough to solve our problems. There must be a joy of doing something beautiful."

In the waiting room scene at sunrise, Dr. V is simultaneously the fellow villager that he once was, and continues to be, and the extraordinary healer he has become. For a moment, his hand rests reassuringly on the arm of a frightened elderly woman. He explains a surgical procedure to a man. He nods to people and keeps the line moving. He cautions the children to be careful of others in their play. He is both village elder and hospital chief. He is also keeping an eye on the staff, insisting on their impeccability in service—guiding his superbly honed institution of compassion with a glance, a word, a silent presence, a smile. As Gandhi once said, "My life is my message." So Dr. V's blend of being and doing is his message. He continually seeks to be an instrument of imbuing the physical world with Living Spirit.

"India will enter the 21st century with 13 million of her people needlessly blind," says Dr. V. "Intelligence and capability are not enough to solve our problems. There must be the joy of doing something beautiful. If you allow the divine force to flow through you, you will accomplish things far greater than you imagined."

Dr. V and his staff perform 92,000 cataract surgeries a year and nearly 850,000 out-patient treatments. That's over 300 surgeries a day and 2,800 outpatients registered and seen each day. At the Seva Foundation, hundreds of our members help support special people like Dr. V and their noble work in underprivileged communities around the world. The Aravind Clinic has become a factory of caring for human beings. Their tall building of cement and steel and large plateglass windows is a shining monument to Western technology. But it is also, like Dr. V himself, a blend of being and doing.

From my experiences with Dr. V and the Aravind family, I have deepened my understanding of a basic tenet of the Seva Foundation—that one need not forego doing for being, or being for doing. In Madurai I found myself immersed in a demonstration of the successful integration of these two aspects of life—actions involving the best skills and technology balanced with caring hearts rooted in a sweet spiritual presence that is embracing of all fellow souls. It is a great teaching.

Want to help restore sight to people in India, Nepal and Tibet; help indigenous people in Guatemala and Chiapas, Mexico preserve their culture and build sustainable communities; support the development of a holistic approach to diabetes for Native Americans, or attend a retreat for social activists? Call the **Seva Foundation** at 510-845-7382.

Small Acts for Big Change: The Oxfam Fast

STORYTELLER: SARAH BACHMAN

Nathan Gray believed that small acts could bring about big change. This 25-year-old community organizer had seen it work. For four years he had lived as a volunteer, working with poor village people in Latin America. In Guatemala, he was impressed by the gentle strength and determination of one village leader, Francisco Basival. Under his leadership, the village had been quietly organized, and had achieved once impossible goals like reintroducing the Mayan technique of using sawgrass to stabilize hillside irrigation.

Back in the States, Nathan thought of Francisco. Although poor and uneducated, he was a genius at getting people to help themselves while working entirely from behind the scenes. There must be a way to help Americans understand and empathize with people like Francisco. "There's got to be a way to have people feel a higher sense of belonging, of humanity," Nathan thought. He had read about Mohandas Gandhi, who whenever he wanted to express his displeasure with British rule and injustice would simply stop eating. The Colonial British hated Gandhi's simplicity, his massive demonstrations and his fasts, and eventually gave in, granting India its freedom in 1947.

"Perhaps Americans would feel empathy for the poor if they fasted," Nathan thought, "if they shared their daily experience of hunger, even for a day." A fast could help people in the wealthy United States connect with grassroot leaders like Francisco in the third world. If people were encouraged to fast for a day in solidarity with people like him, they could donate the money they saved to support self-help projects in poor countries. The feeling of connectedness would benefit everyone. "Let's create a big fast!" Nathan thought. "Get lots of people fasting, raise money and consciences."

Oxfam-America, the international organization Nathan had helped start in Massachusetts, had heard about the Oxfam England organize small fasts for years. However, the then-stodgy Oxfam-American board thought a big, organized fast would be too undignified. As far as the board members were concerned, the idea was a inappropriate. But Nathan was determined.

He proposed a name—The Fast for a World Harvest—and set a special date: a week before Thanksgiving. To pay for publicity, he sold old greeting cards and baskets made by Oxfam-supported Third World groups. Then he had a stroke of inspiration: every major religion advocates fasting as a way to cleanse the soul and focus the thoughts on the humble essentials of life. Nathan sent a mailing to 10,000 college chaplains, inviting them to get involved. The chaplains responded immediately. All over the country, they began organizing fasts, teach-ins and money-raising activities.

To create the biggest fast in America, Nathan realized, he needed help getting the word out. Nathan visited AP and UPI, the largest wire services; the *New York Times* and CBS, then home of the top-rated evening news program, hosted by America's favorite anchor, Walter Cronkite. Nathan's father, a distinguished-looking lawyer, accompanied with his son to lend him credibility and support.

The idea took off. Anthony Lewis, *New York Times* syndicated columnist, embraced the fast and promoted it in his column. The *Times* endorsed it, mentioning tiny Oxfam-America alongside much larger charities. Walter Cronkite dedicated an amazing 4½ minutes of the evening news to the Fast.

Finally, the big day came. It was the Thursday before Thanksgiving, 1974, and

250,000 people joined together to give up one day's meals. The Fast was a huge success, generating enormous publicity for Oxfam-America and almost $1 million in donations. From a small idea, the Fast had grown into a national cause, especially on college campuses.

The Oxfam Fast continues today, a quarter-century later. It remains the largest nonreligious fast in America, and is especially popular on hundreds of college campuses. It has generated many millions of dollars, which have empowered grassroots leaders like Francisco. In today's world, many students think: "World hunger is overwhelming. What can I do?" However, when they participate in the Fast, they feel connected with real people doing real work, and they find inspiration and hope.

A couple of years after the first Fast, Nathan felt the impact of his work firsthand. A huge earthquake had just shaken Guatemala, killing 30,000 people in the capital, Guatemala City. He delivered some Oxfam relief supplies and worked with Francisco to distribute them. Together, they dragged bodies from the rubble. They restored the roofs of houses. It was exhausting work, but they boosted each other's spirits. After a couple of long, tiring days of emotional and physical strain, Nathan and Francisco were sitting alone together one night. They were both too tired to sleep. Suddenly, Francisco, a man of few words, ventured a question. "Whose money is helping us recover and rebuild after this earthquake?" he asked.

Nathan searched for the words to explain the Fast. "Well, a lot of people gave up eating for just one day. Then they took the money they would have spent on food, and gave it to Oxfam, to spend on people like you." Francisco still looked puzzled. "Why would people in the world's richest country give up eating?" he asked. Foregoing the logical response, Nathan spoke from his heart. "We wanted you to know how much we care about you and support you," Nathan said. They rose and hugged each other, tears etching lines in their dusty faces. The next day they worked together with a new strength, knowing they were making a difference, one small step at a time.

* * *

Instead of thinking about: How do I earn a living? . . .
how do I survive? . . . we ought to say, what is it that my experiences
teaches me that could bring advantage to all humanity?

—R. BUCKMINSTER FULLER

Oxfam-America's Fast for World Harvest's annual kick-off is the Thursday before Thanksgiving. To organize a learning experience or event at your church, school, college or company, call 800-597-FAST.

Kennedy and the Peace Corps

STORYTELLER: HARRIS WOFFORD

"Ask not what your country can do for you: Ask what you can do for your country." With these words, the young President launched what has become one of the most successful social inventions of this century: the Peace Corps.

When John Kennedy first gave voice to the idea of the Peace Corps, circumstances did not hint that history was about to be made. It was in the final weeks of the 1960 presidential campaign. After a television debate with Richard Nixon, Kennedy traveled to the University of Michigan. He wasn't supposed to speak, but a crowd of 10,000 students and faculty awaited his arrival—at nearly two in the morning.

Moved by the crowd, Kennedy decided to speak to them. He challenged the students to use their educational training as teachers, doctors and engineers to help people in far away lands. "How many of you are willing to spend five or ten years in Africa, Latin America or Asia working for the U.S. and working for freedom?"

Their response was an enthusiastic ovation. The next morning two graduate students, Alan and Judy Guskin, sat at their student cafeteria and wrote a letter to the college paper asking readers to join them in working for a Peace Corps. Their phone rang day and night with offers of help. Within days, 1,000 students had signed a petition saying they would volunteer if a Peace Corps were formed.

News of the student's petition spread to the Kennedy campaign. Spurred by this spontaneous outpouring of support, Kennedy decided to make a major speech in San Francisco expanding on the idea. At the Cow Palace, he promised, if elected, to create a Peace Corps of talented men and women who "could work modern miracles for peace in dozens of underdeveloped nations."

On his way back to Washington, Kennedy met with the Michigan students. They presented their petitions, and Kennedy was impressed with the long list of names. When he began to put the petitions in his car, he sensed some discomfort from the Guskins. "You need them back, don't you?" he asked. It was before photocopying had been invented and they only had one copy of the names and addresses.

As the students shared their ideas about the Peace Corps with the Kennedy staffers, they were told, "You'll be the first to go—that's a promise!" And some of them were—Judy and Al Guskin were among the first volunteers sent to Thailand.

Campaign promises are often forgotten, but not this one. After Kennedy was elected, the White House received more mail on the Peace Corps than any other subject, and it was wildly popular in the polls. But support for the idea was far from universal. President Eisenhower derided it as a "juvenile experiment" and journalists called it a "Kiddie Korps."

Few expected that young people of the "silent generation" would volunteer, or that they could make a difference if they did. But Kennedy knew that young people would rise to the challenge. To a reporter's skeptical question, one of the first Peace Corps volunteers said, "Nobody asked me to do anything unselfish, patriotic and for the common good before. Kennedy asked."

President Kennedy appointed his brother-in-law, Sargent Shriver, to organize the Peace Corps. Shriver joked that Kennedy picked him because it was easier to fire a relative than a political friend, but in truth Kennedy couldn't have made a better choice. Shriver was a man of vision and practicality with incredible energy and imagination. He knew the Peace Corps would have only one chance to work. "As with the parachute jumper, the chute had to open the first time," he used to say. He proposed a big and bold start to capture the imagination of the potential volunteers and the public.

I was lucky to be on the team Sargent Shriver assembled to turn Kennedy's idea into a living program. Shriver's guiding premise was never to accept "no" as an answer. When he asked the State Department experts how long it would take to get the first volunteers overseas, they estimated at least two and a half years. Shriver said, "We're going to show them. In five months we'll have 500 volunteers in at least five countries." And that's exactly what happened.

Beating the bureaucracy became the name of the game. "You guys had a good day today," a civil service expert helping us wryly remarked one afternoon. "You broke fourteen laws." Instead of waiting for Congress to pass a law, we recommended that Kennedy create the Peace Corps by executive order as a pilot and then ask for legislation. He agreed, and on March 1, 1961, six weeks after he was sworn in, the Peace Corps was born. In his State of the Union address, he said "Nothing carries the spirit of American idealism and expresses our hopes better and more effectively to the far corners of the earth than the Peace Corps."

Unfortunately, Kennedy did not live to see the Peace Corps grow to 15,000 volunteers. Since 1961, about 150,000 Americans have served in more than 100 countries in the Peace Corps. Millions of people in Asia, Africa and Latin America now enjoy better education, safer water, more productive land and greater economic prosperity because of their service. Currently the Peace Corps is at work in the former Soviet Union and Communist China. It continues to provide a world-wide training for Great Citizens—volunteers who return home with the skills and determination to help solve problems in America.

Another high hope of the President's is at long last beginning to be realized. After sending off the first Peace Corps Volunteers from the White House lawn, President Kennedy said, "The logic of this idea is that someday we will bring it home to America." At last that day has come.

Today 25,000 Americans from many walks of life, most of them young, are teaching kids, fighting crime, building homes and cleaning the environment through service in AmeriCorps. Created by Congress and President Clinton in 1993, AmeriCorps is often called the "domestic Peace Corps." Indeed, in creating AmeriCorps, we often turned to the experience of the Peace Corps for guidance. The Peace Corps set the precedent for the government playing a vital role in creating opportunities for citizens to serve— in local community programs under local leadership.

The secret to American success has always been our belief that we can change things, we can make things better, that we can solve our most serious problems by working together. Through the Peace Corps, we are spreading that spirit around the world. Through AmeriCorps, we are renewing that spirit here at home. As we enter a new century full of challenges, we must do everything we can to keep that spirit going and growing.

Want to help others while having an unforgettable opportunity for personal and professional growth? Serve in the **Peace Corps**, call 800-424-8580.

Global Village

What is this fascination we have with people from foreign lands, and they with us? Is it just their rich culture, lively music and dancing, exotic foods and colorful festivals? Is it just our rich lifestyle, our fast foods and action-packed movies, money-making schemes, and modern conveniences? Or is it our shared sense of humanity, our desire to learn from each other and our generous spirit, welcoming each other into our homes and our world?

Marshall McLuhan predicted that all the world's people would one day live in a "global village," thanks to modern technology's ability to instantaneously transmit information. While the media informs us about our neighbors in foreign lands, too often we only hear about their national crises, political turmoils and environmental disasters. Sometimes this unsettling news overwhelms us, leads to "compassion fatigue" and a questioning of how we can actually manage this global village. Sometimes we wonder how we can help people in other countries when we have so many problems at home.

The stories in this chapter offer a ray of hope and a myriad of opportunities we can learn from. Some of our foreign neighbors are addressing tough problems, often with very limited resources. Even in the poorest of nations, the simple act of people joining with one another to solve the problems they face is bringing about astounding change.These amazing grassroot initiatives are slowly, quietly transforming countries around the world. These global heroes are some of the world's greatest treasures, offering us valuable lessons. When such progress can be made in places where natural resources and capital are scare, just think what could happen in a nation as rich, as blessed as ours?

This chapter offers an "advanced course" of *Stone Soup for the World*, bringing hope to those in this country who wonder if it's possible to change an entire nation. Many of these global heroes have risked their lives, influenced whole countries and sometimes even changed the course of history. Here you will find stories of ordinary people who became global heroes just by taking one step at a time toward their dream of bringing social and economic justice. Even after spending 27 years in South African jails, Nelson Mandela still believes that "Man's goodness is a flame that can be hidden but never extinguished."

Some of the stories in this chapter tell how global heroes are rekindling their traditions and spiritual values while encouraging their countrymen to rebuild their lives and their villages. Filipinos call their tradition of giving back *Bayanihan*: working together for the common good. A *Bayani* is a community hero, one who works for the good of all. In Japan, some people speak of *kyosei* to describe a vision of living together in harmony and interdependence with others.

Children all over the world are told the Stone Soup story of people helping other people, working together to make a better life for themselves, their children and their countrymen. In the Philippines, the story Sopas Na Bato, is legendary. Instead of carrots, potatoes and onions, rice, chicken, vegetable leaves and jalapeno peppers are added to the soup. While their recipe may be a little different than ours, they build the same community spirit with their "magic" stone. In China, the Stone Soup story teaches children a lesson about the power of changing our minds about what we think we can give.

These stories also show the positive impact new immigrants are making in America. Most of them have a Stone Soup story to tell, how each generation gives to the next, continuing this honorable tradition, preserving family unity and creating a strong sense of community.

In these stories, we see how their giving to those outside their families inspired

Americans to join with them. From building schools for street children in Nicaragua to bringing dances for peace to refugee children in Bosnia, they rise above the horrors of war and help build a world that works for everyone.

As you read these stories, you will discover how much we can learn from each other. Countries which are striving to build new democracies, inspire us to rebuild our own. Those who are using their pain to help others bring about peace can inspire us to heal the wounds in our own communities. Those renewing their cultural and spiritual traditions, remind us to rekindle ours. These stories give new meaning to the "global village" and new ideas for how to fulfill its promise.

- When you travel abroad, be sure to look for the hopeful stories and bring home the good news along with your postcards and memories.
- And when you meet new immigrants, ask them to tell you a Stone Soup story from their country.
- By taking the time to get to know one another and share our stories, we will bring out the best in each other and discover how to live together on one planet.
- Our children and grandchildren can then look forward to a more hopeful future.

The Courage to Care

STORYTELLER: ALLAN LUKS WITH PEGGY PAYNE,
adapted from *The Healing Power of Doing Good*

"Please, may I come in?" asked the woman at the door. It was dark and she was frightened. Magda Trocme opened the door. "Come in," she said. Later she admitted, "I did not know it would be dangerous. Nobody thought of that." The woman at the door was *Juif*—a German Jew. She had come to this village in the mountains of France to hide until the danger of the Nazi regime was over.

Andre Trocme, a Protestant minister, and his wife Magda wanted to help. "Will you hide the Jews?" Andre had been asked. "Is your village prepared to do that?" He had gone to the town church council and in minutes they had agreed. Now the test was here. A German Jew was at the door seeking shelter.

Le Chambon-sur-Lignon sits on a plateau surrounded by the high mountains of south-central France. During World War II and the German occupation, the community of Le Chambon made a collective decision to hide Jews who were fleeing Hitler's wrath. They refused to identify their Jewish neighbors and instead created a haven for Jewish children and families from all over the world. Not one refugee was ever turned away or turned over to the authorities. Instead five thousand Jews were rescued and hidden, a number equal to the total population of the town.

In Le Chambon, Jewish children went to school with Gentiles. They played together, sometimes with a pig that they called Adolf. At night, the Jewish children hid and slept in the barns and stables of farms around the town. In the morning, they would emerge from their hiding places to go to school. A young village boy was put in charge of the signal to let Jewish children know when the road was safe. When the shutters to his room were open, the road was open. When the shutters to his room were closed, they were to return to their hiding places.

Over and over the residents of Le Chambon were pressured to turn in the Jews and each time they refused to cooperate with the Nazis and the occupation government. As a pacifist, Andre Trocme had urged his parishioners and neighbors to resist violence with "weapons of the spirit." When he was asked for a list of the names of Jews in hiding, he declined, saying, "The Jews are my brothers." For his strong convictions, he was imprisoned. When the police came to take him to prison, Magda invited the gendarmes to sit and eat while she packed her husband's suitcase. To offer them such a kindness was nothing extraordinary, according to her. "There we were, and it was time to eat. It was nothing at all."

Years after the war was over, movie director Pierre Sauvage came to Le Chambon to learn more about this story. Sauvage had his own special reasons for this visit, "It was in Chambon that I was born, in March 1944, a Jewish baby," he says. "I was very lucky to see the light of day in a place that was committed to my survival at the very time when much of my family was disappearing into the abyss." Sauvage interviewed the aging survivors of World War II for his documentary, *Weapons of the Spirit,* about Le Chambon and the rescuing of the Jews. In his interviews, Sauvage sought to discover why the citizens had acted as they did. What had given them the courage to care and to risk their own lives to save these Jews?

Many of the villagers were Huguenots, French Protestants whose ancestors had been persecuted by the Catholic kings of France. The stories they'd heard all their lives of what their forebearers had been through helped prepare them to take a courageous stand. When it came time to do so, they were eager to help others who were being persecuted. At the same time many other congregations across Europe were closing their eyes to what was occurring around them, the people of his church understood the word of God to mean that they should help their brothers, the Jews. And the example set by one church was heroically accepted by all the townspeople, many of whom were not Huguenots.

As he asked the same question again and again, Sauvage often received the same response—a slight shrug of the shoulders and these simple words of explanation: "It was the right thing to do."

To learn more about **Le Chambon-sur-Lignon**, read the book and watch Pierre Sauvage's documentary, *Weapons of the Spirit.*

The Oasis of Peace

STORYTELLERS: NINA MERMEY KLIPPEL AND SHARON BURDE

In the heart of a land known for conflict and violence, there exists a symbol of hope. Its name is its message. In Hebrew, it is *Neve Shalom.* In Arabic, it is *Wahat al-Salam.* In English, it is The Oasis of Peace.

Located halfway between Jerusalem and Tel Aviv, The Oasis of Peace is a haven for Palestinians and Jews who have chosen to live and work together in peace. Only a precious few have made the choice to live in this bilingual, bicultural village. But they have created a model of coexistence that inspires people everywhere.

For generations, Jews and Arabs have struggled over the biblical land of Palestine. For Jews, it is the promised land of their forefathers. For Arabs, it is the home where they have dwelled for centuries.

After World War II, thousands of Jewish Holocaust survivors arrived in Israel with hopes of a more peaceful future. But the Palestinians resisted this massive immigration into their precious homeland. When the Jews asked for the state of Israel to be recognized by the United Nations, bitter fighting erupted and a tragic cycle of violence developed. Today, the people of Israel live with a fragile commitment to peace and the fear of a continuing legacy of violence.

Against this backdrop, Neve Shalom/Wahat al-Salam is a miracle. Throughout most of Israel, Arabs and Jews live completely apart—separated by community, language, culture, and schools. But, in this unique village, Jewish and Palestinian families live side by side, sharing their gardens and their homes. Since both Hebrew and Arabic are taught in school, children at play call out to each other in both languages.

Neve Shalom/Wahat al-Salam started as the vision of one very gentle man with an unusual heritage. Father Bruno Hussar was born a Jew in the Moslem land of Egypt. He converted to Catholicism, became a monk, and devoted his life to building understanding between Christians, Jews, and Muslims. After building partnerships between different religions and cultures with organizations like the Vatican and the United Nations, Father Bruno wanted to make his dream of peace become a reality for ordinary people.

He pictured a village where Moslems, Jews, and Christians would live together in peace: a place where their very diversity would be a source of enrichment rather than dissension. By living together, they would learn to break down the barriers of fear and ignorance and build bridges of trust, respect, and understanding.

Father Bruno obtained a ninety-year lease on a plot of land from the Abbott of the Monastery at Latrun, a stony, brambly hillside without water or shade. It was hardly an oasis, but for him it was the Garden of Eden. At age sixty, he and a few friends took up residence in this desolate place, living at first in empty packing cases. Word of this new community of peace spread. Gradually, a few pioneering Jewish and Arab families came and built houses. In 1972, Neve Shalom/Wahat al-Salam was born.

The soul of the village, the School for Peace, is a magnet for Jews, Palestinians, and peace-seeking people from all over the world, one of whom was an Arab boy named Ahmad Hijazi. This young Palestinian grew up in an Arab village in northern Israel. When he was sixteen, his class came to a School for Peace workshop. For the first time, he and the Jewish students met face to face in a safe, supportive environment. Just to see Arab and Jewish teachers working together in harmony was an eye-opener.

In the workshop, the young people, led by skilled facilitators, got to really know each other. They talked, argued, and in the end, were able to tell each other, with total honesty, of the mutual distrust, fear, and anger they bore. Many cried, remembering friends or family members who had been killed or injured by one side or the other. "As we envisioned steps to a more peaceful future," says Ahmad, "we saw each other with new eyes, as human beings. For the first time in our lives, we could see that peace was possible."

The experience changed Ahmad's life. After going to the university, he moved to the village and joined the staff of the School for Peace. He became the general secretary of the village, a job similar to that of mayor, which rotates between Jewish and Palestinian citizens. He and his Jewish colleagues travel to the U.S., Europe, and Japan sharing with people everywhere their dream for peace. "Although governments sign peace treaties, ordinary citizens still have to learn to overcome their fear and prejudices in order to build a peace that endures," Ahmad points out.

Since its founding in 1979, the School for Peace has trained over twenty thousand young people in the ways of peace: Jews, Arabs, and even inner-city youth from America. Teachers from the School for Peace also serve as ambassadors, sharing their training in Northern Ireland, the barrios of Los Angeles, and other troubled places. They hope to spread their message of tolerance, mutual respect, and understanding to all war-torn areas.

The village has a long waiting-list of families who want to move in. The primary school, the only comprehensive Arabic-Hebrew bilingual school in Israel, has become a model for other schools in Israel. Children from nearby towns as well as from the village are taught here.

Neve Shalom/Wahat al-Salam has been nominated five times for the Nobel Peace Prize. It has been honored with prestigious awards in Italy, Japan, Germany, Austria, Sweden, and the United States. The great humanitarian Elie Wiesel said,

“Neve Shalom/Wahat al-Salam deserves our warmest support, for it justifies our highest hopes.” As Palestinian leader, Faisal al Husseini says “ I would like to see the moment when there would be such a thing as Neve Shalom/Wahat al-Salam not only between the Palestinians and Israelis, but between all the people in the Middle East.”

Father Bruno, who died in 1996 at age eighty-four, lived to see his oasis nourish people throughout the world. He once said, “I have just sown the seeds; others have cultivated the plants they have produced.” In the village, a new crop is sprouting: the Jewish and Arab children who are growing up in Neve Shalom/Wahat al-Salam share their languages and cultures and, most important of all, a commitment to peace. With young people like these to lead the way to the twenty-first century, could we hope that the Middle East itself might one day become an Oasis of Peace?

Raise your voice for tolerance and democracy in the Middle East. Become a partner for peace by calling the **American Friends of Neve Shalom/Wahat al-Salam** at 212-226-9246 or e-mail: afnswas@compuserve.com.

Hunger Can't Wait

STORYTELLER: PETER MANN

Herbert de Souza spoke the truth when he told his fellow Brazilians, "If we want a democratic country, we must fight poverty." Known affectionately as *Betinho* by his countrymen, de Souza was a frail, sixty-year-old man with gray, wavy hair and deep, luminous green eyes. Betinho was one of three brothers, all hemophiliacs, who contracted the HIV virus from blood transfusions. In the last years of his life, Betinho was often very sick from the disease, but he was a man with a cause, and the urgency of his cause kept him going. "Hunger is in a hurry," he said. "Hunger cannot wait!"

Over the years, Brazil has become a land of paradox. Its people live in one of two worlds: the life of luxury or of misery. Rich in agriculture, Brazil is one of the world's largest food exporters, yet thirty-two million of its people, more than one fifth of the country, go hungry every day. Until recently, the people of Brazil had closed their hearts to the desperate plight of their fellow countrymen.

But in 1993, mass demonstrations forced a powerful, corrupt president to resign. Amazed at their newfound power to fight for a better life, people were ready to take the next step. It was an ideal time for Betinho to challenge his people. "In the past we have tolerated poverty and misery," he said. "We have tried to explain it away. But now we must fight against it—and make this a priority!"

As an invitation to stretch their newfound democratic muscle, Betinho created Citizen Action: A Campaign Against Hunger and encouraged people to organize local committees to fight hunger. "We'll help you, but we won't tell you what to do," he told them. The response was overwhelming. Thousands of local initiatives developed all over the country. In Rio de Janeiro, seven thousand cyclists "pedaled against hunger" and collected sixteen tons of food. In São Paulo, middle-class citizens joined their shantytown neighbors to organize food distribution networks in the slums. The comfortable learned where the hungry were, where the food was, and how to get it to the hungry. Most of all, they got to know hungry people personally. When one committee discovered that twelve thousand of their one hundred thousand people were destitute, they donated food and clothing. Then these middle-class families "adopted" poor families, helping them to deal with their specific problems. "We are replacing the map of hunger with the map of solidarity," Betinho says. "Poverty now has a human face."

The impact of Citizen Action has been extraordinary. Today, three million people are involved in campaign committees and thirty million more support the campaign. Everyone gives what they can. The Small Farmers Union in San Paolo created a "green belt" to grow food for the hungry. Workers at one company started by donating their monthly meal vouchers to buy food for five hundred poor children at a nearby school, then they offered training courses to help their parents get jobs. Companies with industrial kitchens created Project Our Soup, providing soup for thirty thousand each day. For many, it is their only meal. Even prisoners at a tough jail contributed by going without one meal each week. In solidarity with their poor countrymen on the outside, they sent them rice, beans, flour, and cooking oil.

As the program takes hold, people eventually discover the connection between feeding the hungry and helping hungry people to become self-reliant. "After the first year, we realized we couldn't continue to give food away indefinitely," Betinho said. "With the slogan 'Food against hunger. Jobs against misery,' local committees responded with much needed jobs. They created entrepreneurial projects such as bakeries, small vegetable gardens, microenterprises, and paper recycling ventures. This way even the poorest people can experience their own power and dignity and then give back to the community."

Growing up as a young boy in a conservative Brazilian town in the 1950s, Betinho learned about the miserable plight of the masses from the Catholic church. While at a Catholic university, he cofounded Popular Action, the first progressive non-Communist party in Brazil. But in 1970, when a military dictatorship took over Brazil, he was forced to flee, returning nine years later when a general amnesty was declared.

Now, the campaign against hunger crosses all social and political lines. For the first time, instead of waiting for their political party, union, or church to take action, people are experiencing their own power as active citizens. "The committees did more than just give food to people," Betinho said. "They started breaking the cycle of poverty by providing housing and sanitation, by educating the children, and by helping the elderly."

From the beginning, Betinho knew that the media were key to the campaign. When a major São Paulo newspaper decided to back the campaign, hundreds of committees sprang up throughout the city. One television station wove the hunger campaign into the story line of a popular soap opera. PR agencies pooled their efforts to donate advertising, creating commercials that show Brazil's "two worlds." One of them, shot in stark black and white, shows a luxury car stopped at a traffic light on a busy Rio street. An elegantly dressed man looks straight ahead. Then he glances to his side and quickly pushes a button to close the car window. As the glass rises, you see the reflection of a child, begging, an empty dish in hand. The child keeps looking, hoping, but the man doesn't look back. He waits for the light to change, then drives away. No words are spoken, just the closing trailer: "Hunger doesn't just isolate the hungry—you are a prisoner of poverty, too."

Today, people in Brazil speak of Betinho as a saint. When he died in 1997, the campaign of nearly three million workers and volunteers, was an impressive success. In areas where campaign committees are at work, hunger has been reduced by as much as one-third. "This period will be remembered as the era when citizenship was awakened," Betinho said. Watching him work, and seeing the good he has done brings to mind Homer's words from *The Iliad:* "Whatever you do that is kept in the minds of the people who come afterwards, you will be alive."

This nation is looking for a vision.
We had 'manifest destiny.'
We built the railroads, industry, won two world wars.
We're looking for something grand and good to do.
Feeding the world could be that thing.

HARRY CHAPIN, FOUNDER OF WORLD HUNGER YEAR

Learn how you can work with others to fight hunger in your community. **World Hunger Year** asks the question, "Why does hunger, poverty, and homelessness stalk this bountiful planet?" Call us at 1-800-5-HUNGRY.

Adagio in Sarajevo

STORYTELLER: RICHARD DEATS
adapted from *Fellowship,* the magazine of The Fellowship for Reconciliation

It's hard to believe that not too long ago, Sarajevo was looked to as a model of religious and ethnic harmony. The world marveled in 1984 when athletes came to this exquisite city to compete in the Winter Olympic Games. Here Orthodox and Muslim, and Catholic and Jew peacefully lived and worked side by side in a unique atmosphere of tolerance and goodwill. The ancient city of Sarajevo, with over a half a million people, had been a cultural haven for Croats, Serbs, and Muslims for centuries.

How could it all have changed so quickly? By 1990, Yugoslavia was disintegrating into rival ethnic states and Sarajevo, the jewel of Bosnia, was surrounded in a siege that was slowly destroying the city. Unending civil war engulfed the region; its people were subjected to regular shellings and unpredictable sniper fire. Food and supplies were scarce at best.

Waiting hours on the street for a single loaf of bread was a regular routine. One day in May 1992, a long line at a Sarajevo bakery stretched outside and snaked down the block. As the people waited they spoke about the war, about hunger, and about their children trapped at home, too afraid to go to school. At 4 P.M., their conversations ended abruptly. A shell exploded directly in the middle of the line, killing twenty-two people and wounding over one hundred.

The world was shocked, and for the families, the grief overwhelming. Still, people needed to eat. So the next day, the bakery once again opened its doors. As the hour of 4 P.M. approached, people in line became tense and silent. But instead of another shell, they were surprised to be "hit" by the sounds of music. Exactly at 4 P.M., Vedran

Smailovic, the principal cellist of the Sarajevo Opera, arrived at the bakery, carrying a chair and his cello. Dressed in a formal black suit and white tie, Smailovic played the majestic yet sorrowful lines of Albinoni's *Adagio,* and the music fed the people's souls. Every day for twenty-two days he came and played again at the same time: one performance for each victim of the attack. With his music, he honored those who had died there, affirming the indomitable spirit of life even in the midst of death. He also set into motion a series of musical and artistic homages to those victims.

The place of what is known as "the bread line massacre" has become a shrine, marked by wreaths, candles, and pieces of paper holding the names of the victims who died there. Not far from where the bread line was is a ruined city square, remembered for being a place where a Muslim mosque, a Roman Catholic cathedral, and an Orthodox church once stood. In April 1993, Joan Baez was the first major artist to visit Sarajevo since the siege began. With Smailovic accompanying her on the cello, she sang "Amazing Grace."

How do people respond to unspeakable acts of violence? Monks pray, workers strike, and artists raise awareness by doing what they do best. Half a world away, Seattle artist Beliz Brother heard the story of Vedran Smailovic and wanting to respond through her own art, she created a sculpture to memorialize the massacre. On a street corner in Seattle, she built a ten-foot-high stack of bread pans, with twenty-two loaves scattered about. In front of them she placed a coffin-looking cello case and covered it with flour and pieces of mortar. Symbolically, her sculpture depicted the building rubble from the destroyed bakery and what she called "the whiteout of ethnic cleansing."

In solidarity with Smailovic, Brother also arranged for Seattle cellists dressed in formal attire to perform the *Adagio* at twenty sites around the city. Their only props were baskets of bread and bouquets of flowers. She repeated the gesture for the 1993 inauguration of President Clinton, persuading twenty-two cellists to perform the

Albinoni's piece at various places around Washington, D.C. From federal buildings to sites of terrorist acts, from city squares to the White House, the *Adagio* cried out. And in the midst of the inaugural festivities, the siege of a great Olympic city was not forgotten. In 1995, to commemorate the thousandth day of the siege of Sarajevo, Smailovic performed at the Statue of Liberty, to remind the world that we should not rest until peace has come once again.

In April 1994, cellists gathered at the International Cello Festival in Manchester, England, to hear the renowned cellist Yo Yo Ma perform *The Cellist of Sarajevo*, a piece for unaccompanied cello written by the English composer David Wilde. When Ma had finished, the deeply moved listeners sat in stunned silence. Then he walked into the audience and embraced a man with long, wild hair and a huge mustache. The man was dressed in a stained and tattered leather motorcycle jacket; his face was old beyond his years, creased with pain and suffering. Then the audience realized this was Vedran Smailovic—the cellist of Sarajevo himself!

They rose as one in a wave of emotional release: clapping, weeping, shouting, embracing, and cheering. And in the center of it all stood these two men, embracing each other, both crying freely: Yo Yo Ma, the suave, elegant prince of classical music, flawless in appearance and performance, and Vedran Smailovic, who had just escaped from Sarajevo, disheveled and defiant. His cello, it turned out, had held more power than bombs and guns and all the ugly instruments of terror combined. With his music, the cellist of Sarajevo had defied the power of death itself, inspiring many to resist despair by celebrating love, life, and that spark of human spirit that can never be destroyed.

Help bring peace to Bosnia by supporting the **Bosnian Student Project.** Contact them at the **Fellowship of Reconciliation**, Box 271, Nyack, NY 10960 or visit http://www.nonviolence.org/~nvweb/for.

Awakening

Storyteller: Marianne Larned

A. T. Ariyaratne stood before a group of villagers in Sri Lanka. They were in despair: their irrigation system was in shambles and the government had ignored their pleas for help. For years, they had gone without enough water for their animals, their crops, and their children. Now they could wait no longer. Their village was dying and they needed a miracle. Ari knew that by working together could they create one. He asked, "who can feed one person by sharing his meal with another?" One by one, several hands went up. "Who can feed two, three, or four?" A few more hands went up. Gathering materials in the same way, Ari organized a work camp for the villagers to repair their own water system, save their village, and begin to make history.

In 1958, Ari had the idea of bringing his upper-caste high school students to remote poverty-stricken villages to help rebuild them. For two weeks, these privileged young people lived and worked side by side with people of the lower caste. They learned practical skills while developing compassion for their countrymen. From these work camps, Ari began a crusade. He called it *Sarvodaya,* a term Gandhi used for "awakening of all." Ari wove Gandhian and Buddhist principles together to create a powerful volunteer service and grassroots human development organization and created the *shramadanas* (work camps) as "gifts of labor."

As a child growing up in a tiny Sri Lankan village, Patrick Mendis had heard stories about this man. By 1972, everyone in every village in Sri Lanka knew about the good works of the Saravodya. Since the government was ignoring the needs of small villages, the Sarvodaya was the only hope for the "little people" of Sri Lanka. Patrick says, "When we heard that the Sarvodaya was coming to our small village in Polonnarauwa, we were ecstatic! It was like Santa Claus was coming. We'd ask ourselves, 'Is it really going to happen in *our* village?!' It gave us hope, because we knew now things would get done."

Patrick was only twelve years old, one of the youngest of thirty young boys who participated in a one-day shramadana. Since he had been left by his parents as an infant and raised by his grandparents, he'd always struggled with feeling like an outsider. Here he was the only Christian in a group of Buddhists. To his surprise, they welcomed him warmly. "Everyone called each other *mali* or 'brother,'" he says. "We lived as one big family, practiced sharing, and treated everyone as equals."

These thirty youngsters planted gardens, dug latrines, connected the village's road to the main highway, and had fun working together, happily and enthusiastically. "We didn't have a plan, a design, or a blueprint," Patrick says. "We just talked about our ideas and what we'd like to see in our village and worked together until we got it right. We started the day with a Buddhist chant, a loving kindness meditation, and finished with a meal. From early morning until late at night, everyone worked together to improve life in the village. At the end of the day, everyone was jubilant," Patrick says. "We'd become friends. We had built more than roads, we had built a family, a community, and a spirit in our village. We created a sense of hopefulness in our village." Patrick was particularly moved by the deep connection he felt with his new "brothers".

A few years later, Patrick left Sri Lanka for America to get a Western education. He was fortunate to study at the best universities. He became an accomplished researcher and teacher of international development and foreign affairs. He had a wonderful wife, two beautiful children, and a good life in Minnesota. But something was missing. In the back of his mind, he kept thinking about that special day from his childhood.

He started writing about the Sarvodaya, publishing articles and even a book about this practice. "What is happening to me?" he wondered. There were other books he was supposed to be writing, but memories of his experience with the shramadana kept returning. Finally, he decided it was time to write to Ari and introduce himself.

By 1995, the Sarvodaya had become well known as the world's largest volunteer movement. Over seven million people, half of Sri Lanka's population, were working together to improve over eleven thousand villages throughout the country. They had one hundred coordinating centers, each serving the needs of twenty to thirty villages, implementing programs in education, health care, transportation, agriculture, and technologically appropriate energies like windmills and methane generators. In one year, Sarvodaya built three times as many roads as the government had, linking many underdeveloped villages for the first time with the outside world.

Ari was pleased to hear from Patrick and invited him to come home for a visit, as his guest. It would be Patrick's first visit in over twenty years. He was a bit nervous and very curious. "When I arrived at Ari's house, he bowed his head to me," Patrick said. "I was shocked. I thought I should be bowing to him. Then Ari put his hands together and called me 'Mali,' and told me to call him *'Ayya,'* or 'big brother.'" "This is our home; it is open to you," Ari told Patrick. "Here, we are one family." Patrick felt the same wonderful connection that he had when he was as twelve-year-old boy.

One day, Ari asked Patrick to join him at a Sarvodaya family gathering. There, people would talk about their village's problems and share ideas about how to make things better. When they arrived, Patrick was invited to come up to the podium. He was nervous and embarrassed. He hadn't spoken his native Sinhalese for many years.

"You can speak any language you want," he was told, "we will translate."

"This is our guest: Dr. Patrick Mendis from the United States," Ari told the people who were gathered. "He is from Polonnararuwa. A long time ago, he worked in the Saravodya." Patrick told the expectant crowd, "I came to learn from you." Then he told them of his experience as a young boy at the shramadana and how his life had been changed by the sense of connection that he experienced in that one very special day. "Saravodya awakens young people like you and me, who then awaken their families, their communities, then the world," he said, "but the awakening must start first with each one of us."

Everyone loved hearing Patrick speak, even though he mixed up the two languages. Some wanted to shake his hand. Others wanted to know how he got to America. "They thought I was a big shot," Patrick says. They wondered how I could end up in the U.S. coming from a tiny village in Sri Lanka. They wanted to know my secret." Patrick told the villagers that the secret was there for them, right in their own village. And that coming to America wasn't the key to happiness. Smiling, he reminded them of the Sarvodaya saying: "We build the road and the road builds us."

We must be the change we want in the world.

GANDHI

If you would like to create an awakening in your life, come experience a shramadana work camp at the **Sarvodaya** in Sri Lanka. E-mail Dr. Ariyaratne at arisar@sri.lanka.net or Sarvodya USA at STEVODAYA@aol.com.

Turning Leftovers into Lifesavers

STORYTELLER: CARRIE CATON PILLSBURY

After 20 years in America, Mohamed Ahmed couldn't believe his eyes. With the violent overthrow of Ethiopia's King Haile Selaissie, the military had taken over everyone's land in this stunned country. Ethiopians lost their incentive to work, production bottomed out and starvation was epidemic. Businessmen like Mohamed's father, who owned a small salt factory, were labeled enemies of the state and many were imprisoned.

In the midst of this nightmare, Mohamed's father lost his life. One morning he awoke with acute, unexplainable pain and was rushed to the Dessie Regional Hospital, where poverty had wiped out any available medicine or supplies. Here Ethiopian physicians were attempting to treat 100,000 refugees with nothing but tongue depressors and stethoscopes. The doctors had to send Mr. Ahmed's diagnostic tests via bus across dusty, one-lane paths to Addis Abbaba, more than 250 miles away. The letter revealing his fatal diagnosis of bone cancer finally arrived back in Wollo, Mohamed's home village—10 days after his burial.

As Mohamed stood over his father's grave, he remembered the Ethiopia he had left 20 years ago. His plan then had been to obtain a U.S. education and return home to teach young Ethiopians at the university. But he had soon realized that his dream was not to be. His future students were busy waging war against the dictators who wreaked havoc on his homeland. Now, beside his father's grave, Mohamed wept—for the father he had loved, for the country he had all but lost, for his dying people who could not be saved at hospitals bereft of the tools of healing.

The doctors had told his family, "We are in Ethiopia—there is nothing we could do for him." But Mohamed Ahmed didn't like feeling helpless. In that moment he swore to do everything in his power to see that no Ethiopian family would ever have to hear those words again.

Returning to America to hunt for resources, Mohamed contacted fellow Ethiopians in his newly adopted home of Dallas to enlist their aid. He then called close friends in an effort to raise more money. But he quickly realized that galvanizing the forces needed to save his far-away village was more than a one-man job.

Desperate for ideas, he remembered reading an article in the *Dallas Morning News* about a group of people committed to improving health care in developing countries. He soon found himself on the doorstep of MEDISEND. The goal of this Dallas non-profit organization was to transform America's medical surplus into life-saving supplies for third-world countries. Mohamed was most definitely in the right place at the right time.

At MEDISEND Mohamed met Dr. Martin Lazar, a neurosurgeon who, in 1987, had witnessed firsthand the abysmal conditions of health care facilities in developing countries. Dr. Lazar also knew firsthand of the excessive waste in American hospitals. He flinched as perfectly usable medical supplies were thrown away due to strict American safety standards. Untouched packets of cotton gauze exposed only to air, and expensive, but outdated, orthopedic supplies were constantly being thrown into overflowing landfills. In the United States, $6.5 billion worth of surplus medical supplies are needlessly dumped into these landfills each year.

Dr. Lazar knew that a once life-giving, heart-lung machine now gathering dust in a Texas hospital storage room could be refurbished and shipped to a hospital in Africa, Eastern Europe or Asia to save many more lives. He also knew that rubber gloves, unused and discarded during a surgical procedure in a Washington D.C. hospital could be resterilized and used for as many as ten operations in other countries. "Imagine the impact of 1,000 pairs of gloves could have in hospitals in those countries," he thought. In 1990, Dr. Lazar founded MEDISEND to "turn leftovers into lifesavers" and become "a life-saving force for our neighbors throughout the world."

Mohamed Ahmed and Dr. Lazar shared a common dream—extending medical care and hope to lands of poverty. They worked together to make that dream became a concrete reality for the hospital in Mohamed's village. Soon the supplies that could not be used in America were being shipped to Ethiopia.

"There are many people who feel a common bond of humanity and are willing to extend a helping hand out of moral conviction," says Mohamed. "The supplies and equipment MEDISEND sent made the difference between having nothing and having a lot. They gave our hospital the chance to survive and serve its community."

It was one more humanitarian and environmental success story for MEDISEND. To date, the organization has shipped 150 tons of medical supplies and equipment valued at more than $4.3 million to 106 hospitals in 50 developing countries. The value of the human lives these shipments have saved is priceless.

As Mohamed recovered from grieving for his father, he started a family of his own. And having experienced the profound fulfillment of reaching out to others, he made sure to pass these values along to his own children. A quarter of a century after the death of the grandfather they never knew, Mohamed's 12-year-old daughter, Sophie, and 8-year-old son, Amir, showed the same generosity and compassion as their father. They saved their allowances and birthday gifts, and managed to pool together a life savings of $515. They donated it to MEDISEND, explaining that they wanted to help more poor people get medical attention.

The overworked doctor or nurse in Ethiopia who opens that new parcel of post-op products with a note that reads "from Sophie and Amir with love" might not know the story of how the whole thing started. But surely they will see that miracles can come out of expressions of love. And maybe it will give them hope that someday their beloved homeland will be the healthy place it once was—-a miracle they are all working towards.

You start with one step and it's amazing how wonderful people will rise to the occasion.

MARTIN LAZAR, M.D.

If you want to help **MEDISEND** "turn leftovers into lifesavers" and identify new sources of usable medical surplus or be part of our distribution channel, call 214-696-0901 or e-mail Medisend@airmail.net.

Step by Step

STORYTELLER: GIL FRIEND

Karl-Henrik Robèrt, a Swedish doctor specializing in pediatric medicine, was tired of seeing children die of cancer. As a noted medical researcher, he wanted to know why. Like many of his colleagues, he had developed a certain professional detachment from the daily agony of watching young children waste away. But, one day, when another young girl died of leukemia, something in him snapped.

"*Why* are so many little ones dying this way?" he wanted to know. Most of his patients were far too young to have developed the type of at-risk lifestyle often associated with cancer. There was growing evidence in the medical community about the role of the environment in disease. He had heard the endless scientific and political bantering; was this substance the main culprit, or that one? How many parts per billion of this toxin or that were "acceptable"? Dr. Robèrt became impatient with the debate: he decided to *do* something about it.

"Much of the debate over the environment," he later wrote, "has had the character of monkey chatter amidst the withering leaves of a dying tree. In the midst of all this chatter, very few of us have been paying attention to the trunk and branches. . . . if we heal the trunk and the branches, the benefits for the leaves will follow naturally."

Dr. Robèrt decided to study the "trunk of the tree"; the fundamental and inarguable principles, underlying our environmental problems. He organized the basic facts and circulated a draft to leading Swedish scientists. Then he asked them to add their ideas, correct what was wrong, and include anything important that might be missing.

The scientists responded to his call. Dr. Robèrt added their ideas, revised the paper, and circulated it again and again. Ultimately he repeated the cycle twenty-one times. He never argued his point of view. He just asked, listened and revised, until all the scientists agreed they had identified the "trunk of the tree"—and the healthy environment it needs to grow. They concluded that putting the laws of nature at the heart of our economy and into our daily lives is essential for the sustainability of our world.

Dr. Robèrt then took on an equally challenging task. Knowing about a problem is one thing: doing something about it is entirely different. He knew he must share the message in a way that everyone in Sweden would want to get involved. In 1990 he founded The Natural Step to provide ordinary people with the information they need to help improve their country's environment.

Then in another creative leap, Dr. Robèrt approached Swedish television, asking, "If I had the participation of our leading musicians, actors and business executives, would you broadcast an environmental message?" The answer was an enthusiastic yes. He then enrolled the country's most noted musicians and actors, "If I had the television air-time, and the support of leading businesses, would you appear on a show to help the environment?" Intrigued by the cause, they agreed. He then approached business leaders, and got them involved too.

Together, they created a television program that documented why every Swedish citizen was needed to help create a healthy environment. To show people how they could help, they developed a booklet and audio tape and mailed it to every household in the country. Step by step, the project has become a huge success, affecting millions of people and catalyzing creative initiatives throughout the country.

The Federation of Swedish Farmers took a goal of growing the "world's cleanest agriculture." They are helping farmers to reduce the use of chemical fertilizers and pesticides, and shift their production to organic farming. This shift is not only healthy, it is profitable: Sweden's agricultural exports have significantly increased.

Dozens of local governments have created ambitious programs for environmental improvement, with many declaring themselves "eco-municipalities." And they are building voluntary agreements with residents, retailers, and manufacturers to help meet those goals. One town developed a plan to reduce the burden on municipal water treatment systems. Residents of this town are educated to shop for cleaning products that generate less toxic waste, and retailers are encouraging their suppliers to come up with cleaner products. The result is a chain reaction of ecological activism, exactly what Dr. Robèrt wanted to inspire.

Dr. Robèrt has also inspired corporations to invest in redesigning their products with the environment in mind. The IKEA retail furniture chain now conducts environmental life cycle analyses on all their products. They are also asking their suppliers to change their manufacturing processes and materials "to meet ecocyclical requirements." So every employee can understand and contribute to changes and explain them to customers, the company's entire workforce as well as its suppliers is receiving basic environmental training.

By 1996, seven years after Dr. Robèrt began his effort, more than 60 major companies and 50 municipalities in Sweden had adopted The Natural Step as a guideline for improving the environment through their operations. TNS has had a tremendous impact on some major manufacturing operations including Electrolux, the world's largest appliance manufacturer. Electrolux didn't exactly enter the game eagerly. One of their largest customers refused to sign a major contract when they concluded that Electrolux products did not the "system conditions" for sustainability. When Electrolux executives found out why they had lost the account, company executives angrily demanded a meeting with Dr. Robèrt. "What are you doing?" they demanded. "You've cost us millions!"

Dr. Robèrt patiently shared the basic science underlying the TNS strategy with the Electrolux executives. As good scientists and engineers, they had to admit that his non-negotiable scientific principles were . . . well . . . non-negotiable! Having no choice but to acknowledge their validity, they embarked upon the great challenge of bringing their company into alignment with the laws of nature.

Electrolux is now redesigning household appliances, such as dishwashers, to dramatically conserve the precious resources of water and energy. Their annual report insist that it is not a "green" company; they say it is simply taking prudent steps to meet business goals and build shareholder value! The fact that those "prudent steps" serve environmental interests is beyond the imagining of most environmental activist five years ago. Electrolux calls their billion kroner investment in Natural Step initiatives the best financial investment they have ever made.

The Natural Step is simple, yet powerful. One man's idea has helped to change an entire nation—by getting people to focus on what they can agree on, instead of how they disagree. Imagine what could happen if everyone—farmers, companies, governments and citizens—in your community did the same. If we put the laws of nature into the heart of our enterprise and into our daily lives, we could build a healthier world for everyone to enjoy.

If the people lead, the leaders will follow.

DWIGHT EISENHOWER

Learn more about how you can take the next step toward improving the environment in your community. Call **The Natural Step** at 415-332-9394 or send e-mail to: tns@naturalstep.org.

Pathways to Peace

STORYTELLER: MASANKHO BANDA

My passion for peace through social justice was born when my father was imprisoned for speaking out for democracy in Malawi, West Africa. "We will lock him up until he learns to be quiet," said the President. My father languished in a cell for twelve long years: another voice for freedom silenced.

At the time, there was little I or anyone could do. For thirty years, Malawians lived in terror under the cruel dictatorship of our president. Relatively speaking, my father was one of the lucky ones. Today he is one of only three surviving members of the twenty in Malawi's first Cabinet, formed in 1964. Most of the others disappeared without a trace. As children we were considered outcasts and were prohibited from going to school.

At 18, I fled Malawi and its political persecution. Arriving alone in the United States, I carried the weight of my family's suffering. I wanted to connect with other young people whose lives had been shattered by war, but I didn't know where to go. One day a friend said to me, "Masankho, if you want to work with someone who is truly making a difference in children's lives around the world, call Avon Mattison." It turned out to be the most important telephone call of my life.

Although Avon was from America—the other side of the world—she was a kindred spirit. When she told me her remarkable story, I was deeply touched. It turns out Avon had been another child caught up in the nightmare of war. When she was born in 1941, the darkness of World War II covered the whole earth. On her fourth birthday, Avon looked out the window and made a silent wish for peace.

Avon's wish was answered by a most extraordinary vision! As she looked out her window, the little girl saw a beautiful image of the planet Earth as a living being. She saw an image of people of all ages and countries living harmoniously with the earth and with one another. When she wondered what they were doing, a voice inside told her they were building pathways to peace for future generations.

Young Avon wondered what her birthday message and "pathways to peace" meant. So she tried to tell the grownups what she had seen and asked them for an explanation. However, she was told that it was just her childish imagination. Her voice was not heard.

As a young adult, Avon began asking how people could make peace a practical reality for future generations. She met with leaders from the United Nations, corporations and government agencies, military officials and scientists, asking them all the same question. Many of them were too busy preparing for and fighting wars to answer her. But, in time, she found one or two brave souls from each walk of life who were willing to see what they could do together to build pathways to peace.

In the mid-1970's, Avon decided to bring these kindred spirits together so they could unite their strengths with and for the children. For the last 20 years, Avon's organization, Pathways to Peace (PTP), has coordinated a peacebuilding initiative involving 200 global organizations. PTP has co-sponsored several International Children's Conferences and has sent young people as its official representatives to U.N. Conferences.

Avon's greatest joy comes from working closely with young people, preparing us to become leaders of the 21st Century. She believes that we have the greatest stake in creating peace since we will be the ones who have to live with the decisions everyone is making today.

Like me, young people have come from all corners of the earth to meet Avon and ask for her guidance. Many of us have lived through the horrors of war. All of us long for a more peaceful world. Avon takes each one of us under her wing, focuses our energy and opens doors so that our young voices can be heard in the corridors of power and influence. Together we build unique peace-building initiatives with diverse peoples and organizations from around the world.

At our very first meeting, Avon began training me as a facilitator for the upcoming Children's Conference on Human Rights in Vienna. She wanted young people to be the ones who were recognized at this historic world conference. She wanted us to present our own perspectives and recommendations concerning the rights of children.

Four weeks after meeting Avon, I found myself on a plane to Vienna. Avon had given me her ticket and her place at the conference. I realized that in so doing, she was passing the torch to me, she was living her commitment to putting young people first.

In Vienna, I met 140 other young people, many of whom had been traumatized by years of war. At first, some of the youth had trouble even speaking their names. But in time they came to trust each other and their transformations were dramatic. For example, at the beginning of the conference, Liliana, a shy 15-year-old high school student, could barely introduce herself. But by the fifth day she was leading workshops with strength and authority. Igor and Vladimir, Bosnian and Serbian teenagers who had each lost a close relative in the war, led a joint workshop on tolerance and forgiveness. At one point, Igor turned to Vladimir and said "You and I are here, we are friends. Our people have done horrible things to each other. We can create something different. Instead of revenge, we need to talk about reconciliation. Instead of destroying, we can rebuild our country." When they hugged, there was not a dry eye in the room.

Each night, I worked with the children from Croatian refugee camps, teaching them songs and universal dances of peace. On the last night, they gave a special presentation for everyone. These children who had known only war in their lives were dancing for peace. We all danced and sang together; and spoke of peace, love, and reconciliation. We all knew that this was the way things should be all the time.

After the dancing, Ivana, the Croatian children's chaperone, walked over towards me. Tears running down her face, she smiled and embraced me. "Masankho, these children have been in the refugee camps for two years," she said. "This is the happiest I have ever seen them. Please come dance and sing with the children we have left behind." So we designed a children's peace education project for the Croatian refugee camps. We have made three trips to the camps, and have touched the lives of over 1000 children.

Through PTP, I've had the opportunity to see facets of Avon's childhood vision become a reality. I also see through her example and my own experience that the potential for peace leadership is in each and every one of us. Although the pathways to peace are difficult to build, I now know that you and I can make a difference. I truly believe that one day peace will prevail on earth.

Life is no brief candle to me;
it is a sort of bright torch which I have got hold of for a moment
and I want to make it burn as brightly as possible
before handing it on to future generations.

George Bernard Shaw

The Heavens Open

STORYTELLER: MARIANNE LARNED

Like many Americans who watched the peaceful revolution in the Philippines in 1986 on CNN, I was spellbound. When People Power was born, it brought hope for the rest of the world. Watching a courageous housewife like Cory Aquino become a president was truly inspiring. Her heartfelt invitation for Americans to help her fragile country touched my heart. Before I knew it, I was on a journey that changed my life.

When I arrived in 1987, the Philippines was a magical place. Everyone was eager to share their moment in history. Each taxi ride became a history lesson. Profiles in courage and determination, patience and faith, against insurmountable odds, were everywhere.

For almost twenty years, Filipinos had suffered as President Marcos sold their country to the highest bidder. But when Ninoy Aquino, their imprisoned hero, was assassinated, they'd had enough. Prominent Filipino women started questioning their values, talking with their friends, and gathering facts about the corruption, greed, and deception their country was drowning in. They banned together, gaining strength in numbers, and chipped away at the status quo. In the process, they risked their personal security and comforts: their marriages, their families, and even their lives. They encouraged their influential husbands to use their business powers to stop Marcos. Everyday for three years, they prayed for a more hopeful future. In February 1986, their prayers were answered.

At first, it looked like the Philippine Revolution would be a bloodbath. Soldiers, guns, and tanks were everywhere. Marcos cut off all communication with the outside world. The people were terrified, but a local radio announcer coaxed them to join together in Manila's streets. For one day, these frightened souls became a mighty army.

Teenagers put their bodies in front of tanks, befriended the soldiers, and placed flowers in their guns. Singing, "All we are saying, is give peace a chance," they rekindled the spirit of the 1960s, showing how to make love, not war—slowly, gently.

For nearly a year, I worked alongside these Filipinos, learning their secrets. One of my greatest teachers was Marietta Goco. A tall, strong woman from a privileged family, she had a generous spirit, a clever mind, and a deep commitment to making the system work for those less fortunate. She used her political savvy to build bridges between poor villagers and global funders.

Marietta took me under her wing and welcomed me into her world. Each day we'd meet with those who were planning the country's future. We traveled together to some of the seven thousand Philippine islands, listening to business, government, and community leaders as well as farmers, educators, and laborers. Each night, we would share the lessons we were learning with each other.

One of the toughest lessons was the cost of ignoring the problem. Twenty years of Marco's greed had left the country in shambles. UNICEF's report on malnutrition in the Philippines had first awakened the international community to the country's crisis. These global funders were shocked, thinking that their millions had been improving life for the poor. Their refusal to continue funding the deceptive Marcos dictatorship helped topple it. But the horrendous twenty-eight million dollar debt was strangling any hope for the future of the Filipinos. The gap between the haves and the have-nots had grown to a chasm. Almost half of all Filipino families were destitute. Unless they resolved this inequity, it was clear that their newfound peace would be short lived.

People were euphoric about bringing down Marcos, but were angry with the destruction left behind. They were excited by the opportunity to rebuild their country's democracy, but feared an unknown future. Some were in despair, questioning if the Revolution had been worth it. Where they had once been united against a common enemy, many were lost without one. But as we listened to these people, we heard a common refrain: they all wanted a better life for their children. They longed to keep alive the transformational spirit of the peaceful revolution. Most important, they wanted peace for more than just a day—for a lifetime.

One night, Marietta awoke as if from a deep sleep. "My father used to tell me about *Bayanihan*, one of our traditional Filipino values," she told me. "To help me understand, he used to tell me stories about people who worked together for the common good. These people were called, *Bayani*: a hero, for our country. What made them special is they had a willingness to think of others instead of themselves, to perform a kind of selfless service." She ended her story by saying that, "My father told me that *Bayanihan* gave people the courage to face their fears, stand up for their convictions and make choices that bettered their family, community, and the world."

As Marietta reflected on her father's words, she said, "Over the years, we've forgotten about the importance of working together for the common good. If we're ever going to create lasting peace in the Philippines, we'd better remind our people, and teach our children, about *Bayanihan*."

Marietta's story resonated deeply inside me. I realized this was the special secret I'd been searching for, the unspoken reason for my journey to the Philippines. When I returned home to the United States a few weeks later, it was with a sense of purpose and a commitment to awaken this value in my own country.

After Cory Aquino's close friend and ally, Fidel Ramos, was elected president, he asked Marietta to help create his Philippine 2000 vision. As a military man and a West Point graduate, he knew the key to long-lasting peace was for all people to have a stake in it. In 1995, he asked Marietta to develop a plan to bring the disenchanted into the mainstream. And he gave her a goal: to decrease poverty by 10 percent in five years.

Marietta accepted her new role in shaping her country's future with passion and determination. She decided to use Filipino values like *Bayanihan* to rally her countrymen and to make this goal to eradicate poverty their own. She designed a re-education program to help people remember their God-given talents, honor their capacity to realize their own visions, and encourage them to give back: to be a *Bayani*. She invited each person to create a personalized plan for how they would meet their own basic needs and help rebuild their country. Some started with simple steps: quit smoking, learn how to read, or be a better father. Others made larger goals: help their neighbors, care for their community, or run for local government. Together, they came to see that when each person gave a little of themselves, it made a difference for everyone.

At first, it wasn't easy. As Marietta's deputy, Chukie, remembers, "Over the last twenty years, people had forgotten the basic goodness of Filipinos. It took time for them to trust again and to believe in each other and in her. But after awhile, Marietta's sincerity touched people's hearts. It was like coming home. She helped you remember your own goodness."

And in just three years, this values-oriented program has transformed the lives of an amazing two million people. Marietta's plan is working so well that they've reached their 10 percent goal two years ahead of schedule. It's become the heart of the Philippines' social and economic success. With an annual economic growth of 7 percent, they were ranked the best place to invest among ten Asian-Pacific nations.

With a robust economy and a hopeful future, they've transformed their image from the "sick man of Asia" to one of its "flying tigers." For the second time in history, the Philippines have become our teachers. Their lesson is that when we all work together for the common good, everyone wins.

"Marietta's leadership opened the door to a whole new world of opportunities," Chukie says. "It's not always easy to be with her. She's super energetic, and she never gives up. She doesn't allow you to choose the easiest way, nor does she allow conflicts to fester. But sometimes, when you don't think you can keep up, she lifts you up again and again." Marietta is now invited to speak to leaders at the United Nations and around the world, opening their eyes to what can happen when you empower people to change their lives.

As a true Bayani, Marietta muses, "It's not that I want to do this, I just can't do anything but this. It becomes a choiceless choice: a calling. And once you make the decision, the heavens open."

Bayanihan, it's the goodness in every Filipino.
Bayanihan, each one helping each other.
Bayanihan, let's learn to give and take.
Bayanihan, this is the hope for our country.

JIM PARADES

If you would like to learn more about this Bayanihan spirit, and help support the poorest of the poor in the Philippines, call the **Presidential Commission to Fight Poverty** at the Office of the President of the Philippines at 011-632-735-1601 (or 2) or 736-0226.

Revolution of the Spirit

STORYTELLER: LESLIE KEAN

It was August 1988, and Aung San Suu Kyi's speech to the massive rally at Rangoon's Shwedagon Pagoda began with a minute of silence. Five hundred thousand people took a moment to honor the students who had recently lost their lives demonstrating for freedom and democracy in Burma.

On March 18 hundreds of schoolchildren and college students had marched along the bridge on Inya Lake, singing Burma's national anthem. They wanted to end the harsh military rule that had been in place since a 1962 military coup. Riot police arrived in steel helmets and beat many of the protesters to death. Those who managed to escape into the lake drowned. After demonstrations intensified, thousands fled Burma. British television referred to those left behind as "forty million hostages."

Aung San Suu Kyi arrived in Burma when the military were crushing these nationwide demonstrations. She had returned home from England to nurse her dying mother. Many would have seen this tragedy as a clear indication to return to England. But she was the daughter of Aung San, the hero who had won Burma's freedom from the British in 1947, and she felt an undeniable inner call to bring peace once again to her homeland.

Years of misrule had reduced the once prosperous Golden Land to one of the world's most economically destitute nations. The government now wanted to turn the country into the next Asian "tiger," by forcing more than two million people, many of them children, into slave labor. Human rights abuses were rampant, but so far the world had not taken notice.

Aung San Suu Kyi started traveling around the country, bringing her vision of freedom, personal responsibility, and compassion to huge, electrified crowds. Her charisma and brilliance captivated the world. At last, the plight of Burma began to receive international attention. The Burmese people finally began to show signs of unity. However, this one gentle woman struck terror in the hearts of the totalitarian government.

One night, as she walked home, she encountered a group of soldiers. The officer ordered her shot unless she turned back. The soldiers aimed their rifles at her heart. Without fear, Aung San Suu Kyi walked calmly forward. As she came closer and closer, the soldiers saw only compassion in her eyes. Still, orders were orders. A senior officer intervened at the last possible second, sparing the brave woman's life.

Aung San Suu Kyi's growing popularity seriously threatened the ruling junta. In 1989, they placed her under house arrest. She would not walk freely beneath the sun for six long years. But she had no time to grieve for her own freedom. Forty young democracy activists from her headquarters had also been imprisoned. Following the example of Gandhi, she employed one of the most potent forms of nonviolent protest available: fasting for justice. She ended her hunger strike only when she was assured that her supporters would not be tortured. During her long years of house arrest, she refused to allow her spirit to be imprisoned. She meditated daily and a flame of purpose and dedication burned within her.

In 1990, when elections finally came, Aung San Suu Kyi's party, the National League for Democracy, won a landslide victory. The generals not only refused to honor the results; they threw most of the newly elected parliament into prison.

In 1991, on International Human Rights Day, Aung San Suu Kyi was awarded the Nobel Peace Prize in absentia. As she was still in captivity, her son traveled to

Oslo and accepted the prize for her, on behalf of all the people of Burma. He said, "I know if she were free today, my mother would, in thanking you, also ask you to pray that the oppressors and the oppressed should throw down their weapons and join together to build a nation founded on humanity in the spirit of peace."

The international press has recognized Aung San Suu Kyi as the world's most famous political prisoner since Nelson Mandela and called the human rights disaster in Burma "the new South Africa." After six years in detention, Aung San Suu Kyi was finally released in July of 1995. Still the center of Burma's struggling democracy movement, she is now encouraging her country's military rulers to seek dialogue and reconciliation. She believes a very different Burma will emerge within her lifetime.

"The last six years have afforded me much time and food for thought," says Aung San Suu Kyi. "I have come to the conclusion that the human race is not divided into two opposing camps of good and evil. It is made up of those who are capable of learning and those who are not. Learning is a process of absorbing those lessons of life that enable us to increase peace and happiness in our world. As we strive to teach others, we must have the humility to acknowledge that we too still have much to learn. And we must have flexibility as we change the world."

Aung San Suu Kyi works vigilantly each day to share this wisdom with her followers. Her message is simple and direct: "We're in this together. If you want freedom and democracy, you must work for it. It will not be given to you. To get freedom we must be unified. I can only point the way." Following the example of their leader, they are consciously cultivating the Buddhist practice of *metta,* or "loving kindness." Some wear T-shirts that say: "Fear is a habit; I'm not afraid."

There are always new challenges. "We are increasing the momentum of our work, and they are increasing the momentum of arrests," she says. But Aung San Suu

Kyi never loses sight of the underlying spiritual aims of their struggle. "The quintessential revolution is a revolution of the spirit," she says.

The nonviolent approach does not immediately change the heart of the oppressor.
It first does something to the hearts and souls of those committed to it.
It gives them a new self-respect:
it calls up resources of strength and courage that they did not know they had.
Finally, it reaches the opponent:
and so stirs his conscience that reconciliation become reality.

DR. MARTIN LUTHER KING JR.

Join Aung San Suu Kyi's revolution of the spirit and help support human rights and democracy in Burma. **The Burma Project USA**, in Mill Valley, California, can be reached at 415-381-6905 or via e-mail: burmausa@ix.netcom.com.

The Pied Piper

STORYTELLER: KAREN ANDERSON

Myron is a twenty-year-old father of five. Until last year, he'd been living a life of crime—drugs, guns, the works—as one of Baltimore's toughest, most misguided, most troubled youths. Myron met his own father only once, a few years ago. As a kid, he got by on his own with his street smarts. Myron is the kind of young man that Joe Jones has dedicated his life to helping.

For hundreds of young men on the streets of Baltimore, Joe Jones is their role model, mentor, and moral compass. Sometimes he looks like a pied piper, with young kids and adults alike turning their heads as he passes, some trailing along behind. He's always searching for ways to get kids off the streets and back into society.

Joe knows what its like on the streets. He was only eleven years old when his parents divorced and he began his seventeen-year career as a drug addict. He credits support systems for turning his life around. "When my father left, our extended family stepped in," he says. "Later, it was a treatment center that helped me turn away from drugs."

Joe started helping others by taking care of young men dying of AIDS. He then helped addicted mothers and their children—first as a substance abuse counselor, then with the Healthy Start program. To Joe, working with some of the city's poorest unwed mothers felt like a never-ending turnstile. Some of the fathers would come in with "their women" and Joe realized there was nothing he could offer them. "There were all these maternal and child health care programs available, but something was missing from the equation," Joe says. "If we really want to reduce infant mortality, we can't forget the young men." Joe set out to balance the equation.

For the last three years, Joe has run the Men's Services program for the Baltimore City Healthy Start program that works with some 450 young men—many who were jobless, directionless, and fathering a whole new generation of potentially disenfranchised children. "Too often, they care little about the mother of their children, and maybe even less about themselves, so we focus instead on the child," Joe says sadly. "The first thing I ask is 'Do you want your child to have a real father?' Usually, they answer 'Yes.'"

The formula for the Men's Services program is simple. It targets the fathers of the children of the many young mothers who come into Healthy Start. It provides a support system, sometimes a "kick in the butt," but mostly positive feedback. "These young adult males virtually raised themselves in the streets. As toddlers and adolescents they were raised in poverty and never trained to be positive," Jones explains. "These guys are leaders, they have tremendous skills, but they have never been given the guidance to put those skills to work in a positive way."

When Joe met Myron, he was meandering through Baltimore's juvenile court system. For the past two years, with Joe's constant vigilance, Myron has been trying to focus on being a father to his children and a positive role model to other young men in the community. It was Myron's special leadership quality that prompted Joe to bring him on an educational trip to Kingston, Jamaica, as part of the Lessons Without Borders program at the U.S. Agency for International Development (USAID).

Lessons Without Borders was launched in June 1994 to foster an exchange of the community development lessons the agency has learned from working in developing countries over the last three decades. Baltimore Mayor Kurt Schmoke and many of the city's frontline people had been learning from these lessons. Through

Lessons Without Borders, Joe visited Jamaica and saw firsthand how a country with far less resources than we have was dealing with issues similar to those in his own community. One of the more powerful programs Joe observed was a community policing program in downtown Kingston that Joe thought could have a positive impact back in Baltimore. In 1996, Joe made a return visit with Myron, in the hope that Myron could help Joe translate his vision back on the streets of Baltimore.

Jamaica may seem like an unlikely place for Baltimore to learn from, but there is more in common than meets the eye. In the heart of Kingston, Jamaica, is Gold Street, an area of burned-out buildings and dilapidated shacks that marks the borderline between two warring gangs. Infamous for its crime and violence, most Jamaicans shudder at the thought of venturing near there.

In the last few years, the Kingston Restoration Company had been working with support from USAID to restore the devastated community. They reclaimed the downtown public areas and initiated economic development ventures. They have also begun to counter the violence and rebuild the community's social fabric with cultural, educational, health, and family-planning programs. The Gold Street police station has become a focal point of the community's healing process. Kingston police walk the beat so they can talk, rebuild trust, and create friendships with the young people through tutoring, mentoring, and after-school programs right in the police station. Confronted with the poorest of the poor and the baddest of bad, they are instilling hope and a sense of what's right into the hearts and minds of these unfortunate kids living in this desolate neighborhood.

Joe wanted Myron to witness firsthand how the program worked so he could help translate it back onto the streets of Baltimore. At first, Myron was awestruck by the poverty and crime he saw among people his age and younger. "I thought I had it bad back home, but it's nothing compared to what's happening there. Yet these kids are determined to do the right thing," he said. Myron was impressed with the relationship between the police and street kids. It was nurturing and positive, not combative and punitive.

In bringing these lessons home to Baltimore, Joe emphasizes that "each of us, and especially cops, can have a positive impact on the lives of young kids simply by showing that they care. Solutions don't always cost a lot of money; sometimes all it takes is a helping hand and the moral support to make kids feel like they're really worth something." For young people like Myron, that makes all the difference.

As we look at the lessons that have been learned from our work overseas,
I'm convinced that many of those lessons can be learned and applied in America.

FIRST LADY HILLARY RODHAM CLINTON

Help us find the best solutions to common problems in community development. Whether the solution is from Baton Rouge or Bangladesh, good ideas know no borders. Send your good ideas to **USAID, Lessons Without Borders**, 2201 C Street NW, Washington, D.C. 20523.

Oskar Schindler

Adapted from the *Schindler's List Study Guide from Facing History and Ourselves*

People were suspicious of the stories told of a Nazi war profiteer who rescued Jews. Oskar Schindler had come to Krakow, Poland, from his native German town of Zwittau. Unlike most of the carpetbaggers, he took over a factory that had lain idle and in bankruptcy for many years. In the winter of 1939–1940, he began operations with four thousand square meters of floor space and a hundred workers, of whom seven were Jewish.

Production started with a rush, for Schindler was a shrewd and tireless worker. During the first year, the labor force expanded to three hundred, including 150 Jews. By the end of 1942, the factory had grown to forty-five thousand square meters and employed almost eight hundred men and women. The Jewish workers, of whom there were now 370, all came from the Krakow ghetto. "To avoid life at the camps, it had become a tremendous advantage," says Itzhak Stern, Schindler's Jewish bookkeeper, "to be able to leave the ghetto in the daytime and work in a German factory."

Word spread among Krakow's Jews that Schindler's factory was the place to work. Schindler helped his Jewish employees by falsifying the factory records. Old people were recorded as being twenty years younger and children were listed as adults. Lawyers, doctors, and engineers were registered as metalworkers, mechanics, and draftsmen—all trades considered essential to war production.

From behind his high bookkeeper's table, Stern could see through the glass door of Schindler's private office. "Almost every day, from morning until evening, officials and other visitors came to the factory and made me nervous. Schindler used to keep pouring them vodka and joking with them. When they left he would ask me in, close the door, and then quietly tell me whatever they had come for. He used to tell them that he knew how to get work out of these Jews and that he wanted more brought in. That was how we managed to get in the families and relatives all the time and save them from deportation."

Then, on March 13, 1943 came the orders to close the Krakow ghetto. All Jews were moved to the forced-labor camp of Plaszow, outside the city. Conditions there, even for those who had been in the terrible Krakow ghetto, were shocking. The prisoners suffered and by the hundreds either died in camp or were transported to Auschwitz-Birkenau.

Stern, along with Schindler's other workers, had also been moved to Plaszow from the ghetto but, like some twenty-five thousand other inmates who inhabited the camp and had jobs on the outside, they continued spending their days in the factory. Falling deathly ill one day, Stern sent word to Schindler, urgently pleading for help. Schindler came at once, bringing essential medicine, and continued his visits until Stern recovered. But what he had seen in Plaszow had chilled him. Nor did he like the turn things had taken in the factory.

Increasingly helpless before the frenetic Jew-haters and Jew-destroyers, Schindler found that he could no longer joke easily with the German officials who came on inspections. The double game he was playing was becoming more difficult. Troubling incidents happened more and more often.

The increasing frequency of unpleasant incidents in the factory and the evil his eyes had seen at the Plaszow camp probably moved Schindler into a more active role. In the spring of 1943, he began the conspiring, the string-pulling, the bribery, and the shrewd outguessing of Nazi officialdom that finally was to save so many lives. It is at this point that the real legend begins. For the next two years, Oskar Schindler's ever-present obsession was how to save the greatest possible number of Jews from the Auschwitz-Birkenau gas chambers, only sixty kilometers from Krakow.

His first ambitious move was to attempt to help the starving, fearful prisoners at Plaszow. Other labor camps in Poland had already been shut down and their inhabitants "liquidated." Plaszow seemed doomed. At the prompting of Stern and the others in the inner-office circle, Schindler one evening managed to convince one of his drinking companions, General Schindler (no relation) that Plaszow's camp workshops would be ideally suited for serious war production. The general fell in with the idea and orders for wood and metal were given to the camp. As a result, Plaszow was officially transformed into a war-essential concentration camp. And though conditions hardly improved, it came off the list of labor camps that were then being done away with.

But by the spring of 1944, the German retreat on the Eastern Front was on in earnest. Plaszow and all its subcamps were ordered closed. Schindler and his workers had no illusions about what a move to another concentration camp implied. The time had come for Oskar Schindler to play his trump card, a daring gamble that he had devised beforehand.

He went to work on all his drinking companions and his connections in military and industrial circles in Krakow and in Warsaw. He bribed, cajoled, and pleaded, working desperately against time and fighting what everyone assured him was a lost cause. He persisted until someone, somewhere in the hierarchy, perhaps impatient to end the seemingly trifling business, finally gave him the authorization to move a force of seven hundred men and three hundred women from the Plaszow camp into a factory at Brennec in his native Czechoslovakia. Most of the other twenty-five thousand men, women, and children at Plaszow were sent to Auschwitz-Birkenau, there to find the same end that more than one million other Jews had already discovered. But out of the vast calamity and through the stubborn efforts of one man, a thousand Jews were saved temporarily. One thousand half-starved, sick, and almost broken human beings had had a death sentence commuted by a miraculous reprieve.

The *Schindlerjuden* (Schindler Jews) by now depended on Schindler. His compassion and sacrifice were unstinting. He spent every bit of money still left in his possession, and traded his wife's jewelry as well, for food, clothing, medicine, and schnapps with which to bribe the many SS investigators. He furnished a secret hospital with stolen and black-market medical equipment, he fought epidemics, and he made a three-hundred-mile trip himself carrying two enormous flasks filled with Polish vodka, bringing them back full of desperately needed medicine. His wife, Emilie, cooked and cared for the sick and earned her own reputation and praise.

Perhaps the most absorbing of all the legends is one that graphically illustrates Schindler's self-adopted role of protector and savior in the midst of general and amoral indifference. Just about the time the Nazi empire was crashing down, a phone call from the railway station came late one evening, asking Schindler whether he cared to accept delivery of two railway cars full of near-frozen Jews. The cars had been frozen shut at a temperature of five degrees and contained almost a hundred sick men who had been locked inside, ever since the train had been sent off from Auschwitz-Birkenau with orders to deliver the human cargo to some willing factory. But, when informed of the condition of the prisoners, no factory manager would hear of receiving them. Schindler, sickened by the news, ordered the train sent to his factory siding at once.

The train was awesome to behold. Ice had formed on the locks and the cars had to be opened with axes and acetylene torches. Inside, the miserable relics of human beings were stretched out, frozen stiff. Each had to be carried out like a carcass of frozen beef. Thirteen were unmistakably dead, but the others still breathed.

Throughout that night and for many days and nights following, Oskar and Emilie Schindler and a number of the men worked without halt on the frozen and starved skeletons. One large room in the factory was emptied for the purpose. Three more men died, but with care, warmth, milk, and medicine, the others gradually rallied. All this had been achieved surreptitiously, with the factory guards, as usual, receiving their bribes so as not to inform the SS commandant.

Such was life at Brennec until the arrival of the Russians on May 9 put an end to the constant nightmare. In the early morning, once certain that his workers finally were out of danger and that all was in order to explain to the Russians, Schindler, Emilie, and several of his closest Jewish worker friends discreetly disappeared and were not heard from until they turned up, months later, deep in Austria's U.S. Zone.

The film Schindler's List *focuses on the years of the Holocaust—*
a time when millions of Jews and other men, women, and children were murdered
solely because of their ancestry. It is one of the darkest chapters in human history.
Yet an appalling number of people, young and old, know little if anything about it.
Even today the world has not yet learned the lesson of those terrible years.
There are far too many places where hate, intolerance, and genocide still exist.
Thus Schindler's List *is not just a "Jewish story" or a "German story"—*
it is a human story. And its subject matter applies to every generation.

Schindler's List *is simply about racial hatred—which is the state of mind that attacks not what makes us people but what makes us different from each other. It is my hope that* Schindler's List *will awaken and sustain an awareness of such evil and inspire this generation and future generations to seek an end to racial hatred.*

—STEVEN SPIELBERG, AMBLIN ENTERTAINMENT, INC.

To receive a **Schindler's List Study Guide** call **Facing History and Ourselves** at 617-232-1595 or visit their website at www. facing.org to learn about the dangers of indifference, the values of civility, creative approaches to the challenges we face, and opportunities for positive change.

Steven Spielberg created **Survivors of the Shoah Visual History Foundation** to videotape and archive interviews with Holocaust survivors all over the world. For more information, please call 800-661-2092.

The Healing Power of Doing Good

A pessimist, they say, sees a glass of water as being half -empty;
an optimist sees the same glass as half -full.
But a giving person sees a glass of water
and starts looking for someone who might be thirsty.
"If you don't, who will?"

G. DONALD GALE

Do you remember the last time a young child gave you a gift? A flower, a drawing from school, or even a hug? In his innocent way, he was saying, "Be my friend. I love you. Thank you." Did this simple act of giving touch your heart? Did it make you want to give something back?

Young children are born with a natural instinct to give, to help and to love. Their little faces light up with joy each time they do. Sometimes as we grow up, we get so busy we forget the magical power of giving. Sometimes we don't even realize that what we do really matters.

The stories in this chapter remind us how good it feels when we give of ourselves. We are inspired by those who sometimes sacrifice their personal gains for the good of their fellow man. We marvel at those who stopped complaining about "the system," waiting for someone else to fix it, and just did it! We applaud those who take risks, and overcome obstacles, not just for themselves, but for others. We are thrilled to hear of people who made miracles happen, just by giving back. We are touched by those who use their personal pain as a lever to first change their own lives and then, the world. Our soul is nourished and our faith in humanity is restored. We feel hopeful knowing there are ordinary people who are improving the world, one step at at time. Just reading these stories makes us feel better and gives us courage to give what we can.

Why do some of us look and feel young at 65 and others old at 35? Research shows that when we help others, we can be physically and mentally energized. In his book, *The Healing Power of Doing Good*, Allan Luks described how people experience a "helper's high," similar to a runner's high, which improves their body's immune system and their health. By helping others for as little as two hours a week, they achieve similar physiological and psychological benefits as they did from exercising. And the smile on a child's face, the joy in a person's eyes or a simple thank you, makes us feel like a million!

In this chapter, some of these "helping heroes" discover the amazing life-changing benefits from helping others. A busy mother finds the time to hold babies at a hospital nursery and experiences the magical healing power of love. Inner city teenagers who help others gain self-esteem, dignity and personal mastery in their lives. A cynical student fills the emotional and spiritual hollowness in his life by volunteering in a soup kitchen. Being part of something greater and more meaningful than their own little universe, brings them the kind of happiness they've always wanted.

True healing happens for the giver and the receiver when we slow down and really connect with each other. The smallest acts of kindness bring a sense of calm, self-esteem and joy to our lives. People who take the time to give from their hearts feel less pain, depression and disease, and have more energy to live their lives. Even people who've been ill sometimes receive a new lease on life by helping someone else. And those in the helping profession with "helper's burnout" renew themselves by refocusing on the special human being they are with. In that moment, knowing we've made a difference in someone's life is a real gift.

Sometimes we find it easiest to help strangers. We feel fewer expectations and more freedom to choose how we want to give. Yet, as a wise friend once told me, if we want to change the world, the best place to start is with our own families. Given the daily ups and downs of families, they offer an ideal training ground for learning how to care for others. In our fast-paced world, we often have too many things to do, places to go, and people to meet. When we remember to take time for each other, our families and our neighbors, we receive many blessings: loving relationships, happy children and healthy communities.

Dr. Caroline Myss tells a funny story in her book, *Why People Don't Heal and How They Can* about how we sometimes get lost in our lives. There was this group of people who wanted to make the world a better place. Having learned a few lessons about helping others, they decided to begin by healing themselves first. They hired a big boat, called *Heal Thyself First,* and headed off on their journey. After awhile, they'd became so fascinated on the boat that they decided to stay on it, forgetting all about their original goal of helping the rest of the world. By telling this story, Dr. Myss urges her patients not to get too caught up in healing themselves. She reminds them that real health and happiness comes when we help others and the planet.

In *Love, Medicine and Miracles*, Dr. Bernie Segal tells his patients that when they get to heaven, they will have to answer two questions, neither of them about what they have acquired during their lives. *What did you contribute?* and *How much of your potential did you use?*

* Each one of us has special gifts we can give.
* When we give our gifts, freely from our hearts, we will realize our full potential and help build a better world.

From a Cynic to a Server

STORYTELLER: ANDREW CARROLL

Despite the benefit of a Quaker education and two extraordinarily generous and loving parents, I left home for college at the age of eighteen a rather cynical young man. I wasn't bitter or angry; I just believed that the world, especially as it appeared on the nightly news, was a brutal place, and that nothing would ever change.

Cynicism, as I saw it, was the easiest route to happiness. It seemed daring and adventurous, unrestrained by rules or responsibilities. Best of all, it demanded nothing of me. It didn't ask me to sign petitions, recycle old newspapers, or feed the homeless. I didn't have the energy to get involved anyway. I was too busy having fun and living for the moment. It was all very intoxicating. But underneath my cavalier confidence was a suspicion that something enormously significant was missing in my life.

Then I came across a book that changed the way I saw the world: Robert Bellah's *Habits of the Heart: Individualism and Commitment in American Life.* This book explores the emotional and spiritual hollowness of living selfishly. After reading it, I began to look at people differently and see their positive qualities, not just negative ones. I also noticed how many people—those whom I had previously ignored—were working selflessly to improve their communities.

Inspired by the commitment I saw in others, I decided to give it a try myself. I started by volunteering at a soup kitchen in the basement of a local church. The volunteers, cooks, servers, and organizers all went about their work quietly and dependably, never asking for recognition or appreciation. For the first time in my life, I started to feel I was part of something greater and more meaningful than my own little universe.

To my surprise, it wasn't difficult to find the energy to volunteer—in fact, volunteering *gave* me energy. It was like a spiritual oxygen that nourished and invigorated me. It taught me that even a cynic like me could find hope. But it was easy to have hope when things were going well. The question was whether I could be as optimistic during the hard times.

I was challenged with that question just a few days before Christmas—when our house burned to the ground. I'd never been much for Christmas spirit, I liked it only because it meant plenty of gifts. By the age of eighteen, I felt that Christmas had lost its magic for me. Now with the devastating fire, I had even more reason to hate it. Everything I had owned was destroyed: my books, clothes, and CDs; the letters from friends and loved ones; the silver pocket watch from my grandfather; the cherished photographs; and all the other personal items that meant something to me were gone forever.

But as I was mourning the loss of all my material possessions, I realized that something even more significant remained: my newly discovered sense of idealism. It helped me to see that a lot had survived the fire. Most important, everyone had gotten out of the house unharmed. Even our cat, Claude, escaped without injury.

We found a place to stay over the holidays and during the time the house was being rebuilt. But the fire made me think about those who didn't have a home to go to—at Christmas or anytime. When I returned to school after the break, I continued to volunteer at the soup kitchen, but I wanted to do something more.

The next year, remembering what it was like to lose everything just before Christmas, I decided to donate some gifts to Toys for Tots, a program that distributes gifts to poor and homeless children for Christmas. I thought, at the very least, I could give some child a toy and make theirs a happier holiday. Much to my dismay, I discovered that our school didn't have such a program.

With the help of some friends and the school's volunteer program, we decided to start one. We called it the ABC Project; ABC stands for "A Better Christmas." We put up flyers and spread the word in classes and at churches. We even convinced the college newspaper to print a full-page ad asking for donations.

The response was extraordinary. Toys and books came pouring in. Students, professors, fraternities, sororities, and even people who lived in the neighborhood made donations and offered to help. I was overwhelmed by the community's generosity. I had never realized how much people really want to give of themselves. It just takes someone to ask them.

For me, the ABC Project was all about giving but it wasn't long before I realized that the more I gave, the more I received. The day before I left to go home for Christmas break (almost one year exactly since the fire), I received a handwritten note with no return address. It came from a homeless mother who'd recently suffered a great loss. She wrote: "Thank you ABC for the toys you gave my children. All we had was stolen last week. I had no toys to give them, but now I do. You don't know how much I appreciate it. Thank you so much, and have a Merry Christmas."

These simple words were the best Christmas gift I have ever received. The letter from this woman made me realize that at long last I had discovered the true joy of the season. How many times had I heard that it is more blessed to give than to receive? But it was the heartfelt gratitude of this one woman that returned the Magic of Christmas to me. And I knew as I read her letter, that her gift and my newfound hope, would inspire me for a lifetime.

Help **The American Poetry & Literacy Project** (**APL**) to distribute free poetry books in public places like hospitals, libraries, schools, and jury waiting-rooms or donate books for homeless children or at-risk young people, call 202-338-1109.

Baby Magic

STORYTELLER: ALLAN LUKS WITH PEGGY PAYNE,
adapted from *The Healing Power of Doing Good.*

Twelve years ago, Lynn was suffering from chronic back pain. No matter what she did, the pain just wouldn't go away. One day, she found herself lying in traction in a hospital bed. Her doctor was recommending surgery. Lynn listened carefully and thought about her options. She'd heard about a program at the Rusk Institute for Rehabilitation Medicine in New York City. There people learned how to cope with stress and control most back problems. Lynn decided to refuse the surgery, opting to join the program instead. She found that the relaxation techniques helped ease the pain. But the periodic flare-ups continued—until she began to help with the babies.

At first, Lynn didn't think she would have the time. She lived a full and stressful life. In addition to being a wife and mother of two teenagers, she carried heavy professional responsibilities. As the director of a private preschool, she worried about competing for students, pleasing worried parents, and placating her school's supervisors. It seemed impossible to add one more regular commitment to her schedule. But she did.

Now, once a week after work, Lynn takes a fifteen-minute walk to a nearby urban medical center. Once there, she puts on gloves and a bright yellow sterile gown. Then, for the next two hours, she holds, feeds, and diapers new babies; babies who have no one else to care for them. Most days Lynn arrives to find ten babies in the room: four being fed and the rest crying. They are so small, their crying resembles the mewing of kittens. Some of the babies, abandoned by drug-addicted mothers, are shaking from withdrawal symptoms. Many are born outside of a hospital to mothers without medical care. Here, they sleep in metal cribs, each tagged with a sticker giving the baby's last name and a few statistics.

Even with all of their problems, these babies are uncommonly beautiful. Their huge eyes and little bodies are a constant reminder of how precious and fragile life really is. Lynn leans over to a waist-high crib and picks up a baby. Today, it is Madison, a tiny, dark-skinned, week-old baby boy. He is awaiting the results of a drug test, then placement in a foster home. She can feel his tiny bones in her hands. "It's so scary to hold some of them," Lynn thinks as she cradles him.

As Lynn rocks back and forth feeding him, Madison latches onto a bottle with surprising vigor. When he is finished, she gently pats him to sleep and puts him to bed. A new baby is brought in. He's half-an-hour old, big, pink, and howling. This little linebacker looks so startlingly healthy, that the others seem even smaller. By severe contrast, the baby nearest him, Sanchez, born with heart and liver problems, lies helpless in an incubator. At birth, Sanchez weighed a little over two pounds.

Leaning over to pick up Dupree, Lynn makes no effort to protect her back. Dupree has curly black hair and features that look almost grown-up. He is two weeks old and trembling, sometimes faintly, sometimes in shudders that move through his whole body. "I'm sorry, I'm sorry," Lynn whispers as she holds his little body.

Lynn spends her entire two hours in the nursery, lifting and lowering babies, feeding and diapering. When she arrived, her back had been a little stiff. But now, the pain has vanished. As she gets her coat to leave the hospital, she notices her hands still smell of babies. "Baby Magic," she says, taking a sniff. "Baby Magic has changed my life."

A baby is God's opinion that the world should go on.

CARL SANDBURG

Discover the joy and experience the healing from holding babies. **Call your local hospital** and ask how you can join their volunteer program, helping out in their nursery.

The Quilt

Storyteller: Marianne Larned

There is a quilt on Cleve Jones' bed: he's had it all his life. In one corner, stitched in yellow thread on a blue background, are the words: "Emma Rupert—age 78—1952." Emma was Cleve's great-grandmother, born in Bee Ridge, Indiana in 1874. The quilt she sewed for him, her first great-grandchild, was a wonderful quilt for a little boy: a crazy quilt sewn from scraps of grandpa's pajamas; with hundreds of brightly colored tigers, horses, dolphins and dragons.

Cleve thought of this quilt the night of November 27, 1985 as he stood in the San Francisco Civic Center Plaza surrounded by a sea of candles flickering in the chilly fog. Thousands of people marched, as they march every November 27th, holding their candles as they proceeded down Market Street in memory of Supervisor Harvey Milk and Mayor George Moscone.

Harvey Milk was California's first openly gay elected official. He and Mayor Moscone were assassinated in their City Hall offices on November 27, 1978. As word of the murders spread throughout the city, first hundreds, then thousands, then tens of thousands of San Franciscans made their way to Castro Street to join the silent march to City Hall.

In November of 1985, as they prepared for the annual tribute to Milk and Moscone, articles in the *San Francisco Examiner* were reporting that 1,000 San Franciscans had died of a new disease called AIDS. Cleve knew many of those first thousand to die. They were his friends, neighbors and colleagues. They were dying too quickly, too painfully; and often, they died alone.

As he stood at the corner of Castro and Market Streets, Cleve knew he was at the center of a terrible human tragedy, a cruel plague accompanied by a parallel epidemic of hatred and bigotry and fear. It seemed to him that he and his friends would all be dead long before the world awoke to the awful challenge it faced. He wanted to do something, to find some way to let people know they had been here. Cleve wanted to give a voice to those who were silently disappearing.

That night, as the marchers gathered with their candles for Harvey and George, Cleve asked everyone to take a placard and write the name of someone they knew who had been killed by AIDS. They marched to City Hall and stood in silence there for several moments; then they marched on to the Federal Building, where they had earlier hidden extension ladders and rolls of tape. They placed the ladders against the gray stone walls of the Federal Building and climbed three stories up, taping the placards with the names of their dead to the walls.

When it was done, and the walls were covered with placards, Cleve stepped back and looked at the patchwork of names covering the building. "It looks like a quilt," he thought. It reminded him of his great-grandmother—and of the gentle ladies who brought their quilts to Quaker meetings in Indiana to raise money for the poor. To Cleve it seemed the perfect symbol of traditional middle-class, middle-American family values. A perfect symbol to match with this disease that was killing gay men, black children, hemophiliacs, and drug users. A perfect antidote, if not to the virus, perhaps to the hatred and fear growing in our country.

A year later, Cleve created the first panel of the AIDS Memorial Quilt in memory of his best friend, Marvin Feldman, who died in October, 1986. And on October 11, 1987, the NAMES Project AIDS Memorial Quilt was unfolded for its first display on the National Mall in Washington, DC. It contained 1,920 names.

When Cleve returned to San Francisco he found letters from all over the world:

letters from anguished parents who had lost their children, letters from community leaders uncertain of how to mobilize their communities against the epidemic, letters from gay men who had been abandoned by their families, letters imploring him to bring the Quilt to their hometowns.

So Cleve and his friends bought a truck named Stella, loaded up the Quilt, and began to travel across this country and around the world displaying the Quilt as the centerpiece for locally coordinated educational and fundraising campaigns. Out of their travels grew an extraordinary network of chapters and international affiliates, uniting diverse peoples from every nation in the global struggle against the HIV disease.

While they had first thought of quilting as a particularly American folk art, they learned that similar traditions exist in many other cultures. In the years since, they have used the Quilt to encourage international solidarity in the fight against AIDS. Today, the names of Cleve's gay friends from San Francisco are stitched in next to panels memorializing housewives from New Jersey, farmers from Uganda, shopkeepers from Thailand, street kids from Brazil; men, women, and children of all races, faiths and nationalities.

Over six million people have visited the Quilt in its thousands of displays worldwide. Wherever it is seen, the Quilt sparks a dialogue between those who make the panels and those who view them. A gift from the hearts and hands of Americans has touched millions of people and moved them to act. They have cared for the sick, comforted the dying, built hospices, joined speaker's bureaus, written checks, signed petitions, demonstrated, testified, been arrested, worn red ribbons, sewn quilt squares for their own loved ones and raised their own candles against the darkness.

Nominated for the Nobel Peace Prize in 1989, the Quilt is the largest community art project in the world. It illustrates the enormity of the worldwide AIDS crisis by revealing the individual lives behind the statistics, offering a powerful symbol and eliciting a compassionate response. In October 1996, the Quilt was displayed once again on the National Mall in Washington DC: it had grown to have 45,000 panels, covering more than 27 acres, the size of 30 football fields. A litany of the dead, 70,000 names, was read by 2000 readers; it took three solid days.

In Edinburgh, Texas, a small town on the banks of the Rio Grande, the display consisted almost entirely of panels created for people from South Texas, joined by several panels sent from Mexico City. Cleve watched as thousands of families from both sides of the border walked silently through the fabric walkways of the Quilt; young parents with small children, gay and lesbian couples, grandparents, teenagers. A hot wind was blowing dust from the desert, but no one complained, they just listened carefully to the reading of the names. One woman approached Cleve with a bundle of fabric in her arms. "This is my son," she said as she handed me the cloth. "He is gone now, but he lives on—in my heart and in the Quilt."

Her impulse—to keep alive the memory of a loved one—is the same one that motivated Cleve's great-grandmother so many years ago. At the age of 78, she knew she wouldn't always be around. With her act of love, she touched Cleve, now a twenty year survivor of AIDS, and inspired him to reach out to others. Cleve and his friends discovered the power of humanity to overcome fear, hate, prejudice—and yes, even death. They created a gift that now reaches out and touches the whole world.

The Names Project urges you to join our fight for a world without AIDS. Call 415-882-5500, for information on how to get involved with the AIDS Memorial Quilt.

Changing People's Minds

STORYTELLER: SUSAN KEESE

Joseph Rogers could be mistaken for Santa Claus. This forty-five-year-old man with his bushy white beard and robust manner is often called the "Mother Teresa of the consumer movement" or the "Martin Luther King of mental health." But, despite all that he's accomplished, Joe still struggles with his illness.

Joe remembers the day he was diagnosed as a paranoid schizophrenic. "It was like a death sentence," he says. He was only nineteen when he was told he'd spend most of his life in a mental institution. "While most people my age were planning for their future, I was told, 'You might as well apply for social security.'" Thirty years later, he has become a nationally recognized leader in a movement that's recreating the mental health care industry from the ground up. Many would find it hard to imagine that this powerful and respected advocate, who has conferred with presidents, testified before Congress, and consulted with foreign governments, was once homeless, wandering the streets of New York City and fishing through dumpsters for food.

Raised in a troubled household on the outskirts of Orlando, Florida, Joe left home at thirteen. As he drifted, he became increasingly disorganized, isolated, and depressed. At nineteen he met an understanding youth worker who helped him begin the long road to recovery. But his entrance into the mental health system was only a beginning. Throughout his twenties, he bounced from one mental hospital to another, enduring many painful experiences. Between hospitalizations, he struggled through classes at New Jersey Community College. "I got lots of insights into my life from the courses I took in psychology," he says. But his recurring bouts of mental illness, and the lack of progress in his recovery, made it difficult for him to finish his degree.

One day, a professor convinced him to use his insider's knowledge of how the system works (and, too often, doesn't) and how to make it better. Joe decided to volunteer at a small community mental health center in New Jersey that was struggling to cope with the aftermath of severe government budget cuts. "Suddenly, this little center designed for family counseling was expected to take care of people with serious mental illness. Many had been institutionalized for a long time," Joe says. "Folks at the center weren't prepared for this new challenge. Something needed to be done, so I said, 'Let me work on this.'"

Joe remembered how he had felt when he first came out of the hospital. So, he spent time with these people, sharing his story and listening to theirs. People found it comforting to talk with someone who had "been there." Joe made them feel less alone, less afraid. The next step was to create self-help programs for people in halfway homes. Joe's first experience was memorable. "It was at an underfunded place, where residents helped run things on the weekends. They had to. No one else was there to do it." From this successful experiment, he created a model and set up a series of self-help groups with former patients to inspire each other to rebuild their own lives.

But ironically, even as Joe's reputation began to spread, he had to hide his own background. "I had all this experience with inpatients and outpatients, but I couldn't tell anyone how I got it," he says. That changed when he moved from New Jersey to Philadelphia, accepting a job with the Mental Health Association of Southeastern Pennsylvania (MHASP). There, he created Project SHARE (Self Help and Advocacy Resource Exchange) to help people who had lived with mental illness design programs to meet their own needs. "Hearing the success stories of people whose problems are similar to your own gives a kind of hope you can't get from professionals," Joe maintains. "Many professionals don't really see us as equals. They see us as children at best or mentally retarded at worst. It's a threat to them to have former patients saying, 'This is what I want' or 'This works best for me.'"

Through Project SHARE, thousands of mental health consumers have transformed themselves from helpless recipients into helpers and wage earners. Many have also become powerful advocates for mental health care as well as role models for others who share similar struggles. Joe estimates that already over five thousand people have been helped by Project SHARE on their way to a better future. "Many people come into our programs, literally homeless and hopeless," he says. "They start as volunteers, then become paid facilitators. They go to school, get new skills, and end up with a new lease on life."

Project SHARE has spawned hundreds of peer counseling–support groups and serves as an umbrella organization for twenty projects run by mental health clients such as housing programs, drop-in centers, job training, outreach, and advocacy. They've also created a national clearinghouse to help consumers around the country organize their own self-help and advocacy groups. In one program, formerly homeless individuals now help those people who still live on the streets. Joe's message is simple, "Helping others is often the best therapy."

In 1992, Project SHARE was blended with MHASP. Five years later Joseph Rogers became the executive director of what is now the largest mental health association in the world. "The hybrid has SHARE's hard-hitting activism and MHASP's long-standing credibility," he says.

Part of Joe's lesson plan for the mental health establishment includes a simple course in finance. In 1987, he helped lead the effort to close the infamous Philadelphia State Hospital and wrangle fifty million dollars from the state to create a system of community care to take its place. "Our Community Companion program costs one thousand dollars *a year* to monitor a match between a volunteer and a consumer. It costs up to five hundred dollars *a day* to hospitalize someone." The math is pretty straightforward for Joe. "For what it once cost to warehouse five hundred people in the state hospital, we're now serving three thousand in a community setting."

"Joe Rogers is a visionary who saw the future and pushed for it to happen," says Ilene Shane, director of the Philadelphia-based Disabilities Law Project. "He's made Pennsylvania a model for consumer–run mental health programs around the country and the world."

Joe still suffers from random hallucinations and sometimes hears voices that no one else does. Every day, he and millions of others must try to make it through life while they wait for a cure. But, thanks to Joe and Project SHARE, at least the wait is more hopeful, and the life is certainly more meaningful. By helping each other, they are a shining example of what it means to be our brother's keeper. And by educating others about the reality of mental illness, and advocating for change, they are building the road to a better future.

Whatever you can do or dream you can, begin it:
Boldness has genius, power and magic in it.

GOETHE

Help Yourself! If you have a mental illness—believe in your abilities: organize a self-help/advocacy group for yourself and others who are working toward recovery. Call the **National Mental Health Consumers' Self-Help Clearinghouse** for information on getting organized, getting funding, and more at 800-553-4539, ext. 290.

Caring for Our Families

STORYTELLER: MARIANNE LARNED

Caring for others has always been a tradition in the Carey family: new neighbors were greeted with Grammie Carey's pecan rolls. New mothers would find my aunt Betty's lasagna on their doorstep. Lonely friends were invited to share a Thanksgiving meal. Grieving families receive sweet treats and warm hugs.

As children, we often begrudged the loss of goodies from our kitchen, as if something were being taken from us. Too young to realize, we were learning one of life's most important lessons: caring for others multiplies love like the loaves and fishes.

For many years, our extended family came together for christenings, graduations, weddings, and funerals. Since the four Carey siblings had a total of twenty-eight children, there were lots of special occasions to celebrate. These family gatherings glued us together and kept us whole. They made the joy more wonderful and the pain more bearable. We laughed and cried, ate and drank, and sang and danced together.

Like many families who grew up between the 1950s and the 1990s, we often struggled to make sense of all the changes. As we each searched for our own uniqueness, our differences sometimes collided. Too often, we ended up confronting each other and parting with deep resentments. As the years went by, we lost track of what we had once shared in common. In the process, we lost our connection, forgetting how much we needed each other. Somewhere along the way, our family's tradition of caring seemed to fade.

Caring is such a simple thing, yet it is so often neglected. In our fast-paced world, we all have too many things to do, places to go, and people to meet. We forget to take time for each other and for our families. But, as a wise friend once told me, if we want to change the world, we can start with our families. They're the best training ground for learning life's lessons. They're also a great place to start learning how to care for our communities. I wasn't sure how to begin with my own family, but I knew I had to try.

One day, my mother, Aunt Betty, and I confided in each other our concern and our sense of loss. We'd had more than our share of heartaches. Loved ones, fathers, and children had been painfully taken too soon, some before we got to say good-bye. We could not bear to lose anyone else and we could not wait any longer, hoping that healing would just happen on its own.

We decided it was time for a family reunion. To start, we sent a flyer inviting all twenty-eight cousins and their thirty-five children. It was to be a Fourth of July celebration at Aunt Betty and Uncle Connie's camp on Lake Champlain in Vermont. We were eager to see how our family would respond.

To our great delight, they came! From California, Florida, and all over New England, they came to see if the Carey magic was still there. Some hadn't seen each other for years. Many had never met their cousins' new spouses or children. People who hadn't spoken in ages let go of the past and renewed old friendships. Love and caring was everywhere, and an annual tradition was born.

Pretty soon we outgrew the camp. Now, each year, we search for the perfect spot somewhere in New England: a secluded campground with a big fireplace, picnic tables, and a swimming hole for the kids. No shopping for thirty miles and no televisions or telephones. Instead, for a few days, we chop wood, carry water, cook over fires, pitch tents, and sleep on the hard ground. Each family brings their favorite food and veggies from their garden. From a basket comes a tablecloth, some candles, and good wine. Voilà! A Stone Soup feast! Living simply, we remember the importance of each one pitching in to make life better for everyone.

After dinner, we sing songs and make s'mores around the campfire. Everyone listens as we retell childhood stories: Uncle Francis building these campgrounds as a teenager in the 1930s as a part of FDR's Conservation Corps, me growing up in the idealist 1960s, and Nancy, who came of age in the 1970s era of sex, drugs, and rock 'n' roll. Ben, a teenager now, helps prepare us for the future. As we share our stories, we renew our common values and vow to raise our children with them.

Our hearts are touched seeing a grandmother's eyes or an uncle's smile passed from one generation to the next. New babies are welcomed into the clan. One mother gives another time out: without saying a word, she takes a cranky child for a walk or a swim in the lake. Last year's toddlers are running with the "big kids" now. New friendships blossom. Photographers run to capture magic moments, like when two five-year-old cousins meet and become friends.

"Mom, that boy keeps following me," says Simon, a bit confused. His mother patiently explains, "That's your cousin, Taylor, and he wants to play with you." Once Simon understands he has a new playmate, they become inseparable. They explore the woods, play monster in the water, and bury themselves in the sand. They giggle, laugh, tease, and torment each other. They are adorable. Their contagious friendship causes aunts and uncles to smile, remembering the fun they had together with young cousins. Our family spirit is reconnected and rekindled. There are hugs—lots of them; we stock up for months.

When it's time to leave, everyone is too busy packing to notice that Simon and Taylor aren't around. Suddenly, Simon's watchful Mom calls out the alarm. The entire family joins in a frantic search for the boys. Relief comes when Hershey chocolate bar wrappings lead to the hiding place of two chocolate-covered smiling faces. The boys are surprised by all the fuss. They're just finishing the eight candy bars left over from last night's s'mores.

And then it's time to say good-bye, but the boys don't want to go. As Taylor walks off and cries quietly to himself, Simon is puzzled once again. Not knowing what else to do, he sits beside his cousin and puts his tiny little arm around his shoulder. We never knew what words, if any, transpired. He was just there with him, caring. After all, that's what cousins do.

How many years has it been since your extended family got together? Take the time to organize a family reunion and try to make it a regular event. You'll be glad you did.

Compassion, Their Precious Treasure

STORYTELLER: ROBERT THURMAN

Maybe it was the majesty of the land itself: the largest and highest plateau on earth, ringed by the world's tallest peaks. For centuries, Tibet has been known as "the rooftop of the world." Her gentle people became a symbol of inspiration because of their mystical talent for finding the sacred dimension in everyday life. The rich culture, spirituality, and language of this land of snows were uniquely and beautifully her own.

Then in 1950, Chinese forces invaded. The occupation quickly changed into a campaign to eradicate the Tibetan identity. The Tibetan language was forbidden, and all aspects of Tibetan culture were rigidly suppressed. Worship was banned, and almost all monasteries and holy sites were destroyed. Tibetans who continued to follow their own religion were tortured or slaughtered. For nearly fifty years, the world has remained mostly silent as the Tibetan genocide unfolded.

Tibet's leader, the fourteenth Dalai Lama, born Tenzin Gyatso, was forced to flee the country in 1959 along with thousands of his followers. He established a Tibetan government-in-exile in Dharmsala, India, and has since worked diligently to preserve Tibetan arts, scriptures, and medicine. To millions of people of all faiths from all over the world, the Dalai Lama has become an inspiration. With his deep wisdom and compassion, he leads a nonviolent struggle to regain his homeland.

The year 1985 witnessed an extraordinary experience between this spiritual leader and his people. Two hundred thousand Tibetans risked the arduous journey over the mountains to Bodgaya, India: the mecca for Tibetan Buddhists to celebrate one of their most sacred ceremonies, the Kalachakra initiation. To ensure their prompt return, the Chinese government held the families of the pilgrims as virtual hostages.

For many, it would be the first time they would see His Holiness, the Dalai Lama, a moment they had anticipated their entire lives. Yak herders, shoemakers, peasants—people who had undergone unspeakable horror and violence—had endured even more hardship in order to keep this sacred commitment. The buses were overcrowded and the roads treacherous. Nepalese and Indian police along the route forced the travelers to pay unlawful tolls. But after days of strenuous travel, they finally arrived to see and hear the Dalai Lama.

The task before Tenzin Gyatso seemed insurmountable. He knew he must speak to his people about the Buddhist teachings of tolerance and compassion for their enemies. Yet he was acutely aware that he was talking to people who had been tortured, who had witnessed the rapes and mutilations of their families, and who had spent long years in wretched prisons. As he sat close to his people, you could almost feel the Dalai Lama's own heart break wide open. He implored the people to respond to their enemies without violence or hatred. He asked them to find compassion for their oppressors and overcome their instinct to strike back. He acknowledged that their families had been violated and their land, their life, their country, and their religion had been taken from them. Yet, he beseeched them to employ their suffering as a spur to conquer any vindictive, hateful, or destructive tendencies within themselves.

"I'm not suggesting to suppress it, but to take that warrior energy and defend yourself against becoming outraged and revenging yourself on the enemy. Be careful not to sink to the level of the enemy by torturing, killing, or being violent to anyone," he said.

"This is war, but it is an internal war. It may seem the world has forgotten us, allowing the Chinese to do this to us. But we can win the war by completely conquering our inner enemy. If we wage this war against our natural instinct for revenge and conquer the vengeful egotism we have within ourselves, then we will have done something very special. Then the world will have to recognize our stand against the endless cycle of violence. The world will then see to it that there will be justice. But it must be done without vengeance against the Chinese."

As he spoke, the Dalai Lama, usually composed and calm, was openly weeping. So were the majority of the two hundred thousand assembled before him. You could see the struggle in the faces of the children and teenagers. They did not know whether to believe this man or not. The Chinese had worked hard to turn them against him and his teachings, but the Dalai Lama had touched them so tenderly with his open heart and his message of love and compassion that they accepted the wisdom of his message.

When the pilgrims returned home, it was as though His Holiness was sending an army of guerrilla fighters back into Tibet. Their war was to conquer themselves: to do battle in their own hearts. It was astounding to see these enraged people wholeheartedly internalize such high aspirations, giving a new, transcendent meaning to the sacred path of the warrior.

Four years after this amazing scene, the Dalai Lama received the Nobel Prize for Peace. In his acceptance speech he reaffirmed his belief in the path of tolerance and compassion.

"I accept the prize with profound gratitude on behalf of the oppressed everywhere and for all those who struggle for freedom and work for world peace," he said. "I accept it as a tribute to the man who founded the modern tradition of nonviolent action for change, Mahatma Gandhi, whose life taught and inspired me. And, of course, I accept it on behalf of the six million Tibetan people, my brave countrymen and women inside Tibet, who have suffered and continue to suffer so much.

He continued, "They confront a calculated and systematic strategy aimed at the destruction of their national and cultural identities. The prize reaffirms our conviction that with truth, courage, and determination as our weapons, Tibet will be liberated."

The Tibetans' struggle has touched the hearts of ordinary people around the world. As each year passes, they gain greater recognition and support. In the journey to social justice, small steps sometimes lead to unexpected leaps of progress. Recently, the Walt Disney Company refused to be bullied by China's leaders into suppressing the release of *Kundun*, a Martin Scorsese film that tells the story of the Dalai Lama. By having the moral courage to tell the story of the Tibetan people, Disney will influence history in a way other leaders have been reluctant to do.

The Tibetan people have something more than their rich culture. They have a unique treasure with the potential power to transform the world. Their precious secret for transcending violence through compassion may be their most valuable treasure of all.

Love and compassion are the basis of hope and determination.

HIS HOLINESS, THE DALAI LAMA XIV

If you want to help the Tibetan people and preserve Tibet's precious civilization, call the **Tibet House,** the Dalai Lama's official cultural organization in America at 212-213-5592 or write to 22 West Fifteenth Street, New York, NY 10011 for their membership materials. Pray for peace and develop compassion in your heart.

Wise Beyond His Years

STORYTELLER: ROBERT WUTHNOW,
adapted from the Independent Sector's report,
What it Means to Volunteer; Lessons from America's Youth

Dexter Wellman lives with his mother, father, and sister in the low-income area of a prosperous midwestern city. Their home is a tiny, one-story clapboard house with walls so thin the ice-cold winter air blows right through. Dexter sleeps in a small room with a mattress on the floor, a couple of posters on the wall, and some plastic milk crates stuffed with books. There is no other furniture. It isn't much to look at, but as Dexter points out, at least it's a home. That's a luxury this ninth grader hasn't always had.

When Dexter was twelve, both his parents lost their jobs. After falling too far behind on rent and utilities, the Wellmans were forced out into the street. They stored what few belongings they had at his aunt's apartment and became homeless. Fortunately, the African Methodist church to which they belonged ran a shelter for the homeless.

The facility provided refuge, but, as Dexter quickly learned, it was no place for a child. Surrounded by so many unfortunate people who seemed to have lost their will to live, Dexter was terribly afraid. Not wanting to end up like them, he looked for a way to stay busy and keep his spirits up.

One day, while wandering around the church building, Dexter noticed some unused classrooms. Seeing the empty spaces, he thought of the many children in the shelter, most of whom couldn't read or write. He remembered playing school in the park near his old home. He'd always enjoyed helping other kids with their homework. Perhaps, Dexter thought, he could do it again.

When the woman who ran the shelter agreed to his plan to create a tutor center, Dexter went to see his school principal. He got some workbooks that were going to be thrown away. Then, he asked a community agency to bring over a few desks. Before he knew it, Dexter was in business. Soon, every afternoon, evening, and all day Saturday, the kids would come. In all, there were about twenty at a time. Dexter helped them with their homework, taught them to read, and had them practice in their newly acquired workbooks.

He fondly remembers one of his first pupils. "When I first started living at the shelter, I met a four-year-old girl named Sarah. She was the youngest student I ever had. At first she couldn't read or write. But, within three days, she was reading easy books, like *Cat in the Hat* and *Green Eggs and Ham*." Her progress was remarkable, thanks, in part, to Dexter's creativity: "I taped my voice while reading a book. Then, she played the tape and read along with it." Dexter felt really good knowing that he had done something to help someone. During the nine months he lived at the shelter, he grew very close to the other children.

It was painful for Dexter when his pupils moved on, going from shelter to shelter. "Just when you'd get used to someone, they'd move out," Dexter says. Of little Sarah he recalls, "I was really upset when she and her mom left for another shelter. But, I gave her the read-along tape and the book and told her to keep on reading."

Although two years have passed since Dexter and his family moved out of the shelter, he still goes back every day to tutor his kids. When he's not with them, he can be found helping the children in his own neighborhood with their schoolwork. And, the few books Dexter keeps in the plastic milk crates in his bedroom are his lending library.

Now sixteen, Dexter is wise beyond his years. He has already experienced more as a child than most people would ever want to in a lifetime. When asked why he does volunteer work, he replies, "Like they always say, you do something for somebody else, you always get something back." Then he pauses, as if somehow he has been trite. "People have always helped me," he adds. "So I thought that it was time to give something back."

It is not possible for civilization to flow backwards
while there is still youth in the world.

HELEN KELLER

About one-third of all homeless kids can't attend school regularly. Let Dexter's actions inspire you to spend a few hours a week at a homeless shelter helping these kids keep up and receive the extra emotional support they need. Call your local homeless organizations, your county Homeless Coalition, or Volunteer Center at **800-VOLUNTEER** for a referral.

Learning to Love Again

STORYTELLER: JUDITH THOMPSON

For the first eight years of his life, Arn Chorn enjoyed a luxury too valuable to take for granted: the gift of a peaceful childhood. Each night he would lay in his bamboo house in Cambodia's Battenbon province and watch stars ablaze in the warm and silent sky.

Then came his ninth birthday. He remembers the moment the Khmer Rouge first rode victoriously into town. At first the people welcomed them. But when they got a closer look, they noticed something eerily hard and cold about the faces of these young warriors. It was almost as if their very souls had deserted them.

This fanatical Cambodian Communist group sprang up in the countryside during the troubled years of the U.S. war with Vietnam. While hiding in the jungle with their brutal leader, Pol Pot, these boys were schooled in layer upon layer of hate. Each learned how to turn a deaf ear to the voice of his own conscience. The day the Khmer Rouge took over in Cambodia began one of the cruelest bloodbaths in history. Those who survived watched in horror as their beautiful homeland earned a new name, and Cambodia came to be known worldwide as "the killing fields."

Little Arn Chorn was taken from his family, forced to march into the countryside, and taken to a child labor camp. For the next four years, his life became a living hell. The Khmer Rouge began the systemic slaughter of millions of Cambodians. People were executed for wearing glasses, for having light skin, or for being teachers or monks. People were executed for crying when a family member was killed. Thrust into the front lines of combat, forced to witness the murder of thousands of children, Arn says, "I had to kill my heart in order to survive."

In the chaos that followed the Vietnamese invasion into Cambodia in 1979, Arn was able to escape into the jungle. There he lived alone for many months; his only friends were the monkeys. Arn learned how to survive in the jungle by watching them, seeing what they ate, and eating only the fruits they did. He came to trust these monkeys more than he had human beings. The tenderness and unconditional love they showed him was the first he had experienced in years. Inside, a tiny part of Arn started to heal.

One day, Arn miraculously stumbled across the border into Thailand. He was close to starving to death when rescue workers discovered him and brought him to Sakeo, a large refugee camp. Arn could scarcely believe his fortune when he became the first Cambodian orphan permitted entry into the U. S., a country that had always seemed at least as far away as the stars. When he arrived in October 1980, he started healing his past

When I met Arn, I was moved by his ability to share his story and by his extraordinary desire and ability to inspire others. For one so young, Arn impressed me with his desire to reach out to those like himself who had endured the nightmare of human madness. Before long, we decided to create Children of War, to provide an opportunity for these forgotten children, to heal their lives and reclaim their futures.

We began by working day and night with young people from Cambodian refugee communities. As Arn listened to their stories, he began to heal from his own pain. The Khmer Rouge had killed people for expressing any feelings. To survive, Arn had been forced to cut off his own capacity to feel. Hearing these young people's experiences softened his own frozen feelings and opened the closed doors of his heart. He discovered a deep connection and compassion for them.

In 1982, when he was just sixteen, Arn spoke before a riveted audience of ten thousand people in New York's Cathedral of St. John the Divine. "It seems almost unbelievable that I could forgive and forget what happened to my people," he said. "Sharing with other young people who've endured similar horrors has helped me to feel again: their pain as well as my own." He closed by saying, "I'm alive after all these years, because I can love again." These simple words carried more power than Arn could have possibly imagined. Before he knew it, he was sharing his story at the United Nations, before Congress, and with people from across the country. From there the movement took off.

For the next several years, Children of War provided the vision, training, and support so that young people from Beirut, South Africa, and Guatemala, as well as U.S. inner cities, could begin to heal from their deep grief so they could rebuild their lives. In the process, they discover what Arn calls the "common bonds of suffering" which unites them. Surprisingly, their own painful sharing gives way to a much deeper joy. They begin to see themselves in each other's stories and realize for the first time that they are not alone. They also discover that they share a common dream: for children like themselves to be able to live in peace.

These young people become Children of War leaders, traveling across the U.S. educating and motivating their peers. That's how Arn met Jacob Smith, a boy from Bedford-Stuyvesant, one of New York's toughest neighborhoods. For several years, Jacob had gone the way of guns, drugs, and violence and had ended up in the New York juvenile justice system. "When I met Arn and all the other Children of War participants, I began to dream about my future again," says Jacob. "When I was acting out I didn't have time to dream. But when I met Arn and began thinking again, I just started to feel real good. Every time my good feeling increased, I realized the violent feelings decreased."

Now Arn and Jacob work as a team in inner-city high schools. They encourage young people to share their stories and come to understand the despair that drives them to acts of violence. They give victims of violence the opportunity to become visionaries. By being exposed other youths like Arn, these kids can begin to see their own lives in a new light. For his work with Children of War, Arn received the Reebok Human Rights Award and the opportunity to travel worldwide on behalf of children whose lives had been torn apart by violence.

In 1990, Arn returned to Cambodia for the first time, where he came face-to-face with the memories of his early nightmarish experiences. "Sometimes I feel like I want to die," Arn said. "The weight of the past is so great. But then I tell myself that I can do something good to help other people and that keeps me going." So, Arn rolled up his sleeves and organized youth in Cambodia so they could create healing as they rebuilt their country. Today, there are fifty thousand young people who are part of his program, Cambodian Volunteers for Community Development. Arn is now in Boston, helping Cambodian youth, hoping to build partnerships with those back in Cambodia. "These people have all suffered so much. It will take awhile for them to learn to trust and love again," says Arn. "The Khmer Rouge took that away from us. It will take time, but I am committed. We have to learn to love each other again. That's the only way."

May you live all the days of your life.

—JONATHAN SWIFT

If you want to help young people heal from the violence in this country and around the world and help them rebuild their lives and reclaim their futures, call Arn Chorn and Judith Thompson at the Institute for New Leadership at 617-648-1276, which is carrying on the legacy of **Children of War**.

A Healing Moment

STORYTELLER: BROTHER DAVID STENDL-RAST

New York City had never seen anything like it. Close to one million people were demonstrating against the insanity of nuclear arms. It was 1982 and The Cold War was raging. The superpowers continued their expensive, seemingly uncontrollable arms race. Yet, in the midst of all this, hundreds of thousands marched for peace.

The march led from the United Nations headquarters to Central Park. It took us half a day to walk those few miles. The crowds with their banners and bands moved slowly enough, but we were slower still. My walking partner, the Vietnamese Zen monk, Thich Nhat Hanh, had asked that we make every single step of the march a meditation for peace.

Thich Nhat Hanh had been a leader in the nonviolent movement for peace in Vietnam. He believed that mindfulness, insight, and altruistic love should be the foundation for any political action. After meeting him in 1964, Martin Luther King Jr. had resolved that the civil rights movement would be nonviolent, and, in solidarity with his new friend, Dr. King took the controversial step of supporting the anti–Vietnam War movement. Later, when he nominated Thich Nhat Hanh for the Nobel Peace Prize, he said, "His ideas for peace, if applied, would build a monument to ecumenism, to world brotherhood, to humanity."

Our silent band of Buddhist and Christian monks had set out with the first marchers, but our walking meditation was moving so slowly, that group after group caught up with us and passed us by. We were enjoying the crowd: the colorful array of streamers and signs, the clowns surrounded by children, the musicians and singers, and the mothers wheeling their infants, the Veterans of Foreign Wars, and even the poodles and collies displaying peaceful slogans on their backs. Grandmothers for Peace and groups in masks and costumes: one by one they all got ahead of us.

Eventually, a policeman politely pointed out that we were walking too slowly and suggested a shortcut. We didn't mind. We took the shortcut and found ourselves once again near the head of the march. As group after group that had passed us before passed us again, they reacted with surprised laughter and cheers.

It was a day of pure joy. We felt like one big happy family of a million members and behaved accordingly. On the evening news of that historic day, New York City's chief of police made a brief statement. He praised the demonstrators for cleaning up every scrap of trash along their route, right down to the gum wrappers, and admitted that he and his friends could not have left their backyard in better condition after a barbecue. And a party it had been for the whole city: a celebration of the love of life uniting all humans.

Why not leave it at that? Why introduce a sour note into festive singing? A Pax Christi group of students from Columbia University with whom I set out the next morning had grappled all night with this issue. Not without pain we had reached a consensus: there are times when we are allowed to forget for a while what divides us, but at other times we must face and oppose what separates us. Only then can healing take place.

This reasoning determined our plan of action. In nonviolent direct action we were going to obstruct access to the office of the French delegation to the U.N. Other groups were doing the same at offices of the other countries who were keeping the arms race going. A confrontation it was to be, yet in the form of a celebration. We would celebrate what we shared and share it even with those who opposed us.

As a symbol of our message, we brought bread to share: baskets and baskets of fresh, fragrant home-baked loaves of bread. The banner above us read, "Bread Not Bombs." We sang and prayed and broke the bread, offering it to people on their way to work. Most of them rushed by, but some looked up at our banner and stopped long enough to share this communion.

Soon a police squad moved in and surrounded the entrance to the building. They asked us to clear out. We stayed. "Do you want to get arrested?" they asked. "We want to stay here," we said, "even if that means getting arrested." They lowered the visors on their helmets and grabbed their clubs. We knelt down and refused to move.

This was a strange configuration, these two lines of people confronting each other, face to face, less than two feet apart. In my memory this has become a figure in a dance: one movement of a strange choreography suspended in time. All motion stopped. An hour went by, then another. We sang. We prayed the Lord's Prayer aloud, over and over: "give us this day our daily bread, and forgive us . . . as we forgive. . . ." Another hour passed.

We had gotten up off our knees by now, but imagine standing face to face with someone for so long! We came to know the buttons on those uniforms in far greater detail than we'd ever known the ones on our own coats. Behind the visor opposite me, I could see into the eyes of a young man: Puerto Rican, I guessed. In a different context, I might have called those eyes gentle. I imagined his mother proudly showing her neighbors a photo of her son in uniform. By now, I felt like a brother to him.

But why had we not been arrested and taken off in a paddy wagon hours ago? Why this deadlock? Later we learned that more arrests had been made that day than ever before in the history of New York City. Every police van and even school buses had been pressed into service to cart off the demonstrators. When it was our turn, there were simply no vehicles left to take us to jail. This was the practical reason, but a deeper reason may have been that we were waiting for an event: a healing moment.

Many employees of the French offices had passed us by. Then one small, gray-haired gentleman in a gray business suit, complete with vest and tie, stopped. Looking down the long row of helmets that was facing an equally long row of unprotected heads, I could see the man's face exactly where the lines converged. At first, he eyed with a timid expression the row of demonstrators face to face with the police. But then something happened. It was as if a high voltage had built up between the two poles—so close, yet not touching—and, suddenly, a spark jumped. The man's face lit up. He read the banner, "Bread Not Bombs," took off his hat, and bravely and proudly held out his hand. He took a piece of bread and put it in his mouth, solemnly almost, as if it were Holy Communion. It was as if an inner voice seemed to say, "Go in peace, your courage has healed you."

Shortly after that, the police took off their helmets, shook our hands, and simply let us go home. One of the officers gave us the victory sign. But what I will never forget is the moment when the gray-haired man's face lit up: the victory of his own private conviction and his own healing.

Touching the present moment is the door to everything.

THICH NHAT HANH

Your gift to the hungry may be small but find out how you can give it the greatest leverage by contacting **Bread for the World** at 800-82-BREAD or contacting us via e-mail at bread@igc.apc.org, or visiting the website at: http://www.bread.org.

If you want to learn mindfulness with **Thich Nhat Hanh** by attending a retreat or if you wish to receive a list of his books and tapes, contact the **Community of Mindful Living** at Parallax Press, P. O. Box 7355, Berkeley, CA 94707.

Doing Well by Doing Good

What would you do if you made $1 billion in just nine months? Would you join with Ted Turner and give it to your favorite charity? Would you help rebuild your homeland, like George Soros is doing with Eastern Europe's emerging democracies? With today's robust stock market gains, just think what could happen if more of us found imaginative ways to give back!

There is a saying in business: make your money while you are young and give it away when you are old. Some new millionaires are deciding not to wait and are having fun sharing their wealth—like beneficiaries of Microsoft's stock-option policy with their Seattle community. Some generous people are now renewing the age-old tradition of tithing 10% of their income. Wayne Silby and his friends founded the Calvert Social Investment Fund so ordinary Americans could invest their money for social good. In Tom Cruise's box office hit, *Jerry Maguire*, he challenges his colleagues: being more honest and doing more for others will bring far more happiness than a few more dollars in the bank.

The business community, especially investors, could become the next champions for building a better world. "Philanthropy from the private sector is rapidly becoming the most practical source of long-term change in America," says Claude Rosenberg, Jr. in his book, *Wealthy and Wise*. A successful investor, Rosenberg realized he could share a lot more of his wealth than he ever imagined and enjoy giving more to deserving causes. After discovering that the nation's top earners give less than 10% of what they could easily afford to give, he started encouraging them to share their good fortune and help make the world a better place.

Business leaders in the 1970s set a powerful precedent for how they could impact our country's health and well-being. When corporate America realized they could reduce their health care costs if employees changed their lifestyles, they led the charge to get Americans healthy. The three-martini-lunch was replaced with low-fat diets, bottled water and workouts at the gym. To rally national support, corporate leaders forged alliances with unions, schools, government and the media. Getting America healthy became our national goal. People across the country joined the fitness revolution. Today, many more of us are making healthy choices and living longer by exercising, watching what we eat and drink.

If we could work together to improve our personal health, we surely can improve our country's health too! If the business community led this charge with a powerful call to action, they could invite all Americans to join in and rally our country to help build a better world.

This chapter offers successful examples and a wealth of ideas for how to begin. These stories show how business heroes like Aaron Feurerstein, Judy Wicks and Arnold Hiatt have combined their head and heart and used their resources to improve their communities. Corporate giants like George Draper Dayton built a legacy of charitable giving and inspired his company to continue the tradition for over 50 years. Dayton Hudson has kept its promise, even during economic downturns, of giving 5% of their profits to the community. They've also encouraged other Minneapolis companies to form the 2% Club, to counteract the corporate giving trend of giving only 1.3%. Organizations like Business for Social Responsibility encourage companies to renew their corporate citizenship by investing in educating children and building healthier communities.

The stories in this chapter describe various ways companies can contribute to communities. NationsBank finds building partnerships with community organizations multiplies their investments and maximizes their effectiveness. Companies like Home Depot who encourage employees to volunteer in their communities build a strong team spirit in the workplace. Working Assets' customers vote on which social action and environmental organizations they want the company to support. Bonneville International offers listeners of their radio stations opportunities to give back to their community. Multinational companies like EDS extend their tradition of being good neighbors as they expand their business abroad.

Money is one the most important tools we have to create positive change in the world. While we can't all be Ted Turner or George Soros, there are hundreds of ways each of us can invest our time and our money in our communities. We will make the world a better place, when we revolutionize the way we think about giving.

What if more of the business community decided to champion the building of a better world? What if we channeled our collective resources, organized our business skills and rallied the best and the brightest to support what is working in the world? Just imagine what would the new millenium look like? What a gift we would give to future generations!

There comes a time in each of our lives when we must choose: to continue on the path we're on, or take a look at the world and ask ourselves:

* What is most important in my life?
* What kind of life do I really want to live?
* What kind of world do I want for my children and my grandchildren?

With the millenium just around the corner, now is the time. And it's your turn to choose.

* Dare to share.
* Act with your pocketbook.
* Write the check. Just do it!

Stone Soup Magic

STORYTELLER: A. E. HOTCHNER

Think of him as a master chef cooking up magic for the whole world. "I like to take what I've got and spread it around," Paul Newman says. He has the old-fashioned notion that a man ought to give something back. So, he does. He donates every penny of his after-tax profits from his company, Newman's Own, Inc., to good causes. Since 1982, his charitable contributions have totaled over eighty million dollars.

"Newman's Own began as a lark, a joke more or less, and soon became a challenge," says the movie star. "I had no idea that my salad dressing would out-gross my films. Today there's an entire generation that may know me more for my popcorn than for my movies," he adds with a grin.

"Newman's Own furnishes people with wholesome, all-natural foods that they enjoy," Newman explains. "The after-tax profits from the company are then given to organizations serving people who, because of poverty, sickness, old age, or illiteracy, desperately need assistance." Newman has funded programs for health, education, the homeless, the environment, the arts, and children. Thousands of organizations have received grants from the company, with the majority of grants being made to smaller, obscure organizations that are often overlooked by mainstream charities. "What makes this business great is the mutually beneficial recycling from the haves to the have-nots," says Newman.

Among his favorite endeavors is the Newman's Own and Good Housekeeping Recipe Contest, in which winners receive ten thousand dollars to donate to their favorite charity. When a first-grade class at the Terra Linda School in Beaverton, Oregon, learned about the recipe contest, they decided to try their luck.

That week during story time, their teacher, Mrs. Clement, read them the classic children's folk tale, *Stone Soup:* "A hungry traveler feeds himself and a whole village, starting with just one magic stone and a pot of water. When each of the villagers gives a little, there is plenty for everyone." Twenty-four six-year-olds listened carefully, sitting cross-legged on mats surrounding their teacher. Their wide eyes studied the pictures she showed them. When she finished reading, they talked together about the book. The children agreed that their favorite illustration was the very last one. Above the words, *The End,* an entire village was feasting upon this very special soup.

Then Mrs. Clement had a great idea: what if the class entered their own recipe for Stone Soup in the contest? The kids were very enthusiastic. Working together, they chalked a list of their own special ingredients upon the blackboard; your basic soup ingredients, except for two: One was a twenty-six-ounce jar of Newman's Own Sockarooni Sauce. The other was a stone. "It wouldn't be right without a stone from Oregon," said ten-year-old Jessica Stewart.

The Stone Soup recipe made the first-graders winners. "When Mrs. Clement told us we had won the contest," Jessica remembers, "we screamed, shouted, and danced around the classroom."

The students knew exactly what they would do with their $10,000 in prize money. They would give it back to their own school. They purchased books for the library, keyboards for the music department, and a weather station. They stamped each and every item with the words *Newman's Own.* Now, when students check out a book or play the keyboards, they can remember how good it felt to help their school and work together as a team.

As for Jessica, her days of giving have just begun. "Winning $10,000 as a kid made a big difference in how I feel about giving. It made me want to help others now and when I get older," she says. "Now that I'm in the fourth grade, I'm on the student council. Each year we give our time and energy to help others. We've collected money to buy school supplies for the flood victims in the Oregon flood. We've collected pop cans to raise money for Keiko the whale. We bring in Campbell's Soup labels to get balls for our playground."

Mrs. Clement is happy that the contest gave the children an opportunity to give back to their school. "An important part of what we teach in the classroom is sharing, giving, and helping others," she says. "The students also learn that to be successful in life, it's necessary to listen, work together, and solve problems." The Stone Soup story gave them lots of food for thought.

Mrs. Clement is very grateful to Paul Newman. "He gave these children a once-in-a-lifetime opportunity," she says. "The books and keyboards will grow old and out of date, but the memory of what the students were able to do for their school will stay with them always. He could have just made a donation, but by helping others to give, he gives so much more than just money. The greatest gift Paul Newman gave my students was a lesson in the value of giving. He planted the seeds for them to do great things in their lives."

Mrs. Clement's First Graders' Stone Soup Recipe

- 1 magic stone
- 10 cups water
- 1 10½ oz. can broth
- 1 tsp. salt
- 1 tsp. pepper
- 2 lbs. stew meat
- 1 large onion, sliced
- 1 26 oz. jar Newman's Own Sockarooni Sauce
- 4 carrots, sliced
- 4 celery stalks, sliced
- 10 small new potatoes, cut in small chunks
- 1 12 oz. package Italian green beans
- 1 cup uncooked ABC pasta

* Place stone in small amount of water (2 cups) with broth, salt, pepper, stew meat, and onion in an 8-quart soup pot. Simmer on low heat for approximately 2 hours.
* Add Newman's Own™ Sockarooni Sauce and vegetables. Continue to simmer for 20 minutes, until vegetables are tender.
* Add ABC pasta and cook for another 10–15 minutes until pasta is al dente. **Don't forget to remove stone before eating or teeth may get hurt.**
* Serve with warm bread and butter. Serves one first-grade class of 24 or 8 adults.

Give the children in your life an opportunity to give back. Cook up a winner for your favorite charity. Enter your best recipe using a Newman's Own™ product in the **Newman's Own/Good Housekeeping Recipe Contest.** For more information, call 800-272-0257.

From Street Kids to Wall Street

STORYTELLER: MATTHEW MALONE

Show Steve Mariotti a group of young people bright enough to rob a man and get away with it, and he'll show you a group of potential business people needing direction.

Jogging down a busy New York street, full of the city's normal hustle and bustle, Steve was stopped by a gang of youths who wanted his money. Somewhat dazed after handing over his wallet and watching them run away, he was shaken by an equally powerful thought: What if the energy these kids had for illegal and destructive activities could be channeled productively?

A successful business man, Steve recognized that the creativity and drive they possessed, however misguided, were the same qualities needed in the business world. They were aggressive, focused, and they were working together to achieve a common goal. Unfortunately, tonight their goal was his wallet. But Steve knew that with the proper training and encouragement, these kids could reach higher (and more productive) goals in the world. He left his successful import-export business behind and set out to be the teacher he had always wanted to be.

One of his first classes was held at the Central Ward Boys & Girls Club in Newark, New Jersey. And one of his first students was fifteen-year-old Felix Rouse. Felix was instantly impressed with this out-of-place short white man who was carefully explaining business concepts like supply and demand, buying wholesale, and profit. To this bunch of kids, the business world was another planet. As Steve laid the groundwork for his "mini M.B.A.," his students immediately began to tune in.

The students quickly caught onto the basics of running a business. They opened checking accounts, got business cards, and discussed the delicate art of customer relations. They visited Wall Street, met with wholesalers, and were challenged to come up with plans to start their own businesses. Within a few months, Felix and a friend began turning their mutual passion for comic books into detailed business plan, outlining the costs, prices, and strategy for a comic book store. Steve provided $100 in capital, and for two years, they operated their business out of office space provided by the Boys & Girls Club. The boys did all the buying, selling, bookkeeping, and inventory. "Though we didn't make a ton of money, I never had to borrow any," Felix says. "I learned very quickly to take care of myself, and I developed the skills to be successful."

In 1986, Steve created the National Foundation for Teaching Entrepreneurship (NFTE) to help spread his successful program to other inner city youth. By 1996, NFTE had 186 teachers and fourteen thousand sponsors replacing the dead ends of drugs, crime, and teenage pregnancy for 10,000 students with a vigorous pursuit of success in the business world. Through NFTE, inner-city kids are taught the ABCs of business while learning lessons for life along the way. And while the business knowledge they gain through the classes is invaluable, so is the personal attention from someone who cares. "Steve was always in the mix," Felix says. "He knew about my struggles and was always there to listen. He cares about all of us on a very personal level."

Like many other NFTE students, Felix has experienced some bumps along the road. During his senior year in high school, his adoptive father passed away. A year later, his older brother was shot and confined to a wheelchair. Despite these personal tragedies, Felix had the courage and strength to stay the course. In 1996, he graduated from the University of Pennsylvania with a degree in political science. Today, he is the first graduate of NFTE to be trained as an entrepreneurship teacher, teaching at the Boys & Girls Club where he first encountered Steve.

Felix now shares Steve's message with a new generation of students. In him they see a twenty-three-year-old who overcame obstacles similar to ones they face and triumphed. In them, Felix sees the dawning of a very bright future. They all thank Steve for helping them discover their potential and giving them a chance to avoid the kinds of lifestyles that are better left behind.

For the thousands of kids like Felix who have experienced the NFTE program, the outlook is anything but "underprivileged." The knowledge, skills, experience, and hope they have gained has made their chances of success skyrocket. As one graduate put it, "My dream is not to die in poverty, but to have poverty die in me." Day by day, student by student, NFTE is helping to make that wonderful dream a reality.

A coach is someone who tells you what you don't want to hear
and has you see what you don't want to see
so you can be who you have always known you could be.

TOM LANDRY

Want to help a child learn how to start a small business, get **NFTE**'s entrepreneurial curriculum into the hands of at-risk youth, or sponsor a teacher to be NFTE trained? Call 800-FOR-NFTE.

The Robin Hood of Wall Street

STORYTELLER: TERRY MOLLNER

Wayne Silby was introduced to the world of high finance at the age of eight. His father bought him twenty shares of stock, and Wayne carried the confirmation slip around with him, knowing it was important. He treasured it more than his baseball cards, which was saying something for a boy raised in a small Iowa town. By the time Wayne was fourteen, he was picking his own stocks. At age thirty, he was probably the youngest chief executive officer of a billion-dollar investment fund.

In the 1970s, most people were still putting their money in savings accounts. Wayne and his buddy John Guffey dreamed of creating a better way for the common man to save: an investment fund of some kind. What they needed was a strategy for a safe as well as lucrative return. They found it when the Small Business Administration (SBA) began selling many of its loans in the late 1970s. Wayne realized that where most interest rates stayed the same for twenty or thirty years, these interest rates were scheduled to go up and down each day, depending on market conditions. He borrowed ten thousand dollars from his father, and he and John raised the one hundred thousand dollars in start-up money to launch the First Variable Rate Fund In Government Securities. Within a couple of months it was the top performing all-government money market fund in the country. Among other things, they put small ads revealing this in the *Wall Street Journal* and *New York Times* and within a few years the fund had over one billion dollars invested in it.

While Wayne and John were building what became known as "The Calvert Group of Mutual Funds," I was trying to figure out how to educate average Americans about their potential power to do good in the world with their money. I met Wayne at a conference in the mid-1970's and we became friends instantly partially because of our common interest in finance. One day, Wayne came to Boston to visit and explore ideas about socially responsible investing. In the afternoon we took a long walk in a park, talking about the state of affairs in the world and what we could do to make things better. As we talked, we thought how nice it would be to have an investment fund that was an expression of something from our generation. Our 60's generation was very focused on making the world a better place for everyone. Then the idea of creating a mutual fund that only invested in companies which had healthy relationships with their employees, the community, and the environment came out of Wayne's mouth. Suddenly, our feet stopped. Our eyes met. We knew instantly that that was exactly what needed to be done and what we wanted to do.

Months later Wayne called me and invited me to help him create the Calvert Social Investment Fund inside his company by serving on its board of directors. Little did we know that it would grow to also become over a billion-dollar fund, spawn a whole new industry, and attract millions of supporters. "That's what happens," Wayne once laughed with me, "when you just decide to do the right thing!"

When Wayne and John first presented the idea to their management team, it was rejected. They were told that their small company would be laughed out of the Wall Street community. "Well," Wayne responded, "since we own the company, we will do it anyway only as a special project." To set it up, they spent hundreds of thousands of dollars, knowing it would be many years of losses before they would reach the thirty-million-dollar break-even point.

We started it with one particularly bold decision: to not invest in any company doing business in South Africa. Calvert was the first mutual fund to make such a commitment. For decades, apartheid had been the country's official policy of discrimination against black Africans. In 1982, only a few brave souls were trying to put an end to it. But within a short few years, a huge movement of investors—including city and state governments, universities, and other business and financial institutions—also came to refuse to invest in companies doing business in South Africa. Since the Calvert fund was initially the only mutual fund in which people could invest with a clear conscience regarding this issue, it reached the thirty-million-dollar mark years before we thought it would.

The impact on South Africa is historic. "The divestment movement in America was a significant factor in ending apartheid," says Nelson Mandela. And, according to Dr. Louis Sullivan, founder of the anti-apartheid movement's Sullivan divestiture principles, "The Calvert Group deserves a great deal of credit, they were the first to pressure companies and to help us confront the government of South Africa."

Today, socially responsible investing is a legitimate part of the professional investment community and it is growing rapidly. You can walk into any brokerage firm anywhere in the U.S. and find someone to help you set up a socially screened portfolio. In 1975, you would have been sent to the offices of a local charity because you were not solely interested in making money regardless of how it was done.

From the beginning, we not only wanted people to have the option of achieving the same financial return while being socially responsible but also to have the investment option of accepting a lower return so we could provide dollars to poor families to work their way out of poverty. In 1990, Calvert shareholders voted to begin making loans with up to 1 percent of the assets in our socially responsible funds at low interest rates (3-4 percent) to local community loan funds around the world. This had a tiny effect on the performance of the fund but those millions of dollars had a very big effect in poor communities. The local community funds re-loan the money to poor families in "micro loans"—sometimes initially as small as twenty-five dollars—to help them start their own businesses. The program was so successful—we have not lost a penny since inception—that we created Calvert Community Investments within a foundation we established alongside the Calvert Group. Now it is possible for anyone in the world to invest solely for the purpose of ending poverty.

The lives of thousands of people have been transformed by these loans. One of them is Joite, a woman I met in a Bangladesh village. "A few years ago, my children and I were living under a tree by the road. We had nothing. Nothing!" she says emphatically. "With your help, I now have a house, chickens, goats, cows, a fish pond, banana trees, and a husband. My children go to school. We are happy…and alive."

While Robin Hood stole from the rich to feed the poor, we have invited the rich and all investors to join us to assist the poor to pull themselves up and out of poverty permanently while the investor receives a reasonable return. In so doing we have created yet another investment sector on Wall Street called "community investing"—investment to end poverty. The number of people who have responded is once again beyond what we imagined. Thus, today, in the private sector, there is now a mutually respectful hand-up, rather than hand-out, industry putting an end to poverty.

A few years ago you couldn't find any legitimate socially responsible investment options in the Wall Street investment community. Today, many can be found. And this new industry is spreading around the world.

Wayne Silby had the courage to take the lead in creating a place for socially responsible investing even though all but the dreamers were against him. Because of his courage and imagination, it is now possible for small investors to follow their hearts while fattening their wallets, something that once was hard to do. "People naturally want to do the right thing," Wayne often says. "If they are given a choice, many will choose to make money by helping the good guys. All we did was give them the ability to make that choice."

To invest your money with companies who have healthy relationships with their employees, the community, and the environment, call the **Calvert Family of Socially Responsible Mutual Funds** at 800-368-2750. To invest to help people work their way out of poverty permanently, call **Calvert Community Investments** at 800-248-0337.

Jim's Big Secret

STORYTELLER: SHEILA RICHARDSON

Jim Guest is a great guy who had been hiding a big secret. For the past fifteen years, he's worked hard to be a valued employee at Ames Rubber Corporation. His supervisors knew they could count on Jim to learn just about any job. They knew he would get it done—in record time. What they didn't know was that Jim couldn't read. But he wasn't alone. Over forty million adults in the United States can't read either.

Jim will be the first to admit that he was never very interested in school. He had other things on his mind. As a child, it was playing. As a teen, it was partying and having a good time. No one knew Jim couldn't read or write, and he tried to keep it that way. "When you don't know how to read, you find ways of getting around it," he explains. "People who can't read have a bag full of tricks to hide their handicap. To pull it off, you actually have to be pretty smart. Being illiterate is definitely not the same thing as being stupid."

Jim hid his secret well, until one day when it came crashing in on him. He was chosen to participate in a special company project and was asked to take notes at a meeting. Jim was trapped with no way out. He decided to tell his boss, Bob Kenna, the truth—the three words he had been hiding his whole life: "I can't read." He didn't know what to expect. Would his boss understand? Would he be throwing away years of hard work and loyalty?

When his boss said, "Don't worry about it, we'll work something out," a great weight was lifted from Jim's shoulders. After hiding the truth for so long, he was finally free. A few months later, Bob asked Jim if he wanted to learn how to read.

He explained that several Ames teammates had been trained as tutors by Literacy Volunteers of America. He could work with one of them and learn to read on company time. Jim was overjoyed. "I jumped at the chance," he said.

Under the guidance of his tutor, Sandy Rocheleau, Jim began taking reading lessons for an hour and a half every week. He learned the skills most people acquire in grade school. At first, his progress was slow, but gradually he improved. For two years, Jim was faithful to his weekly tutoring sessions. He had a special goal that kept him going. He wanted to be able to read to his new son, Kyle.

Several months passed, during which Jim and Sandy hadn't spoken. Then one day Sandy received a phone call from Jim. He had just finished reading his first novel, *Robinson Crusoe*. "Thanks for making it possible," he said. Sandy remembers that as one of the golden moments of her life. "It just doesn't get any better than that," she says. "I'm so proud of Jim. And I've gotten as much out of it as he has."

"It's hard to express how I feel," Jim says. "Words like pride, accomplishment, self-respect, self-confidence, and security come to mind, but also hard work, drive, challenge, and commitment. It has not been easy, but it sure was worth it."

As a result of Jim and Sandy's success, Ames is giving this gift to others. Their tutors now work with any employee or Sussex County, New Jersey, resident who wants to learn to read and write. And Jim has become their greatest cheerleader, encouraging everyone to learn to read. "There is no shame in not being able to read," Jim tells others. "The shame is in not taking advantage of an opportunity to learn."

"When you can't read, your whole life is a continuous balancing act, memorizing on the one hand, hiding the handicap on the other. What's frightening is that I couldn't even read medicine bottle labels for the correct dosage. Thanks to Sandy and Ames, I don't have to hide any more. I owe them a lot for all they've done for me.

"At bedtime, as I hold my son in my arms, a lot of things go through my head," he adds. "'I have to change the oil in my car.' 'What will I plant in the garden this year?' 'I need new work boots.' But all these thoughts fly out of my head when Kyle tosses *The Cat in the Hat* in my lap. A few short years ago, I could not read even the most simple story to him. It won't be long now before his mother finds us sitting at the kitchen table doing homework together. Tonight, he said, 'Come on Daddy, let's read *Green Eggs and Ham* next.' You can't imagine how good it makes me feel to be able to do that for him."

The Boulder in My Life

All through my life, a boulder was in my way.
I tried to move it. It wouldn't budge.
I tried to pick it up, or break it.
I could only chip at it.
So, for most of my life, I managed to work around it.
Then one day, there was no way out.
I looked at it, and admitted it was a problem.
Help came.
Together we chipped away at the boulder.
Then, we pushed it, tugged at it.
We managed to move it, slowly at first.
It started to roll, then faster and faster.
It rolled off a cliff and broke in pieces.
Today I can read.
And though I still have some problems, there's help.
Thanks for the help.

JIM GUEST

Give someone the gift of reading; call **Literacy Volunteers of America, Inc.,** at 315-445-8000 for the LVA group nearest to you. If someone you know could benefit from their free and confidential services, have them call LVA, too.

Giving Them a Chance

STORYTELLER: DIANE VALLETTA

Ladell Johnson was a casualty of a factory line shutdown; just another unemployed inner-city African-American woman who faced a bleak and uncertain future. Quiet and timid, Ladell's potential was shrouded in a deep-seated lack of confidence. She worked hard and kept looking for a new job because the welfare of her three children depended on it. All she wanted was a fair chance.

Thanks to Rachel Hubka, she got it. The owner of Rachel's Bus Company, has a special gift for recognizing people's hidden talents. For Rachel, interviewing an unemployed person with no related job experience was not unusual. After all, she chose to locate her company in North Lawndale, a Chicago neighborhood with a 60 percent unemployment rate. Rachel actively recruits welfare recipients and the seemingly unemployable to drive her school buses.

Thanks to the support of her parents, Rachel grew up convinced that, "I could do anything, as long as I had an opportunity." She now extends that same confidence and enthusiasm to her employees. "When I opened my business, I wanted to create opportunities for those the system had left behind. They needed work, and I needed employees. I knew that with the right training they could become valuable members of society."

Rachel believes in helping people help themselves. Her guiding principle is the adage: "Bloom where you are planted." By training, inspiring, and encouraging her employees to take on more responsibility, they move up in the company. Rachel also fosters an entrepreneurial spirit by giving drivers opportunities to earn commissions by bringing in charter business. She helps these men and women with marginal work histories and minimal skills become proud, productive, and committed employees.

Helping others work has worked for Rachel. Her seven-year-old company has grown to a staff of over 140 and a fleet of 125 buses. In 1995, she received the prestigious Business Enterprise Award honoring business owners who combine their social conscience with sound management practices. She is also a national spokesperson for Welfare to Work Reform.

When Rachel hired Ladell, it dramatically changed Ladell's life. "Rachel stirred something inside me," Ladell says. "Her faith in my abilities woke me up to what life was all about. For the first time, I felt I could really live instead of just going through the motions." But Rachel did more than just give Ladell a job. From the start, she encouraged Ladell to stretch herself. She gave her new opportunities and guided her along the way. Rachel asked Ladell to take her place at meetings with school administrators, chief executive officers, and other business and community leaders.

For Ladell, who had lived a life of solitude and had rarely interacted with the community around her, the opportunity was challenging and difficult. At first, she went reluctantly, but later she went with increasing self-assurance and enthusiasm. Slowly, she began to develop a natural ease with others. From her first job as a personnel clerk, Ladell quickly rose to become head of the Human Resource division. Now, she looks for ways to make a positive impact on the company, her coworkers, and the community.

In only a few short years, Ladell lowered employee turnover by screening applicants and matching them with the right jobs. She helps get people registered to vote and urges other employees to take active roles in their community. On her own time, as a lay minister, she helps those who are ill or just want someone to talk to.

Ladell, someone whom society might have written off, even received the Sister

Thea Bowman Humanitarian Award that is given to people who do things for others "just because." She credits Rachel for the opportunity and inspiration to make her life a successful one. In a note of thanks she sent to Rachel, Ladell wrote, "I recently met two young women who reminded me of the old me. Both in their early twenties, their lives in a downward spiral. One was in an abusive relationship; the other, struggling to find her way as an adult. I reached out to them. Now the three of us are finding our way by enriching the lives of others. And it all began with you."

Give **Welfare to Work Reform** a chance and make a positive impact on your community and the nation's economy. Help people off the welfare rolls and onto the tax rolls. Call Welfare to Work Partnership at 800-USA-JOB1 (872-5621) or visit its website: www.welfare to work.org or call Business for Social Responsibility at 415-537-0888.

A Culture Of Giving

STORYTELLER: ANN M. BAUER

For eight years, Esther Diaz has risen early two days each week and dressed for her job at the Target store in Lavern, California. There she serves customers from behind the counter on "Food Avenue," folds towels, hangs clothes, marks prices, and always earns the highest marks from her superiors. Esther is a remarkable employee who just happens to have a mental disability. And she's in good company, thanks to a recruiting program called "I Can Do That."

It began in 1988 when Dwight Bonds, a high-school teacher, devised a plan to help Esther and three of her classmates who were developmentally disabled make the transition from graduation to the workforce.

"I called Target's regional office and explained what I was looking for," Bond says. He was pleased with the response he received. "They said, 'We'll make them a part of our family,'" he says. "Target offered them regular jobs with the same benefits and wages paid to other employees."

The store came through with frontline jobs and job coaches. Bonds prepared the students by drilling them on practical skills such as money counting and alphabetic filing. Within five months the arrangement was so successful that twenty-five more mentally challenged students were placed in thirteen California locations.

Bonds calls it a win-win-win situation: young people get jobs, parents who feared their kids would be dependent for life see that they are able to work and be productive, and businesses find out that the disabled can make great employees.

Esther Diaz continues to be a success story. Her managers have discovered she is dependable and attentive to every job she is assigned, even those at which other workers might lose interest. "You never see Esther just standing around," comments her current supervisor, Hope Cantwell. "She's always working hard."

The program has grown by leaps and bounds. Today there are more than 1500 severely disabled workers in 736 Target stores nationwide. Customer response has been fantastic. Letters pour into the national office complimenting the workers and praising the company for giving them a chance.

Minneapolis-based Dayton Hudson, owner of Target, has been a national leader in charitable giving and social action for more than fifty years. George Draper Dayton began this culture of giving in 1909 by donating five hundred thousand dollars from his department store to charity. "Success by contribution is open to everyone," wrote Dayton. "The thrills of relieving distress, of encouraging the young or ministering to the aged, of easing the footsteps of the weary—are these not rewards greater than the knowledge you have added thousands of dollars to your hoard?"

Fortunately, the heirs to Dayton's growing empire inherited their grandfather's generous spirit. In 1946, they created the "5% Rule," under which 5 percent of the corporation's pretax profits are set aside and reinvested in the community. So strong is their commitment to giving, that in 1974, a particularly hard year for the retail industry, Dayton employees voted to keep the 5 percent covenant even if their salaries had to be cut.

Thanks in part to Dayton's leadership, the Twin Cities ranks as one of the most giving corporate communities in the United States. The Greater Minneapolis Chamber of Commerce sponsors the 5% Club for companies like Honeywell, Piper Jaffray Cos, and over 200 other members.

In 1996, Dayton Hudson celebrated their fiftieth anniversary of giving with the "50 Acts of Giving Day" in which more than one hundred stores across the country helped their communities. Employees rolled up their sleeves donating time and energy to various local causes. "We put our people power together," says Chris Park, director of the company's foundation.

When a district team leader, Kim Dicicco, and her southern California colleagues learned that the Special Olympics would be held on the same day as the 50 Acts of Giving Day, she rallied to take them on as a joint cause. Thanks to her recruiting efforts, more than four hundred Target employees from seventy stores volunteered for the weekend events. On opening night, they formed a huge cheering section to welcome the athletes. For the next two days, during the competitions, they shouted encouragement from the sidelines and handed out medals. "We did a lot of screaming, yelling, and high-fiving," remembers Kim.

Ian Eaton, a young man hired through the I Can Do That program, ran with the Olympic torch in front of the store where he works as a cart attendant. "When Ian was coming down the street, we announced it over the loudspeaker. Everyone just poured out the doors," recalls his supervisor, Karla Burgess. Even customers left their shopping carts and ran outside to cheer for Ian.

"That was fun!" Ian told his supervisor. "I saw you waving to me!" The week after the race, Ian's supervisor had to slow him down a few times, because he was still running through the store. Karla smiles and says, "He just forgets he's not still on the track with all of us cheering him on."

Small kindnesses make a community whole and lift up all of its members.

AMB

Create a culture of giving by becoming involved in your own community: meet your neighbors and volunteer for school functions and community events. To become a **Special Olympics** coach, call 800-700-8585.

Waking Up to Coffee

STORYTELLER: LAURA BROWN

Paul Katzeff believes in trying to do the right thing. He'd worked as a social worker in East Harlem for ten years before moving to Aspen Colorado in 1969, with the intent of brewing the best cup of coffee around. He discovered that in order to accomplish his goal, he had to buy an old roaster and roast his own beans. The cafe failed, but, his roaster in tow, he migrated to Mendocino, California, and, with the help of his wife, Joan, started building Thanksgiving Coffee. In those early days, Paul and Joan had very little idea of the effect the American coffee industry was having thousands of miles away.

Coffee farmer Francisco Javier Saenz lived with that reality every day. When Paul invited him to speak at a 1985 industry discussion of the subject of "Coffee, Human Rights, and the Third World Economy," Saenz saw an opportunity to educate the American businessmen and invited all 120 participants to visit his Nicaraguan fields. There, challenges facing his family and community were devastating. Nicaraguan coffee growers were effectively forced to sell to a handful of giant coffee brokers, which resulted in coffee prices so low that it was hardly worth selling the beans.

Paul was the only one who took Saenz up on his offer, and when he arrived in Nicaragua, it didn't take him long to see through Francisco's eyes. As they left the airport, homeless street children in filthy, tattered clothing chased after his car, begging him to purchase cookies or drinks. One look in these children's eyes, and he knew they might go to bed hungry if he didn't.

The next day in the mountains, Francisco introduced him to coffee pickers who were even more destitute. Their homes had dirt floors and cardboard roofs. The only windows were holes pushed out of the walls. In the corner of one hut, an exhausted, barefoot woman was making tortillas. Francisco explained that the women often spent three hours a day pounding out tortillas for their families.

Paul was forced to take an honest look at the coffee industry. For every pound of gourmet coffee sold in the U.S., the growers were getting from thirty-five to fifty cents. A coffee picker's family might earn four hundred dollars to six hundred dollars per year, barely enough to buy the most basics necessities of life. Paul was distraught to find out that his company, Thanksgiving Coffee, was selling a product that was doing very little to help the very people who produced it.

It was especially disturbing because he had been raised to never tolerate a situation like this one. His family, hard-working Russian immigrants in New York City, were deeply involved in labor union organizing, political activism, and war relief for Jews in the Soviet Union. "My family taught me that you can accomplish anything if you try," Paul says in his gruff New York accent. "I never saw them give up."

He decided to give something back to the coffee pickers. After much soul searching, he came up with the Coffee for Peace program. The program was simple and straightforward: fifty cents of each coffee bag's purchase price would go directly back to the villages where the coffee came from. Thanksgiving Coffee's program makes it possible for each family to receive at least enough extra to buy some livestock or plant their first garden. The program also sponsors village banking, lending money for people to start their own small businesses. It created a nursery where small farmers can grow coffee trees to expand their crops. The company also helped the village purchase a tortilla machine. Now, instead of spending three hours a day making tortillas, the women can do it in just ten minutes. Nicaraguan coffee farmers like Francisco are happy to see that Thanksgiving Coffee is living up to its name.

But Paul realized that returning cash to the farmers to help them improve their lives wasn't enough. He had seen the environmental destruction caused by coffee crops and knew that if it continued, coffee pickers would soon be living in a dangerously wounded environment. He learned that in the 1970s, plantations had begun to cultivate a new kind of coffee plant that only grew in direct sun. So they began cutting down the forests; and without the large shade trees, thousands of songbirds and other plants, animals, and insects lost their homes and died. Where 150 to two hundred species of birds used to live in shaded coffee plots, only five to ten species now live in the sun-grown coffee trees. Sadly, these are the same delicate songbirds that migrate north to the U.S. and sing to us so sweetly every spring.

And that wasn't all. Paul saw pesticide runoff from the fields polluting streams and rivers, and the coffee pulp clogging the waterways, consuming all the oxygen in the streams and killing healthy plants and fish. Something had to be done. With the help of experts, he developed a system of standards and incentives that would encourage coffee farming practices that protected the environment while improving the quality of the coffee and earning more for the farmers. Farmers can earn points by growing coffee in the shade, refraining from using harsh chemical pesticides, or implementing solar coffee pulp dryers so the pulp can be used as a natural fertilizer. By caring for their land, they earn extra money while investing in the future.

Today, Thanksgiving coffee is a six million dollar per year business that returns about sixty thousand dollars per year to benefit the health and well being of the coffee producers. Because of its success, other coffee companies are beginning to realize that they, too, can make a difference. Thanks to Paul, Joan, and their close family of employees, hundreds of thousands of farmers are now living a better life and together they are protecting the earth for generations to come.

"We think of coffee as just something to drink," says Paul, "but twenty-six thousand square miles of the Earth are planted with coffee and that affects millions of people's lives. Coffee can represent hope for these people." A little awareness goes a long way. Next time you're drinking your coffee, think about Francisco and that your decisions about what you buy can make a huge difference in the world.

Who gives a man fish feeds him for a day;
who teaches a man to fish feeds him for a life.

You can find **Thanksgiving Coffee** at quality food outlets nationwide, or visit their website at www.thanksgivingcoffee.com and www.songbirdcoffee.com. If you want to help improve living conditions for the children and their families in coffee producing communities, including education, health programs, and microenterprise development, call **Coffee Kids** at 800-334-9099.

The Power of Giving

STORYTELLER: GREGORY S. GROSS, ED.D.

As seven-year-old Van Truong Le looked over the rail of the boat, his homeland was quickly disappearing from view. He, his family, and a hundred others were running from war, seeking peace. When Van arrived in America, he felt like he was in a movie. There were no bombs, there was no war; just lots of big cars.

Before the war, Van's father had been a successful businessman and landowner in Vietnam. But he had lost everything and had to start over as a janitor in America. At the time, Van could not even dream of the life that lay before him or of Arnold Hiatt, the man who would play an important supporting role in his life.

Arnold Hiatt was a businessman who always wanted to do more than just make a profit: he wanted to make a difference. With little formal business training, Hiatt built a prosperous children's footwear company. When the Stride Rite Corporation wanted to acquire his company and have him assume the presidency, he agreed—on his terms.

As president of the Stride Rite Corporation, Hiatt concluded that by serving employees, stockholders, and the community as one, he could build his business on a solid foundation of shared values and principles by, as he says, "doing unto others as we would have them do to us." Under Hiatt's leadership, Stride Rite set a precedent for how business could make a difference in the community. He convinced his directors to first give 1 percent and then 5 percent of the company's pretax earnings to social initiatives in the community. By creating the nation's first on-site corporate day-care program, he helped Stride Rite workers and gave jobs to residents of economically troubled Roxbury. Stride Rite was also the first company to establish an intergenerational center, providing opportunities for seniors and children to be cared for together. A strong advocate for mentoring, he also encouraged Stride Rite employees to work with inner-city youth at the company's expense during work hours.

Stride Rite's sales increased dramatically, and, for several years, the company was in the ninety-ninth percentile of financial performance on the New York Stock Exchange. "People started to wonder if there was a correlation between treating people fairly and doing well," Hiatt remembers. Over the years, he became one of the nation's champions for greater corporate social responsibility. He was a founder of the organization Business for Social Responsibility to help other companies become more responsive to their workers, their community, and the environment.

But Hiatt's favorite program, and the one that changed Van Truong's life, is the least well known. Hiatt was concerned that young people should learn to be responsible citizens. So he invited his alma mater, Harvard, to become partners in providing scholarships so that low-income students could do public service work in the inner city. The Stride Rite scholars have been serving in homeless centers, AIDS wards, juvenile offender programs, and shelters for abused women and children.

Van Truong, whose hard work and tenacity earned him a place at Harvard, was one of the forty students who received a Stride Rite scholarship that year. When he realized that there were housing projects near Harvard, he used his scholarship funds so he could work at one, Jefferson Park. He wanted to help other young people overcome obstacles like those he'd faced. Every summer for four years, Van Truong lived with these youngsters. "These kids live in a tough inner-city environment," he says. "Because of my own childhood experiences, I could relate to them." Over time, Van gave hope to those who had very little and became a living example of what they could become. He tutored them and took them on field trips, giving them a glimpse of a different world. By teaching them to write their intimate feelings in personal journals, he helped them find their "voices." Van was happy to see that, "at nine or ten years old, these kids had great dreams for themselves and for their future."

During the course of his work in the projects, Van was amazed that Hiatt, the head of a multinational corporation, would take the time to meet with him, ask about his summer, and get to know him. Hiatt wanted to see for himself how these scholarship students were making a mark on their community. During one of Hiatt's visits, Van told him about a serious problem that was undermining the program. Harvard was reducing financial aid for students receiving the Stride Rite scholarships and the students were caught in the middle.

Hiatt was troubled by what he heard. He informed Harvard officials that Stride Rite funds would continue *only* if they were never used to displace other student aid. He challenged Harvard to match Stride Rite funds, generating additional funding for work-study grants. He also created a fellowship program for graduating students to continue their public service work. Thanks to his strategic support, public service has become a multiplying force for change at Harvard and in the community. And the lives of the young people he touched have been forever changed.

Van Truong, for one, was profoundly influenced by his mentor and his commitment to public service. "Arnold Hiatt showed us how to be public spirited and not forget our community," he said. "Working closely with him strongly affected my beliefs, my values, and my career goals. He actually altered the course of my life. In the money crazy 1980s, he was a visionary role model for us all."

Van has since decided to dedicate his life to public service. A recent law school graduate, he is now a clerk for a Boston federal court judge. And one of Van's former Jefferson Park students is now pursuing his own dream of going to college. Van is grateful for Hiatt's example of a life lived in pursuit of something more than material wealth. He's learned about pursuing a quieter, richer dream: a life given to serving others. It is a gift he will treasure all his life. Van says, "Arnold Hiatt taught me the power of giving back, one person at a time."

Everyone can be great, because everyone can serve.

DR. MARTIN LUTHER KING JR.

Companies who want to launch or improve community service initiatives can call **Business for Social Responsibility (BSR)** for information, tools, resources, and technical assistance. Ask for Elissa Sheridan at 415-537-0888.

Reaching for the Dream

STORYTELLER: SUZANNE APPLE

The final notes of the closing ceremonies hovered in the humid air over Centennial Olympic Stadium as the final day of the Olympics came to an end. The best athletes in the world—more than eleven thousand of them from 197 countries—were enjoying every second of their final farewell party. At that moment there were no winners or losers, only champions who had reached for their Olympic dreams.

Down the road, in a brand new three-bedroom home, another celebration was just beginning. In the community known simply as Peoplestown, Wrandell Jackson was also reaching; he was reaching toward the dream of owning his own home. Like the athletes at his backdoor, he too had raced against great odds and cleared innumerable hurdles to cross the finish line.

Jackson had worked hard, holding down two jobs to pay the rent and feed his five children. During the day he worked in a kitchen, then he cleaned office buildings at night. Help in financing a new home meant he could quit the night shift and be home for his family when they really needed him. And with his home came a new sense of belonging to a neighborhood where everyone was beginning all over again.

The wood-framed house at 899 Washington Street is a tiny piece of an extraordinary legacy that grew out of the 1996 Centennial Olympic Games. Over the course of six years, local businesses rose to the challenge and transformed a blighted swath of downtown Atlanta into a twenty-four-acre urban park. The rights to televise the games helped fund construction of a state-of-the-art stadium, and Habitat for Humanity deployed an army of volunteers into impoverished inner-city neighborhoods to build one hundred homes for those who had none.

It was an unparalleled undertaking by Habitat, and the worldwide nonprofit organization gave itself eighteen months to accomplish the task. When it came time to select partners, The Home Depot was invited to construct one of the original houses and to build the one hundredth home, which was for thirty-year-old Wrandell Jackson and his family.

The Home Depot was selected because of its total commitment to help build affordable housing. In less than twenty years, the company has opened more than five hundred do-it-yourself stores in the United States and Canada, and its volunteer force, made up of one-hundred-thousand associates, helps communities in many ways. They partner with local nonprofit organizations, such as Habitat for Humanity and Christmas in April, to build and repair homes for low-income families, the elderly, and the disabled.

No one keeps track, but it seems as though everyone at The Home Depot volunteers—sales associates, managers, and officers alike. When company president and cofounder Arthur Blank put out the call for volunteers to build the one hundredth home in the company's hometown, forty-five officers from across North America and thirty-five of their spouses signed up to help. Together, they worked side by side with Wrandell in the sweltering heat to "blitz build" his home in six days. Chief Financial Officer Marshall Day hammered nails, hung trusses, and installed windows.

"It was a phenomenal experience," says Marshall. "We'd pick up our tools just after sunrise and finish around dinner time. It seemed every day was hotter than the last. But as a team we kept on going, hammering, measuring, and making things fit." On Monday morning 899 Washington Street was just a concrete foundation. By Saturday afternoon it was a home. When they handed Wrandell his keys, there wasn't a dry eye in the place. The paint was still fresh on the peach-colored house when

Marshall signed up to build another Habitat home.

In Peoplestown, with the Olympic stadium in full view, the Jackson household realized their dream with a lot of reaching and a little help from their friends. As a family, they're now fixing screen doors and learning how to care for daisies and pansies.

"Before we moved in, we would drive by here all the time," says Wrandell. "The kids were always asking, 'When are we moving in, daddy, when are we moving in?' And now we're here, living in our own home. It's a dream come true."

Help a low-income family build a home and realize their dream, call your local **Habitat for Humanity** affiliate, visit their web site at www.habitat.org, or call 800-422-4828.

Focus: HOPE

STORYTELLER: JIM YOUNG

Maia Cherry, a twenty-five-year-old African-American student, is a ray of hope in Detroit. But when she first came into this world, there wasn't much hope there. Five years earlier, race riots had nearly torn the city apart.

Born to a single mom, Maia is the youngest of five children. A bright student, she loved sports and got good grades in school—most of the time. But when she didn't get the attention she needed from her busy mom, she had lots of problems. "I didn't have any motivation, so I wasn't consistent," she says. "I wasn't happy. Sometimes, I was even suicidal." Then Maia found a way through the darkness. "I knew there had to be more to life," she says. "So I started reading the Bible, going to church, and letting God direct my steps." She's glad her steps led her to Focus: HOPE.

Focus: HOPE was born on the road from Selma to Montgomery, Alabama. In 1964 Father Bill Cunningham had traveled south in response to Dr. Martin Luther King's call for help in building racial harmony. For Father Cunningham, being on that historic march left an indelible mark. Three years later, in the summer of 1967, when he saw his own hometown being destroyed, he knew in his heart that he had to find a way to build racial harmony in Detroit. One of his parishioners, Eleanor Josaitis, a housewife raising five children, was touched by his passionate commitment to overcome racism, poverty, and injustice. In 1968, Father Cunningham quit his teaching job and Eleanor left her comfortable life in the suburbs, moving her family into Detroit's volatile inner city. They started simply, by feeding people in a church basement. "We felt we had a moral responsibility to feed the children and the elderly," Father Cunningham said. Since then they've made inroads into combating racism by giving young people the skills they need to get good jobs and create a better life for themselves.

After thirty years of hard work, Focus: HOPE has grown into a charitable empire including a state-of-the-art technology center with a six-year engineering degree program and four manufacturing companies, as well as a food distribution center, a preschool, and a day care center. It has transformed the landscape of Detroit and become an engine for the city's economic renewal.

Everyone Father Cunningham met was greeted with an invitation, "Come join us," and thousands of volunteers did. One of these was Hulas King. He came for a visit and stayed for a year. As the director of industry partnership programs for EDS Unigraphics Division, Hulas was a "loaned executive" to Focus: HOPE. The loaned-executive program is just one of the ways that EDS reaches out to help communities. EDS Chairman Les Alberthal came from a small town where everyone knew everyone and helping your neighbors was, as he says, "as natural as pulling on one's cowboy boots." Alberthal encourages this sense of neighborliness among his ninety-five thousand employees who volunteer all over the world, living out the philosophy that healthy communities and healthy business go hand in hand.

"EDS is known as a systems integrator. We're also helping to integrate urban minority youth into mainstream society through technical training," says Hulas. "Our corporate partnership with Focus: HOPE helps us achieve this goal." At Focus: HOPE, students use the most advanced equipment, receive real-work experience, and learn from the best teachers. Retired engineers from Detroit supervise them, helping them to become well-rounded manufacturing engineers and the best machinists in the world. "Since the technology center's founding in 1981, more than five thousand young people have completed these programs, moving out of poverty and forward in their lives. For kids once on welfare and walking the streets, that's an incredible future," says Hulas.

During Hulas' year at Focus: HOPE, he spent lots of time with the students. When Maia first saw him, she was surprised. "We deal with thousands of important people at Focus: HOPE, even presidents of companies. But they are usually white. Hulas is one of the top people, and he's black. I was impressed!" she says.

Early on, Hulas reached out to Maia. They developed a special mentor relationship. "He would ask me how was I doing, how my grades were, and he would give me some advice. He told me 'Stay focused and do your job, be on time, and be responsible. Be a 110 percent kind of person,'" she says. "He told me as a young black woman, I may face racism and sexism, but I should still be a lady and never lower my standards." Hulas also helped Maia gain a realistic perspective about life. "Don't look for somebody to shake your hand after you do something," he'd say. "Your rewards will come. Just do your best, keep on moving, and enjoy your life." What Maia appreciated most was knowing Hulas was there for her. "If you need anything, anything at all, let me know," he told her. Hulas certainly knows the importance of helping the next guy—or gal. "I grew up in East St. Louis, one of the most deprived cities in America. We all shared the same poverty, so we stuck together. When a kid got out of line, the whole community stepped in to discipline him," Hulas says. "To be able to help students and then have the pleasure of watching them assume positions of responsibility is really wonderful," he adds. "When you nurture them to be on their own, they can then reach back and help someone else." This continuity is part of what makes the mentoring such rewarding work.

Maia has big plans for how she wants to give back to other young people in Detroit. Having finished her undergraduate studies, she hopes to one day get her doctorate. After that, she plans to build her own business and work in the corporate world for a while. Eventually, she plans to teach the three As: Academics, Attendance, and Attitude. "I want high school students to learn that engineering isn't as hard as people make it seem," she says. Maia readily admits that she isn't a math whiz. "It just takes practice," she says.

"There are so many smart young people, and they don't even know their potential. A lot of kids stop themselves by thinking 'I couldn't do it.' I want them to know, if you have the desire, you can do it!"

Carrying on Father Cunningham's tradition of inviting others to join in, Maia encourages others to come to Focus: HOPE. "If we all give back, we can make Detroit really great," she says. From Dr. King to Father Cunningham, from Hulas to Maia: people are reaching out to each other and making dreams come true.

Over the years, Father Cunningham and Eleanor Josaitis faced many challenges at Focus: HOPE. When things were difficult, they shared a special ritual that gave them the courage to carry on. They would, quietly, without anyone noticing, hand each other a penny. The simple inscription "In God We Trust" helped them remember that they were never alone.

Continuing her leadership at Focus: HOPE, Eleanor recently told a special story at Father Cunningham's funeral. She asked the gathered mourners to think of him when they saw a penny, so his spirit would live on forever. The next week, several Army trucks delivered more than one million pennies to Focus: HOPE. One for each of the millions of lives he had touched.

★

Make a career of humanity . . . and you will make a finer world to live in.

DR. MARTIN LUTHER KING JR.

Reach out and help someone to find the road to success. Companies who want to build partnerships that give young people the gift of technology and bring hope to their communities should call Lloyd Reuss at **Focus: HOPE** at 313-494-4430.

We Can Do It

Storyteller: Anne Colby

What makes Cabell Brand different from the average ambitious businessman who builds a small family company into a multimillion dollar corporation? For the best answer, you need to come visit the Roanoke Valley in Virginia. But, if you can't make it any time soon, here is the next best response.

Cabell believes in the American system of entrepreneurship, but while most of his colleagues are interested in how well the system works for them, Cabell wants to make it work for everyone. While building his shoe business, he spent over a quarter of his time in community activities. Since he sold it in 1986, he's spent nearly all his time helping others, some say, as a kind of "community entrepreneur."

It all started for Cabell in 1965. "I'll never forget watching the *Today Show* interview with Sargent Shriver, who had just been appointed director of the War on Poverty. 'What the hell is this . . . this War on Poverty?' I thought. I'd seen poor people in slums but had never really thought of it as a serious problem. When I read about President Johnson's Economic Opportunity Act, I thought, 'I didn't realize all this was going on.'" Cabell learned that, "the federal government was going to make money available, but that local people had to get organized to benefit. If you didn't get organized, the money went somewhere else." He began to think about the poor people he'd seen in the poverty-stricken Roanoke Valley.

Scheduled to make a major presentation to Roanoke Valley's prestigious Torch Club, he dropped his prepared speech and spoke instead about the new poverty program. Then he took three months off from his business to apply for the federal funds, realizing the program could bring desperately needed resources to Roanoke Valley. His time paid off: the funds that would lay the foundation for a revitalized community were granted.

But Cabell didn't stop there: he's been organizing resources ever since. For over thirty years, he was the volunteer president and chairman of the board for a local group called Total Action Against Poverty (TAP). They are as committed to building a profitable community as any corporate board is to building a profitable company. For Cabell, TAP, and the people of Roanoke Valley, that means starting from the ground up.

According to TAP, success means a community with good early childhood education, high literacy, low unemployment, and accessible health care. It means programs that offer new beginnings for drop outs, ex-convicts, and drug users. It also means home weatherization and food banks for the tough times, and community centers for the good times. It's ultimately about preparing for the future and dealing with people's real problems, not just the symptoms of poverty.

Perhaps TAP's most dramatic undertaking was bringing water to the thousands of rural valley homes that had none. As Cabell describes the situation, getting water to these areas was just the beginning of the magic. "Once there was water in the area, all kinds of good things began to happen. Roads were built, developers came in, and there were new job opportunities. When people went to work, their families were no longer isolated, and they kept their kids in school." When Charles Kuralt showcased them on his *Good Morning* show, viewers saw a thriving community.

The battle is far from over. "Can you believe it?" Cabell asks. "We've still got over 79,000 families with no water, no wells, nothing!" If anyone can find a solution, though, he's the one. "He's a walking brainstorm," says TAP executive director, Ted Edlich. "He never stops thinking. He never stops generating ideas. He's got more energy than any human being I know." That's saying quite a lot, when you consider that Cabell is nearly seventy-six years old. From time to time, he does get a little tired and discouraged. Fortunately, he has a great support system in his wife, Shirley. "She has always been there for me. She challenges me to keep going and sustains me in the difficult times."

Cleo Sims, Roanoke Valley's Head Start director, is one who has benefited from that support. Cabell Brand has been her mentor for thirty-one years. "Running Head Start is a tough, demanding job, and I've weathered lots of storms, especially the ups and downs of funding," she says. "This man has never wavered. He has always been there. He works very quietly, behind the scenes. But he's a giant in this community. He lives by the motto: 'We can do it.'

"Now that people are starting to realize we need our communities to help local people," Cleo explains, "we really need more business people like Cabell—people who ask us, 'What can I do?' and 'What needs to be done?'

"Even though he's retired now," Cleo says wistfully, "he never forgets us. To see how much he's given to help people I've known, touches me. It's people like Cabell who inspire me and give me the strength to keep going."

Cabell likes to quote the popular slogan "Think globally, and act locally" to describe his approach of applying local solutions to social problems. "I have always been conscious of what I'm going to leave as a legacy," he says. "It's the everyday lessons, the building blocks of progress, and the community process." From his perspective, "The bigger the problem is, the bigger the challenge is, and the more important it is to get started.

"The problem is that not enough people are helping," he says. As he sees it, "If our communities are to become and stay profitable, more people have to get involved." He admits that tackling the large issues in community development can be intimidating to many people. But there is a system that can help overcome any obstacle," he points out. And if you could see the changes put in motion by this one man's efforts, you'd understand where his optimism comes from.

This country will not be a good place for any of us to live in
unless we make it a good place for all of us to live in.

THEODORE ROOSEVELT

Work with one of the 1000 Community Action Agencies nearest you to build partnerships that last. Call the **National Association of Community Action Agencies** at 202-265-7546. To reach the **Roanoke Valley Community Action Agency,** call Cabell Brand at 540-387-3402 or Cleo Sims and Ted Edlich at 540-345-6781.

Serve First

STORYTELLER: LARRY C. SPEARS

Many years ago there lived a gentle man named Leo. He was an unassuming man who joined a group of spiritual travelers as their servant. He fixed the meals, carried the heaviest of their belongings, and did many other chores for the group. Leo was also a musician, keeping the traveler's spirits high with his joyful songs. All went well with the journey, until one day Leo disappeared.

At first, the group of travelers thought they could continue on their way, without him. However, they soon discovered, the good spirit they shared had disappeared overnight. People who had been the best of friends began to argue over little things. Before they knew it, no one could agree on much of anything. The group fell apart and abandoned their journey.

Many years later, one of the travelers happened across Leo and was overjoyed to see him. Leo took the seeker to the headquarters of the spiritual organization which had originally sponsored the journey. Once inside, the seeker was surprised to discover that Leo, whom he had known as his servant, was in fact the head of this organization: its guiding light. Leo was a great and noble leader.

—*Journey to the East* by Herman Hesse

This story, first told by the German writer in 1956, was read some years later by an American Quaker businessman, Robert Greenleaf. Greenleaf, a former AT&T executive, had been on a similar journey, searching for a new kind of leader. He found him in Hesse's story. He was impressed that Leo put the needs of others first, the group went further, did more, and had fun. By sacrificing his own needs to take care of others, they were freed up to focus on the bigger picture and achieve a shared goal. Without his help, they lost sight of what really mattered. And, in the end, they failed.

Greenleaf tried to imagine a world where the people we value most highly are those who best serve others: the teacher who inspires a student, the nurse who cares for a patient, and the boss who takes a few minutes to ask about an employee's sick child. Greenleaf's quest sparked the simple, yet profound idea for servant-leadership. He thoughtfully created a series of questions that guided his life decisions as a servant-leader: Do those I serve grow as people? Do they become healthier, wiser, more autonomous, and more likely to become servants themselves? How am I benefiting the least privileged in the group? Then he wrote a small book, *The Servant as Leader,* introducing the concept. Over time, Greenleaf's humble questions influenced hundreds of thousands of people and revolutionized companies and organizations around the globe. TDIndustries, a construction and service company in Dallas, Texas, is just one.

Their chief executive officer, Jack Lowe Jr., enthusiastically shares his story in a lighthearted, southern drawl. "My dad, Jack Sr., was a servant-leader before it was even called that. In 1946, he built this company to be owned by its employees. He thought that was only fair. In the 1970s, he stumbled across Bob Greenleaf's book on servant-leadership and felt a special kinship with its author. Dad started giving away copies of the book, hundreds of them, to employees in discussion groups and to leaders at community meetings." One day, Bob called him, Lowe recalls with a laugh, "He was wondering why a construction company was his biggest customer. 'What are you doing down there in Dallas?' he wanted to know.

"For the past twenty-five years, we've been using Greenleaf's work as the foundation for our training programs," Jack Jr. explains. Before then, many of our supervisors struggled as leaders. They were highly skilled in their trades, but unprepared as managers or foremen," he continued. "The construction business is tough, and so are the men who work in it. Some of the guys thought being a supervisor entitled you to be a bully or that getting promoted went hand in hand with getting respect. They didn't understand: you've got to earn respect.

"By learning to serve first, TDPartners, as TDI employees are called, have done just that. The result: everyone wins. The partners feel valued, they support their supervisors, and, together, they build a stronger team and a healthy company. Today ninety-three percent of our partners say their supervisor is fair in dealing with them, compared to only sixty percent nationally.

"Servant-leadership has helped us build a great company," Jack explains. "If you're going to succeed in today's business world, you've got to have a lot of trust between employers, employees, suppliers, and customers. Servant-leadership has helped us build a trusting culture and has allowed us to create change, embrace diversity, enhance quality, and integrate technology. It's also gotten us through some horrible situations."

In the late 1980s, the construction market collapsed and every major bank in Texas failed, including TDIndustries' bank. "When our bank went under, we owed the Feds sixteen million dollars. We didn't have it," Jack remembers. "We did everything we could to stay afloat. We even asked our partners to consider investing their own retirement funds back into the company. It was a lot to ask, since they would be risking everything to help us try and turn the company around. We were amazed, and deeply moved, when nearly every associate said, 'Yes!' Our partners took over 1.25 million dollars out of their retirements and invested it back into the company. In less than a year, with everyone's help, we made it," says Lowe.

The TDPartners were making a statement. TDI's service supervisor, Jerry Lynn says, "What surprised me was how much people gave back to the company. The seeds for their generosity were planted by a company who built trust with its people. Today, business is fabulous! TDIndustries just celebrated its fiftieth anniversary and we were honored as one of the one hundred best companies to work for in America." A high level of trust, built on servant-leadership, has supported the company through both the good and the bad times. But Lowe isn't resting on his laurels. He's always looking for ways to make his employees happier and his business better. "Our best years are yet to come," he promises, "and it's going to really be fun."

Each human has his lifetime to invest—to realize the potentials of her various freedoms and choices, to be employed to the advantage of all human beings, in order that we may fulfill our mission on this planet.

—R. BUCKMINSTER FULLER

If you want to learn more about serving-and-leading others, call **The Greenleaf Center for Servant-Leadership** at 317-259-1241 for a free information packet, or visit the website at www.greenleaf.com.

A Lesson in Giving

STORYTELLER: LAURA GATES

I'll never forget the night my husband walked out on me. I felt like someone had punched me in the stomach. Even though we had separated on and off over the past year, I had assumed that eventually we would be able to work things out, that we would reconcile our differences. As I sat there sobbing on that cold December night; I thought my heart would break. I felt completely alone in the world. I had few close friends of my own and I was far away from my family. Even though I had started a successful marketing business, I wasn't happy with my work. My whole world had revolved around my husband. Now that he was gone, I felt completely powerless, like I had nothing left to hold onto, nothing left to live for.

What scared me most was the rage I felt inside. I was afraid that if I let it out, I might never stop. I thought, "Thank God I don't have a gun in the house." Realizing that I actually wanted to hurt another person, especially someone I claimed to love, was terrifying. Somehow things had gone very wrong in my life.

I wondered how I had gotten so lost. As a young girl, I had always felt that I had important work to do in this world. But here I was crying all the time, afraid to even leave the house. Sometimes, I didn't have the energy to get out of bed in the morning.

One day I forced myself to go to lunch with a friend. When she asked me how I was, I started to cry, telling her what was happening in my life. She told me about this woman, Claire, and how she had helped her cope with the pain of divorce while teaching her some valuable lessons about relationships. Claire Nuer, a Frenchwoman in her sixties, was a Holocaust and cancer survivor who had lived through and learned from the pain in her life. She had also worked with thousands of people like me, teaching them how to use their difficulties as levers to change their lives. I knew I had to study with this woman.

Shortly after, I attended a seminar where Claire asked a few seemingly simple questions, "What do you want in your life? . . . in your relationships? . . . in your family? . . . in your work? and . . . in the world?" Then the questions became more challenging, "What changes could you make in your life today that would create a more humane world fifty years from now?"

Like most people, I wanted to be loved, recognized, respected, and appreciated by others. I wanted good personal relationships, and I wanted to be creative, to do work I loved, to travel, and to make a good living. I also wanted my life to have meaning. This seemed simple enough, but in asking myself the questions Claire posed, I realized my life had become just the opposite. I had tried desperately to get the love of one man, and, in the process, I had narrowed my world and let go of everything else important to me. And now he was gone.

With Claire's guidance, I realized that I often struggled between two extremes: either trying to get something from others for my own gain or else running away from others, afraid they wanted to get something from me. As a result my relationships were often superficial. It was depressing to see how this had happened in my business as well as my personal life. As a marketing consultant, I was helping companies inflate their images by glossing over their problems. Increasingly, this way of working left me feeling empty. What had happened to the young woman who wanted to build a better world?

One day Claire said something that touched me very deeply. She looked at me with clarity and determination in her eyes and said, "One person can be the rock that changes the course of a river." This simple idea had helped Claire overcome impossible odds surrounding her health, her family, and her life. This tiny woman, once a child hidden from the Nazis and not able to complete school, was now counseling some of the world's leaders in academia, government, and business. She had become well-known and respected around the world for her workshops that taught people how to open doors to better, happier, and healthier lives.

Claire's commitment to building a better world had inspired her to take on impossible tasks time and again. In 1995, she gathered over three hundred people at Auschwitz so they could learn how to transform the wars in their daily lives. In just a few days, managers of companies and their employees, parents and their children, Jews and Palestinians, and Serbs and Croats learned a new way of being together so they could create peace in the world. If Claire had the courage to live her dreams, I decided, so could I.

I wanted to be that rock in the river, too, so I decided to start with my own life. My biggest challenge was to learn how to be compassionate and giving, instead of playing the "getting game." My commitment was tested many times—once from a business client. The president of a manufacturing company that employed one hundred people had hired me to improve their image, tarnished after bankruptcy several years earlier. Since then, the company had more than doubled in size and revenues, but their work environment had deteriorated. The fear, in-fighting, and competition among employees was palpable. While I wanted to say something about this tense atmosphere, I just did my job and kept my opinions to myself.

Then I remembered my goal of being the rock. A little voice inside reminded me to ignore my fear and share my observations with the company president, even if it meant losing him as a client. I gathered all my courage and went into his office. Before I could even say a word, he started telling me about his concerns. "Something's lacking in this company since we've grown," he said. "When we first came out of bankruptcy, we had a sense of teamwork, even intimacy among our employees. Somehow, we've lost that—and I want it back."

I was surprised by his openness and his willingness to be so honest with me. I realized how much I actually cared about this man and his company and how much I wanted them to succeed. I decided to take the risk and share with him what I'd been learning from Claire about giving and getting. I took a deep breath and asked him, "Do you think that maybe you've become too focused on *getting* results?" I paused for a moment and thought about my experience with his employees. "Your employees seem to be competing against each other instead of working together as a team. If you want people to give of themselves to the company, you need to give them something: they need a larger goal, something they can hold onto, one that gives them hope that they can make a difference in this company."

"What you're saying is important," he said, listening intently. Over the next few weeks we talked about possible improvements he could make in the company. Then one day he called me into his office again and said, "I've been thinking about what you said. Today, I'm holding a company-wide meeting so people can tell me about their fears and concerns.

"I've also decided to take three employees to lunch each week, so I can hear people's feedback individually. I also want to create a company mission that will help motivate people and move us in the right direction." He paused and said to me, "You know, Laura, I really listened to you because you seem committed to the people here. That goes beyond what we pay you. It's like you're part of the family."

It's been rewarding to see his company grow and expand in a way that included and nurtured his employees. And I learned that by giving more of myself and staying focused on my goal of creating good relationships, I could put aside my own fears and actually make a difference. I thought back to the night my husband left, about how angry and desperate I had been, even ready to commit violence. I realized that if someone as peace-loving as I was able to feel rage, it was hardly surprising that the world was in such a sorry state.

But that same furious energy, when understood and then turned around, was capable of becoming the rock that changed the course of the river. The impact I was able to have with one company—simply by being compassionate and giving rather than getting—was hopeful. Just imagine what could happen if I lived this way every day with all my relationships! And if each one of us made this kind of a commitment, collectively we really could build a better world and create world peace, if not in our lifetime, then perhaps for our children.

If you want to bring your deepest aspirations into action in your workplace, family and the world, contact **ACC International Institute** for upcoming leadership training programs at 415-789-8802; P. O. Box 335, Larkspur, CA 94976-0335.

A Mensch

STORYTELLER: JEANNE WALLACE

The telephone had been ringing for hours in mill owner Aaron Feurerstein's kitchen when he and his wife, Louise, opened their front door. Feurerstein answered the phone. He had been quietly celebrating his seventieth birthday at a small surprise party thrown by his family. During the celebration, one of his top managers had gotten word of a small fire at the mill. A few others were told, but nobody passed the word to Feurerstein. Nobody wanted to ruin his party. "The mill's burning, Aaron. The whole mill's on fire," said the manager. Feurerstein hung up, pale and shaking. "I've got to get up there," he told Louise. "I've got to do something."

News of the fire raced through the mill workforce the morning of December 12, 1995 as fast as the flames had destroyed the mill the night before. Many stood outside in the bitter cold, drawn to the devastation as though the mill were a dying family member.

Joseph Melo, a thirty-three-year-old machine operator, had worked in the mill since high school. His father, Manuel, had spent his life in the mill and his stepfather, sister, and cousin had also worked there. As he stood outside that morning, looking at the damage, Joseph wanted to believe the mill would be saved and everyone would go back to work.

Feurerstein, realizing the city of Lawrence could become a ghost town with more than three thousand people without work, vowed to rebuild the plant in the city—the twenty-sixth poorest in the nation. In the days and months ahead, this third-generation mill owner, driven by pride, religious conviction, and a sense of family, did something nobody in modern times had attempted: he rebuilt a giant textile plant in an old New England mill city. To concede defeat would be against everything he and his family had stood for in over ninety years of mill ownership. In the process, Feurerstein and his mill became a national media story. But behind the sentimental headlines, the battle for the heart and soul of a new Malden Mills was a tough fight with wide-ranging implications for workers and American industry.

Founded in 1906 by Feurerstein's grandfather Henry, Malden Mills had stayed put in the 1950s when nearly every other textile mill in New England had shut down or moved away. It had nearly gone out of business in the early 1980s when one of its mainstay products, fake fur, went out of fashion, forcing the business into bankruptcy protection. Aaron Feurerstein battled back, restructuring the mill around two revolutionary new products: Polartec and Polarfleece. These unique wool-like synthetics, developed by his workers out of recycled plastic, quickly grew in demand for their lightness and warmth. It was Polartec that put Malden Mills in the forefront of textile technology, generating two hundred million dollars in sales in 1995, about half the company's total.

Rebuilding the mill when he could have settled for the insurance money is indeed noble. But, what was even more amazing was his commitment to his employees while the mill was being rebuilt. Three days after the fire, Feurerstein made a major announcement at a local high school gym that would stun his company and capture the attention of the media nationwide. He told his people that he would pay all thirty-two hundred employees for thirty days, including health benefits—at a cost of fifteen million dollars. Later he would extend this generosity for another two months. "When he did it the first time, I was surprised," said Bill Cotter, a nineteen-year veteran of the mill. "The second time was a shock. The third . . . well, it was unrealistic to think he would do it again." But, Bill's wife Nancy notes, "It was the third time that brought tears to everyone's eyes." Not only did it bring tears, it brought intense loyalty to the hearts of mill employees.

To rebuild quickly, Feurerstein insisted, "We need to keep our people together." Malden Mill's people reflect the city from which many come. Rich in textile and labor union history, Lawrence had become a city of vacant mill buildings and poor workers with too few jobs and too little hope. The exception was Feurerstein's mill. It had made dreams in this city as well as textiles, providing a way for countless blue-collar workers to become part of America's middle class. Many had limited English language skills or trade skills outside textile-making. Eight hundred sixty-three of the workers were minorities and many were first-generation immigrants who came from twenty-one different countries. Like Joe Melo, they found in Malden Mills a way to earn a good living and begin raising a family. In a city of low wages and few opportunities, with the average $12.50 an hour pay (the highest in the industry) plus overtime and benefits, was a godsend to these people. Failure to rebuild the mill would be like an economic death sentence.

"It's the right thing to do," is how Feurerstein assured his managers and how he answered the question, Why?, that followed him wherever he went. "There is a need to know that corporate America is interested in the welfare of the worker as well as the shareholder," he says, adding, "I consider our workers an asset, not an expense. If you close a factory because you can get work done for two dollars an hour elsewhere, you break the American Dream," he says. "It would have been unconscionable to put three thousand people on the streets and deliver a death blow to the cities of Lawrence and Methuen."

Feurerstein's employees repaid his loyalty with their own. "If he had the guts to rebuild," said one, "we decided we would do whatever we could." By the end of February, the entire mill complex, with its sense of utter destruction just two months earlier, had come alive with energy and a sense of mission. And people across the country rallied to help. Hundreds of state, federal, and local licenses and zoning changes were obtained at breakneck speed.

In order to keep the business open, employees had to meet production demands with only a fraction of the prefire staff and equipment. "Our people became very creative," said Feurerstein. Incredibly, Polartec began running off a fire-damaged machine just three days after the fire. It was only a test, but it had symbolic importance. "We're back in business," a manager said. Before the fire, one plant had produced 130,00 yards a week. A few weeks after the fire, it was up to 230,000 yards in a temporary facility seven days a week. Not only were the employees creative, they were committed. "They were willing to work twenty-five hours a day," said Feurerstein. He sees this as "a direct result of the goodwill and determination of our people to show their gratitude to Malden Mills."

Nearly five months after the fire, Feurerstein had to convince the furniture retailers in South Carolina—who account for 50 percent of the mill's business—that he could deliver. He traveled there, knowing that his commitment to his 3100 workers to rebuild his mill and bring everyone back to work were hanging in the balance.

In High Point, South Carolina, and elsewhere in the state, Feurerstein has become famous for his generosity. His picture adorns the front of many showrooms in this furniture-crazy town. Feurerstein has a big reputation and a lot friends here. He needed both. When he met with his customers, he asked, "Would you stick with us now?" "Absolutely," said one company president, greeting Feurerstein like an honored relative. "Anything we need to do to make it work, we'll do." Another had heard all about it and was impressed, "Anything we can do to be part of it, we will." Still another tells Aaron that his company is using the now-famous Malden Mills name in its marketing. "They are like 'Made in America' tags; people feel good about it because of Aaron."

As of December 1997, all of Malden Mills' employees, along with 200 new people are back on the job. Feurerstein has promised to rehire the remaining employees when the mill is back up to full capacity. In the meantime, he has supported those he was unable to take back with retraining, extended benefits, and job-search assistance. Bill Cotter has known his boss, Aaron, for a long time. As a factory worker and sometime union official, Cotter has dealt with the chief executive officer across a bargaining table and chatted with him on the shop floor. But Bill never really knew Aaron until the fire. "Aaron gave us a chance," he says.

Aaron and his mill will go down in American history as one of the most courageous tales of corporate commitment our country has ever seen. And Aaron started a kind of fire of his own, sparking a renewed collective faith in the American people. Thousands of letters have poured in from well-wishers across the country. Dozens of local and national organizations have rushed to recognize him. Twelve universities have awarded him honorary doctorate degrees, and he was the personal guest of President Clinton for his 1996 State of the Union Address.

In Yiddish there is a special word for a very decent human being: a *mensch*. But Aaron downplays his own role in his company's recovery. It is the workers, he says, who are responsible for that. "They wanted a miracle to happen and it did. That's all I can tell you: It did."

To support the **Malden Mills Employee Relief Fund**, call Ken Gallant at 508-682-5296 or write to him at P. O. Box 527, Lawrence, MA 01841.

A Little Company Makes a Big Difference

STORYTELLER: KEVIN BERGER

Laura Scher could barely contain her excitement. The thirty-seven-year-old chief executive officer of Working Assets was presenting a fifty-five-thousand-dollar check to Planned Parenthood President Pamela Maraldo at their headquarters in New York. Standing next to her was one of her heroes, women's rights leader Gloria Steinem.

The check was one of thirty-six donations, totaling one million dollars, that the company made to nonprofit organizations in 1993. But to Laura it represented much more. Eight years earlier, as the one and only employee of Working Assets, she had dreamed of the day when her little company could make a big contribution to a cause she believed in with her heart and soul. As Laura handed over the check, her nervous excitement gave way to a beaming smile. Her dream had come true. "I was so proud," says Laura. "Our donation helped Planned Parenthood keep up its great work for women's health and freedom." She adds, "We also showed the world that you really can create a successful business *and* be committed to social change."

Laura has turned Working Assets from a vision into a $100 million company. Founded in 1985, the telephone long distance and credit card company was designed to give customers the opportunity to contribute to social change. Today, ten cents of every Working Assets credit card purchase and 1 percent of all long distance bills is donated to nonprofit groups.

Remembering the excitement of starting Working Assets, Laura says, "It is such a perfect product: just by people talking on the phone or buying a book, we can build a community of kindred spirits with enormous impact." Over time, Working Assets has indeed built such a community. In ten years it has raised over ten million dollars for nonprofit groups. In 1995 alone it donated two million dollars. Practicing what Laura calls "democracy in action," their customers nominate the organizations they want to receive the donations and then vote on how much money each one receives.

"Working Assets has created a wonderful vehicle for supporting social change," remarks Pamela Maraldo. "Their contribution to our organization helped us increase access to reproductive health care for women, troubled teens, the sexually abused, and the underserved. We were particularly grateful to be the highest vote getter on a long list of very effective and worthwhile grantees. To us, it's a vote of confidence from the American people."

Working Assets customers can also increase support to nonprofit groups by rounding up their monthly phone bills to the highest dollar. In March 1993, they sent the extra money—more than fifty thousand dollars—to the humanitarian group MADRE, which aids rape victims and refugees in Bosnia. Laura says that she was impressed that "a simple message on a bill like, 'Round up your check,' can change the lives of people who live half a world away."

Working Assets also helps its customers stay informed. Each month's phone bill highlights two crucial issues under debate, explaining what's at stake and who to contact to make a difference. If you have something to say on either topic all you have to do is pick up the phone and speak your mind—and Working Assets will pick up the tab. Or, if you prefer, the company will send a "CitizenLetter" on your behalf. By flooding Congress and corporate boardrooms with their calls and letters, customers brought attention to sweat shop conditions, wasteful government spending, and America's vanishing wilderness.

Laura always wanted to work for a company that treated its employees well and was conscientious about the environment and developing countries. But her ambitions cast her as a lone wolf among her classmates at Harvard Business School. After all, Laura had graduated in the top 5 percent of her M.B.A. class at the height of the greed-is-good '80s. Even before she graduated, she was wined and dined by recruiters from Fortune 100 corporations who promised salaries of over one hundred thousand dollars a year, right out of school.

"But I didn't want to sell laundry detergent," she says. "And I didn't want to work on Wall Street. I wanted something valuable to come out of my work. We don't need one more company to figure out how to invent one more cereal. We need to figure out how to solve some of the world problems."

So instead of, as Laura says, "sitting in an office on Wall Street with a view of the Hudson River," she and her husband furnished a dusty one-room office with an old desk and a filing cabinet. "We didn't have enough money to pay the landlord to renovate the space," she says, "so we had to live with orange shag carpet and bright orange bookcases. But I did talk them into at least cleaning the curtains."

As its chief executive officer, Laura's challenge has been to demonstrate to vendors that Working Assets is legitimate. The banks that issue its credit cards and the major phone companies that lease its fiber-optic cables are tough business folks. "People in the business world have a hard time believing that consumers will make buying decisions based on their social convictions," she says. "But time after time we've convinced them that people will use a credit card and choose a phone company based on their beliefs." Indeed, Working Assets' annual revenues recently topped $100 million. As Laura guides the company into its next decade, she wants the company to reach an annual donation budget of ten million dollars.

Laura is proud of the success she has achieved and credits her parents with teaching her that responsibility means taking your social values into the workplace. Her father, who ran a water-based chemical company, and her mother, an economics professor, taught her to have concern for others and the world around her, instead of being self-absorbed.

Laura wants to pass on to her daughter the same values she learned from her parents. "I want her to know that she can do anything she wants with her life," she says. "And I want her to understand that everyone doesn't have the basic comforts of life, so it's up to the rest of us to create a more just and equitable world."

It is by spending oneself that one becomes rich.

SARAH BERNHARDT

To join **Working Assets**, the phone company that connects people to a better world, call 800-788-8588.

Table for Six Billion, Please

STORYTELLER: SUSAN DUNDON

Judy Wicks was five years old when she ran a string of extension cords down the driveway, hooked up her record player, turned it up full volume, and sat in a little chair waiting to see who might come along. That was the opening of her first "restaurant," and her first customer was a neighbor, Johnny Baker."

Five years later, on a sunny spring morning in 1957, the feisty ten-year-old girl with a passion for baseball was just itching to play on the first day of the season. "Class," her gym teacher announced, "it looks like a great day out there. Time to play ball! Guys down to the field; girls go over there and practice cheerleading." Judy was dumbfounded. She stood dejectedly behind the backstop watching the boys play.

She was outraged by the notion that anyone should be excluded. For Judy Wicks, now the owner of the White Dog Cafe in Philadelphia, her first experience with discrimination was a defining moment, and for the next forty years, she's been bringing people together, making sure that everyone gets to play the game.

Running a restaurant may seem like an odd enterprise for a woman who once refused to cook and rebelled against having to take home economics by leaping out the classroom window. But then, Judy would never have been satisfied with running, as she says, "just a restaurant." For her, food is the magic power that brings people and communities together.

The White Dog Cafe started simply, as a take-out muffin shop. One morning when Judy leaned out her apartment window above her shop, she noticed there was a line of people waiting to be served. She brought a table and some chairs from her apartment and invited everyone to take a seat. It was an impulse that came naturally. One chair led to another and Judy now has two hundred chairs in her restaurant, situated in three attractive townhouses on a lovely tree-lined street. The music that lured Johnny Baker up the driveway is always part of the festival atmosphere at the White Dog, whether it's the music of *Noche Latina* [Latin Night] or tunes from other multicultural, intergenerational events held there. But the real heart of the White Dog Cafe, where people gather for fun and lively conversation, lies as much outside its walls as within. Judy throws back her head and laughs when she says that she uses good food "to lure innocent people into social activism."

Judy had always wanted to create one big city-wide community. She thought that by getting people from different worlds to sit down to a good dinner and talk, they could begin to appreciate their similarities rather than fear their differences. She asked around, and community leaders suggested several minority-owned restaurants. The first was Daffodil's in North Philadelphia.

Daffodil's is located in what the local media have dubbed the "Badlands." It is sandwiched between a sad-looking Shiloh Apostolic Temple and a garage whose door is badly in need of repair. Owner Daphne Brown remembers Judy just walking in the door one day, introducing herself, and sharing her idea about bridging cultural and ethnic gaps by bringing people together to join in a meal. To start, they arranged an evening of entertainment at the Freedom Theater, one of the oldest African-American theaters in the country, followed by dinner at Daffodil's. Several dozen White Dog customers, mostly white and affluent, came and had a lot of fun. As the first participants in the White Dog Sister Restaurant Program, they still return from time to time. And, they've even brought Daphne new catering jobs.

With the addition of more sister restaurants in Philadelphia—a Latino restaurant in the barrio and a Korean American restaurant in Olney—Judy sees her community dream growing, and it isn't confined to Philadelphia.

Judy's busy adding more chairs for her extended community around the world. Her invited guests have included people from Nicaragua, the former Soviet Union, Vietnam, Cuba, Thailand, and Mexico. She calls her international sister restaurants program, with tongue in cheek, "Eating with the Enemy." Most come from nations which have policy misunderstandings and disputes with the U.S. Government and Judy wanted to know why.

To find out, Judy takes a scouting mission to "enemy" territory each year under the auspices of a nonprofit organization such as Global Exchange. The following year, she and a group of twenty White Dog customers return. During their two-week visit, the White Dog's "sister" restaurant where they can get to know ordinary people in the "enemy" country. Through their explorations, they learn how U.S. policy affects people in that country. They come to appreciate each other's hardships and learn first hand about the misunderstandings that exist between cultures and nations.

One White Dog customer who has accompanied Judy on trips to Vietnam, Cuba, and Mexico is Harriet Behringer. "These experiences have increased my understanding and knowledge of my world," she says. "I've laughed and learned and cried. Above all, I've discovered that we are not eating with the enemy, but with friends."

It isn't certain yet what new friends will join Judy's community next or what countries she will travel to next. Bosnia, perhaps, or Indonesia. It doesn't matter. Wherever Judy goes, the extension cords will go on connecting, the music will play, and there will always be room for another chair at the table. Everybody in the world will have a place.

This is Judy's vision. Its real name is, "Table for six billion, please!"

Most politicians will not stick their necks out
unless they sense grassroots support . . .
neither you nor I should expect someone else
to take our responsibility.

KATHARINE HEPBURN

Learn how to mix social activism with sound business and good food. Call us at 215-386-9224 and ask to receive our quarterly newsletter, *Tales from the White Dog Cafe.* Come and taste our delicious foods when you visit Philadelphia.

If You Don't, Who Will?

STORYTELLER: G. DONALD GALE, PH.D.

The elderly couple came through the door at Broadcast House in Salt Lake City, holding hands. The man carried a small coin purse. They opened the purse and together emptied a few coins into a slotted wooden box labeled "KSL Quarters for Christmas." Their smiles were warm, satisfied, happy.

"We don't have much," the man explained. "And we never had children of our own. We save coins to help buy shoes for youngsters who need them. It makes Christmas more meaningful for us."

For thirty years, KSL Radio has conducted the Quarters for Christmas campaign to raise money for shoes for needy children. Every cent collected goes to buy shoes. Each year the campaign elicits the kind of heartfelt response like that of the elderly couple. It is as if thousands of listeners are looking for ways to do good and KSL provides an easy way for them to express their goodness.

In New York City, hundreds of children and their parents gather in a Salvation Army auditorium. It's the week after Thanksgiving. At the front of the auditorium are literally thousands of children's coats: some new, some used, all freshly dry-cleaned. People at social service agencies distribute the coats to needy youngsters.

At the back of the room stands Mark Bench, manager of radio station WDBZ. He beams, "Look at those youngsters smile. For some, this is the first warm coat they've ever had. What a joy to be the voice for 'Coats for Kids.' Our entire radio family feels lucky."

Once again, Bonneville's New York station provided the bridge between listeners who want to help and children who need warm coats. Collection bins are placed in area shopping malls. On-air announcements urge listeners to deposit new or used coats in the bins for children who need them.

Similar stories can be told at every division of Bonneville International Corporation (BIC), owner-operator of seventeen radio and television stations. Ever since their founding in 1964, Bonneville has taken their community values seriously and every year, they publish a Values Report which chronicles the community service activities of company stations in five cities across the country. The report describes literally hundreds of examples each year where the company and its employees create opportunities for many thousands of people to give back.

"We don't have the resources to respond to every request for help, but we can reach out to bring together the people who do and who want to help those who need it. So often, people want to help but don't know how to go about it," says BIC President and CEO Bruce Reese. "They need only a little encouragement and assistance to complete the circle. We think of ourselves as facilitators. Our broadcast stations give us a voice in the community, and we use it to say, 'Sure you can help, and here's how.' It works every time—both among our employees and among our viewers and listeners."

Like most men and women, Bonneville employees care about their communities and need only a little encouragement to turn their caring into action. One of the company's six core values is service. Employees know that when they volunteer in their communities, the company will back them with time and resources. Bonneville believes it takes both individual involvement and corporate commitment. People must want to serve and the corporate culture must give service high priority.

A company-sponsored public service campaign running on all its broadcast outlets announces the theme: "If you don't, who will?" The messages talk about simple things: slowing down in school zones, voting, being a courteous driver, reading to children, and discarding fast-food wrappings in garbage containers instead of on the sidewalks. "If you don't, who will?" applies to everyone at every level, whether it's buying shoes for disadvantaged children or raising millions of dollars to care for sick children.

The elderly couple with their purse full of coins know they cannot afford to buy even one pair of shoes for a needy child, but by pooling their quarters with the quarters of many others, they can put shoes on thousands of needy youngsters. KSL provides them a way to multiply giving. The benefits go beyond simple problem solving; it's the time-proven personal rewards of serving.

A pessimist, they say, sees a glass containing water as being half empty; an optimist sees it as half full. But a giving person sees water in a glass and starts looking for someone who might be thirsty.
If you don't, who will?

Channel your goodness by tuning into one of **Bonneville International Corporation's** stations in New York, Washington, Chicago, Salt Lake City, Los Angeles, or San Francisco. To learn about their community service projects, call 801-575-5690. Encourage your favorite broadcast station to use their voice to serve the community.

Footprints in the Sands of Time

STORYTELLER: JAN BOYLSTON

Driving by the four hundred boarded-up apartments of Dallas' Wynnewood Gardens, it was easy to see why neighborhood residents wanted it torn down. The former public housing complex was an eyesore and a security threat to surrounding homes. But Duane McClurg saw something very different. "I could imagine children playing and hearing the neighbors chatting," he said. Turning his vision of much-needed affordable housing into reality wasn't going to be easy. Duane had to convince neighbors that a mixed-income apartment community would enhance the area. Then the renovations would take a huge investment. As president of Dallas City Homes, Duane turned to the one bank with a wealth of experience in community development: NationsBank.

Almost twenty years earlier and nearly one thousand miles away, Hugh McColl, NationsBank chairman and chief executive officer, had a similar vision. The once beautiful Fourth Ward in Charlotte, North Carolina, had become a neighborhood of deteriorating Victorian homes and increasing rates of crime. McColl decided to tackle the daunting task of reversing the neighborhood's deep, downward spiral.

Creating the first Community Development Corporation (CDC) of its kind, McColl forged a partnership with city government, citizens, and preservationists that led the way to a remarkable transformation. People worked together to restore shabby and haunted-looking flop houses to their original, decorative grandeur. Like a spring garden, fresh paint in pinks, blues, and yellows blossomed new life in their neighborhood. The snow-white accents on the gingerbread lattice said, "Welcome Home."

Dr. Mildred Baxter Davis, who had lived in neighboring Third Ward for more than twenty years, was intrigued by what she saw happening. Her neighborhood also had suffered harshly from various social and economic pressures. Prostitutes walked the border streets and a thirteen-acre working scrapyard blighted the neighborhood. Determined to act, she organized a small group of concerned neighbors and asked for McColl's help. McColl seized the opportunity. The CDC constructed new townhomes. An abandoned foundry was converted into offices, galleries, and pubs. The neighborhood blemish—the scrapyard—is now the well-manicured practice fields of the Carolina Panthers. The stadium is just beyond.

"We wanted a community for all people, a place for anyone and everyone: black, white, young, and old," Dr. Davis says. "What we've achieved is really wonderful. People here care about their homes and their neighbors. This is what a neighborhood should be." When Charlotte's assistant city manager, Del Borgsdorf, compares the before and after, he says, "Both of these neighborhoods were places no one wanted to walk through, let alone live in. Now they're vibrant places: real neighborhoods where people really want to live."

As NationsBank grew, it carried its vision to other communities. Once forgotten areas like The Parklands in Washington, D.C., Atlanta's Summerhill neighborhood, Baltimore's Lexington Terrace, and Nubia Square in Houston are being rejuvenated. Because of NationsBank's vision, migrant worker families in Immokalee, Florida; low-income families in East Point, Georgia; and senior citizens at Villa de San Alfonso in San Antonio have decent, affordable rental housing. In the last five years, their nearly $20 billion in community development loans and investments have helped thousands of people realize their dreams. The CDC has developed more than 10,000 affordable homes and apartments. "Business people generally don't leave many footprints in the sands of time," McColl says. "Projects like these are real footprints."

A wise businessman, McColl points out, "Profits give us the resources to get things done like investing in the lives of our neighbors. By strengthening our neighborhoods, we strengthen our communities. And that's good for business." But the real success is measured in people's lives. Thousands of first-time home buyers or low-income renters now enjoy clean, safe, and affordable homes. "What's heartwarming," McColl says, "is that we always find residents who still have hope of someday improving their neighborhoods. They just need help."

For years, Rodney and Colette Brown lived in Richmond, never imagining it would be possible to own their own home. Then one day, they attended a course sponsored by the bank and the NAACP for first-time home buyers. They learned how to straighten up their credit and save for a down payment so they could buy a house. "God used NationsBank and the NAACP to plant seeds in our lives," says Colette. "We learned how to make our dream come true," she adds. "Our whole family now has a sense of pride and belonging. We call our home our 'lighthouse': it draws us together, as a family and with our neighbors."

McColl says, "Rebuilding our most troubled neighborhoods is essential for the health of our cities and our country. No one company, nonprofit group, or government agency can do it alone. Each has an important role to play; each has certain resources and expertise to bring to the table." Challenging other corporate leaders, McColl says, "More players need to get off the sidelines and join in. At the end of our careers, the real test will be, 'Did we matter?' I think everyone wants to be able to answer 'Yes!'"

When Duane celebrated the reopening of The Parks at Wynnewood in Dallas, he could see the rewards. Oak trees shade the trimmed lawns where childrens' laughter fills the air. Neighbors meet regularly at the community center. Residents exchange greetings as they go to and from the laundry rooms. A neighborhood has been reborn.

McColl credits his grandmother and mother for instilling in him a sense of responsibility and desire to help others. Decades of community development work bring reflection for McColl. "I really wish I could talk with them again," he says, wistfully. I now realize all they taught me and I wish I could thank them."

Want to leave tracks? Help address the critical need for affordable housing by building a partnership with your local **Community Development Corporation.** Call the **National Congress of Community and Economic Development** at 202-234-5009.

The Hundredth Monkey

STORYTELLER: KEN KEYES, JR.
adapted from *The Hundredth Monkey*

The Japanese monkey, *Macaca Fuscata*, has been observed in the wild for over 40 years. In 1952, on the island of Koshima, scientists started feeding the monkeys by dropping sweet potatoes in the sand. While the monkeys liked the taste of the potatoes, they didn't like the sand.

An 18-month-old female named Imo found she could solve the problem by washing the potatoes in a nearby stream. She taught this trick to her mother and to her playmates, who also taught their mothers. Over a period of several years, all the young monkeys on the island learned to wash the sandy sweet potatoes to make them more palatable. But only the adults who imitated the children learned this trick. Other adults kept eating the sandy sweet potatoes.

Then something startling took place. In the autumn of 1958, a certain number of Koshima monkeys were washing their sweet potatoes—nobody knows how many. For the sake of the story, let's suppose that when the sun rose one morning there were 99 monkeys on Koshima Island who had learned to wash their sweet potatoes. Let's further suppose that later that morning, a hundredth monkey learned to wash the potatoes.

That's when it happened. The additional energy of this hundredth monkey seemed to create an ideological breakthrough for the entire species. By that evening, nearly every monkey in the tribe was washing their sweet potatoes before eating them.

But that's not all. The most surprising thing observed by the scientists was that the habit of washing sweet potatoes somehow jumped overseas. Soon colonies of monkeys on other islands, and the mainland troop of monkeys at Takasakiyama were also washing their sweet potatoes!

Although the exact number may vary, the "Hundredth Monkey Phenomenon" means that when a limited group has a certain realization, it remains the conscious property of that few. But, at a certain point of "critical mass," when just one more mind tunes-in to the new idea, the field is exponentially strengthened, and the awareness is picked up by almost everyone!

Just think what this bit of science can mean for mankind. Every time we adopt a new habit or belief that helps our community, we increase the collective wisdom of humanity and get one person closer to changing the world!

Share the Stone Soup Spirit

We invite you to let yourself be touched by these stories. Take the time to let them open your heart and renew your spirit.

Try walking a mile in a community hero's shoes. Feel the healing power of their love. See how they inspire and challenge you to think about what you could do to make the world a better place.

When people read these stories, their eyes usually soften and sparkle. You can see their hearts have been touched. Everyone has a few favorites, ones that made them laugh or cry, or remind them of someone from their own lives. For some, it was a kind person who reached out to help them. Others remember the warm glow they felt when they helped a child, a friend, a neighbor or a stranger. Take a moment to give thanks for all those who've given to you and helped you become the person you are today. Take the time to share your special memories with that person, your friends, your colleagues.

Catch the Stone Soup spirit! Use your "magic stone" to make a difference in someone's life. Get involved with one of the organizations featured in this book, or start your own. Decide to do something every day to make the world a better place. See how much better you feel and how much more hope you have for our future.

Spread the good news! Share these *Stone Soup for the World* stories with a friend. Send them to someone who needs a good dose of hope in their lives. Invite them to join you in building a better world. We would love to hear from you about how the stories in this book have touched you. We are collecting new ones for future editions of *Stone Soup for the World.* If you would like to submit a special story about someone who touched your life or a community hero you admire, please send it to us:

The Stone Soup Foundation
P. O. Box 4301 • Vineyard Haven, MA 02568
Tel: 508-696-8514 • Fax: 508-696-9460
Website: http://www.soup4world.com

A Special Invitation to Kids

There are lots of wonderful kids doing great things in the world. Some of them are featured in this book. David Levitt was only 11 years old when he first spoke to the school board in Tampa, Florida and convinced them to give leftover cafeteria food to local soup kitchens. Fifteen-year-old Andy Lipkis turned his concern for Los Angeles' dying trees into an opportunity to bring people in Los Angeles together—to plant a million trees. Our youngest community hero, Isis Johnson, was only 4 years old when she started collecting food for hungry children in New Orleans. Arn Chorn was a 16-year-old Cambodian refugee when he invited young people to transform their painful memories into lessons for teaching peace.

Young people have been involved with all aspects of *Stone Soup for the World*. They nominated their favorite community heroes, wrote some of our best stories and polished them until they shined. They also reviewed all the stories in the book to make sure kids would relate to them and be inspired to help build a better world.

When young people read these stories, wonderful things happens. A class of second graders in Texas were so inspired when their teacher read them the stories, they started looking for their own heroes. Sixth graders in an English class on Martha's Vineyard read the stories and then wrote one about someone who'd made a difference in their lives.

This book is dedicated to young people—to each one of you and to my 19-year-old brother, Chris—in hopes that all kids will discover the joy of helping others.

You are invited to become an ambassador of hope in the world.

Let us know which stories touch your heart, give you hope and inspire you to help others. Share these stories with your friends. Bring this book to your school and show your teacher. Send us stories about your favorite community heroes for our next book.

Share the Stone Soup spirit! And thanks—for making the world a better place!

Stone Soup Resource Guide

National Days of Service

Join with the millions of Americans who spend one day working together to build a better country.

The Big Help Campaign 212-258-7080 The Big Help is Nickelodeon's year-round campaign gets kids involved in their communities through volunteering. Each year, Nickelodeon airs The Big Help-a-thon, a live, televised extravaganza when kids call 800 numbers to pledge their help. In 1997, 8 million kids called in and pledged 85 million hours of service. Nickelodeon also provides teachers with The Big Help Classroom Kit, local community leaders with educational materials and information about local volunteer activities through a traveling Helpmobile. They partner with 23 national organizations dedicated to helping kids serve. The Big Help Week is April 18-25, 1998. Call the Big Help Hotline or visit the www.NICK.com.

Christmas in April 800-4-REHAB9 Deliver a dream to an elderly neighbor who needs you—grab a hammer or a paintbrush to restore joy and hope in homes across the country. Christmas in April preserves neighborhoods, reduces institutionizations and builds stronger communities in partnership with community groups, business, labor and everyday Americans. Lend a hand and make a difference. "We're love in action."

Day of Caring 703-836-7100 The United Way in over 400 communities conducts one or more Days of Caring each year, typically in the fall. Individuals and groups volunteer to work in day-long projects at local agencies—delivering meals to the elderly, reading to children, repairing and painting houses even rebuilding a baseball field. The day combines the camaraderie of side-by-side work with coworkers, friends, or new acquaintances with exposure to the good works of agencies in your community.

Make a Difference Day 800-VOLUNTEER An annual day of doing good in which more than one million Americans volunteer and organize service activities in their communities. The event, created in 1992 by USA WEEKEND magazine in partnership with The Points of Light Foundation, rallies corporations, government leaders, charitable organizations and everyday Americans. Volunteer efforts that capture the spirit of the day receive charitable awards from a pool funded by USA WEEKEND magazine and Newman's Own. The day takes place the fourth Saturday of each October. In 1998 Make A Difference Day is Saturday, October 24. Call their hotline or e-mail: usaw.usaweekend.com or visit www.usaweekend.com.

Martin Luther King, Jr. Day 202-606-5000 In the spirit of Dr. King's commitment to service, the King Holiday in January is a national day of service. This day, sponsored by the Corporation for National Service, is also an opportunity to raise awareness about human rights, interracial cooperation and youth anti-violence initiatives. On the third Monday of every January, people and organizations will keep the "Dream" alive by opening their hearts and offering their hands to bring diverse peoples together. Call Rhonda Taylor at 202-606-5000 ext. 282 or visit http://www.nationalservice.org.

National Youth Service Day 202-296-2992 Celebrate the power of young people to change our country block by block, neighborhood by neighborhood. Held on April 21 in 1998, National Youth Service Day is the largest service event in America, engaging 2 million young volunteers in more than 9 million hours of community service. An annual public education campaign, sponsored by Youth Service America in collaboration with 34 national youth organizations, it promotes the benefits of service to the American people through youth service and volunteering in communities. Call Omar Vellarde-Wong at 202-296-2992 ext. 34 or visit: www.SERVEnet.org.

Stand for Children 800-663-4032 Stand for Children helps people who care about children become effective grass roots leaders for children as part of Children's Action Teams (CATs), which engage in ongoing local service, awareness-raising, and policy change initiatives. Each year on June 1, Stand For Children coordinates local activities all across the country. Visit www.stand.org or e-mail tell-stand@stand.org.

Take Our Daughters To Work Day 800-676-7780 On the fourth Thursday of April, parents and other adults across the country take their daughters or other young girls to work for the day. Sponsored by the Ms. Foundation for Women, this day gives girls get a first-hand glimpse into what the work day looks like, celebrates girls' work by educating them about their wide range of life options and help girls become self-confident and resourceful during their teen years. Call Gail Maynor or visit http://www.ms.foundation.org.

Trick or Treat for UNICEF 212-922-2646 For over 48 years children across America have been celebrating Halloween by collecting coins to help provide medication, vaccines, clean water and sanitation, nutritious food and basic education to millions of children in over 106 countries. During the month of October, the U.S. Committee for UNICEF provides educators and families with a myriad of opportunities to teach children about global issues and celebrate cultural diversity that surrounds them in their classrooms, communities, and the world. To order the free trademark orange Trick or Treat for UNICEF cartons or educational materials, call or visit http://www.unicef.org.

Growing Nationally

To get involved with exciting programs in your community, call one of these national organizations who are connecting people across the country.

Alliance for National Renewal 800-223-6004 The Alliance is a unique coalition of 194 community-building organizations, institutions, communities, and people from the public, private and nonprofit sectors who are re-engaging citizens in community life and working together towards a shared vision of improving communities. The Alliance is a program of the National Civic League. Call 800-223-6004 or visit www.ncl.org/anr.

America's Promise: The Alliance for Youth 800-365-0153 The goal of this national campaign is to propel the mission of the Presidents' Summit into the 21st century. America's Promise is a growing alliance of hundreds of organizations making commitments to the goal of ensuring that at least two million additional young people (particularly those most in need), between the ages of 0-20 are connected to the five fundamental resources of a healthy start, safe places to live, adult mentors, training in marketable skills and opportunities to serve. Mentor programs need more volunteers. To connect with a mentor program in your community. call 888-55-YOUTH.

Connect America 800-VOLUNTEER Connect America is a collaborative effort that brings together the energies and resources of nonprofit organizations, businesses, and community volunteers to help build the connections that are critical to solving many of society's problems. To learn about volunteer opportunities in your community, visit the Connect America section of the www.pointsoflight.org.

Corporation for National Service 800-942-2677 A public-private partnership that collaborates with local and national nonprofit organizations to sponsor service projects that respond to the needs of the communities they serve. They oversee three national initiatives: AmeriCorps: a year of community service for citizens 17 and over; Learn & Serve educational resources and models for kindergarten through college and the National Senior Corps for people 55 years and older. Call 800-942-2677 or visit the national service web site at www.nationalservice.org.

The Giraffe Project 360-221-7989 The Giraffe Project is a national nonprofit organization that finds, honors and publicizes people who "stick their necks out" for the common good, like Stone Soup story, Steve Mariotti, National foundation for Teaching Entrepreneurship. The Giraffe Program provides educational materials to children in 46 states and American schools in Italy, Spain, the UK and on Guam. E-mail office@giraffe.org or visit http://www.giraffe.org/giraffe/

The Independent Sector 202-223-8100 Comprised of 800 nationally-oriented foundations, nonprofits, charities and philanthropies, the Independent Sector researches and reports on trends in giving and volunteering; labors to safeguard advocacy rights for nonprofits; educates the public on the integral role of nonprofits in society and provides a forum for interaction and collaboration between the nonprofit, business and government sectors.

One to One: The National Mentoring Partnership 202-338-3844 One to One serves as a resource for mentoring initiatives nationwide and advocates the benefits of expanding mentoring programs. To start or expand a mentoring program call 202-338-3844 or visit www.mentoring.org.

The Points of Light Foundation and Volunteer Centers 800-VOLUNTEER The Points of Light Foundation is a nonpartisan, nonprofit organization dedicated to engaging more people more effectively in volunteer service to help solve social problems. The Foundation and its member Volunteer Centers around the country are working together to mobilize people and resources to deliver creative solutions to community problems. Their Stone Soup story spotlights Phil Stevens and his work with Native American Indians. The Volunteer Centers connect over 1 million people each year to volunteer opportunities. To learn about volunteer opportunities in your community, call your local Volunteer Center or 800-VOLUNTEER or visit www.pointsof light.org.

What One Person Can Do

You, too, can make a difference in someone's life! Call one of these organizations to learn how.

American Association of Retired Persons 202-434-3219 AARP has a national Volunteer Talent Bank that matches people ages 50 and older with volunteer opportunities based on their interests, skills and geographical location. Their database matches volunteers with service opportunities in literacy, sciences, legislative and legal assistance, health, housing, arts and cultural, intergenerational and environmental activities. To become a volunteer, call 202-434-3219 and ask for a registration packet.

Big Brothers Big Sisters of America 215-567-7000 Big Brothers Big Sisters of America's 500 agencies nationwide provide more than 100,000 children from single-parent homes with positive adult role models. Become a caring friend to a child in your community so they can succeed in the world—through BBBSA's One-to-One mentoring program or through the School-based Mentoring Program.

Boys and Girls Club of America 800-854-CLUB Boys and Girls Club of America is a nationwide affiliation of organizations working to help youth of all backgrounds, especially those in disadvantaged circumstances, to develop the qualities needed to become responsible citizens and leaders.

Catholic Charities USA 703-549-1390 Catholic Charities USA is a national nonprofit network of 1,400 local, independent agencies, which in 1996 provided social services to more than 12 million people in need—regardless of religious, ethnic, or social background. As the largest, private, social services network, they provide housing, refugee and immigration assistance, employment programs, pregnancy and adoption services, counseling and food.

Family Service America 414-359-1040 Family Service America strengthens family life through 280 local agencies in the U.S. and Canada. Volunteers mentor young people to reduce teenage pregnancy and drug/alcohol abuse, serve as counselors for marriage and parent-child relationships and help with foster care, adoption and crisis hotlines for family pressures related to aging, child abuse, or family violence.

Jewish Community Centers Association of North America 212-532-4949 The Association offers a wide range of services and resources to enable its 275 affiliates—Jewish Community Centers, YMHA, and YWHA's and summer camps across the U.S. and Canada—to provide educational, cultural and recreations programs to enhance the lives of Jewish people.

Jewish Family and Children's Agencies Jewish Family and Children's Agencies provide family services to people in need regardless of their faith. Volunteers help feed the hungry, visit hospital patients, serve as companions to the elderly, and work with disadvantaged children, at-risk youth and people with disabilities. They also help resettle Jewish families from other countries and work at improving intercultural relations.

The United Black Fund 800-323-7677 There are 39 United Black Funds around the country who work with nonprofit organizations to meet the unmet needs in communities such as child care, literacy, crime prevention, drug and alcohol programs, mentoring programs for youth and support programs for the elderly people and those with disabilities.

Many of these organizations have been helping your community for many years. Give them a hand. Check your phone book for the one nearest you.

American Red Cross 212-737-8300 The American Red Cross is a volunteer-led humanitarian service organization, which annually provides almost half of the nation's blood supply,certifies more than 8.5 million people in vital life-saving skills, mobilizing relief to victims in more than 68,000 disasters nationwide, providing direct health services to 2.8 million people, assisting international disaster and conflict victims in more than 40 countries, and transmitting more than 14 million emergency messages to members of the Armed Forces and their families.

Girls Inc 212-689-3700 Girls Inc., a national youth advocacy organization, helps girls become "strong, smart and bold" in an equitable society. They provide educational programs, i.e. developing leadership skills, encouraging science, math, technology studies to 350,000 young people at 1,000 sites, particularly those in high risk, underserved areas.

Girl Scouts of the U.S.A 212-852-5000 The Girl Scouts are committed to helping all girls from every background develop the confidence, determination and skills needed to thrive in today's world.

Hugh O'Brian Youth Leadership 310-474-4370 HOBY is a nonprofit organization that provides more than 20,000 high school students from private and public high schools the opportunity to meet with distinguished leaders to discuss democratic and economic systems, education, entrepreneurship, media, and communications.

National 4-H Council 301-961-2800 In 4-H, teamwork and leadership skills are developed through hands-on learning projects in the environment, gardening, nutrition, raising animals as well as public speaking and citizenship. More than 5.6 million youth, ages 5-19 participate in 4-H's co-educational programs every year.

The Salvation Army 703-684-5500 The Salvation Army is a national nonprofit organization motivated by a love of God and a concern for people in need, regardless of color, creed, gender or age. Volunteers in their 10,000 centers help with crisis hotlines, emergency disaster services, day care centers, summer camps and youth programs for low-income children, as well as food banks and shelters for the homeless. During the Christmas season, they distribute food to the homeless along with toys and clothing to disadvantaged children.

Volunteer Centers of America 800-899-0089 Volunteers of America serves over one million people each year through our community-based affiliates which offer a variety of programs including day care centers for abused and neglected children, emergency shelters for the homeless and "meals on wheels" for the frail elderly. We are also the nation's largest non-profit affordable housing provider for low-income families, the elderly and persons with disabilities.

YMCA (Young Men's Christian Association) 312-977-0031 The YMCA helps men and women of all ages, incomes, abilities, backgrounds and religions grow in body, mind and spirit. Volunteer with one of the 2,000 YMCAs nationwide to help them provide tutors, mentors and offer alcohol and drug prevention programs, health and recreation programs, day camps and child care, food banks and job training.

YWCA of the U.S.A. (Young Women's Christian Association) 212-614-2700 The YWCA is dedicated to the empowerment of women and girls. With 363 member associations in thousands of sites in all 50 states, the YWCA works with more than a million women, girls and their families nationwide with parent and peer counseling, child care, health care, teen pregnancy prevention, domestic abuse and career counseling.

United Neighborhood Centers of America, Inc 216-391-3028 United Neighborhood Centers of America serves 153 neighborhood centers by cultivating leadership and accrediting quality day care, youth/family/elderly programs and other services improving conditions for all neighborhood residents.

Doing Well By Doing Good

Dare to share. Act with your pocketbook. Write the check. Just do it!
Join these organizations who are building a better world.

Co-op America 800-58-GREEN The National Green Pages. directory features 2,000 socially and environmentally responsible companies and organizations including the Stone Soup story, Thanksgiving Coffee, that are changing the way America does business.

The Business Enterprise Trust 650-321-5100 Each year, The Business Enterprise Trust honors business people who combine sound management and social vision. Stone Soup stories include: Judy Wicks, White Dog Cafe and Rachel Hubka, Rachel's Bus Company. Please call to nominate an outstanding business leader or receive information about the Trust's educational materials.

The Greenleaf Center for Servant-Leadership 317-259-1241 An international, not-for-profit organization whose mission is to improve the caring and quality of institutions through servant-leadership. The center offers a wide array of programs, publications, and other kinds of resources on servant leadership. Contact them for a free information packet.

The World Business Academy 415-227-0106 The World Business Academy celebrated its 10th year in 1998. Since business has become the dominant force in society, WBA urges members to seek to avoid or solve our most pressing problems including sustainability. An international membership organization, it is open to anyone committed to maximizing their human potential and implementing the new paradigms. Their Stone Soup story, "We Can Do It," honors businessman Cabel Brand.

Social Venture Network 415-561-6502 SVN is a part of an international organization of business and social entrepreneurs dedicated to promoting progressive solutions to social problems and changing the way the world does business. SVN members strive to be effective business people and catalysts for social change by integrating the values of a just and sustainable society into their day-to-day business practices and use their enterprises and create new ventures to improve the world.

Community Cooperation

The next time you get together with your family and friends, try talking about what you could do to improve things in your world. Call these organizations to learn how you can create community cooperation.

Center for Living Democracy 802-254-1234 The Center for Living Democracy works to inspire and support the active participation of citizens in problem solving across all arenas of public life, from schools and workplaces to government and community affairs. The Center is a national organization offering guides and models for effective engagement like the Stone Soup story about Elena Hanggi and her leadership at ACORN: the Association of Community Organizations for Reform Now. Call 802-254-1234 or visit: www.livingdemocracy.org.

Institute for Food and Development Policy: Food First 510-654-4400 Food First empowers citizens to address the root causes of hunger, poverty and environmental decline. Our research and educational materials teach people how to change anti-democractic institutions and belief systems which promote hunger and environmental deterioration. Call us or e-mail: foodfirst™igc.apc.org. or visit: http://www.netscape.org/

Grassroots Leadership 704-332-3090 Be passionate for justice. Learn the skills of community empowerment. To receive books, tapes, CDs, from Grassroots Leadership write to: Box 36006, Charlotte, NC 28236 or call 704-332-3090 or www.grasslead.org.

National Civic League 800-223-6004 Help your community prepare for the future through a citizen's visioning and strategic planning process. Call the National Civic League and ask for their catalogue of books, conferences and tools including: 98Things You Can Do For Your Community.

National Coalition for the Homeless 202-775-1322 NCH is a national advocacy network of persons who are or have been homeless, activists, service and housing providers committed to ending homelessness. NCH works to meet the urgent needs of person who are (or at risk of becoming) homeless as well as creating systemic and attitudinal changes to prevent and end homelessness. Call, e-mail nch@ari.net or visit: http://nch.ari.net.

Robert Wood Johnson Community Health Leadership Program 617-426-9772 Each year, the Community Health Leadership Program honors ten outstanding heroes of community health care, like the Stone Soup community hero, Dr. Juan Romagoza and his work with the Hispanic community in Washington D.C.. Call us for information on how you can nominate an outstanding health leader.

Cultural Healing

Take small steps towards healing our country. Challenge your friends and family to think and act more compassionately. Call these organizations to learn how you can create cultural healing in your community.

Teaching Tolerance This project of the Southern Poverty Law Center helps teachers promote interracial and intercultural understanding. Half a million educators receive its free magazine and more than 50,000 schools have used its free multimedia kits. For more information write to: 400 Washington Ave. Montgomery, Alabama 36104 Fax: 334-264-3121.

Anti Defamation League's A World of Difference 212-885-7700

The Interracial Democracy Program 802-254-1234 A program of the Center for Living Democracy links and encourages groups that focus on interracial dialogue that bridges America's racial divides to solve community problems.

Conflict Resolution International, Inc. 412-687-6210 CRCI is a world-wide web of cutting edge mediators, teachers, arbitrators and dispute resolution specialists bridging conflict and peace on every continent. They draw on the accumulated wisdom and experience so that wherever you are, whatever your problem, the solution may be available to you. Visit http://www.conflictnet.org/crci.

Educators for Social Responsibility 617-492-1764 ESR is nationally recognized for promoting children's ethical and social development to shape a safe, sustainable and just world—through conflict resolution, violence prevention, intergroup relations and character education. A leading voice for teaching social responsibility as a core practice in the schooling and upbringing of children, they offer professional development, networks, and instructional materials to educators and parents.

National Coalition of Latino Health Organizations 202-387-5000 COSSMHO's network of over 400 organizations and 800 providers have a 25 year history of connecting communities and creating change to improve the health and well being of Hispanics in the United States. They operate national information and referral hotlines, provide training on cultural competencies, conduct policy and research studies, and fund programs throughout the nation to create strong healthy Hispanic communities.

Global Village

Take the time to get to know people from different countries. Call one of these organizations to discover how we can live together on one planet. Our children and grandchildren can then look forward to a more hopeful future.

Heifer Project International 800-422-0474 HPI helps more than 1 million struggling families worldwide to become self-reliant by giving the gift of livestock and training in their care. HPI joins with people of all faiths to work for the dignity and well-being of all people.

Mennonite Central Committee 717-859-1151 MCC connects people around the world who suffer from poverty, conflict, oppression and natural disaster with those in North American churches. We strive for peace, justice and dignity of all people by sharing our experiences, resources and faith.

Quaker Information Center 215-241-7024 The Center provides a list of volunteer/service opportunities, internships, workcamps and life changing experiences with a wide variety of Quaker and non-Quaker organizations like American Friends Service Committee in the U.S. and around the world. Call, fax: 215-567-2096 or visit: http://www.afsc.org/qic.htm.

Save the Children 202-221-4079 Save the Children Federation empowers 2 million disadvantaged children and their families in 39 countries and 15 U.S. states to take control of their lives. Their 2000 professionals provide education, health, economic opportunities and humanitarian response and community self-help assistance.

Trickle Up Program 212-362-7958 We give the poorest of the poor the opportunity to start their own businesses. In twenty years, over 250,000 people in 112 countries have lifted themselves out of poverty by starting over 47,000 businesses.

US Committee for UNICEF 800-FOR-KIDS We are working for the survival, protection and development of the world's children through education, advocacy and fundraising projects. To join in any of these activities, call us or visit us at www.unicefusa.org.

World Peace Prayer Society 212-755-4755 Unite with people all over the world through the universal prayer, May Peace Prevail on Earth! To bring the Peace Pole Project to your community or learn about the Peace Pals program for children, call or visit: Peacepal@worldpeace.org.

Additional Resources

American News Service 800 654-NEWS The American News Service, a pioneer of solutions-oriented journalism, provides stories of innovations in public problem solving to hundreds of major media outlets. Media and individual subscriptions are available. Call or visit www.americannews.com.

Hope Magazine 207-359-4651 A bi-monthly magazine about humanity making a difference.

Who Cares Magazine 202-628-1691 This bi-monthly magazine reaches 50,000 readers providing information to help people create, grow and manage organizations for the common good and to foster a sense of community among social entrepreneurs.

Yes! A Journal of Positive Futures 206-842-0216 Connect with thousands of others in the US and around the world who are turning hope into action for a sustainable, just, and compassionate future. Join Positive Futures Network, call, fax: 206-842-5208, or visit: www.futurenet.org.

Books

The Soul of a Business, Tom Chappell, New York, Bantam Books
It Takes a Village, Hillary Rodham Clinton, Simon & Schuster
Some Do Care, Anne Colby and William Damon, The Free Press
The Call of Service, Robert Coles, Houghton Mifflin
Oasis of Peace, Neve Shalom/Wahat al-Salam, Laurie Dolphin, Scholastic, Inc.
The Measure of Success, Marian Wright Edelman, Harper Perennial
On Leadership, John Gardner, The Free Press
Emotional Intelligence, Daniel Goleman, Bantam Books
Newman's Own Cookbook, Nell Newman and Ursula Hotchner
World Class, Rosabeth Moss Kanter, Simon& Schuster
The Young Entrepreneur's Guide, Steve Mariotti, Times Books
50 Things You Can Do to Save the Earth, Earth Works Press
Most of All, They Taught me Happiness, Robert Muller, World Happiness and Cooperation
Building Communities From the Inside Out, John Kretzmann and John McKnight, ACTA Publications
The Quickening of America, Frances Moore Lappe, and Paul Martin Du Bois, Jossey-Bass Inc., Publishers
The Kid's Guide to Social Action, Barbara Lewis, Free Spirit Publishing
The Simple Act of Planting a Tree, Andy and Katie Lipkis, Jeremy P. Tarcher, Inc.
Revolution of the Heart, Bill Shore, Riverhead Books
Streets of Hope, Holly Sklar and Peter Medoff, South End Press
The Different Drum, Scott M. Peck M.D. Simon& Schuster
A Way Out of No Way, Andrew Young, Thomas Nelson Publishers

The Storytellers

Jonathan Alter is a senior editor and columnist at *Newsweek* . He often writes about community service. This is the first time he's written about his mother, Joanne Alter.

Karen Anderson is the director of Public Liaison for the U. S. Agency for International Development. She has developed their Lessons Without Borders program so U.S. communities can benefit from lessons they have learned from developing countries.

Suzanne Apple is Director of Community Affairs for The Home Depot. In 1994,she accepted the 1995 President's Service Award in a special White House Rose Garden Ceremony on behalf of Team Depot.

Sarah Bachman is an editorial writer for the *San Jose Mercury News* . She has reported on women, development, and child labor in Bangladesh and other countries. She dedicates her story about Oxfam America to all those she met while volunteering in Bangladesh.

Masankho Bandho, co-vice president of Pathways to Peace, is a graduate student of theology in Berkeley, California. Through dance and theater, he helps children work for peace and justice in the U.S. and Europe.

Rosalind E. Barnes is the director of communications and public affairs for INROADS, Inc. She is an INROADS graduate and has spent the past nine years as a mentor encouraging young adults to pursue a lifetime of excellence.

Ann M. Bauer is a Minneapolis-based writer and communications consultant to the Dayton Hudson Corporation. She is actively involved in making public schools inclusive for all children.

Melba Pattillo Beals is a communications consultant in San Francisco, a former NBC reporter, and author of *Warriors Don't Cry*, her memoir about the struggle to integrate Central High School in Little Rock, Arkansas. She recently adopted two children with special needs.

John Bell is a founding staff member and the director of training for YouthBuild USA. He is the proud husband and work partner of Dorothy Stoneman.

Nancy Berg is a widely published writer, poet, and creative writing instructor living in Santa Monica, California. She was an editor for *Stone Soup for the World* and *Chicken Soup for the Woman's Soul.*

Kevin Berger, author and senior editor of *San Francisco* magazine, found Laura Scher, a business leader as concerned with social and environmental issues as the bottom line, a breath of fresh air.

Jan Boylston is the Senior Vice President for public policy at NationsBank. She consistently volunteers with numerous community and civic programs in Charlotte, North Carolina.

Patricia Broughton was a freelance writer and photographer before joining Bethel New Life as its Director of Resource Development. She has learned the power of transforming silence into language and action.

Laura Brown is a freelance writer living in Washington, D.C. She urges you to join her in buying from businesses that do well by doing good.

Matt Brown, Executive Director of City Year Rhode Island, worked on the national service legislation with Senator Kennedy. As a child, Matt's mother brought him to peace and political rallies and involved him in non-violent, community development activities.

Sue Bumagin, a mediator and systems theory psychologist, links ideas to action and helps health organizations move to their next developmental stage. As the former deputy director and co-creator of the Robert Wood Johnson Community Health Leadership Program, she was inspired by community health leaders like Dr. Juan Romagoza.

Sharon Burde, a public policy mediator with expertise in ethnic relations, has worked in the United States, former Yugoslavia, and the Middle East. She is the former Executive Director of the American Friends of Neve Shalom/Wahat al-Salam, the support organization for the Oasis of Peace.

Jeb Bush is the chairman and **Brian Yablonski** is the communications director for The Foundation for Florida's Future, a non-partisan, grassroots-based public policy institute guided by the principles of personal responsibility, strong families and communities.

Andrew Carroll is the executive director of the American Poetry and Literacy Project, based in Washington, D.C., and the author of *Letters of a Nation.*

Jimmy Carter, former president of the United States, is the Founder of the Carter Center.

Navin Chawla works for the Indian government as a senior civil servant.Educated both in India and in England at London University and the London School of Economics, he has enjoyed a varied and challenging career that includes having worked with Mother Teresa.

Dan Carothers is a writer and editor, living in Cincinnati. His profile of Ernie Mynatt was adapted from *Perceptions of Home*, a traveling multimedia exhibit about Appalachian migrants.

Alex Counts recently returned from Bangladesh, where he lived among the poor for more than five years, to become the executive director of the Washington, D.C.-based Grameen Foundation. He remains in close contact with the men, women and children in Bangladesh who befriended and inspired him.

Leslie Crutchfield is editor of *Who Cares* magazine, the tool kit for social change, the nation's leading magazine for community leaders who want to make a difference.

Ram Dass is founder of the Seva Foundation and the Hanuman Foundation. He is the co-author of *How Can I Help?* (with Paul Gorman) and dedicates his time in service to others..

Richard Deats is an author, lecturer, workshop facilitator and editor of the *Fellowship* and coordinator of communications for the US Fellowship of Reconciliation. He has worked all over the world for nonviolent social change and reconciliation.

Tom Dellner is the editor-in-chief of *Golf Tips* magazine and a regular contributor to *Rolling Stone*. He dedicates his story to his mother Jeanne, who taught him the value and rewards of community service.

Susan Dundon is the author of a novel, *To My Ex-Husband*, and an essayist whose work appears in numerous magazines and newspapers. Her face, on the other hand, frequently appears at the White Dog Cafe.

Jonah Edelman is the executive director of Stand for Children, where he works alongside his mother, Marian Wright Edelman, to build a strong movement to Leave No Child Behind. They created a national network of grassroot children's activists who plan local activities all across the country for Stand for Children on June 1 each year.

Gil Friend is president of Gil Friend and Associates, a consulting firm helping companies and communities prosper by putting the laws of nature at the heart of enterprise. He can be reached at 510-548-7904 or gfriend@eeo-ops.com.

Donald C. Gale, Ph.D. is vice president of Bonneville International Corporation and a former university professor. He serves on the boards of a dozen community service organizations, with emphasis on education and young people.

Arun Gandhi is the grandson of Gandhi and founder/director of the M.K. Gandhi Institute for Nonviolence, and an author and lecturer on the philosophy of nonviolence.

Laura Gates is a marketing and management consultant dedicated to creating a more human workplace in which people's potential and creativities are realized. She has volunteered with ACC

International Institute for three years.

Rick Glassberg and Susan Spence, longtime summer visitors to Martha's Vineyard, became year-rounders in 1993. They were "Barn Busters" for the new Agricultural Hall and recently authored *Magic Time*, a family guide to the best of Martha's Vineyard.

Gregory S. Gross, Ed.D., is president of the Jacksonville Jaguars Foundation and serves on the Harvard Outward Bound Advisory Board. He dedicates this story to Arnold Hiatt and to those who have taught him by example.

Marc Grossman, a media consultant in Scaramento, California, was Cesar Chavez's longtime personal aide and spokesman. He still handles press duties for the United Farm Workers.

Jane Harvey is editor of the quarterly publications *Volunteer Leadership* and *Connect America* for the Points of Light Foundation. She sings in her church choir and volunteers at a food pantry.

Jo Clare Hartsig, a United Church of Christ minister, recently moved to Denver, Colorado with her family. She writes a regular column in *Fellowship* magazine and consults to non-profit foundations.

A. E. Hotchner is a long-time friend and cooking conspirator with Paul Newman. They founded Newman's Own, Inc. and the Hole in the Wall Gang Camp for seriously ill children. "Hotch" has authored screenplays and books such as the bestseller, *Papa Hemingway.*

Janet Hulstrand is an editor who lives in New York City. Her clients have included Andrew Young and Caroline Kennedy. She is the mother of two, and is currently reading them the *Stone Soup* folktale.

Dawn Hutchison is the co-founder and chief operating officer of KaBOOM! and has worked with communities and corporations nationwide to build a better future for children. She enjoys writing, organizing service projects, and seeking creative ways to bring people together.

Rosabeth Moss Kanter, a professor at the Harvard Business School and author of several prize-winning books, is a proud member of City Year's National Board of Trustees and loves to participate in their annual Serve-a-Thons.

Leslie Kean is a journalist and co-author of the photographic book *Burma's Revolution of the Spirit.* For two months in 1996, she attended Aung San Suu Kyi's weekend speeches. Leslie hopes that one day the current ban will be lifted so others will be inspired by her.

Susan Keese is a freelance writer and columnist who has written for numerous newspapers and magazines. She encountered Joseph Rogers while reporting for the American News Service.

Ken Keyes, Jr. is a successful author whose books now total over a million copies, including *The Handbook to Higher Consciousness* and *The Hundredth Monkey.*

Nina Mermey Klippel has written for *House & Garden*, *House Beautiful,* and other magazines, as well as newspapers across the country. She learned about Neve Shalom/Wahat al-Salam at an inspiring benefit event hosted by Richard Gere, and loves to share her excitement about the Oasis of Peace.

Frances Moore Lappe's efforts to understand the roots of world hunger led to her 1971 *Diet for a Small Planet,* many other books, and to the co-founding of The Center for Living Democracy. Its American News Service spreads stories of bottom-up initiatives through news media nationwide.

Trude Lashe was Eleanor Roosevelt's friend and co-worker for over 40 years. She is co-chairman with Arthur Schlesinger, Jr. of the Franklin and Eleanor Roosevelt Institute, and former director of the Eleanor Roosevelt Institute. Her late husband, Joseph Lash, wrote many books about the Roosevelts and received the Pulitzer Prize for *To Eleanor and Franklin.* Mrs. Lash received the first Eleanor Roosevelt Medal.

Allan Luks is executive director of Big Brothers Big Sisters of New York City; author of four books on social and health issues, and a lawyer who has initiated laws that have become national models. He also volunteers regularly.

Jeffrey Madison is a Harvard-educated writer who volunteers at Food from the 'Hood, where he discovered that he is the sum of everyone around him and they, the sum of him. He's now turning that into action.

Matthew Malone graduated from Connecticut College with an economics degree and is pursuing a writing career in Colorado. As he developed business stories for *Stone Soup*, he discovered that when "capitalism is coupled with compassion, it's a marriage with an exciting future."

Nelson Mandela, author of *A Long Road to Freedom*, is an international hero whose lifelong dedication to the fight against racial oppression in South Africa won him the Nobel Peace Prize and the presidency of his country.

Peter Mann is international coordinator for World Hunger Year. He works with hunger activists around the world and is a proud member of a community-supported farm in New York.

Robert Marra is coordinating an immigrant health and access coalition at Health Care for All, the nationally recognized health advocacy organization. He came to Boston as a medical student and then worked with Judith Kurland at Boston City Hospital for her five years as Boston's Commissioner of Health and Hospitals.

John McKnight directs the Asset Based Community Development Institute at Northwestern University. He is committed to discovering the gifts, capacities and resources in local neighborhoods.

Ashley Medowski is a seaglass jeweler living on Martha's Vineyard. Author of the forthcoming children's fairytale, *Merangel*, she was also an editor for the sampler of stories of *Stone Soup for the World* for the Presidents' Summit for America's Future.

Jenny Midtgaard is the former Lifestyles editor for the Gavilan Newspapers and a Gilroy Garlic Festival volunteer for the past thirteen years.

Dr. Terry Mollner, a pioneer of socially responsible investing and community development for over twenty-five years is the president of the Trusteeship Institute, founding board member of the Calvert Social Investment Fund and co-chair of the Calvert Foundation.

Dennis Morgigno is a writer and broadcast journalist in San Diego. He reported one of the first television stories on Father Joe Carroll's attempts to reinvent homeless shelters and became a believer, a donor, and supporter of Father Joe's crusade.

Dr. Robert Muller, Chancellor of the University of Peace in Costa Rica, former Assistant Secretary General to three Secretary Generals of the United Nations and author of several books, is a great humanitarian and a prophet of hope for the 21st century.

Suki Munsell, Ph.D., an inspired colleague of Anna Halperin for 23 years, brings transformational healing into her fitness programs at the Dynamic Health and Fitness Institute in Corte Madera, CA.

David Murcott is the former vice president of The Journey Foundation, a non-profit resource group helping college students prepare for the road ahead. He is currently a partner in a professional development company in San Diego.

Niki Patton is a former New York media producer turned Martha's Vineyard writer, musician and performer. She believes that when we find our creative path we will make a positive difference in the lives of others.

Carrie Caton Pillsbury, formerly with MEDISEND, is now a project manager on EDS's Community Affairs team, helping non-profit organizations and the communities they serve. She and her husband volunteer at her local church mentoring college students.

Jennifer Pooley grew up in New England and graduated from Colgate University in 1997. A freelance writer living in Orlando, she's especially interested in improving children's programming.

Sheila Richardson is an editor, book reviewer, freelance copy-writer and children's story writer who believes that books are the windows to the world. Sheila is a trained tutor for Literacy Volunteers of America.

Kimberley Ridley is the senior editor for *HOPE* magazine, a magazine about humanity making a difference in Brooklyn, Maine. She writes about people in communities who are working together to solve local problems.

Joseph L. Rodriguez, executive director of Human Resources for GenCorp Inc., serves on the Board of Directors of the Lewisville Habitat for Humanity and volunteers his time mentoring Latino students. He wishes to thank his family and God for his success.

Dick Russell is a Boston-based author and award-winning environmental activist. A personal friend of Alejandro Abando, his story is dedicated to the children he met on a memorable visit to Nicaragua.

Diane Saunders is vice president of the Nellie Mae Fund for Education. After six years volunteering in Botswana, she wrote short stories for two anthologies, *Eyes on Africa* and *Patterns of Africa*.

Billy Shore is the founder and executive director of Share Our Strength. In his book, *Revolution of the Heart*, he describes his personal transition from traditional politics to innovative community service and his prescription for community change.

Marion Silverbear, a development consultant, artist and poet, wishes to thank Ada Deer, and everyone who helped with her story, and the Encampment for Citizenship community for contributing all of their unique flavors to the soup.

Holly Sklar, a Boston-based writer, is the co-author of *Streets of Hope: the Fall and Rise of an Urban Neighborhood*, the story of the Dudley Street Neighborhood Initiative. She shares DSNI's commitment to make democracy work for everyone through true community empowerment and government accountability.

Larry C. Spears, executive director of The Greenleaf Center and editor of four books on servant-leadership, also serves on the board of *Friends Journal* , a Quaker magazine.

Steven Spielberg, a principal founder of DreamWorks SKG, produced, executive produced, or directed eight of the top twenty highest grossing films of all time. He touched millions of people's hearts with *ET The Extra-Terrestrial* and dedicated the seven-time Academy Award winning *Schindler's List* to the memory of the Holocaust so that it would never be forgotten or happen again.

Brother David Stendl-Rast, a Benedictine monk, author and lecturer is a charter member of Bread for the World. His books include *Gratefulness, the Heart of Prayer*, *A Listening Heart,* and, with his Buddhist brother, Robert Aitken Roshi, *The Ground We Share*.

Judith Thompson, co-founder of Children of War, has been a mentor to youth leaders internationally for almost 20 years. She considers herself a "social artist" with Arn Chorn as her muse.

Robert Thurman, professor of Buddhist Studies at Columbia University, friend of the Dalai Lama for thirty-five years, the father of five children and the author of many books. As a co-founder of Tibet House in New York, he works for the freedom of Tibet and the future of life on earth.

Peggy Townsend is a feature writer for the *Santa Cruz County (CA) Sentinel* where she focuses on children's issues, especially children in neighborhoods where Nane Alejandrez began his work.

Skye Trimble is the Youth Services Program Coordinator at the Vineyard Haven Library in Martha's Vineyard. After working with Frances Vaughn on the *Christmas in April* story, Skye and Frances became enthusiastic pen pals.

Diane Valletta, owner of a Chicago-based communications firm and member of the National Association of Women Business Owners board of directors, often writes about the contributions of women-owned businesses in service to the community.

Elaina Verveer, publications assistant at the Corporation for National Service, is pursuing graduate studies in English. In the spirit of the Foster Grandparent Program, Elaina currently tutors children at a local elementary school.

Patricia Parrott West is a freelance writer committed to community newsletters and their ability to forge bonds among neighbors. The 1991 Oakland Firestorm stopped just 10 houses short of her own home. Her husband, Charles, is project manager for the Fire Prevention District formed during the fire's aftermath.

The Reverend Cecil Williams is Minister of Liberation of Glide Memorial United Methodist Church in San Francisco, California. He has been on the forefront of change for more than thirty-four years as a minister, community leader, activist, advocate, author, lecturer and television personality.

Harris Wofford, C.E.O. of the Corporation for National Service, has dedicated his life to making citizen service a common expectation and experience for all Americans. He has served as a U.S. Senator from Pennsylvania and assisted President Kennedy in creating the Peace Corps.

Robert Wuthnow is a Gerhard R. Andlinger professor of sociology and director of the Center for the Study of American Religion at Princeton University. He is the author of a number of books including *Acts of Compassion* (1991) and *Learning to Care* (1995).

Andrew Young was a close friend of Dr. Martin Luther King Jr. An ordained minister of the

United Church of Christ, he served as the executive director of the Southern Christian Leadership Conference. He has also served as a congressman and mayor of Atlanta, U.S. Ambassador to the United Nations and as co-chair of the Atlanta Committee for the Centennial Olympic Games.

Jim Young is the assistant to the Chairman of EDS. a $15 billion information services company with operations worldwide. Jim is active in the community both locally and nationally, particularly projects in connection with education and the needs of young people.

Editors

Nancy Berg is a widely published writer, poet and creative writing instructor living in Santa Monica, California. She was an editor for *Chicken Soup for the Woman's Soul*.

Janet Hulstrand is an editor who lives in Brooklyn, New York. Her clients have included Andrew Young and Caroline Kennedy. She is the mother of two children, and is currently reading them the *Stone Soup* folktale.

Dori Hutchings has been an elementary school principal, a student and teacher of the Unity Church. She's now a grandmother who writes poems and meditations and loves to play tennis. She shares her life with friends on Martha's Vineyard and her family in California.

Ashley Medowski is a seaglass jeweler living on Martha's Vineyard. Author of the forthcoming children's fairytale, *Merangel*, she was also an editor for the sampler of stories of *Stone Soup for the World* for the Presidents' Summit for America's Future.

David Murcott, a partner in a professional development company in San Diego, has edited stories for various inspirational books. His work with the Journey Foundation, where he has helped prepare college students for the road ahead, has given him a special appreciation for this book project.

Story Reviewers

To make sure that each one of these stories would realize our goal of touching people's hearts and inspiring them to help others, we asked twenty-five people to give each of them the "taste test." People from all walks of life, from various cultures and life experiences—students and teachers, a minister, a bankteller. a financial executive; an artist, a craftsperson, a filmmaker, a restaurant employee, a store manager and a real estate broker; a nurse, a health care executive and a Chamber of Commerce director. Their thoughtful feedback helped us choose the best hundred stories and make each one the best it could be. A very special thank you to young people who worked with us to make sure this book would touch teenagers' hearts and inspire them to help build a better world.

The story reviewers are: Sonia Attala, Christy Bethel, Shirley Bickell, Molly Bishop, Betty Blouin, Kolsown Brown, Autumn De Leon, Anne Durigan, Melissa Kite, Judy Lane, Margaret Larned, Frank Logan, Matthew Malone, Ashley Medowski, Reverend Alvin Mills, Sherry Peyson, Jennifer Pooley, Sheri Scott, Elisa Tebbens, Donna Thatcher, Peg Thayer, Skye Trimble, Randi Vega, Alfredo Villa and Paula Wexler.

Story Nominators

Thanks also to the more than 100 friends and colleagues who nominated more than 2000 "community heroes" to be considered for this book. The following people nominated stories in this book: Suzanne Apple, Jeff Ashe, Donna Bajorsky, Jeff Bercuwitz, Del Borgsdorf, Richard Deats, Lucy Durr Hackney, Judith Kurland, Frances Moore Lappe, Lawrence Jordan, Josh Mailman, Melinda McMullen, Dr. Patrick Mendis, Barbara Gaughn Muller, Jennifer Pooley, Charlie Rose, Shirley Sapin, Linda Rohr, Elisa Tebbens and Jim Young.

Nominating Organizations

The following organizations helped us select just one story from the hundreds they work with every year: Co-op America, the Robert Wood Johnson Foundation's Community Leadership Project, The American News Service, The Business Enterprise Trust, The Giraffe Project, The Fellowship for Reconciliation, The Independent Sector, The Points of Light Foundation and The World Business Academy.

The Author's Journey

For as long as I can remember, I've felt if we each did our best, gave what we could and all worked together, the world would work. As a child, I learned from those who showed me how. The great leaders of our time inspired me to reach out and help others. When Martin Luther King, Jr. asked the nation to create equality for all people, I volunteered to tutor black kids learn how to read. At first, it was a shock, traveling with my mother each week from our safe, suburban community to Boston's dangerous, inner city of Roxbury. But as a twelve year-old Girl Scout, I learned a valuable lesson: the joy of making a difference in someone else's life. The summer I turned sixteen, I had an opportunity to help with poor families in the "hollers" of Appalachia. Again I was shocked by their poverty, and touched by their ability to make light of their troubles. The songs we sang around the campfire still echo in my heart.

When Cesar Chavez invited people to join the grape boycott, I learned how I could help immigrant farmers in California over 3,000 miles away. To support them, our middle-class New England family stopped eating grapes for a long time. It was John F. Kennedy's call to action that touched me the most: "Ask not what your country can do for you, but what you can do for your country . . . " His words left an indelible mark on me. When he told the country we needed more teachers, I decided to become one. First, I taught handicapped children, then adults who wanted to change their unhealthy lifestyles, and later corporate executives and government, hospital and community leaders who wanted to build healthier communities.

Learning, teaching and serving have given me a strong foundation for my life. After learning to heal from a life-threatening disease, I realized that if we could each heal ourselves, we could help heal the planet. As a consultant to major corporations in the '80s, I learned we could build a national movement to get Americans healthy. After the peaceful revolution in the Philippines, I learned with Filipino business, community, and media leaders how a nation of people could actually rebuild a whole country. Working with business, hospital, and community leaders in the 1990s, I learned how to create public-private partnerships that met their community's needs. Using the Stone Soup folktale as a teaching tool, we discovered how to do more with less: when we worked together and pooled our resources, we helped build healthier communities.

In the beginning of each new project, I would ask the same question: What will it take for you to get others more involved in your community? People would respond by saying they wanted to know how others had faced similar challenges and worked together to resolve them. They wanted to learn about what was working in the world. So I would tell them stories, about leaders and ordinary people who were working together to make their world a better place. These inspiring stories gave them new ideas, as well as the hope and courage they needed to get started. It was immensely rewarding to watch these people rally their communities, rebuild their own can-do spirit and tackle the tough issues they faced. Their pride and joy was contagious! It renewed my own faith in our work together.

But when I listened to the news and read the statistics, I often felt concerned. I was especially upset about how our country's children were starving: for food, for love, for a good education and hope for their future. In my heart, I knew it didn't have to be this way. From what I'd seen in the communities I'd worked in both here and abroad, it seemed that we knew what needed to be done and what it would take to build a better world. We just needed the will power and the people power to do it. I wondered how could we spread the good news of "what works" to more people, so they, too, would have hope that we really could make things better for children, our country and around the world.

It wasn't until 1990, when I met a Frenchwoman named Claire Nuer that I discovered why all this mattered so much to me. In Claire's leadership training program, I realized how my own childhood had given me a unique compassion for the world's children. When my forty-six-year-old father died and left my mother to care for our big family, it changed my life. At the age of nineteen, I felt a profound responsibility to carry on my father's dream: that we would all make something of ourselves. Having already lost two siblings, I realized how fragile a child's life can be. Then when my youngest brother, Christopher, died at the age of nineteen, it devastated my family and left a huge hole in my heart. For many years I tried avoiding the pain by filling it, with important people, places and projects. I couldn't bear the thought of losing any more children in the world, so I kept myself very busy. With Claire's help, I learned how I could face my pain and use it as a lever to change my life and the world.

As a Holocaust and cancer survivor, Claire's commitment to creating a more humane world had given her the courage to take on impossible tasks, time and again. When she asked training participants, "What changes could you make in your life today to create a more humane world fifty years from now?", it was a powerful wake up call for me. I realized how much I longed to be part of a community of people who were committed to building a better world for all the children. The next day Claire challenged us again saying, "One person can be the rock that changes the course of a river." Her simple words helped me see that if she had the courage to live her dreams, so could I. In that moment I decided to be one of those rocks to change the course of the river.

Strengthened by my new commitment, I felt a growing urgency as we neared the year 2000: What kind of world are we leaving for our children? I wondered. What kind of legacy are we passing on to them? What are we been teaching them, by our actions, as well as our words? Are they learning about about the great leaders who've dedicated their lives to making the world a better place? Are we giving them opportunities to serve and make a difference in someone's life? Are we teaching them how to solve problems in their communities?

To ponder these questions, I took some time off from my fast-paced life and returned to my New England roots. Walking the beaches of Martha's Vineyard, I kept asking myself what I could do. One day I found a magnificent stone on Lucy Vincent Beach. It's fossilized imprint is like the tree of life. It fit perfectly in the palm of my hand. Like magic, it reminded me of Claire's words, and my commitment to be one of those rocks to change the course of the river.

A few months later, I spent the Christmas holidays with my dear friends, Georgia Noble and Jack Canfield in Santa Barbara, sharing stories about our lives, and talking about the state of the world. I found myself saying to Jack, "Just think what could happen if the 10 million people who read your *Chicken Soup for the Soul* books took the next step, from healing themselves to healing the planet!" He immediately responded, "Great idea. You should write a book about it!" Stunned, I realized he was right—and also that I was nervous. Jack gave me his vote of confidence, and told me the four most important things he'd learned from writing his books: keep it simple; touch people's hearts; inspire them; and choose a great title.

Returning home to the Vineyard, I held my special stone and pondered Jack's challenge. Then I called my mother, shared his idea with her and asked her to tell me the Stone Soup story again. She laughed and said, "Your life is a stone soup story. You're always getting people to make something out of nothing. You've always said that if we each gave a little, there would be enough for the whole world." My mother's words helped birth this book, *Stone Soup for the World*.

To begin, I invited 100 friends and colleagues to join me on this adventure. I sent a letter asking them to nominate "community heroes" and friends who could tell their stories from the heart. Over the last two years, we collected more than 2000 stories about people who've made a difference in the world. After sorting through them, we selected a good sample—something for everyone. Thirty friends and colleagues reviewed each story, giving them the "taste test" to make sure they each realized our goal of touching people's hearts and inspiring them to help others. Thanks to these friends and colleagues, we assembled a wonderful collection of 100 stories of people who are making the world a better place.

As we created the book, we built a wonderful community.To the community heroes and storytellers featured in the book, thank you for bringing hope to me and millions of people every day. I'm grateful for the great teachers who nurtured my soul along the journey, many are featured in this book. To the kindred spirits who've supported this book and participated in the Stone Soup gatherings in New York, San Francisco, Washington D.C. and Los Angeles as well as at the President's Summit in Philadelphia, a special note of gratitude.

My dream is for each of us to become like a traveler in the folktale, Stone Soup, discovering our own magic stone and a way to pitch in. For curious, first-time travelers, I hope this book gives you new ideas, inspiration and direction. For our young people, I hope you enjoy meeting some of the real heroes of our time and will discover the joy of making a difference in someone's life. For fellow seasoned travelers, I hope these stories nourish your soul and give you strength to carry on. For all of us, may these stories rekindle the joy of giving and the power of working together to build a better world.

Marianne Larned
Martha's Vineyard
November 1997

ACKNOWLEDGMENTS

Writing this book has been an amazing Stone Soup experience. Many people generously gave of themselves, their time, their ideas, their support. I will be forever grateful to each and every one of you. A special thanks to the community heroes and storytellers featured in this book for your trust in me, your faith in the process and your commitment to building a better world.

My deepest gratitude to my parents for instilling in me the importance of helping others. Special thanks to my mother, who first read me the Stone Soup story and then brought me to Roxbury each week so I could help someone learn to read. To my brothers, Tom, Chris and David and my sisters, Cathy, Betsy, Diane, Susan, Martha and Peggy and their families for their love over the years. A special thanks to my brother, Tom, and to Ron Huth, for their help in writing the dedication to my brother, Chris.

To Claire Nuer and Sam Cohen, Lara, Marc Andre, Polly, Carole, Laura, Judy, Ed, Sharon, Art, and all the fellow travelers at ACC International Institute who touched my heart and strengthened my commitment to help make the world a better place. To special friends for their extra caring and enduring support during this incredible journey: Sonia Attala, Christy Bethel, Jan Bolyston, Sharon Burde, Andy Carroll, Ray Gatchalian, Marietta Goco, Dori Hutchings, Patty Johnson, Joyce King, Avon Mattison, Georgia Noble, Kristen Pauly, Susan Peebles, Sherry Peyson, Marty Scherr, Sheri Scott, Randi Vega and Arlan Wise. Your love nourished and inspired me each and every day. Thank you all from the bottom of my heart.

Thanks to all my new friends on Martha's Vineyard who invited me into your wonderful community, especially those who attended our Stone Soup gatherings: Jane and Ron Beitman, Anna Eddy, Wendy Culin, John Dunkle, Steve and Georgiana Fox, Zelda and Bill Gamson, Lucy, Sheldon and Virginia Hackney, Roxanne Kapitan, Sonya and Jim Norton, Niki Patton, Shirley Sapin, Heidi Schmidt, Robert Schuman, and Susan Wasserman. My deepest appreciation to the Robinson family from the Wampanoag Tribe: Bertha, Carla and Forest Cuch, Bruce and Adriana Ignacio, Berta and Vern Welch.

A special thanks to Nancy Aronie and her wonderfully nurturing Chilmark Writing Workshop. And to Ann Nelson for her sage wisdom about the world of publishing. I'm especially grateful to the young people—Autumn De Leon, Matt Malone, Ashley Medowski, Jen Pooley, Elisa Tebbens and Skye Trimble—who gave their time, ideas and energy during the early stages of this book.

To Conari Press, for their commitment to publishing books that help build a better world, especially Will Glennon, Mary Jane Ryan, Brenda Knight, Jay Kahn, Nina Lesowitz, Tom King, Laura Marceau, and Annette Madden. Your joyful enthusiasm for this book and extraordinary efforts to bring it to as many people as possible made all the difference. For Emily Miles and Leslie Rossman for your outstanding public relations work. To my agent, Robert Stricker, for his gentle wisdom, with special appreciation to Lawrence Jordan for his early support. Thanks to Nancy Berg, Dori Hutchings and David Murcott for editing some of the more difficult pieces into beautiful stories. A very special thanks to my editor, Janet Hulstrand—it was a real joy working with you. To Jack Canfield, Kim Kerberger, Patty Aubrey, Teresa Esparaza and the Chicken Soup staff, a heartfelt thanks for your special kinship. To story nominators, the story reviewers and the hundreds of friends and colleagues who generously gave their ideas, suggestions and support, goes my gratitude.

Many thanks to all who helped manage the Stone Soup office: Sarah Crafts, Sue Doherty, Diana Gilmore, Cynthia Seymour, Kimberly Rome, Peg Thayer and Skye Trimble—with extra thanks to Shirley Bickel for her faithful support over the miles and the years. Thanks to Brigitte Desouches and Jeanne Jones for their masterful help in keeping the numbers straight. Many thanks to my financial advisors: Bill Hylan, Clement Lambert and Sheri Scott, for their caring and wisdom, especially to Frank Logan for his faithful support over the years. To all those who helped produce the preview copy of the book for delegates at the Presidents' Summit for America's Future, especially to Bethany Burhoe, Sharon Danley, Ed Marston with special thanks to the staff at Tisbury Printer and Keith Hagman, Flagship Press. And thanks to Peter Simon for his wonderful photograph taken at Stonewall Beach on Martha's Vineyard.

To all those who helped keep my body and mind healthy during the journey including: Dr. Nancy Berger, Pamela Danz, Claire Elkington, Dr. Friedlander, Tara Hickman, Dr. Michelle

Lazerow and Andrea Parker. And to all the wonderful musicians whose uplifting music nurtured my spirit. With special thanks to Charles and Marion Guggenheim for sharing their beach cottage with me and giving this book an inspiring home.

A heartfelt thanks to the early supporters and friends of the Stone Soup Foundation: NationsBank, Target Stores, Tom's of Maine, Southwest airlines, United Airlines and for all God's children, as well as Don and Ann Brown, Joel Cohen, Ray Gatchalian, Richard Goodwin, Nathan Gray, Theo Gund, Margaret Larned, Avon Mattison, Claire Nuer and Sam Cohen, Lucy and Sheldon Hackney, Kristen Pauly, Marty Rogal, Robert Stricker, Donna Thatcher and Cathy and Frank Valenti. To those who hosted our Stone Soup receptions: Henry Dakin, Ralph and Lou Davidson, Manfred Esser, Lucy and Sheldon Hackney, NationsBank and Judy Wicks' White Dog Cafe. To Tom Martin for encouraging others to give from their hearts. A very special thanks to my dear friend, Karen Stone McCowen, for her generous support and for always believing in me and this book. Thanks for helping to make the dream come true. May God bless each and every one of you for your love, prayers and support.

Much love and appreciation to all the children in my life for being my greatest teachers—for showing me how to laugh at life, sing for joy and give from my heart. Many blessings to all of you, especially my nieces and nephews: Ladleah, Darcy, Julia, Michaela, Nicole, Leah, Andrew, Simon, Bethany and the littlest angel, Rebecca Marie. Thanks for being a special part of my life.

Imagine all the people living life in peace.
You may say I'm a dreamer,
but I'm not the only one.
I hope someday you'll join us
and the world will live as one.

JOHN LENNON

Thanks for permission to excerpt from the following works:

"Long Road to Freedom," is adapted from *Long Walk to Freedom* ©1994 by Nelson Mandela, Little, Brown & Co.

"Mother Teresa," is adapted from *Mother Teresa* ©1996 by Navin Chawla, Element Publications.

"Peace For Their Grandchildren," is adapted from *Talking Peace, A Vision for the Next Generation,* ©1993 by Jimmy Carter, Penguin USA.

"Letter From a Birmingham Jail," is adapted from *An Easy Burden: The Civil Rights Movement and Transformation of America* © 1996 by Andrew Young, HarperCollins.

"Everyone in America is Helping," is adapted from *How Can I Help: Stories and Reflections on Service,* ©1985 by Ram Dass and Paul Gorman, Knopf, Inc.

"Young Acts of Courage," is adapted from *Warriors Don't Cry: A Searing Memoir of the Battle to Integrate Little Rock's Central High,* © 1995 by Melba Beals, Simon & Schuster.

"The Banker With Heart." is adapted from *Give Us Credit,* © 1996 by Alex Counts, Times Books/Random House.

"We Walk Our Talk," is adapted from *No Hiding Place: Empowerment and Recovery for Our Troubles Communities,* © 1992 by Cecil Williams, published by HarperCollins.

"Baby Magic," is adapted from *The Healing Power of Doing Good: The Health and Spiritual Benefits of Helping Others,* © 1992 by Allan Luks and Peggy Payne, Fawcett Books.

"The 100th Monkey," is adapted from *Hundredth Monkey,* ©1984 by Ken Keyes Jr., Devorrs & Co. Vision Books.

"Adagio in Sarajevo,"is adapted from an article of the same name originally appearing in *Fellowship,* the magazine of the Fellowship for Reconciliation, by Richard Deats, March 1993.

"Miracle in Montgomery," is adapted from an article entitled *God Makes the Crooked Places Straight,* originally appearing in *Fellowship,* the magazine of the Fellowship for Reconciliation by Joseph Lowery, July/August 1995.

"The Forgiveness Party," adapted from an article of the same name originally appearing in *Fellowship,* the magazine of the Fellowship for Reconciliation by Jo Clare Hartsig, July/August 1995.

"Shine on Montana," adapted from an article of the same name originally appearing in *Fellowship,* the magazine of the Fellowship for Reconciliation, by Jo clare Hartsig, January/February 1995.

"Teaching Jazz, Creating Community," is adapted from an article by Leslie R. Crutchfield entitled *Democracy=Participation With Style,* appearing originally in *Who Cares Magazine,* Fall 1995.

About Marianne Larned

Marianne Larned has dedicated her life to helping to build a better world. Over the years, she has served great leaders and worked with wonderful people across the country and around the world. *Stone Soup for the World* honors many of those she has worked with, learned from and admired.

Marianne is a dynamic speaker, masterful trainer and strategic consultant who inspires people and gives them tools to build healthier communities. She truly believes that somewhere on this planet, someone has a solution to each of the world's problems. Connecting people with new ideas and ways of doing things gives her great joy. She loves sharing inspiring stories and rekindling people's enthusiasm for making the world a better place. Using the Stone Soup metaphor, she helps people see that when we work together and pool our resources, we can do more with less—and have more fun. She's like a modern-day Johnny Appleseed, spreading seeds of hope wherever she goes.

Marianne's commitment to helping others started early in her life. As the oldest of 10 children, she discovered the importance of the phrase: "each one, teach one." She discovered the joy of volunteering at the age of 12 when she helped someone from Boston's inner city learn to read and then as a teenager working with families in rural Appalachia. She received an award from Hamilton-Wenham High School for outstanding community service. Her undergraduate studies at the University of Massachusetts, Amherst and the Rudolph Steiner Center in Aberdeen, Scotland prepared her to work with children. Her graduate work at Boston University and California State University gave her the business and organizational development tools to assist corporations become more socially responsible.

For over twenty years Marianne has been helping corporate, government, civic and community leaders develop public-private partnerships to build healthier communities. Her clients have included Southwest General Health Center, the American Hospital Association, and The Healthcare Forum. She also assisted Business Week, the Interactive Video Industry Association, the San Diego and San Francisco Chambers of Commerce in developing public-private partnerships to improve the quality of education in our public schools. Working with the national consulting firm, Health Research Institute, she helped major corporations like

AT&T, Avco, Johnson & Johnson, The Kellogg Company, The Mitre Company, Westvaco Corporation and Wilson Learning as well as health care coalitions in Massachusetts, Michigan and Oregon, contain their health care costs by providing employees with opportunities to improve their health. In partnership with the Phillippine Foundation for Education and Economic Development, she helped develop strategic alliances between business, government, media and community leaders to support their nation rebuilding efforts.

For her pioneering and humanitarian work, Ms. Larned has been recognized as an Outstanding Young Woman of America and World Intellectual of 1993 and is listed in 2000 Notable American Women and the World Who's Who of Women.

An inspiring speaker, she has addressed business, civic, labor and professional associations, school districts, youth and community organizations, hospitals and corporations. Her speeches motivate volunteers, energize public-private partnerships and mobilize resources to build healthier communities.

Marianne's zest for life encourages people to overcome obstacles and follow their dreams. After learning how to overcome a life-threatening illness, she realized that if we can each heal ourselves, together we have the power to heal our planet. Her presentations have inspired people from many walks of life: corporate employees, healthcare workers, schoolchildren, teachers and volunteers of nonprofit organizations. For more information about her trainings, and workshops, or to schedule her for a speaking presentation, please contact:

Shirley Bichel
Larned & Associates
P.O. Box 5354
Larkspur, CA 94977
phone: 415-646-0416
fax: 415-488-9614

Dedication

My brother Chris was the tenth and last child in our family. From the moment he was born, he was larger than life, weighing eleven pounds, with curly blonde hair and a twinkle in his eye. With his take-charge attitude and sense of humor, he lived life to the fullest. What I remember most are his hugs. Real ones, like he meant it.

Chris would do anything for his friends. He always stood up for what he believed in and challenged people to live up to his high standards. As captain of his high school football team, he got his teammates to quit drinking and stop taking drugs when he did. Once he sent a letter to a wayward teacher, challenging him to set a better example for his students.

Chris had a fierce loyalty to his family and brought us together in times of trouble. Just before he died, he organized a family reunion. It turned out to be his going-away party.

Chris wasn't always this way. When he was just 5, our Dad died. This loss left him with a hole in his heart and a chip on his shoulder. Without a father to guide and stand up for him, he struggled to find his way in the world. Growing up, he protected himself with his quick temper, so no one would get too close.

Until one summer when he went to a Young Life camp. Chris loved being with his friends, playing basketball, sailing, water skiing and climbing mountains. But something special happened that helped him put things in perspective. He had a personal revelation that really touched him and and began to fill the hole in his heart. The words "God so loved us, that he gave . . ." really clicked for him. From that summer on, Chris came to see that life was about giving. When he gave to others, he found more meaning, purpose and fulfillment in his life.

Just before Chris died, he wrote a letter to his friend, Toby.

Sitting here, talking to my roommate, listening to Pink Floyd, eating round Doritos. Midterms are coming up this week. I'm hoping for the best. I'm also working for the best, too. Tonight I asked God to show me the right ways to go about preparing for each test, to help me avoid distractions and to give me the strength to do my best. I think he listened. I really ask a lot of him . . . and often feel that I have too little to offer in thanks. I think that by helping other people in this world to utilize the unique assets he gave them, I could help him as he has helped me. It is easy to say.

Through the ups and downs of his brief life, Chris became a young hero in our community. He really believed that if we each pitched in, we could do just about anything. With his infectious smile, he invited you to join him. When he was killed at nineteen in a car crash, his high school created the Chris Larned award, presented each year to the student who has given the most of themselves.

Losing my brother when he was so young and full of promise left a huge hole in my own heart. His tragic death reminded me of the preciousness of life and inspired me to live mine more fully. It also challenged me to do whatever I could to help build a better world for our children. Through it all, Chris has been my hero, giving me the courage to create this book and guide me in my quest to help other young people discover, as he did, the gift of giving.

MARIANNE LARNED